MW00909121

Emunah Nachmany Gafny

DIVIDING HEARTS
The Removal of Jewish Children from Gentile Families
in Poland in the Immediate Post-Holocaust Years

This publication was supported by a grant
from the following organizations:

The Conference on Jewish Material Claims Against Germany

Claims Conference   ועידת התביעות
The Conference on Jewish Material Claims Against Germany

The Memorial Foundation for Jewish Culture
The Adelson Family Charitable Foundation

Emunah Nachmany Gafny

DIVIDING HEARTS

The Removal of Jewish Children from Gentile
Families in Poland in the Immediate
Post-Holocaust Years

Yad Vashem ★ Jerusalem ★ 2009

Emunah Nachmany Gafny

Dividing Hearts

*The Removal of Jewish Children from Gentile Families in Poland
in the Immediate Post-Holocaust Years*

Translated from the Hebrew by Naftali Greenwood

Language Editor: Asher Weill

© 2009 All rights reserved to Yad Vashem
P.O.B. 3477, Jerusalem 91034, Israel
publications.marketing@yadvashem.org.il

ISBN 978-965-308-330-1

Typesetting: Judith Sternberg

Printed in Israel by Offset Shlomo Nathan Press
2009

To my children,
Idan, Inbar, and Aner

Tell your children of it,
and let your children tell their children,
and their children another generation

Joel 1:3

Table of Contents

Acknowledgments

This study had many partners; I wish to express my gratitude to all of them.

I especially want to thank Prof. Dan Michman, my adviser for the dissertation on which this book is based, for his professional assistance, his patience, his constantly open door, his kindly attitude, and, above all, his encouragement at times when I was in need of it. I could not have had a better adviser. I also thank Bar-Ilan University for allowing me to write the dissertation under its auspices. I would also like to thank Dr. Aharon Weiss, who believed in me and went out of his way to help me establish my relationship with Prof. Michman.

This study took me almost seven years to complete and required many hours of research in both Israeli and foreign archives for which I needed the assistance of the archive staffs and their skills. Indeed, only by dint of their meticulous efforts was I able to gather the materials needed. I thank them for their cheerful willingness to help me orient myself in all this wealth of material.

I required a great deal of assistance from different people in order to cross all the t's and dot all the i's, for only thus could I attempt to understand every document and take measure of its historical context and spirit. I want to acknowledge several of those who lavished their time and patience on me: my mother, Aliza Nachmany, Naomi and Erich Lichtman, Mira Erlich, Ruth Bayuk, Aviva and Poldek Maimon, and many, many others to whom I am grateful — even though my words of gratitude do not suffice.

I thank Allison and Thomas Ujejski, Irena and Thomas Tryuk, and Ita Kowalska for their invaluable friendship. They opened their hearts and doors during the many days that I spent in Poland and responded to my numerous requests; demanding and trivial alike.

I thank all the now-adult "children" whose stories are revealed in this book, for having allowed me into their world and giving me their trust. Even as they encouraged me and gave me the energy to complete this study, they also waited patiently for it to be completed.

I thank the small group of colleagues and friends who collaborated with me, shared in my research efforts, and helped me in various fields and at different stages. I acknowledge the help of two of them, Miriam and Chaim Cohn, with special fondness. Their assistance continued during the process of translating the book into English.

My thanks to the heads of the International Institute for Holocaust Research at Yad Vashem, Prof. Dan Michman and David Bankier, and its scholars for having found this study worthy of publication under its auspices. I thank the Institute's administrative staff: Dr. Tikva Fatal-Knaani, Lilach Shtadler, and Eliot Nidam Orvieto for their sympathetic support.

I am very grateful to the director of Yad Vashem Publications, Ms. Gabi Hadar, the editor-in-chief, Dr. David Silberklang, and their staff. Their support and efforts were of utmost importance in bringing this research to fruition. I also thank the former editor-in-chief, Dr. Bella Gutterman.

I wish to thank Naftali Greenwood and Asher Weill, who made it possible to bring my research to the English reader. My appreciation goes to both of them for their sensitivity and understanding of the nature of my text.

And a final word of gratitude to my husband, Zvika, and my children, Idan, Inbar, and Aner, who were ever sympathetic as they listened to my doubts, thoughts, and difficulties, and the human stories laid out on our living-room table.

E.N.G
Yokneam, February, 2009

Introduction

Jan Dobraczyński, director of the Child Care Desk at the Warsaw Municipal Social Assistance Department and a member of the Polish Resistance, was one of those who first broached the idea of removing Jewish children from the Warsaw Ghetto and placing them with Polish families and in convents, thereby hoping to spare them from the inevitable fate of extermination that would otherwise await them. Years later, Dobraczyński reconstructed a talk he had held at the time with one of the leaders of the ghetto:

> In the summer of 1942, I was informed that a representative of the Jews in the ghetto, a Dr. Marek, wanted to meet me. Indeed, we met at Bankowy Square. At the meeting, the man thanked us for what we were doing but accused us of converting the children to Christianity. I replied, "Sir, we must do this, at least for the sake of appearances; otherwise we cannot assure their safety."
>
> "Yes, but what will happen afterwards?" the man asked. I began to laugh and replied, "How can we speak now about what will happen after the war? I don't know if we'll be alive tomorrow and neither do you. But if you want my opinion, I'll tell you that it's the parents who decide on a child's religion. Even though I'm a Christian, I think that if the child's parents come to claim him after the war, they'll bring the child back to his faith. And if none of the child's relatives appear, I don't know and see no reason why the child cannot continue to belong to the Christian faith until he reaches adulthood, and then he'll decide for himself." Dr. Marek answered that these were difficult terms, but he had no choice but to accept them.[1]

Only two years later, and the problems, both overt and covert, expressed in this exchange became one of the most sensitive issues on the Jewish public

---

[1] Ewa Kurek-Lesik, "Udzial Żeńskich Zgromadzeń zakonnych w akcji ratowania dzieci Żydówskich w Polsce w latach 1939–1945" (Lublin: Katolicki Uniwersytet Lubelscki, 1989), pp. 331–332.

agenda at the end of the Holocaust. In this sense, the conversation became a self-fulfilling prophecy.

On the eve of World War II, there were almost 3,500,000 Jews in Poland.[2] Most of the few who survived the war were the last vestiges of their households: "one from a city, and two from a family."[3] As I show below, although the chances of children emerging safely from the decrees intended for them — forced labor and extermination — were slight; some survived nevertheless. A very few emerged from the concentration and death camps; others were saved in convents or by wandering among villages and towns, usually under false identities. Others survived in the forests with the partisans, and some were spared in homes under the protection of Polish citizens. This book deals with the post-war efforts to search for and locate children who had been concealed in the homes of Poles, and to transfer them to relatives or to Jewish children's homes.

Some of the children who had spent the war with Poles were retrieved by family members. There were cases in which the relatives knew exactly where the children were to be found; in other cases they had to search for them at length. Although I found it appropriate to include several of these personal cases in various discussions in the book, they were, after all, the actions of individuals and their scope is hard to estimate. This study focuses mainly on actions of the Jewish "establishment" to track down children and to remove them from the Polish homes.

The totality of themes arising from this study has already been discussed, at length or more briefly, in studies on World War II and the Holocaust era and on the period that followed.

Ephraim Dekel's book *Remnants of the Sword*[4] is the only work that focuses on the actions taken by Jewish organizations in Palestine and elsewhere to rescue Jewish children in Nazi-occupied countries during and after the

---

2   David Engel, *Between Liberation and Escape: Holocaust Survivors in Poland and the Struggle for their Leadership, 1944-1946* (Tel Aviv: Tel Aviv University and Am Oved, 1996, Hebrew), p. 15.

3   Binyamin Tenenboim, who visited Poland after the war and met with surviving children, used this expression (from *Jeremiah* 3:14) as the title of his book. The paradox in the title catches the sensitive eye and focuses the reader's attention on the reversal of reality: under the circumstances of the Holocaust, the survival of two per city and one per family was more likely. See Binyamin Tenenboim, *One of a City, Two of a Family, Selection from a Thousand Autobiographies of Jewish Children in Poland* (Merhavia: HaShomer Hatza'ir, 1947, Hebrew). The testimonies were gathered in Poland in 1946.

4   Ephraim Dekel, *Seridei Herev* (Remnants of the Sword), *the Rescue of Children during and after the Holocaust* (Tel Aviv: Ministry of Defense Publishing House, 1983, Hebrew).

war. Dekel was personally involved in this as a commander of the *Bricha*, the Palestinian underground organization that masterminded the rescue of the Jewish remnant. By relating to all actions — both during and after the war — as "rescue," Dekel reveals his own attitude. To his mind, the retrieval of children was a direct continuation of rescue during the war: the rescue of children from the Nazi extermination policy and from those who had sheltered them was one and the same process. Thus, any effort to restore these children to the Jewish people was an act of rescue.

The issue of assistance to Jews during the war and the extent of the willingness of non-Jews to conceal them have been researched by several scholars from various perspectives. Nechama Tec, for example,[5] focused on analyzing and classifying the motives that prompted Poles to rescue Jews. Eva Fogelman[6] concerned herself mainly with the rescue actions themselves, the psychological and social situation of the rescuers, and their relationship with those they had concealed, and she broadened the discussion to encompass Europe as a whole. Bartoszewski and Lewin[7] discussed assistance to Jews in Poland and their rescue by private individuals and organizations against the background of the situation in Poland during the Nazi occupation. The study by Emanuel Ringelblum[8] is materially different: written from his place of concealment in a Polish courtyard, it focuses on the fabric of Polish–Jewish relations during the war and on assistance to Jews and willingness to conceal them. The above studies deal with adult and child survivors alike. Nahum Bogner's book deals with the rescue of Jewish children during the war in Poland and provides us with an understanding of various, though not all, areas related to that period.[9]

Several studies have been written concerning Polish Jewry in the early post-liberation years, each relating to a specific aspect of the time. Yisrael Gutman[10] surveyed the life of Polish Jewry from the time of its liberation

5   Nechama Tec, *When Light Pierced the Darkness: Christian Rescue of Jews in Nazi-Occupied Poland* (New York and Oxford: Oxford University Press, 1986).

6   Eva Fogelman, *Conscience and Courage: Rescuers of Jews during the Holocaust* (New York: Doubleday, 1994).

7   Władysław Bartoszewski and Zofia Lewin, *The Samaritans: Heroes of the Holocaust* (New York: Twayne, 1970, first published in Kraków: Znak, 1966).

8   Emanuel Ringelblum, *Polish–Jewish Relations During the Second World War* (Jerusalem: Yad Vashem, 1974).

9   Nahum Bogner, *At the Mercy of Strangers: The Rescue of Jewish Children with Assumed Identities in Poland,* (Jerusalem: Yad Vashem, 2000, Hebrew). English edition forthcoming, Yad Vashem, 2009.

10 Yisrael Gutman, *The Jews in Poland after World War II: Studies on Polish Jewry* (Jerusalem: Zalman Shazar Center, 1985, Hebrew).

from the Nazi yoke to the end of the 1960s and the changes that the community underwent during that period. David Engel[11] discussed Holocaust survivors in the first two years after the liberation and the struggle for their leadership. Hannah Shlomi[12] focused on initial organizational efforts by survivors. Yehuda Bauer's book, *Out of the Ashes*,[13] probed the influence of the Jews of the USA on survivors throughout Europe and devoted one chapter to Polish Jewry.

Each of these studies cited political and social developments in Poland against the background of changes that the country's Jewish collective underwent. The topic of Jewish children who survived the Holocaust, including those who had been concealed in Polish homes, is mentioned as part of the discussion of the Jewish population at large and its revitalization. However, since the main thrust of these authors' research is not this particular topic, they deal with it only where it impacts upon the issues which mainly concern them. For this reason, they make scant use of primary sources relating to these issues.

In short, even though the issue of the rescue of children is a theme of material importance on the rehabilitation of post-Holocaust Jewry in Europe, so far it has not been fully studied. In the course of introductory remarks at a workshop on the reclamation of Jewish children from Christians in Poland after the Holocaust, held at the Ghetto Fighters' House in September 1988, the following was stated: "We have not yet heard that anyone in Israel has submitted a Ph.D. dissertation that relates to this important event. Isn't this a puzzling and saddening fact?"[14]

---

11 Engel, *Between Liberation and Escape*.

12 Hannah Shlomi, "Initial Organization by Polish Jews at the End of World War II," *Gal'ed: Collection on the History of Polish Jewry, B* (1975), pp. 287–331 (Hebrew); idem, *Organizational Actions by Jewish Survivors in Poland after World War II, 1944–1950*, in Israel Bartal and Yisrael Gutman, eds., *Continuity and Crisis: the History of Polish Jewry* (Jerusalem: Zalman Shazar Center, 1997, Hebrew), pp. 523–547; idem, "Actions by Polish Jewry to Renew Jewish Life in Poland, January–June 1945," *Gal'ed: Collection on the History of Polish Jewry*, vol. 10 (1988), pp. 207–225 (Hebrew).

13 Yehuda Bauer, *Out of the Ashes: the Impact of American Jews on Post-Holocaust European Jewry* (Oxford: Pergamon Press, 1989).

14 Shmuel Bornstein, ed., *Redemption of Jewish Children from Christians in Poland after the Holocaust* (Kibbutz Lohamei Hagetaot: Ghetto Fighters' House, 1989, Hebrew). The book was published in the aftermath of a workshop on the actions of the Koordynacja. Participants in the workshop noted that the matter had been dealt with not only by the Koordynacja but also by Jewish Brigade soldiers in Western Europe and that some Jews and relatives had taken actions on their own. In these remarks, the speaker did not relate to the actions of organizations other than the Koordynacja in Poland at the time.

The present study is the first one to take a focused look at all aspects of the issue of Jewish children who were concealed by Polish families and survived the war. It discusses the actions taken to remove the children from their rescuers following liberation, with consideration of both the ideological and the humanitarian aspects of the topic.[15]

Structure of the Study

Research on the history of European Jewry immediately after the end of the Nazi occupation highlights the centrality of the hidden children issue. The topic was of considerable importance in the fabric of relations between the Jews and the authorities and also in internal Jewish politics. Poland, with the largest Jewish population in pre-Holocaust Europe, was the main arena for this issue.

This study examines all the issues and organizations that played a role in actions to retrieve Jewish children from the Polish families that had sheltered them during the war and return them to the Jewish people. It begins with a background chapter that reviews the circumstances that drove many Jewish parents to wish to conceal their children during the war, attempts to locate Poles who would agree to receive them, problems that arose in trying to hide them, and the relationships that were created between the rescuers and the children.

The study continues with a discussion of the situation in Poland immediately after its liberation from Nazi occupation and how the Polish state and the remnant of the Jewish population organized themselves. This political and social background had a direct bearing on the conditions under which the actions to remove the children were taken and the status of the rescuers in Polish society.

---

15 There are several studies on Jewish children in other countries. See Joseph Michman (Melkman), "The Problem of the Jewish War Orphans in the Netherlands," in Joseph Michman, *Michmanei Yosef: Studies on the History and Literature of Dutch Jewry* (Jerusalem: The Center for the Study of Dutch Jewry and the Hebrew University of Jerusalem, 1994, Hebrew), pp. 399–418; Sylvain Brachfeld, *A Gift of Life: the Rescue of 56 percent of Belgian Jewry during the Nazi Occupation* (Tel Aviv: Yediot Aharonot and Hemed Books, 2000, Hebrew); idem, *The Children of Life: The Rescue of 500 Jewish Children from the Claws of the Gestapo in Occupied Belgium During the Holocaust* (Tel Aviv: Ministry of Defense Publishing House, 1991, Hebrew); Renée Poznanski, "Retrieving the Children," in *Jews in France during World War II* (Waltham: Brandeis University Press in association with the United States Holocaust Memorial Museum, 2001), pp. 468–469.

Since many organizations took part in the tracing and removal of children from rescuers' homes, the study describes the events that led to recognition of the need to begin searching for Jewish children and how the various bodies were established and organized. The diverse ideological points of departure of the organizations, disagreements between them, their working methods, and problems related to the financing of their activities are described. The organizations' relations in Poland and elsewhere are also shown.

The various principals in the matter — the Polish state, the Polish population at large, and, in particular, the rescuers themselves, held different attitudes toward the search for Jewish children and their removal from the homes of the rescuers. In this work, an attempt to evaluate these attitudes as they took shape is made. The study also discusses the attitude of the Church toward the Christianization of the children and their restoration to Judaism, and the influence of Polish courts in cases where judicial intervention was needed.

The study concludes by asking how the children felt about, and responded to, their removal from their rescuers' homes and their return to the Jewish community, both at the time the actions were taken and in retrospect.

Assumptions, Assessments, and Estimates

Since this is the first focused study to be made on the topic of children who survived the Holocaust by being concealed in the homes of Polish Christians and were subsequently returned to their Jewish origins, it entails the examination of various assumptions and assessments.

First, an attempt is made to present the reader with the broadest information available about each organization that was active in the removal of Jewish children. The information is fragmentary, culled from the testimonies of various operatives, and thus it leads to mistaken assumptions about the extent of the activities that took place.

Second, some Jewish observers entertain generalized basic assumptions about the children and their rescuers, several of which have seeped into historical assessments. Remarks about the Poles are voiced, such as: "they stole the children," "they wanted to convert them to Christianity," "they stole their souls," "they cared for them in order to profiteer," "they extorted money," and so on. Since research thus far has not examined these expressions on their merits, this study attempts to explore the reasons for their evolution.

Third, any discussion of the topic raises questions and estimates about the extent of the actions taken, the number of children who survived in Polish homes, and the number of those removed by the various organizations. During the course of this study, we examine these estimates.

Fourth, the Jewish people in general and the operatives in particular considered each individual Jewish child to be of immense importance. Rabbi David Kahana, head of the Council of Jewish Religious Communities in Poland, expressed this when he said, "The Jewish people is noteworthy for its concern that no branch should fall off the tree. Everything must be done to return each child to the bosom of Abraham."[16] This study will evaluate the working methods used, their efficiency under the prevailing circumstances, and the degree of success in attaining the goals that had been set.

Although the main axis of this study concerns the Jewish children who survived the war, it also encompasses a variety of themes that were relevant to the place and time of the events: the complexity of Jewish society — the survivors, the Jewish *Yishuv* (the organized Jewish community in pre-state Palestine), the Jews in the Diaspora — their outlooks, goals, objectives; and Polish-Jewish relations during and after the war, to name just a few.

Nature of the Study

Together with aspects relating to principle and organization, it is my wish in this study to emphasize the human aspect, especially from the point of view of the children themselves. I allow myself to resort to generalizations only if they do not mask the range of nuances in behavior, choices, reactions, attitudes, and the feelings of people, both young and old. The study offers a profusion of examples to illustrate the human situations that arose. In places — or, more correctly, at emotional or ideological points — where I believe that generalizations, assumptions, or interpretations are widely held, I attempt to explain their origins and how and why they took shape. Although the issues discussed here are emotionally charged, it is the role of a balanced historical study, as opposed to widely held doctrinaire approaches, to understand the personalities at work from the perspective of their motives and contexts, without prejudgment.

16 Kurek-Lesik, *"Udzial Żeńkich,"* p. 344.

Demarcations and Definitions

Age of the children

The word "child" usually denotes a person at the outset of his or her life. More specific terms speak of various periods in childhood, such as infancy and adolescence. The use of these terms is fairly subjective. From the standpoint of parents their range extends beyond the accepted years of childhood; children, in turn, wish to shorten their childhood. To demarcate the age limits of "children" for the purposes of this study, I referred to specific landmarks on the timeline of the period of this study. One such landmark is 1939, when the *Wehrmacht*, the German army, crossed into Poland. Another one, somewhat schematic, is 1942, the year in which most of Polish Jewry was exterminated. A third landmark is 1946, when the actions to locate and remove the children gathered momentum; it was then, too, that the working methods for this removal began to take shape.

The 1939 point of reference is relevant with respect to children who were living in areas occupied by the Germans and who found themselves and their families under the occupier's yoke and decrees. It is true that children living in Polish territory that had been occupied by the Red Army also experienced the trauma of occupation and radical changes in their ways of life. These events, however, were followed by about two years of relative tranquility, until the Wehrmacht entered those territories in June 1941. The 1942 point of reference relates to the question of when the children were separated from their parents. From the standpoint of most Jews, this was the last opportunity to make a decision as to whether or not to send a child out of the ghetto. Since those deported to labor camps were young people who in several cases had children of their own, some among them managed to keep their children with them even though they were increasingly aware of the need to find a way for them to escape.

The 1946 landmark is also less than absolute. Encounters with child survivors had been taking place since mid 1944, and actions to search for children and place them in the first Jewish children's homes to be established, began to take formal shape in 1945. The actions continued in the years following 1946; children who had spent lengthier periods in the homes of their rescuers were removed during that time.

These landmarks lead to the following questions: How old was the child when the war began? (Obviously, this question is irrelevant for children born thereafter.) How old were they when separated from their parents — and, hence, how old were they when they left the home of their rescuers?

For reasons explained below, I decided for the purposes of this study to define 1930 as the earliest limit for the concept of "child," because those born then, constituting the oldest members of the age group discussed in this study, were about nine years old when World War II began and twelve years old at the 1942 landmark — still young enough to be considered as children. Even if we bear in mind that the children grew up fast under the living conditions of the ghettos, they still coped with the hazards and dangers of their life with the tools and logic of children. Admittedly, these children were 14–15 years old or even older by the end of the war, adolescents in fact, when they left, or were removed from, their rescuers' homes. The question of their "removal" depends on the personal circumstances of each case and the extent to which it is possible to speak of the "removal" of an adolescent whose decisions, in the greater part, were made autonomously. This question is less important in terms of the younger children. Notably, however, the age limits that I set for this study are neither equivocal nor absolute. Thus, a child born in 1934 who stayed with his rescuers until 1948 was effectively as old as one born in 1930 who had parted with his or her rescuers in 1944. To allow the reader to gauge the differences in the children's responses to the various situations, I have tried, where possible, to note the age of the children.

Demarcation of the research period

I define the onset of action to find Jewish children as the time of liberation from the German occupation, as Red Army soldiers and Jewish survivors encountered Jewish children. As time passed and the realization increased that there were many such children, deliberate actions to search and care for additional children took on a more formal organizational nature. To determine the end of the research period, it was necessary to examine the state of activity in the field. Theoretically, I could have set the limit arbitrarily to coincide with the establishment of the State of Israel in May 1948. This event, however, did not have a crucial impact on the actions being taken. The newly-formed state was facing a war and suffering from birth pangs. Furthermore, some of the organizations involved in the search for children were non-Zionist; they did not regard the Jewish state as a source of authority. Since the roster of organizations was diverse and not centralized under a single authority, both those associated with the State of Israel and those who were not, continued to operate as they had from the outset, irrespective of the independence of the new state.

I decided to establish the termination of the research period at the end of 1949 because it was then that the government of Poland ordered activities to cease and closed down the offices of the various Jewish bodies and institutions.[17] The search actions died out in response to this unequivocal order. The Central Committee of Polish Jews (*Centralny Komitet Żydów w Polsce*), for example, changed its nature and confined its activity thereafter to the management of children's homes.

The issue of the children resurfaced now and then in the ensuing years, mainly when family members who were not prepared to accept the decree of being cut off from children who remained in Poland, continued to try to reclaim them. There were attempts to induce Israel to continue, by means of state-level initiatives, to search for and remove Jewish children who still remained in Europe, and particularly in Poland. However, these attempts proved fruitless, as Zerach Warhaftig of the Mizrachi movement admitted sadly:

> Recent troubles crowd out earlier ones: the establishment of the state, mass absorption of immigrants, wars of existence and consolidation of society took every drop of energy that Israel's Jewish community had. Diaspora Jewry also mobilized for spiritual and financial action on Israel's behalf. The concern for the redemption of children, the physically and mentally exhausting labor that it required, going from child to child, talking and arguing, became marginal. The nation steadily forgot the Jewish survivors of the Holocaust.[18]

Beset by this feeling, Warhaftig, on November 9, 1949, addressed the Knesset regarding children who had not yet been "redeemed"; the hope that the newly-founded state would take action to return them to the Jewish people, and his fear that the passing years would make their removal less and less possible. He lamented that his speech did not have the intended result. Warhaftig also related that when he was appointed Deputy Minister of Religious

---

17 Cases of searching for children in 1949 were transferred to the care of Yisrael Kopit at the Youth Aliyah office in Łódź, via the Israel Legation in Poland. See Central Zionist Archives (CZA), L58/516.
18 Zerach Warhaftig, *Refugee and Survivor: Rescue Efforts During the Holocaust* (Hebrew), p. 445. There is an eponymous English edition of this book (tr. Avner Tomaschoff, Jerusalem: Yad Vashem, 1988). However, it omits entire subchapters and revises various details. Therefore I cite as my source the original Hebrew edition. As for Warhaftig's claim, it may explain why Israel and the Zionist Diaspora Jews who supported it desisted from their activities. However, it does not explain why organizations that did not give the fledgling state moral and financial support also desisted. It follows that this did not depend solely on the wishes of Israel and of Jewish institutions and organizations.

Affairs in early 1952, he attempted to resume actions for the removal of children, but to no avail.[19]

Focus on children sheltered in Polish homes

The issue discussed in this study is the problem of removing Jewish children from the homes of their non-Jewish Polish rescuers after the war. Thus, the study deals solely with children who found shelter in Polish homes. The discussion makes distinctions relating to the duration of their contact with the rescuers. Not all children who left or were removed from their parents' care during the war are included in this group. Some were doomed to wander from place to place and endured a struggle for basic existence that started anew each day. Others hired themselves out for labor in different villages or found shelter in church-sponsored orphanages. I chose to concentrate on the study of the removal of children who were living with Poles, because these children's new families were, to a large extent, surrogates for their own biological parental homes. Some of the children were privileged to live with warmth and love; others were no more than laborers. Either way, however, the family setting gave them some sense of home, security, and emotional bond. After all, the natural place of a child — until he or she reaches maturity — is in a family setting. The liberation thrust these children onto the horns of a unique dilemma: even if they left the rescuer family voluntarily and more so if they were removed against their will, they had to go through a process of parting and severance of relations all over again. Throughout this period, the child's foster parents stood on one side of the divide and the biological parents or the surrogate Jewish organizations were on the other, each asserting its claim on the child.

Terminology

I chose to typify the actions of gathering the children from the homes of rescuers as "removal," a word that describes the act as such and yet reflects a large degree of neutrality. Those who were actually engaged in the work used different terms to describe their actions, such as *pidyon*[20] and *geula*,[21] both

---

19 Ibid.
20 Interview by author with Yeshayahu Drucker, September 1995; Dekel, *Remnants of the Sword*, p. 697.
21 Dekel, *Remnants of the Sword*, p. 697; Sarah Neshamit, "The Koordynacja for the Redemption of Children in Liberated Poland," *Dapim Leheker Hashoah Vehamered,* second collection (February 1952), pp. 116–142 (Hebrew); Leibl Koryski, "The Zionist Koordynacja for the Redemption of Jewish Children in Poland," in Bornstein, ed., *Redemption of Jewish Children* (Hebrew), pp. 23–33.

of which are the Hebrew terms for "redemption" but with slightly different connotations. In describing cases where rescuers refused to return children, some even used the term "captive."[22] In the course of my research, I investigated the reasons for the use of these concepts and what organization used which of them.

The expressions pertaining to Poles who took in Jewish children during and after the war vary in accordance with the speaker's worldview and the extent of emotional involvement. For example, one father who asked for assistance in removing his daughter from a Polish home wrote, "Do everything possible to have this Jewish girl removed *from the cage*" [emphasis added].[23] Another letter asked the Chief Rabbi of Palestine "[. . .] to save this tender girl from *the talons of strangers* [emphasis added"].[24] These expressions seem to originate not only in personal anguish but also in the fear that the children would remain in Christian society, lost forever to the Jewish people. One of the letters expresses this in the following way:

> There is concern that unless a way to redeem the girl is found at once, she will be lost to her family and her origins, heaven forbid... . To expedite the rescue of this tender orphan from *the talons of spiritual destruction* [emphasis added] that threatens to ambush her from every side and direction...[25]

The ironic description of the rescuers as *merciful goyim* [emphasis added] expresses anguish about gentiles who "managed to plant in the children's hearts hatred of the Jewish people and everything that is sacred and close to a Jewish child's heart."[26] However, appreciation of those who had hidden children from the Germans was also expressed. For example, one girl's uncle wrote, "I do not intend, heaven forfend, to offend the dignity of this Chris-

---

22 David Kahana, *After the Deluge: An Attempt to Revive the Religious Communities in Poland after World War II (1944–1949)* (Jerusalem: Mossad Harav Kook, 1981, Hebrew), p. 16.

23 Letter Hirsz Isaac Kurc, Melbourne, to the Koordynacja in Łódź, September 28, 1948, in the matter of R.Z., Ghetto Fighters' House Archives (GFHA), Correspondence File, 788–790.

24 Letter D. Strauss, Haifa, to Rabbi Herzog, October 24, 1946, Religious Zionism Archives (RZA), Rescue Files; see also letter Eisenberg, Basel, to Akiva Lewinsky, December 20, 1946, CZA, L58/748. The letter speaks of "[. . .] a girl who was captured by goyim and must be rescued."

25 Letter Jakob Abramowicz, Netanya, to Rabbi Herzog, February 20, 1947, in the matter of S.H., RZA, Rescue Files.

26 Eliezer Rubinstein, "The Reckoning of an Era (the Mizrachi Movement and Torah va'Avoda in Liberated Poland) [Łódź, March 1946]," *On the Paths of Rebirth*, C (1989, Hebrew), p. 185. Rubinstein was a leading personality in the Mizrachi Movement in Poland.

tian, because I am convinced that he saved the girl's life and may even have risked his own life on her behalf."[27] Accordingly, many Poles were showered with expressions of appreciation for what they had done, for example, "How immensely difficult it was to redeem them *from their benefactors* [emphasis added]."[28] However, it appears that the longer it took to remove the children, and the harder it became, the less and less emphatic the expressions of appreciation became.

I chose to call the Poles who protected children during the war, thereby sparing them from extermination, "rescuers." Thus, I apply the concept of "rescue" to what the Poles did, as opposed to some sources that invoked the same term to describe the actions of those who removed children from Polish homes after the war.[29] They chose such terminology, apparently, because the Poles were Christian; thus establishing the need to "rescue" the children from them, and, by inference, from Christianity. For example, the following was written about a girl "[. . .] who due to the general woes has assimilated among the idol-worshippers [since . . .] of course, there is Gentile influence here."[30]

Sources

The documentation on Jewish children who survived the war in Poland and the actions of various organizations taken to trace them and transfer them to Jewish institutions is found in several archives, but on different scales of importance.

The most copious documentation is kept with the *Żydówski Instytut Historyczny*, the archives of the Jewish Historical Institute in Warsaw, including the activities of the Child Care Department and the Legal Department of the Central Committee of Polish Jewry — Central Jewish Committee, and cor-

---

27 Letter Gwircman to Rabbi Herzog, December 11, 1945, in the matter of Z.S., RZA, Rescue Files.

28 "500 Jewish Children from Poland Reach France," in *Ha'aretz*, October 18, 1946,] quoted from *The Rescue Voyage* (February-September 1946): *The Journey of the Chief Rabbi of Eretz Israel, Rabbi Isaac Yitzhak HaLevi Herzog, to Europe* (Jerusalem: Dfus Ivri, 1947, Hebrew), p. 83.

29 Letter Strauss to Rabbi Herzog, October 24, 1946; letter Eisenberg to Akiva Lewinsky, December 20, 1946; Dekel, *Remnants of the Sword*, p. 697.

30 Letter Rabbi Findling, Haifa, to Rabbi Herzog, December 13, 1946, in the matter of L.E., RZA, Rescue Files; cable Zvia, Chadash, and Goldberg, Poland, to Golda Meyerson (Meir), January 13, 1945. The date should evidently be January 13, 1946, CZA, S26/1317. The writers asked for the establishment of a "child-redemption fund" due to "the immediate danger of *shmad* [spiritual destruction]."

respondence with Jewish and Palestinian organizations, government offices, and the families of rescuers.

The Central Zionist Archives in Jerusalem contain documentation on contacts between Palestine and Poland and the Diaspora. The material is very diverse, including relations between the Jewish Agency Rescue Committee, and Youth Aliyah, as well as organizations in Poland and Jewish organizations around the world.

Various archives contain documentation concerning the actions of organizations that engaged in the removal of children. The quantity of this documentation is huge in some archives and very sparse in others. However, it should be noted that the quantity of the documents does not necessarily reflect their importance. The Ghetto Fighters' House Archives are the central repository of material on the activities of the Zionist Koordynacja for the Redemption of Children in Poland, an umbrella organization that embraced several Zionist movements. In 1947, the material that had been amassed at the Koordynacja offices in Poland up to then was divided among three operatives who left for Palestine. One-third of the material was lost; the remainder was brought to Israel and is now kept in this archive.[31] There is also a card catalog (incomplete) with information on each child and details about the circumstances of his or her rescue and delivery to the Koordynacja children's home. The Religious Zionist Archives, kept at Mossad Harav Kook in Jerusalem, contain documentation about the activities of Rabbi Isaac Halevy Herzog, the chief rabbi of Palestine, and his office staff, and their relations with the Council of Jewish Religious Communities in Poland. The material includes many letters from public bodies and private individuals in Palestine sent to Rabbi Herzog. I found a small but highly important cache of material on the actions of the Mizrachi movement in the Archives of the Institute for the Study of Religious Zionism at Bar-Ilan University. At the Massuah Archives at Kibbutz Tel Yitzhak I was able to study the personal archive of Moshe Kolodny (Kol), a member of the Yishuv mission to Poland in 1946. In the Moreshet Archives at Givat Haviva, I found testimonies from operatives who were working on behalf of the Hashomer Hatza'ir movement.

---

31 Sarah Shner-Neshamit, *I Did Not Come to Rest* (Tel Aviv: Ghetto Fighters' House and Hakibbutz Hameuhad, 1986, Hebrew), p. 210. The personal card catalog and file of documents were brought to Israel by Leibl Koryski, a Hashomer Hatzair delegate to the executive board of the Koordynacja; another portion of the material and an album of children's photos was taken to Palestine by Sarah Neshamit. The portion entrusted to a representative of the Ihud party was lost en route to Palestine.

Material regarding the relations between American Jewish organizations and the bodies in Poland that acted to remove children is found in the personal documentation file of Zerach (Zorach) Warhaftig of the Mizrachi movement in the Yad Vashem Archives. The Archives of the American Jewish Joint Distribution Committee (JDC) in Jerusalem contain documentation about activities of JDC in Poland, some of which was made available to me. Although limited in scale, the material in the JDC archives is of great importance because it proves that the JDC (known as the "Joint") had not funded the Jewish children's homes, but had been directly involved in the removal of children from their rescuers. JDC also encouraged other organizations to help in the work by providing them with lists of children. Most documentation regarding JDC activity is kept in the archives of the Jewish Historical Institute in Warsaw and, at the present, is being sorted and recorded and is not accessible to the public. Nevertheless, during a visit to Warsaw, the director of the JDC Archives in Jerusalem, Dr. Sarah Kadosh, was allowed to study this material and she sent me documents that she had photocopied. The Labor Movement and HeHalutz Archives — Lavon Institute contain material that answered questions about relations between Yishuv institutions and Poland.

There are some bodies that operated in Poland about which there is no documentation. Testimonies kept with the Oral History Division at the Institute of Contemporary Jewry of the Hebrew University of Jerusalem, the Testimonies Division of the Yad Vashem Archives, and the Moreshet Archives, helped me understand the role of these organizations.

In the initial post-liberation years, most of the individuals involved in the activity wrote articles, memoirs, and testimonies in which they described their working methods, worldview, and doubts during that period. These sources compensate to a certain degree for the missing documentation. Examples are books in which emissaries from Palestine describe their activities in Poland. Some of them, for example, the writings of Moshe Yishai, a Jewish Agency emissary to Poland,[32] and Shimon Samet, a journalist for the Palestine newspaper *Ha'aretz*,[33] are of major importance. Operatives who played significant roles in reclamation actions after the war wrote books about their experiences; examples are Sarah Neshamit,[34] David Kahana,[35] and Levi Arieh

32 Moshe Yishai, *In the Shadow of the Holocaust: Memoirs of a Mission to Poland 1945–1946* (Tel Aviv: Ghetto Fighters' House and Hakibbutz Hameuhad, 1973, Hebrew).
33 Shimon Samet, *When I Came the Day After: A Journey to Poland, 1946* (Tel Aviv: Z. Leinmann, 1946, Hebrew).
34 Shner-Neshamit, *I Did Not Come to Rest.*
35 Kahana, *After the Deluge.*

Sarid.[36] Other operatives wrote articles.[37] Each writer stressed the operations in which he or she had been personally involved and, to some extent, compared them with the actions of other organizations.

I also referred to files of testimonies given by children in their own words and from their point of view, immediately after the war: an example is the testimonies that Lena Küchler-Silberman gathered for her book.[38] She spoke with residents of the children's home that she directed in Poland and recorded their life stories as they recounted them. In the same genre is Binyamin Tenenboim's book,[39] a collection of stories that were related to him by children during his stay in Poland in 1946 as an emissary of Hashomer Hatza'ir. Books of later testimonies should also be included in this group, except that their retrospective view of the war years is problematic. Examples are Wiktorja Śliwowska, *Dzieci Holocaustu Mówią* ("Children of the Holocaust Speak Out"),[40] a book written by members of Kibbutz Megiddo about various people who had been children during the war;[41] and a book by members of Kibbutz Lohamei Hagetaot.[42] Despite their limitations, these later testimonies are important because they assess actions seen with the perspective of time.

To understand the rescuers' motives and feelings, I consulted Michał Grynberg's book *Księga Sprawiedliwych* ("Book of the Righteous among the

36 Levi Arieh Sarid, *Ruin and Deliverance, the Pioneer Movements in Poland throughout the Holocaust and during its Aftermath 1939–1949* (Tel Aviv: Moreshet, 1997, Hebrew), pp. 402–420.
37 See, for example, Devorah Fleiszer, "The Rescue of 24 Children from Christian Hands," in Dov Shoval, ed., *Szebreszyn Community Memorial Book* (Haifa: Association of Szebreszyn [in Polish: Szczebrzeszyn] Jews in Israel and the Diaspora, 1984, Yiddish), pp. 300–304; Neshamit, "The Koordynacja for the Redemption of Children in Liberated Poland," pp. 116–148; Levi Arieh Sarid, "Initial Deployment of Polish Jewish Movements and the Palestine Mission, 1944–1946," in Binyamin Pinkus, ed., *East European Jewry Between Holocaust and Redemption, 1944–1948* (Sde Boker: Ben-Gurion University, 1987, Hebrew), pp. 274–333; Miriam Hochberg-Marianska, "I Cared for Child Survivors," *Yad Vashem Bulletin* 8–9 (March 1956, Hebrew), pp. 12–13; Koryski, "The Zionist Koordynacja for the Redemption of Jewish Children in Poland."
38 Lena Küchler-Silberman, *We Accuse: Testimonies of Children from the Holocaust* (Merhavia: Sifriat Poalim, 1963, Hebrew). The testimonies were written in 1946–1947.
39 Tenenboim, *One of a City, Two of a Family.*
40 Wiktorja Śliwowska, *Dzieci Holocaustu Mówią...*, vol. 1 (Warsaw: Nakładem Stowarzyszenia Dziece Holocaustu w Polsce, 1993).
41 Arye Haran, ed., Ruth Stern (interviewer), *What we Remembered to Retell: 24 Members of Kibbutz Megiddo Testify* (Tel Aviv: Moreshet and Sifriat Poalim, 1988, Hebrew).
42 Zvika Dror (interviewer and ed.), *Pages of Testimony: 96 Members of Kibbutz Lohamei Hagetaot Tell Their Stories* (Tel Aviv: Ghetto Fighters' House and Hakibbutz Hameuhad, 1984, Hebrew).

Nations"), which tells the stories of the righteous gentiles in Poland.[43] Additional books that recount the feats of Polish rescuers were written by Mordechai Paldiel,[44] Alexander Bronowski,[45] Eric Silver,[46] and Peter Helman.[47]

I also consulted books and articles in which survivor children gave their personal testimonies years after the fact[48] and expressed their feelings at the time through the prism of emotional retrospect.

To complement the information and to understand various actions and events for which I could find no documentation, I interviewed operatives in the various organizations that had been involved in removing the children, rescuers or members of their families, and persons who been rescued as children and were now adults.

These interviewees and other persons entrusted me with documents and letters that were of great assistance.

The problem of missing documentation

Most organizations that searched for Jewish children shortly after the war acted without official permission and exploited the uncertainty that enveloped Poland at the time. This had a direct bearing on the problem of documenting, since unlike the relatively complete documentation of the actions of the Central Jewish Committee, the activities of the Koordynacja are only partly documented and those of Agudath Israel and the Council of Religious

43 Michał Grynberg, *Księga Sprawiedliwych* (Warsaw: Wydawnictwo Naukowe PWN, 1993).
44 Mordechai Paldiel, *Whoever Saves One Soul: the Righteous among the Nations and Their Uniqueness* (Jerusalem: Yad Vashem, 1993, Hebrew).
45 Alexander Bronowski, *They Were Few* (Kibbutz Lohamei Hagetaot: Ghetto Fighters' House, 1990, Hebrew).
46 Eric Silver, *The Book of the Just: the Silent Heroes who Saved Jews from Hitler* (London: Weidenfeld and Nicholson, 1992).
47 Peter Hellman, *Avenue of the Righteous* (New York: Atheneum, 1980).
48 See, for example, Donia Rosen, *The Forest, My Friend* (New York: Bergen-Belsen Memorial Press of the World Federation of Bergen-Belsen Associations, 1971); Miriam Perlberger-Shmuel, *This Girl Is Jewish (Memoirs of Marysia)* (Haifa: Organization of Survivors from Wieliczka and the Vicinity in Israel, and Carmelit, 1985, Hebrew); Moshe Frank, *To Survive and Testify: The Holocaust Trauma of a Jewish Boy from Zamość* (Tel Aviv: Ghetto Fighters' House and Hakibbutz Hameuhad, 1993, Hebrew); Shlomo Grzywacz, "To the Bosom of My People," *Bulletin of the Ghetto Fighters' House* (Hebrew), April 20, 1958, pp. 59–65; Esther Wasserstein-Blanker, "After the Holocaust I Didn't Want to Return to Judaism," in Gershon Hel, ed., *Radzymin Memorial Book* (Jerusalem and Tel Aviv: Encyclopedia of the Jewish Diaspora, 1975, Hebrew), pp. 331–335.

Communities, not at all.[49] Furthermore, as the period of activities drew to a close, the Polish internal-security services confiscated documents that they had found in most offices of the organizations that were involved in removing children. I am aware of this shortcoming and tried to surmount it in various ways.

Precisely because I bore this problem in mind, I considered it of great importance to concentrate on gathering primary material. Although the effort made my research more time-consuming than it would otherwise have been, it was definitely worthwhile. Every contemporary document that dealt with a matter on the basis of later testimonies was controversial. Those documents were very valuable in discovering the facts and explaining the conflicting nature of the various testimonies.

In this study, I have attempted to compile the broadest possible picture of issues and problems that were associated with the removal of Jewish children from rescuers' homes by various Jewish bodies and organizations. Many of the issues considered in this study, and others that are more tangential, deserve further and more focused probing. Now that the archives of the Polish governing institutions have been opened to scholars, it will be possible to research the issue comprehensively and thus become better acquainted with the points of view of all parties that were involved with child rescue in postwar Poland.

Many studies concern themselves with the war years and the Holocaust. Even though the research of this horrendous episode in human history has not yet ended, the material gathered thus far suffices to teach us a great deal about it. However, this is not the case with respect to the immediate postwar period, when the effects of the war were still evident. To understand the impact of the Holocaust on shaping the realities of post-Holocaust life, much research still remains ahead.

---

49 Interview by author with Jechiel Granatstein, December 1993, in which said he said: "We gathered no testimonies and papers about the actions taken. Our great mistake was that we did not make a list of the children whom we removed. Even if Leibl [a removal operative from Agudath Israel] asked and knew details about the child, we didn't write it down anywhere."

CHAPTER 1

Circumstances Accounting for the Presence of Jewish Children in Polish Homes

"The woman conceived and bore a son, and when she saw that he was a goodly child, she hid him for three months. And when she could hide him no longer, she took a basket of bulrushes and daubed it with bitumen and pitch, and she laid the child in it and placed it among the reeds on the brink of the river. And his sister stood at a distance, to see what would be done to him."

(Exodus 2:2–4)

Introduction: A Concise History of the German Occupation

The German army entered Poland in early September 1939 and by the end of the month had occupied most of the country. In late October, a civil administration known as the Generalgouvernement was established in central Poland. Areas to the west and north of this zone were annexed to the German Reich, while the Soviet Union occupied the area to the east under the terms of the Ribbentrop-Molotov Pact, which was concluded between Germany and the USSR in August 1939.

The Germans wished to transform Poland and the east into German *Lebensraum* and to destroy the Polish nation by repressing and abusing it in various ways.[1] They categorized the Slavic Poles as belonging to an "inferior race" and considered them uncompromising enemies of the Reich.[2]

In June 1941, the Wehrmacht invaded the Soviet Union and, as it headed eastward, wrested the eastern Polish areas from Soviet control. In August 1941, the province of Galicia was annexed to the Generalgouvernement.[3]

---

1   "Poland," in *Encyclopedia of the Holocaust* (New York: Macmillan, 1990), pp. 1143ff.
2   Yisrael Gutman, "Jews of Poland in the Holocaust," in Israel Bartal and Yisrael Gutman, eds., *The Broken Chain: Polish Jewry Through the Ages* (Jerusalem: Zalman Shazar Institute, 1997, Hebrew), p. 486.
3   "Poland," in *Encyclopedia of the Holocaust*.

At the outbreak of the war, there were approximately 3,300,000 Jews in Poland — some in the areas that Germany subsequently annexed and some in the regions that had been occupied by the USSR. With the beginning of hostilities, many Jews fled eastward for fear of the Germans. Some remained beyond the frontier; others returned to Poland shortly afterward. Under the German population transfer policy, Jews were deported to the General-gouvernement from the areas that the Reich had annexed, from the Czech areas, and from Austria. By the end of September, with the completion of the occupation of Poland, directives and guidelines had been issued in regard to the policy to be applied toward the Jews in the occupied area. (See Reinhard Heydrich: *Schnellbrief*, September 21, 1939).

Upon the establishment of the Generalgouvernement, the governor of the area, Hans Frank, issued orders limiting the freedom of Jews aimed at separating them from the Polish population. A proliferation of abuses, humiliations, and forced-labor abductions followed. As time passed, the economic situation of the Jews worsened. Dispossession, economic restrictions, and ghettoization deprived many of them of their sources of livelihood. In most cases, the areas designated for the establishment of ghettos were congested and in disrepair. Hunger, poor sanitary conditions, and lack of medicines led to diseases and epidemics that claimed many lives. However, the ghettos were differentiated in the ways in which they were isolated. In small towns, where most of the population was Jewish, the ghettos were not hermetically sealed; in others, ghettos were not set up at all. In the latter, relations could still be maintained, albeit limited, with the Polish population.

The Germans accompanied their invasion of the Soviet Union with an anti-Bolshevik and anti-Jewish campaign. The anti-Jewish policy escalated in ferocity with the activation of the Einsatzgruppen and the shooting of hundreds of thousands of Jews. In the areas that they had occupied, after liquidating most of the Jewish population, the Germans established small ghettos for workers whom they needed. In early 1942, the extermination of Jews in the Generalgouvernement and the German-annexed areas began in camps that were especially built for the purpose.[4]

---

4   "The Jews in Poland," in *Encyclopedia of the Holocaust*, pp. 1151ff; Gutman, "Jews of Poland in the Holocaust," pp. 457–460, 464, 470, 474; Leni Yahil, *The Holocaust: The Fate of European Jewry* (New York: Oxford University Press, 1990).

Circumstances Behind the Attempts to Hide Children with Poles

Did the Jews understand that their future was actually non-existent? It is hard to provide a hard-and-fast answer. During the period of repression (1939–1942), the Jews presumably felt that although the situation was dire, most of them could endure the horrors. But as time passed, the estimates of the number of Jews who would be able to survive the war became increasingly pessimistic; the number of weak people climbed steadily, and Jewish existence became more precarious as the situation deteriorated. The German tactics of camouflage and deceit, combined with innate human hope, rendered most Jews incapable of foreseeing the systematic extermination that was about to take place. Even when rumors concerning events in various places began to circulate, some dismissed them as attempts to foment despair, or as provocations that would only make things worse.[5]

The Germans used various methods to separate the Jews from the Polish population at large. Their propaganda system was calculated to strengthen antisemitic elements, stressing the negative image of the Jew and emphasizing the menace that Jews presented to society — all aimed at forestalling any humanitarian response or assistance by the Poles.[6] However, as their distress steadily increased, Jews predictably sought contacts with the Polish population in order to obtain assistance. When it was found that such personal relations were indeed taking place, on October 15, 1941, General Governor Hans Frank issued a directive threatening anyone concealing or aiding Jews with the death penalty. The district governors were entrusted with the enforcement of this directive. In November 1941, the governor of Radom District, Ernst Kundt, announced the imposition of the death penalty on Jews who left the ghetto and Poles who aided them by providing shelter or food. Dr. Ludwig Fischer, the governor of Warsaw District, issued a similarly worded directive. In rural areas, village mayors were charged with implementing the edicts.[7] The very fact that such measures were announced indicates that first attempts to find refuge for both children and adults, were being made.

---

5   Gutman, "Jews of Poland in the Holocaust," pp. 472–473, 481.
6   Ringelblum, *Polish-Jewish Relations*, pp. 192–193; Fogelman, *Conscience and Courage*, p. 41.
7   Fogelman, *Conscience and Courage*, p. 30; Bronowski, *They Were Few* (New York: Lang, 1991) p. 19; "The Jews in Poland," p. 1156, Paldiel, *Whoever Saves One Soul*, pp. 15–16; Bartoszewski and Lewin, *The Samaritans*, p. 12.

When the extermination deportations began, attempts by the Jews to find safety multiplied and the Germans intensified the pressure on the Polish population to refrain from assistance. Posters announcing the death penalty for anyone helping ghetto escapees were distributed across Poland.[8] In Warsaw, for example, the directives were posted on bulletin boards from the onset of the deportations in July 1942,[9] and in some places they were accompanied by the promise of a bounty for betrayers.[10] On October 28, 1942, the Generalgouvernement SS and police commander Friedrich Wilhelm Krüger, issued the same directive and augmented it with a clause extending the penalty to anyone knowing about a Jew in hiding and failing to report it.[11] This added provision could give Poles a pretext for action against would-be rescuers from among themselves. To lend validity to the directives and to frighten the population even more, public executions of rescuers and concealed people were widely advertised.[12] Concurrently, manhunts for escapees were stepped up. These actions amplified the fears of Poles who were already assisting Jews[13] and presumably deterred other Polish citizens from emulating them.

Due to the directives and their implementation, some Poles who had concealed Jewish children regretted having done so. In such extreme danger, a great deal of courage and resolve was needed to continue to help concealed Jews. Under these circumstances, each individual had to reassess the situation — and, on the basis of their assessment, people acted in various ways. Some treated the hidden children as flaming coals and hurriedly turned them

8   Testimony: Binyamin Blustein, Yad Vashem Archives (YVA), O.3/5058.

9   Ringelblum, *Polish-Jewish Relations*, p. 152.

10 Fogelman, *Conscience and Courage*, p. 138; Aryeh Bauminger, *The Righteous among the Nations* (Jerusalem: Yad Vashem, 1990), p. 141.

11 Bartoszewski and Lewin, *The Samaritans*, p. 12.

12 Fogelman, *Conscience and Courage*, pp. 30, 234; Bauminger, *The Righteous among the Nations*, p. 141; Rosen, *The Forest, My Friend*, p 46 in Hebrew edition only. See also Bartoszewski and Lewin, *The Samaritans*, Chap. 20, "The Price of Giving Assistance," pp. 420–433, which lists many instances of punishments for persons who concealed Jews.

13 Ringelblum, *Polish-Jewish Relations*, p. 271; Rosen, *The Forest, My Friend*, p. 46 in Hebrew edition only; Fogelman, *Conscience and Courage*, p. 30; Testimony Mira Bramm, No. S-342, given in 1945 at the children's house in Kraków. The testimony was provided to me by Mira Bramm-Ehrlich and is in my possession. After the war, when she reached the children's house in Kraków, the girl was interviewed and her testimony was recorded on site; Tuvia Lewinsky, "Testimony," in Bornstein, ed., *Redemption of Jewish Children*; Bertha Frederbahr-Salz, *And the Sun Rose* (Tel Aviv: Naye Lebn, 1968, Hebrew).

over to the authorities[14] or sent them back to the ghetto.[15] Despite the difference in the two responses, both were tantamount to a death sentence for the children. Other Poles protected the children while their homes were being searched but afterwards asked them to leave.[16] Their conscience would not allow them to harm the children directly but they could not endure the emotional effort entailed by the act of concealment. Some such people stayed in touch with the children and subsequently even helped them.[17]

During their incarceration in the ghettos, and despite the grim living conditions, few Jews considered entrusting their children to Polish families. A feeling that the Polish population had little sympathy for the Jews in the ghettos may have persuaded many to keep their children with them and to provide them with what little protection they had, believing that no one could do this better than they themselves. Even when starvation, disease, and forced labor shattered the family unit, those who remained, clung to each other. One may conjecture that the commitment and the need to protect the vestiges of the family gave those who remained the strength to continue the struggle for a modicum of a reasonable daily life.[18] In the ghettos, there were welfare institutions that could provide some aid, even though their resources were very limited. In the Warsaw Ghetto in 1941, for example, Centos (National Society for the Care of Orphans) posted notices with the caption, "Our Children Must Live." The notices called on Jews to donate money so as to maintain the organization's institutions: kitchens, diners, care centers, and several childcare facilities.[19] The focus was directed at children due to the

---

14 Paldiel, *Whoever Saves One Soul*, pp. 68–69; autobiography of Chaim Goldmann, Tenenboim, *One of a City, Two of a Family*, p. 199; Chaim Meir Beck, "Testimony: How a Shtetl was Destroyed," in David Stockfisch, ed., *The Book of Kraśnik* (Tel Aviv: Association of Kraśnik Survivors in Israel and the Diaspora, 1973, Hebrew), p. 225.

15 Autobiography of Basha Halpern, in Tenenboim, *One of a City, Two of a Family*, pp. 94–95; Yonas Turkow, "On the Rescue of Children from the Warsaw Ghetto," *Pages in the Study of the Holocaust and the Uprising*, CIS 2, Collection A (1970) (Hebrew), p. 261.

16 Autobiography of Shraga Segal, in Tenenboim, *One of a City, Two of a Family*, p. 204; autobiography Ita Teitz, ibid., p. 70; testimony Sabina Halperin, Moreshet Archive (MA), A.201; testimony Mira Bramm.

17 Bauminger, *Righteous Among the Nations*, p. 141; testimony Sukha Shmueli, MA, A.217.

18 Interview by author with David (Jurek) Plonski, December 1989; Wladka Feygl Peltel Miedzyrzecka, *On Both Sides of the Wall: Memoirs of an Underground Liaison Operator* (Tel Aviv: Hakibbutz Hameuhad, 1993, Hebrew), pp. 117–118 (in English: Wladka Meed, *On Both Sides of the Wall: Memoirs from the Warsaw Ghetto);* testimony Chana Owrucki-Mendelberger, YVA, O.3/5773).

19 Reuven Ben-Shem, "From a Diary of the Warsaw Ghetto," *Massuah*, 10 (April 1982) (Hebrew), p. 50.

need to save them, both as individuals and for the sake of Jewish continuity, and due to their extreme vulnerability. At the time, the concept of "must live" was concentrated on the rescue of children within the ghetto. Had Centos considered that rescue was likely only outside the ghetto, it still might have been possible to utilize pre-war contacts, and the possibilities of rescue might have been greater. Notably, however, people who turned to acquaintances often had their hopes dashed, finding that relations established in peacetime were not necessarily valid in wartime.[20]

As time went on, the Jews sensed increasingly that their children were in especially grave danger. The ghetto population was sorted into those who were "efficient" for labor and those who were not, with children included among the latter. The realization of the need to remove children from the inferno can be traced to the time when rumors about deportations began to arrive.[21] Parents realized that keeping their children with them would not provide security and that as opposed to the hopelessness of rescue in the ghetto as a family, there might be a slim chance of saving them by placing them in non-Jewish hands.[22] So at this point, anyone who could contact someone on the outside did so. The escape was not always carried out at the time of this preparatory step; sometimes parents established the relationship so that it could be invoked at a later time of need.[23]

Parents faced an exceedingly difficult emotional dilemma in the very act of handing over their children to non-Jews. Since many were afraid of what their children would face on the Aryan side without them, some preferred to keep them close by, thus providing them with a sense of security that they themselves did not share, and protect them until death. For example, an operative in an organization that removed children from the Warsaw Ghetto described the torment of a mother who had been offered the possibility of moving her son to the Aryan side:

20 Tec, *When Light*, pp. 129–130.
21 Letter JDC-Warsaw to Central Jewish Committee, May 27, 1949, in the matter of K., in response to letter May 17, 1949, ŻIH, Education Department, Warsaw, File 638; Tuvia Lewinsky, "Memoir: My Wanderings and My Rescuer," written testimony given to me by the witness and in my possession; interview by author with Ella Plonski, December 1989; written testimony and personal card from children's home in Poland of Edward (Yaron) Gruder, given to me by the witness and in my possession.
22 Interview by author with David Plonski, 1989.
23 Śliwowska, *Dzieci Holocaustu Mówią*, pp. 11–12; Ephraim Dekel, "Along the Paths of the Bricha," B, *Ma'arakhot*, Tel Aviv, 1969 (Hebrew), p. 437; letter Adela Schiff, New York, to Central Committee, June 12, 1946, in the matter of H., ŻIH, Education Department, File 638.

Manya... did not reply. Heavily she bent her pale, exhausted face. She was silent for a long time. "No, believe me. I haven't got the strength. I can't send him away.... . I am all my eleven-year-old son has in the world. I watch over him like the apple of my eye. I've already gone through all stages of the German hell with him. No. Without me, he won't survive... ." She breathed heavily. I fell silent.... . Manya... did not reply. Her eyes were downcast. I sensed the emotions that raged in her heart... . Still she did not reply. After a heavy silence, she finally answered in a trembling voice: "No, I haven't got the strength. What will become of me will become of my son. We've gone through so much together. Maybe both of us will find a way to stay alive... and maybe both us will perish... ." She ended in a whisper.[24]

Others chose to keep their children with them for religious reasons; although aware of the dangers, they were afraid of *shmad* ("spiritual murder," i.e. loss of Jewish identity and defection to another religion).[25]

Many Jewish families had Polish live-in nannies with whom they maintained relations even after they moved to the ghetto. Some devoted nannies even moved to the ghetto together with their employers and continued to care for the children, only leaving at a later stage.[26] In most cases, the relations of dependency and love that had formed between the caregivers and the children were impossible to overcome.[27] As the situation in the ghetto worsened, it was natural that the family and the nanny would continue their relationship. Sometimes this happened at the initiative of the family[28] and sometimes it was the nanny who came to the ghetto gate and asked the family

24 Peltel Miedzyrzecka, *On Both Sides of the Wall*, pp. 118–119. The interlocutor was Manya Zygielbojm, wife of Szmul Zygielbojm, a Bund leader in Poland who was in London at the time. Manya and her son perished during the ghetto uprising; David Plonski recounted a similar case in his own family when, for the same reasons, his mother refused to hand his younger brother to him; interview by author with David Plonski, 1989; Ringelblum, *Polish-Jewish Relations*, pp. 140–141; Turkow, "On the Rescue of Children from the Warsaw Ghetto," p. 262.
25 Turkow, "On the Rescue of Children from the Warsaw Ghetto," p. 261.
26 Interview by author with Ceisza Landau, March 1988; testimony Ljuba Timianski, YVA, O.3/5131.
27 Testimony Wiktor, in Küchler, *We Accuse*, p. 37; "A Polish Woman Relates," in Noah Gruss, *Child Martyrdom* (Buenos Aires: Tsentral Farband Fun Poylishe Yidn in Argentine, 1947, Yiddish), pp. 91–94; interview by author with Yehudit Szwarcbach, December 1989.
28 Testimony Michael, in Küchler, *We Accuse*, p. 157.

to allow her to care for the child.[29] There were even cases in which children who left the ghetto turned — at their own initiative, naturally — to their erstwhile caregiver for shelter.[30] Notably, quite a few caregivers who hid their former charges survived the war under great hardship, lacking a secure source of livelihood, hiring themselves out for labor in various homes, while at the same time protecting the concealed children and meeting their needs.[31]

The policy adopted by the Germans in moving the Jews to central locations and from the countryside to towns, from certain towns to cities, and from the annexed areas to the Generalgouvernement, coupled with confinement in the ghettos (which were more strictly sealed as 1942 approached), led to the rupturing of relations with Polish acquaintances. At this juncture, with the critical moment at hand, parents had to make more strenuous efforts to establish new ties and find a place to conceal their children. Especially daunting was the situation in small towns that were relatively close together, where Jews made up a perceptible share of the population, and where villages in the vicinity had commercial relations with the town and people knew each other. It was almost impossible to conceal a child in such a place without fear of identification.[32] Parents and rescuers in such localities had to plan meticulously a way to transfer and hide children without endangering either the child or the rescuer.[33]

On the eve of the deportations to labor and extermination camps, most Jewish families were destitute, having spent several years depleting their resources on food and other necessities of life. A few Jews, however, were still relatively well off, either because they had been more affluent to begin with, and had saved their resources for time of need, or for other reasons such as having an occupation that they could practice in the ghetto.[34] Those who

---

29 Gruss, *Child Martyrdom*, pp. 91–94; Mordechai Paldiel, "Rescuers in the Footsteps of the Rescued: Righteous Gentiles Living in Israel," *Moreshet*, 41 (June 1986) (Hebrew), in regard to Helena Szemet, p. 29.

30 Testimony Michael, in Küchler, *We Accuse*, p. 37.

31 Interview by author with Ceisza Landau, 1988; Lena Küchler-Silberman, *My Hundred Children* (London: Pan Books, 1963), pp. 95–97 (in Hebrew); in regard to Helena Szemet and Gertruda Babilenska, see Paldiel, "Rescuers in the Footsteps of the Rescued," pp. 26, 29; Ringelblum, *Polish-Jewish Relations*, p. 143; Gideon Meron, "Because of that War," *Yediot Aharonot* Friday supplement, June 9, 1995, pp. 50–54.

32 Ringelblum, *Polish-Jewish Relations*, pp. 137–138; Fleiszer, "The Rescue of 24 Children," pp. 300–304.

33 Grynberg, *Księga Sprawiedliwych*, "Jan and Janina Kosuth," p. 257.

34 Turkow, "On the Rescue of Children from the Warsaw Ghetto," p. 261; Tsalek Perehodnik, *The Sad Task of Documentation: A Diary in Hiding* (Jerusalem: Keter, 1993, Hebrew), pp. 41–42.

could not afford the essential preparations for the removal of their children spared no effort to raise the necessary funds. For others, awareness of the need to remove their children to safety was an unattainable dream. Those who had been impoverished to begin with had nothing to offer for the rescue of their children at the critical moment.

Jews who shared their workplaces with Poles tried to exploit the relationship.[35] Others, who were unable to establish relations, chose in their distress to send their children to their fate outside the ghetto, with no specific address.[36] Under the pressure of time and emotional distress, some parents resorted to removing a child from the ghetto and leaving him or her somewhere as a foundling, with a note beseeching the finder to shelter and take care of the little one. An example is the note that a father placed with his young daughter: "The father, Adler Moshe, lives at Leszno 24/54, the mother, Bella Adler Spocznykow, Rysia Adler, my daughter, five years old, is handed over at a critical moment in our disaster. Moshe Adler, for the Joint, date: April 30, 1943."[37] From the wording of the letter, one may speculate that the father hoped that the girl and the information about her would be handed over to the Jewish Joint Distribution Committee after the war. There were also children who gauged the situation by themselves and set out at their own initiative,[38] even though they would have only themselves to rely on. Some of them managed to find a family that agreed to take them

35 Dekel, *Remnants of the Sword*, p. 202; Eliezer Yerushalmi, *Children of the Holocaust* (Haifa: MiMa'amamakim, 1960, Hebrew), pp. 30–32; letter, Organization of Survivors of Opoczno to Rabbi Herzog, March 31, 1946, in the matter of R., RZA, Rescue Files; child card of Jozio (Yosef Aizik) Szrajber, GFHA, catalogue of Koordynacja children's cards, File 800.

36 Grynberg, *Księga Sprawiedliwych*, "Julia and Edmond Bieseada," p. 43; ibid., Józef and Franciszka Kuriata, pp. 284–285; autobiography Withold Wajman, in Tenenboim, *One of a City, Two of a Family*, pp. 131–132; autobiography Ita Teitz, ibid., p. 70; testimony Hela, in Küchler, *We Accuse*, p. 187; interview by author with Chana Martynowski-Gutmorgen, August 1995; Lewinsky, "My Wanderings and My Rescuers."

37 A copy of the letter was published in the Koordynacja newspaper that appeared in November 1946 in one edition only. See *Farn Yiddishn Kind*, pp. 4–5, GFHA, File 798; for further examples, see Dekel, *In the Paths of the Bricha*, p. 437; Mali Kempner, "Only the Baby Survived," in *Yediot Aharonot* Friday supplement, June 8, 1990, pp. 31–33, 56; Ch. Leiberman, "The Heartbreak of a Jewish Mother," in the matter of Igenfeld-Besserman, ŻIH, Education Department, File 638; Noah Klinger, "The Jewish Baby who was Thrown from the Warsaw Ghetto Wall is in Israel," in *Yediot Aharonot*, Friday, February 10, 1989; Gershon Janisz, "The Epic of my Rescued Daughter Shifraleh 'Bogumila'," in Gershon Hel, ed., *Radzymin Memorial Book*, p. 337.

38 Testimony Wiktor, in Küchler, *We Accuse*, p. 37; testimony Zipora Minc, MA, A.262.

in.[39] In such cases, the parents lost contact with their children at the moment of the separation and had no information whatsoever about their fate and whereabouts.[40]

In their uncompromising struggle to save their children from the inferno, Jewish parents sometimes used threats to induce Poles to hide their children from the Germans[41] or, after they had already been hidden, to refrain from betraying them.[42] In these cases, parents exploited the fear of the occupation authorities, on the one hand, and members of the Polish resistance, on the other.

Assistance from Żegota

The heart-searchings, initiatives, planning, and acts of saving children described thus far, were carried out individually by families that attempted to solve their dilemmas in ways that suited their connections, status, and economic ability. It is hard to believe that there was a single parent who did not spend sleepless nights wrestling with the question of how to save the children, even if he or she decided not to part with them. As we have explained, some were willing to endanger themselves while others were paralyzed by fear. Be this as it may, everything was done within the family circle, far from the public view.

An exception to this rule was the organized action, albeit rather limited in scale, that took place in the Warsaw Ghetto mainly after the great deporta-

---

39 Silver, *The Book of the Just*, pp. 123–125; Appeal at decision of Tarnów municipal court, presented by Goldfinger to Tarnów district court, heard by the judge Dr. Nałek, File OP16/46 (Icz361/46), November 22, 1946, in the matter of C.Z. and S.Z., known as Hubel, GFHA, Correspondence File, 788–790.

40 Janisz, "The Epic," pp. 340–341; interview by author with Roma Jarska, Kraków, July 1995. The boy's father, who had been in a concentration camp, did not know where his family had placed the child. The father survived, returned to his hometown, and searched for the boy unsuccessfully. The boy had survived the war but the father died without realizing this. Only recently was contact established between the boy, now an adult, and the rescuers' daughter, and with his relatives in Israel.

41 Fogelman, *Conscience and Courage*, p. 96. The woman at issue threatened, in the event that certain Poles refused to receive her son, to inform the Germans that they were concealing Jews in their home. Both the mother and the rescuers knew that this might cost them their lives.

42 Frederbahr-Salz, *And the Sun Rose*, p. 70. The mother informed the rescuers that she had relations with the Polish resistance and that the resistance was monitoring their behavior with her children.

tions. The Jewish welfare institutions and the staffs of two departments at the Municipality of Warsaw — Welfare and Assistance to Children and Youth — had enjoyed a working relationship before the war and they maintained their relationship even after the ghetto was sealed. The municipal workers were allowed to enter the ghetto,[43] and in some cases, they helped to remove children and place them in hiding.[44] In the aftermath of these initial actions, when extermination deportations began in the summer of 1942, attempts were made to formalize these actions so that children could be removed from the ghetto in an organized way.[45] These operations had to be "institutionalized" because the large-scale extrication of children entailed a mechanism that had to prepare papers, establish exit routes, find sources of funding, arrange hideouts, etc.[46]

Although the institutionalization of these activities took place only after the deportations began, it was based on action by the departments and individuals who had been active beforehand. After its establishment in December 1942, Żegota (*Rada Pomocy Żydom*, the Council for Aid to Jews) extended its patronage to the actions that were being taken. Żegota was also active in Kraków, Lwów,[47] Zamość, and Lublin.[48] Most of the Jews had been extermi-

43 Fogelman, *Conscience and Courage*, p. 197; Bartoszewski and Lewin, *The Samaritans*, p. 72; Turkow, "On the Rescue of Children from the Warsaw Ghetto," pp. 257–258.
44 Grynberg, *Księga Sprawiedliwych*, "Wanda Wyrobek-Pawłowska," p. 626.
45 Jonas Turkow, *Once There Was a Jewish Warsaw* (Tel Aviv: Education and Culture, 1969, Hebrew), pp. 140–141; Kurek-Lesik, "*Udzial Żeńkich*," pp. 329–332.
46 Turkow, "On the Rescue of Children from the Warsaw Ghetto," pp. 258–260; Bartoszewski and Lewin, *The Samaritans*, p. 72; Fogelman, *Conscience and Courage*, p. 216. Fogelman claims that the Dutch resistance group known as "Utrecht," which dealt with the placement of Jewish children in hideouts, initially found it difficult to convince parents to surrender their children due to their mistrust of non-Jews. In Belgium, the resistance surmounted the problem by working with Jews who persuaded parents of the necessity of handing over their children. In Poland, in contrast, the non-Jewish operatives were trusted because the women involved in the activities knew each other and had worked together and in the ghettos before the deportations.
47 "Żegota," *Encyclopedia of the Holocaust*, pp. 1729–1730; Gutman, "Jews of Poland in the Holocaust," p. 491.
48 Bartoszewski and Lewin, *The Samaritans*, pp. 89–91; Adolf Avraham Berman, *From the Days of the Resistance* (Tel Aviv: Hamenora, 1971, Hebrew), p. 190; Joseph Kermish, "The Activities of the Council for Aid to Jews ('Żegota') in Occupied Poland," in Yisrael Gutman, ed., *Rescue Attempts During the Holocaust: Proceedings of the Second Yad Vashem International Conference* (Jerusalem: Yad Vashem, 1977), pp. 377–378. Kermish notes that many parents tried to save their children on their own by moving them to the Aryan side especially during and after the first *Aktion*. Due to Żegota's activities in Warsaw, by late 1943 there were some 600 children on the Aryan side; in the Zamość-Lublin District there were approximately 200 children under their care in early 1943.

nated by then — and since children were the first to be harmed, few children remained alive relative to the survivor population as a whole.[49] Ringelblum, reviewing these actions after he had left the ghetto, complained that the Poles were not doing more to rescue Jewish children. He hoped that the government would move to rescue the few Jewish children who had survived in the ghetto, and when this did not happen he inferred that the Polish public was indifferent and would continue to be so.[50]

The Jewish members of Żegota acted vigorously to canvass those of means in the ghetto for funding for the council's activities and to persuade parents to give up their children,[51] but most of the money was raised on the Aryan side.[52] Fogelman claims that Żegota removed some 2,500 children from the ghetto.[53] After arranging their papers, she says, the organization placed them with Polish families for a trial period, and afterwards usually arranged a place for them in various Polish institutions.[54] Two women members of Żegota, Irena Sendler and Jadwiga Piotrkowska, testified that they had kept records of children who had been moved to the Aryan side and, in order not to endanger them, placed the information in bottles that they buried in a garden so that the children's identities could be established later. After the war, however, only a few of these bottles were found.[55]

Preparations for Separation from the Children

The preparations for separating from their child created horrendous emotional situations for the parents. Typically, their thoughts and feelings were

49 Dekel, *Remnants of the Sword*, p. 65.
50 Ringelblum, *Polish-Jewish Relations*, p. 222; Vladka Feygl Peltel, a liaison officer on the Aryan side, voiced the same accusation. Peltel Miedzyrzecka, *On Both Sides of the Wall*, p. 117.
51 Turkow, "On the Rescue of Children from the Warsaw Ghetto," pp. 258–260; idem, *Once There Was a Jewish Warsaw*, pp. 140–141.
52 "Żegota," p. 1729.
53 Fogelman, *Conscience and Courage*, p. 197.
54 Bartoszewski and Lewin, *The Samaritans*, p. 72.
55 Interview by author with Ita Kowalska, Warsaw, August 1993; Kurek-Lesik, "*Udzial Żeńkich,*" p. 341; the following people, among others, took part in child-rescue actions in Warsaw: among the Jews: Ella Golomb-Grynberg, head nurse at the hospital on the Umschlagplatz, who established the initial contacts; Batya Berman-Temkin, Jonas Turkow, Wanda (Bella Alsteryes), Josef Ziminian (Juzio), Ada Margulies; among the Poles: Julian Grobelny ("Trojan"), Aleksander Dargal, Jan Dobraczyński, Jadwiga Piotrkowska, Irena Sendler.

divided into two: in the first place, to prepare the children for life under a false identity and secondly, to teach them not to forget their real identity. A rescued girl related, "The [false] name that my mother gave me was Marta; my real name was Tamar. Even though I was five years old, I repeated the word 'Marta' many times every day really fast and then 'Tamar' would come out. That's how I remembered the details about myself, even though they told me to forget."[56] Evidently the name Marta was not chosen at random; it attested to the creativity that had been invested in it.

When the moment of parting came, the parents were thrust into an emotional maelstrom. Death was knocking on the door; they thought they might never see their child again. However, they were also relieved to have found a way to rescue their child. To spare children further hardship, and fearing that the emotional turmoil might impede their rescue, parents strove not to share their emotions and anxieties with their children. This made the moment of parting more difficult for the parents than for the child. In most cases, the children grasped the full significance of the separation only later. Their subsequent descriptions of the parting moment are very difficult and convey a sense of something having being sacrificed. Here is how one of the girls described her separation from her mother when she was five years old:

> On the bridge, Mother stopped and began to speak to me. She told me that I should go to a certain address, she wrote it down for me on a scrap of paper, and she told me that if I forgot it — I should show people the note with the address. I stood there in total indifference. I heard what she told me, she didn't even hug me, didn't kiss me, maybe she was afraid to show me any love. I don't know. She sat down next to me so that she'd see my face and she spoke to me.... She gave me the note and a slice of bread and jam wrapped in a rag and told me, "Take care of this because it's the last slice of bread; we don't have any more."[57]

56 Tamar Jacobi-Friedman, "Testimony," in Bornstein, ed., *Redemption of Jewish Children*, p. 56; see also interview by author with Lucia Milch-Rosenzweig, New York, August 1995. Lucia's mother asked her to memorize two addresses: one in Canada and one in New York. As soon as she learned them, however, her mother ordered her to forget them, as well as her Jewish identity. When Lucia, stunned, asked what this meant, her mother replied, "That's how it is... your life depends on it."
57 Testimony Chana Batista, YVA, O.3/5732; see also Dror (interviewer and ed.), *Pages of Testimony*, A, "Lila Hundert," pp. 271–275; Yitzhak Sternberg, ibid., B. p. 734; Gruss, *Child Martyrdom*, pp. 95–96; autobiography Ziva Samet, in Tenenboim, *One of a City, Two of a Family*, p. 121; autobiography Ruth Alpher, ibid., p. 138; interview by author with David Plonski, 1989; interview by author with Rachel Kagan-Plodwinska, December, 1989; Peltel Miedzyrzecka, *On Both Sides of the Wall*, pp. 117–118.

The way the parents viewed the transfer of their children to Poles depended largely on the stage at which the transfer took place. Neither side knew for certain whether the child was being "deposited" for a limited period of time until the family would be reunited, or whether the rescuer would actually determine the child's future.[58] If by the time of the placement the parents no longer believed that either of them would survive, they strove to find a Polish family, preferably a childless one, who would wish to raise their child as its own, thereby perhaps assuring him or her of the appropriate care.[59] Obviously, a family who met these criteria would prefer to have the parents relinquish the child unconditionally and in advance. The dilemma of the parents can be understood by considering the following case: parents who had been sent to the Święciany Ghetto (today in Lithuania) with their four-year-old son found a family that agreed to take the boy in return for a payment for upkeep. After several months, the family returned the boy to his parents, saying that they were afraid to keep him because he had been circumcised. The boy's mother, pregnant at the time, decided to try to save at least the child whom she was carrying in her womb. She found another woman, a childless one, who had adopted a girl at an earlier time but had been forced to return her to her mother, and she contacted this woman and offered her the baby. The woman initially refused, fearful about having to relive the process of bonding with and then parting with a child. However, the mother promised that she would never demand the return of her child and only wanted him to live, even if he were to become a priest. The woman took the boy three days after he was born, had him baptized, and registered him as her son. Later on, she found out that the parents and their four-year-old son had been murdered. The boy stayed with the rescuer, who raised him as her own.[60]

58 Copy of court ruling in Lublin, June 11, 1947, in the matter of J.K. (S.R.); appeal of ruling by court in Nowa Ruda, presented by Helena Fuchsberg to the court in Kłodzko, case mOP1/46, May 5, 1948, in the matter of L.F., who also appears as Z.K. Grzegorczyk. The petition, submitted after the war, discusses the girl's future. The central question in the litigation was the father's intentions when he handed her over, with emphasis on the fact that this had occurred "at a time when the Germans had begun to bring extermination actions against the Jews and quarantine them in prisons and concentration camps." See GFHA, Correspondence File, 788–790; see also Fogelman, *Conscience and Courage*, p. 150; Grynberg, *Księga Sprawiedliwych*, "Ługowski," p. 315.

59 Interview by author with Haim Edelstein, Nazareth, August 1996; Ringelblum, *Polish-Jewish Relations*, p. 143.

60 Amit Reicher, "The Priest Burst into Tears in the Confessional Booth: 'I am Jewish,'" in *Yediot Aharonot*, July 17, 1992, pp. 16–17. The priest discovered his Jewishness only when his adoptive mother was hospitalized in February 1978; see also Dekel, *Remnants of the Sword*, p. 207, where a Pole is reported as having asked parents for a letter affirming the

Hardships of Concealment

The difficulties in locating rescuers were compounded by objective hardships that limited a child's ability to be taken in by potential rescuers and that dictated, to a large extent, the degree of danger involved. Some of the Jews looked Polish in terms of facial features and skin color[61] but many others did not, instead resembling to a greater or lesser extent, the stereotypical Jew: dark, curly hair, long nose, dark eyes, and other perceived "typical Jewish" features.[62] Thus, the task of finding a hideout for a child would be easier or harder depending on his or her appearance.[63]

In many Jewish homes, especially in the *shtetls* (small Jewish towns or *shtetlakh*), Yiddish was the vernacular spoken at home, while Polish was used only in interaction with the surroundings. Children raised in religiously orthodox homes were usually less likely than others to be fluent in Polish, since these circles had less regular contact with the non-Jewish population. This does not infer that all such children could not understand Polish, but they tended to speak a Jewish-inflected Polish that was replete with readily identifiable expressions loosely translated from the Yiddish.[64]

Even Jewish families which led secular lives, maintained social relations with Poles and were immersed in Polish culture, also displayed some Jewish features in their lives at home. Hardly any Jewish children were familiar with Christian practices and prayers, or how to cross themselves, so that they could easily blend into Catholic surroundings.[65] Furthermore, since the Jewishness

renunciation of their child; see also ibid., pp. 206–213; see also responses of Maria Kruszala, Poland, to my questionnaire; testimony Alexandra Plonski-Brandwein, in Haran, ed., *What We Remembered to Tell*, p. 122.

61 Letter B.M. to Koordynacja, Łódź, GFHA, Correspondence File, 788–780; letter Tenenboim, Rome, via Committee of Polish Jews in Italy, to Central Committee, March 3, 1948, in the matter of H., ŻIH Education Department, File 638; Silver, *The Book of the Just*, "Witold Pamięko," pp. 125–127.

62 Autobiography Sabina Shtickgold, in Tenenboim, *One of a City, Two of a Family*, pp. 24–25. When the war broke out, nine-year-old Sabina managed to escape with her younger sister. In her post-war testimony, she explained, "This sister, whose face gave her away as a Jew, caused me a lot of trouble"; see also Shulamit Magen, "First and Last Memory," written in 1992 and provided to me by her husband; Turkow, "*Once There Was a Jewish Warsaw*," p. 145.

63 Turkow, "On the Rescue of Children from the Warsaw Ghetto," p. 261.

64 Interview by author with David Plonski, 1989; letter Marian Bafilis to Koordynacja, Łódź, GFHA, Correspondence File, 788–790.

65 Turkow, "On the Rescue of Children from the Warsaw Ghetto," p. 263; testimony Mira Bramm.

of boys could be readily determined — they were circumcised after all — it was harder to find places of concealment for them[66] than for girls.[67] Desperate to save their sons, some parents began in late 1942 when few Jewish children remained in Warsaw, to perform underground circumcision reversal operations. These procedures did not always end successfully.[68]

Adjustment to and immersion in Polish society was, of course, a precondition for the survival of the children. However, as for centuries Jewish society in Poland had segregated itself from its non-Jewish surroundings, the parents lacked the necessary knowledge to impart to their children for successful concealment. Therefore, the responsibility for conveying fundamental knowledge to the Jewish child and for imparting the culture, daily routines, and the Christian faith in the shortest possible time became the responsibility of the Polish rescuer.[69]

Since most Jewish families had several children, parents found it agonizingly difficult to decide who should be handed over to Poles and sent out of the ghetto; that is to say, which of their children would have the strongest likelihood of survival. Sometimes it was the parents who made the decision and sometimes the rescuers; it all depended on the circumstances. When the rescue action took place at the last moment and the parents had no clear address to which to deliver the child, they usually preferred to send older children. One person who was rescued as an adolescent recalls: "If father hadn't insisted, we wouldn't have gone. He simply threw us out, three of the six, and kept the younger ones at home."[70] It stands to reason that one could send a young child out of the ghetto only if there was someone to receive him or her on the Aryan side. The rescuers actually preferred infants — whom one could

66 Turkow, "On the Rescue of Children from the Warsaw Ghetto," p. 261; idem, *Once There Was a Jewish Warsaw*, p. 145. Turkow relates that Emanuel Ringelblum's son was returned to the ghetto despite his "good" appearance, since children discovered his Jewish identity while he was bathing; Reicher, "The Priest Burst Into Tears," pp. 16–17.

67 Fogelman, *Conscience and Courage*, p. 139.

68 Turkow, "On the Rescue of Children from the Warsaw Ghetto," p. 264.

69 Rosen, *The Forest, My Friend*, p. 46 in Hebrew edition only; interview by author with Ella Plonski.

70 Lewinsky, "My Wanderings and My Rescuer." Ultimately, only the writer, Tuvia, the youngest of the siblings whom the father expelled (b.1932) survived. His sister could not find a hideout and returned to her parents; his brother was denounced and murdered. See also interview by author with Chana Martynowski-Gutmorgen. The Gutmorgens sent their four children aged ten and up out of the ghetto a day before the ghetto was liquidated; they kept their four younger children with them and all were murdered; Binyamin Blustein's testimony tells a similar story.

educate with relative ease — or adolescents who understood the dangers and knew how to maintain silence. It was more difficult with children aged four to ten who might stumble when put to the test. An example is an incident involving the granddaughter of Rabbi Jacob Trockenheim, a leader of the orthodox Agudath Israel who was rescued by a Polish policeman. One Saturday, the policeman rode with her on a streetcar, conversed with Germans in the car, and smoked a cigarette. The girl interrupted their conversation, commenting loudly that smoking is forbidden on the Sabbath and that her father did not smoke on that day. The policeman took advantage of the moment of shock that her comment had caused and leaped from the car into the street, carrying the girl.[71]

It is worth remembering that most of the Polish population, although immeasurably better off than the Jews, were themselves in dire economic straits. Financial considerations also figured in the concealment of children. The youngsters had to be provided with clothing, food, and a place to hide, and sometimes the concealing family had to move to a different address or change jobs.[72] Nevertheless, not everyone who concealed Jewish children received money or goods, even though some rescuers made remuneration a basic condition.[73]

Poles who hid Jewish children in their homes were liable to many forms of pressure. The threat of the death penalty placed them in daily jeopardy.[74] The severest pressure, however, was applied by fellow Poles. Since the Germans usually depended upon assistance from the local population in order to identify or uncover a Jew, German law extended the threat of the death penalty to those who knew about a hidden Jew. For this reason, one may conjecture that a combination of antisemitism and the fear of punishment generated severe ambient pressure against rescuers.[75] Furthermore, it is obvious that

---

71 Eliezer Rubinstein, "Our Children," Religious Zionism Research Institute (RZRI), S.20ID; Fogelman, *Conscience and Courage*, p. 139.
72 Jacobi-Friedman, "Testimony," pp. 56–57; Shneor Zalman Cheshin, *Adoptive Children* (Ramat Gan: Massada, 1955, Hebrew), p. 130; Dekel, *Remnants of the Sword*, pp. 645–651; testimony Chana Owrucki-Mendelberger, YVA, O.3/5773; Grynberg, *Księga Sprawiedliwych*, "Wacław and Halina Tarasewicz," pp. 568–569.
73 Fleiszer, "The Rescue of 24 Children," p. 302; child card of Juzio (Yosef Aizik) Szrajber, GFHA, Correspondence File, 788–790.
74 Gruss, *Child Martyrdom*, pp. 91–94; Paldiel, *Whoever Saves One Soul*, pp. 14–16; Gutman, "Jews of Poland in the Holocaust," p. 492; letter Maria Balcerzak, Poland.
75 Fogelman, *Conscience and Courage*, p. 85; Paldiel, *Whoever Saves One Soul*, pp. 15–16, 25; Kempner, "Only the Baby," pp. 31, 33, 56; Grynberg, *Księga Sprawiedliwych*, "Apolonia Ołdak," p. 387; interview by author with Janina Chryc, September 1994, Jastrzebie, Poland.

the German laws provided an incentive for those who were unsympathetic to Jews in any case and objected to any assistance proffered to them. Rescuers were more fearful of persecution by local antisemites than by the Germans, and it was this factor that ultimately explains the limited results of the child-rescue operation.[76] Support for this statement may be found in the testimonies of many rescuers and survivors who recounted their fear of the people around them[77] and even members of the rescuers' own families.[78] One may perhaps find support for the claim that the behavior of the Poles did not always arise solely from their fear of German punishment, in the fact that even Jews who found a hideout for themselves, thereby not endangering anyone, suffered from Poles who discovered their place of concealment. Sometimes they "merely" harassed them,[79] but many subjected such people to extortion or denunciation[80] and several testimonies refer to Poles who even killed Jews who had gone into hiding.[81] Were this not enough, some Poles made a livelihood out of extortion and denunciation. Known as *szmalcownicy,* they placed both survivors and rescuers under severe pressure.[82] Sometimes the extortion was repeated again and again until denunciation took place.

Polish people who, despite everything, helped Jews and concealed them in their homes or in some other place of refuge, placed themselves in great danger. The range of pressures may be summed up in a picturesque way: "A Jew living in the flat of an intellectual or a worker or in the hut of a peasant is dynamite likely to explode at any moment and blow the whole place up."[83]

---

76 Ringelblum, *Polish-Jewish Relations*, p. 140–147.

77 Fogelman, *Conscience and Courage*, pp. 140–141; Paldiel, "Rescuers in the Footsteps of the Rescued"; Apolonia Ołdak, p. 28.

78 Fogelman, *Conscience and Courage*, p. 138.

79 Testimony Miriam Nakric, YVA, O.3/3921; autobiography Yaakov Littner, 1946, in Tenenboim, *One of a City, Two of a Family*, pp. 97–98; Śliwowska, *Dzieci Holocaustu Mówią,* Marianna Adameczek, pp. 11–12.

80 Testimony Naftali Packer, Massuah Archive, Testimonies 1/23; testimony Binyamin Blustein. YVA, O.3/5058; Magen, *First and Last Memory*; Paldiel, *Whoever Saves One Soul,* p. 78.

81 Paldiel, "Rescuers in the Footsteps of the Rescued," Apolonia Ołdak, p. 28; Śliwowska, *Dzieci Holocaustu Mówią,* Marianna Adameczek, pp. 11–12.

82 Testimony Halina Suchocka, 1946, ŻIH, 301/5192; letter Frania Langnas, undated, to Koordynacja in Łódź at the end of the war, GFHA, Correspondence File, 788–790; Gutman, "Jews of Poland in the Holocaust," p. 492; Rosen, *The Forest, My Friend,* pp. 43–46.

83 The words are Ringelblum's. See Ringelblum, *Polish-Jewish Relations*, p. 226.

Children in their Rescuers' Homes

From the moment they crossed to the Aryan side, Jewish children were at the mercy of non-Jews. This includes those who were lucky enough to survive the war with their rescuers;[84] those who stayed in contact even while in some other place of refuge;[85] those who left the ghetto without a specific destination or did not manage to reach the address given to them;[86] and those who were evicted by Polish families that were no longer prepared to conceal them[87] and wandered in towns and villages. Even if these children did not find permanent asylum, their survival often depended on a moment of mercy. Many did not have this good fortune; they died due to denunciation or extortion, or hunger and the cruelties of weather. Their numbers are unknown.

Due to the danger of concealing children, some rescuers did not divulge their actions even to their closest kin, either due to distrust or to fear that they would refuse to cooperate.[88] For example, one girl told of a Pole who had taken her and her friend into his home, concealed them in a hole dug in the kitchen floor, and did not tell his wife and daughters. To keep the secret, the man had to maneuver carefully as he cared for them: he fed them only when he was at home alone and could remove some boards from the entrance to their hideout. On Sundays, when his wife and daughters were in church, he let the girls out of the hiding place and gave them a warm meal and a chance to shower.[89] Each volunteer rescuer like this acted for reasons of his or her

84 Grynberg, *Księga Sprawiedliwych,* "Władysława and Bolesław Brejna," p. 59; ibid., Chawiński, p. 73; ibid., Koszutska-Issat, p. 258; interview by author with Chana Martynowski-Gutmorgen; recorded interview with Haviva Barak (Luba Owjec), given to me by the witness and in my possession.

85 Perlberger-Shmuel, *This Girl Is Jewish,* pp. 40–58. The diary was written in Belgium in 1947–1948, when the author was about fifteen years old; memoirs Elżbieta Miszczyk, as written to Erella Hilferding-Goldschmidt, December 12, 1994, in my possession. Only recently did Erella trace Elżbieta, with whom her mother had left her; Grynberg, *Księga Sprawiedliwych,* "Skowrońska," p. 491.

86 Fogelman, *Conscience and Courage,* p. 176; testimony Chana Batista, YVA, O.3/5732; testimony Hela, in Küchler, *We Accuse,* p. 187. This refers not only to children whom today we would consider adults; very young children also set out in search of a place where they could stay and hired themselves out for household and farm chores.

87 Testimony Binyamin Blustein, YVA, O.3/5058; testimony Mira Bramm.

88 Testimony Aharon, in Küchler, *We Accuse,* p. 212; autobiography Sabina Stickgold, in Tenenboim, *One of a City, Two of a Family,* p. 24; interview by author with Janina Chryc.

89 Testimony Malka Templer, YVA, O.3/4278.

own; after all, such people had no prior commitment of any kind, economic or emotional, to the parents of the children whom they rescued.[90]

If a Jewish child was allowed to move around openly, a convincing explanation had to be provided. Since Poles, too, were being deported or conscripted for forced labor, some rescuers explained the presence of "new" children in their home by describing them as relatives who had joined them.[91] Sometimes neighbors viewed their actions with sympathy and understanding. In other cases, it was necessary to use imagination and make the story more convincing.[92]

In 1943, many of the small labor camps were liquidated and inmates who had survived the extermination transports were transferred to larger concentration camps. In areas that had been made *Judenrein*, manhunts for hidden Jews gathered momentum and anyone found with a Jewish child in his home was liable to be executed. Cover stories that might deceive neighbors were of no use in such searches, since now the rescuers had to prove the Polish identity of the child by producing the right papers. Some parents had already tried to provide their children with the appropriate documents while preparing for the child's removal from the ghetto, but this was not always possible due to the high price, the need for the right connections, and the time it took to prepare the papers.[93] In view of all this, the Polish rescuers with whom the child was staying had to assume responsibility for obtaining suitable documents, since an undocumented child would endanger them too. Usually, it was impossible to "arrange" such papers without confiding in someone who could make the arrangements.[94] While one could arrange or purchase a false

90 Autobiography of Sabina Shtickgold, in Tenenboim, *One of a City, Two of a Family*, pp. 23–24; Grynberg, *Księga Sprawiedliwych*, "Huczak-Szpringer," p. 187.
91 Fogelman, *Conscience and Courage*, p. 75; Grynberg, *Księga Sprawiedliwych*, "Pelagia Vogelgesang," pp. 590–591; ibid., Leszczyński, pp. 305–306; testimony Chana Batista, YVA, O.3/5732; interview by author with Bozena Szaniewska; correspondence between author and Ayes Walczyńska, Poland.
92 Gruss, *Child Martyrdom*, pp. 91–94. When pressure from her neighbors in the village built up and the Gestapo searched her house, the rescuer loaded the children onto a cart and informed the neighbors that she was planning to drown them in the river. That evening, the woman returned with the children and paid another woman to conceal them in her home. See also Fogelman, *Conscience and Courage*, pp. 148, 250.
93 Perehodnik, *The Sad Task of Documentation*, pp. 42–43; Kahana, *After the Deluge*, p. 117; Grynberg, *Księga Sprawiedliwych*, "Rogala," p. 454.
94 Silver, *The Book of the Just*, pp. 123–125; interview by author with Moshe Tuchhandler, who is now called Morris Chandler, Detroit, USA, August 1995; for the story of Zvi Gryner, today Father Grzegorz Pawlowski, see Bracha Łuków (researcher and stage director), "Upside-Down Roots," Israel Television, Channel 1, 1989 (Hebrew); Grzywacz, "To the Bosom of My People," pp. 59–60.

identity card,[95] this, too, was very hazardous. Since Polish community life centered on the church and since the faithful trusted their priests, many tried to solve this problem by confiding in the priest and asking him to issue the child with a certificate of baptism and register him or her in the community records. The decision about whether to obtain false documents[96] or to have the child baptized depended on the willingness of both the priest and the rescuer.[97] In most cases, church attendance was part of the acceptance of the rescuers' way of life;[98] the children also realized that their Polish-Christian cover story could save their lives. Thus, they played along — in some cases willingly, and in other cases for the sake of appearances.[99]

The war brought to an end the children's lives of childhood and innocence and subjected them to challenges and situations of which they had never dreamed. In most cases, they learned to cope and adjust. Before losing contact with their families, the adults gave them very clear instructions about the absolute need to deny their Jewish identity.[100] Whatever they had failed to absorb from their parents they began to understand with time, as they lived on the Aryan side or wandered from place to place. Many adopted a Polish identity at their own initiative[101] and, with the assistance of someone older

95 Fogelman, *Conscience and Courage*, p. 75.

96 Kahana, *After the Deluge*, p. 17; letter Jadwiga Mazur in the matter of Bigosław-Bigos, August 1995.

97 Grynberg, *Księga Sprawiedliwych*, "Leszozyński," p. 305; Śliwowska, *Dzieci Holocaustu Mówią*, Hanka Grynberzanka, pp. 156–164; Küchler-Silberman, *My Hundred Children*, pp. 16–17; testimony Layla Hundert, in Dror (interviewer and editor), *Pages of Testimony*, A, p. 277; Kahana, *After the Deluge*, p. 121. Kahana, who was both the chief Jewish chaplain in the Polish army and head of the Council of Jewish Religious Communities in Poland after the war, claimed, "By and large, some concealed Jewish children due to pity, but most intended to Christianize them afterwards, to tear them from their roots." He complained that Christianity had exploited the disaster that had befallen the Jewish people; Kurek-Lesik, "*Udzial Żeńkich*," p. 340; Jadwiga Piotrokoswka, an activist in Żegota, described the need to give the children a new, Christian, identity so that the Germans would not capture them due to their ignorance of Christian matters and discover their Jewish identity. The purpose, she stresses, was not to convert them to Christianity so that there would be more Christians, but to wage a supreme struggle for their lives. See testimony Jan Dobraczyński, ibid., p. 331.

98 Grynberg, *Księga Sprawiedliwych*, "Leszozyński," p. 305.

99 Śliwowska, *Dzieci Holocaustu Mówią*, Hanka Grynberżanka, pp. 156–164; testimony Hela, in Küchler, *We Accuse*, p. 190; appeal to Tarnów district court in the matter of C.Z. and S.Z.

100 Dr. Mandelbojm-Hofstetter, "One Story among Many," *Farn Yiddishn Kind* (November 1946), p. 6.

101 Curriculum vitae of the child Rywka Mastbojm, Łódź, October 8, 1946, GFHA, Correspondence File, 788–790; story of Jakob Gutterman in Łuków, "Upside-Down Roots."

or by dint of their own imagination, devised their own cover stories[102] with which they kept their Jewish identity a secret. One ten-year-old who made up such a story, for example, was alone and worked in a village by taking cows to pasture. One winter evening, the Polish woman with whom he had found shelter was sitting at home, weaving strands of linen with her friends and conversing. The boy overheard her telling her friends, "It's heartwarming to see how much the little orphan Staszek loves Christ." From his standpoint, her remark showed that he had won.[103] In other cases, Poles took in children who had introduced themselves as Polish and, although suspecting them of being Jewish, allowed them to continue staying with them, both sides avoiding the issue.[104]

Jewish children who stayed with Poles often had to pass practical inspections of their identity.[105] The more they knew about Polish daily routines and realities, and the more confidence they gathered as time passed, the less vulnerable they became. Mirka Bramm of Kalisz, a fair-haired girl who looked Polish, underwent such an experience. In 1943, at the age of eight, she was delivered to the Red Cross in Chełm as a Polish orphan; from there she was taken in by a Polish family that wished to raise her, not realizing she was Jewish. The head of the household, a man of German origin, wanted the Germans to recognize him as a *Volksdeutsche* (ethnic German). The family was ordered to appear before an approval committee; Mirka went with them. She related:

> Before we went, [the Polish woman] asked me if by chance I was Jewish. Because if I was, the committee would take blood from my ear and they'd

---

102 Interview by author with Rachel Kagan-Plodwinska; interview by author with Lucia Milch-Rosenzweig; testimony Mira Bramm; letter S.A., at children's home in Łódź, to the Poles who had sheltered her during the war, January 6, 1947, GFHA, Correspondence File, 788–790; autobiography Yaakov Littner, 1946, in Tenenboim, *One of a City, Two of a Family*, pp. 97–98; Śliwowska, *Dzieci Holocaustu Mówią*, "Karol Galiński," pp. 150–155; Frank, *To Survive and Testify*, pp. 56–57, 70. The boy, a native of Zamość, was a lone nomad at the age of nine. In the home of one of his benefactors, he overheard that Poles were being driven out of the villages in the Zamość area. Thus, he adopted the identity of one of the evictee families and, in his wanderings, identified himself as their son who had got lost. As time passed, he filled in the missing information about the Polish family by talking with various people.

103 Story of Jakob Gutterman, in Łuków, "Upside-Down Roots"; Grzywacz, "To the Bosom of My People," p. 60; appeal to Tarnów district court in the matter of C.Z. and S.Z, GFHA, Correspondence File 788–790.

104 Testimony Zipora Minc, MA, A.262; interview by author with Sabina Neuberg, June 1993.

know that I was Jewish right away [...]. I decided not to admit it [...].We met several Germans at the office. They asked me all kinds of things, like how I'd lived before the war, what illness my mother died of, what kinds of things we ate at home [in order to identify Jewish dishes] — they asked me all this and looked me right in the eye [...]. Afterwards, they told me to walk back and forth across the room; they claimed you can tell a Jew by the way he walks. Even so, they didn't grasp it and allowed me to become a German [i.e., *Volksdeutsche*] together with the rest of the family.[106]

No one knew in advance how long a child would have to spend with the rescuers. As the stay grew longer and the pressures mounted, rescuers faced the dilemma of choosing between their undertaking and the risks that it created.[107] In most cases, the dilemma was compounded by another consideration: the emotional bond that the rescuer had formed with the child.[108] Such bonding was common, irrespective of the initial motives that had prompted the rescuer to undertake to conceal a Jewish child.[109] This was only natural in view of the social isolation and the binding secret shared by the rescuers and the rescued alike. Furthermore, since the extermination of the Jews created the possibility that the children had lost their entire family, some rescuers wished to adopt them.[110] In most cases, the adoption was not actually carried out during the war due to the rescuer's fear of an investigation. Even so, some Jewish children were adopted during the war after having been removed from a Polish orphanage or if the person who found the child presumed that he or she was Polish.[111]

Notably, whatever money or goods that rescuers had received when they

---

105 Personal card of the child Batya Goldstein, no. 56, card catalog of "Koordynacja children," File 800; letter B.M to Koordynacja. GFHA, Correspondence File 788–790.
106 Testimony Mira Bramm; testimony Wiktor, in Küchler, *We Accuse*, p. 41.
107 Küchler, *We Accuse*, p. 5.
108 Grynberg, *Księga Sprawiedliwych*, "Ługowski," p. 315; ibid., Małecka-Keller, p. 322.
109 Ibid., Gutowska p. 172; recorded interview with Haviva Barak (Owjec).
110 Interview by author with Chana Martynowski-Gutmorgen.
111 Letter Maria Madej, Poland, September 1995; deposition Attorney Heifetz, Canada, in the matter of I.B., April 2, 1949, ŻIH, Legal Department; record of deposition of Jopowicz, Central Jewish Committee, May 8, 1947, in the matter of L.H., ŻIH, Education Department, File 638. Although they were not told so explicitly, Jopowicz and his wife understood that the girl in their possession was Jewish; child card of Eduard Radomski, no. 58, GFHA, catalogue of Koordynacja children's cards, File 800; Dekel, *Remnants of the Sword*, p. 194; Grzywacz, "To the Bosom of My People," p. 62.

took the children did not always suffice to ensure honest behavior when the duration of the child's concealment proved unexpectedly lengthy and financial support ran out. In such cases, the rescuers behaved in various ways. (The distribution of responses resembles that regarding the continued concealment of children after the injunction against hiding and assisting Jews resulted in more assiduous searching.) Some Poles continued to keep the children despite everything;[112] others, regarding the rescue as solely a financial transaction, returned the children to the ghetto, expelled them from their home,[113] or placed them in an orphanage.[114] Some "rescuers" even handed the children over to the German authorities.[115] In any event, the act of rescue was not based exclusively on the financial aspect, since no remuneration could provide compensation for the dangers and the psychological stress that the rescuers continually faced.[116] One should certainly not blame impoverished rescuers for accepting the money that they used to carry out the task they had taken upon themselves. It should also be remembered that some Poles even took in vagrant Jewish children for no remuneration whatsoever.[117] Most children who stayed in the countryside — no matter how young — did farm chores or served as laborers, sometimes doing work that was too arduous for them. Even in such cases, however, the labor was not performed as compen-

112 Magen, "First and Last Memory"; Dekel, *Remnants of the Sword,* pp. 148–151; testimony Halina Suchocka, ŻIH, 301/5192; memoirs Elżbieta Miszczyk.

113 Testimony Chana Owrucki-Mendelberger, YVA, O.3/5773; testimony Aharon, in Küchler, *We Accuse,* p. 209.

114 Responses of Tamar Jacobi to my questionnaire, August 1993.

115 Testimony Aharon, in Küchler, *We Accuse,* p. 209; Neshamit, "The Koordynacja for the Redemption of Children in Liberated Poland," p. 117.

116 Ringelblum, who was concealed in the courtyard of a Polish home, claimed that people who protected Jews for payment alone made an effort, sooner or later, to rid themselves of the hazardous burden, while those who persevered had motives beyond money. See Ringelblum, *Polish-Jewish Relations,* p. 245.

117 Autobiography of Sabina Stickgold, in Tenenboim, *One of a City, Two of a Family,* pp. 20; autobiography Ewa Goliger, ibid., pp. 92–94; Lewinsky, "My Wanderings and My Rescuers"; testimony Chana Batista, YVA, O.3/5732; Peter Hellman, *Avenue of the Righteous* (New York: Atheneum, 1980), "Leokadia Jaromirska," p. 168; Leokadia found the baby at the edge of a wood; interview by author with Rachel Wolf-Wajnsztok, September 1985; testimony Esther Mark in the matter of the son of the author Bornstein; letter of testament by Pola to her daughter, Helena Guzala, whom she had saved. I received the letter from the daughter via Janina Chryc of Jastrzebie, Poland, in September 1994. Grynberg, *Księga Sprawiedliwych,* "Grzybowski," p. 171; ibid., "Paja," p. 391; ibid., "Luczak," p. 313; ibid., "Lerman," p. 302; Shner-Neshamit, *I Did Not Come to Rest,* p. 193.

sation for the risk that the rescuers had assumed, especially since some rescuers had children of their own, who were also endangered.[118]

Poles who continued to conceal Jewish children were exposed to many dangers and lived in constant fear and social isolation.[119] Some paid a very high price for their feats of rescue but did not part from the children who were hidden with them. For example, German police visited a family in a village near Berenzo for the purpose of searching their home, evidently after denunciation. Two Jewish children were concealed in the house: a girl who had been handed over to the family and a little boy whom they had found wandering in the forest. While the search was in progress, the parents, their own children, and the Jewish children hid in the forest. The Germans, failing to find their quarry, set the house ablaze. In the house were the elderly parents of one of the spouses. The family was overcome by both death and destitution. As if they had not suffered enough, their own son died in 1945. Nevertheless, they continued to care for the two Jewish children.[120]

Some rescuers believed that their stress-filled lives during the war had caused them to become ill afterwards. In her will that a Polish woman deposited with her husband in 1954, she revealed to her daughter that she was in fact a Jewish girl that she and her husband had taken in to their home as an infant. The woman described the dangers and fears that had accompanied them during the war and added, "[...] We, along with father, endured a great deal of human evil for you [...]. My beloved daughter! I loved you with all

---

118 Testimony Miriam Nakric, YVA, O.3/3921; Fogelman, *Conscience and Courage*, pp. 75, 141; ibid., Niemiec, pp. 232–233; letter Warsaw Committee to Central Committee, Apr. 25, 1947, in the matter of K.F., ŻIH, Education Department, File 638.

119 Paldiel, *Whoever Saves One Soul*, p. 25; Fogelman, *Conscience and Courage*, p. 141. Fogelman describes the case of a Jewish child who let slip his real name while playing with other children. The children reported this to their parents, who informed the Germans. The rescuers' entire family and the Jewish boy were executed. See ibid., p. 5; Grynberg, *Księga Sprawiedliwych*, "Wanda Rachalska," pp. 446–447.

120 Grynberg, *Księga Sprawiedliwych*, "Kuriata," pp. 284–285; Drucker told about a woman who had received a letter from Rabbi Shapiro confirming that she had sacrificed her life for a Jewish girl. See testimony of Yeshayahu Drucker, YVA, O.3/3249; interview by author with Yehudit Szwarcbach. Her daughter's caregiver became pregnant by a man who threatened to denounce her to the Germans, along with "the Jewish girl that you're keeping," unless she had sex with him; Fogelman, *Conscience and Courage*; Stanisław Włodek, pp. 222–223; ibid., Alexander Roslan, pp. 105–117; Dekel, *Remnants of the Sword*, p. 201. After the war, the rescuer was arrested on suspicion of having collaborated with the Germans. During the trial, it became clear that he had been extorted by a Gestapo man who knew that the girl in his custody was Jewish and threatened to harm her unless the rescuer helped his employers.

my heart, so much so that my sorrow was like a strong blow to my chest and unfortunately I have cancer. But I did not hand you over to the Germans."[121] The direct connection that the writer drew between her terror and the price that she believes she paid for it, attests to the intensity of the experience that the rescuers underwent in the concealing of Jewish children: one that left permanent scars.

Conclusion

Several scholars have studied the concealment of Jewish children during the war from various points of view in Europe generally, and specifically in Poland.[122] Each of them encountered many personal stories in the course of the research. Densely detailed stories materialized around each family, each child, and each rescuer. Each detail is important in order to understand the prevailing situation. After all, every day that parents spent in trying to find a way to save their children, the days of fear, loneliness, and memories and nostalgia for their children, and the lives of the rescuers who refused to submit — all became permanently etched in the hearts of those who lived through them. The period of rescue was described as a time of "Sisyphean labor."[123] The very use of this term suffices to explain how intensely the act of concealing a child entailed daily coping with an immense number of details.

It would be erroneous to think that the act of rescue engaged only the triumvirate of parents, rescuers, and the rescued child. In fact, many people were involved in each rescue story. In most cases, behind every rescued child were several Poles who were partners in the act of rescue, as well as other people whom he or she had encountered for better or for worse along the way. In each of the children's stories following the separation from their parents, one encounters people who gloated at their distress, hounded them, sought to betray them to the Germans, and persecuted the rescuers. However, there were others who took the children into their homes — if only for short periods of time — gave them food, clothing and shelter, and taught them Christian prayers.[124]

---

121 Letter of testament by Pola to her daughter, Helena Guzala.
122 Ringelblum, *Polish-Jewish Relations*; Fogelman, *Conscience and Courage*; Tec, *When Light*; Bartoszewski and Lewin, *The Samaritans*.
123 Ringelblum used this expression. See Ringelblum, *Polish-Jewish Relations*, p. 238.
124 Berman, *From the Days of the Resistance*, p. 189.

The extraordinary singularity of the rescuers is evident not only relative to the negative elements in Polish society, who attacked the survivors willingly, but also relative to those who were indifferent to the fate of the Jews, whether due to an inability to abandon their prejudices, or a general insensitivity to the suffering of the Jews and an innate absence of the quality of pity.[125] It is even possible that the Polish middle class, as a whole, chose not to lift a finger as it stood to gain financially from the plight of the Jews.[126]

Not all children who were transferred to Polish Gentile families remained with their rescuers until the end of the war.[127] Some were forced into nomadic wandering, just like the children who, for lack of any address, were doomed from the outset to nomadic lives. Each child dreamed of the privilege of laying his or her head near a warm fireplace during the cold winters, and some even enjoyed this privilege for some time. However, feeling like beasts of prey, they fled whenever they thought that staying too long in one location might lead to their capture. Eventually, many of them internalized their new identities and blended into the societies in which they found themselves.

Some acts of concealment did not come to light after the war. Since most of the Jewish population had been exterminated, the secret was often lost together with the parent who had handed the child over.[128] To locate such children after the war, someone had to know that they had in fact been handed over, as well as their whereabouts. Aware of this possibility and despite the danger, some parents divulged the addresses of the rescuers to a few people whom they trusted, in the hope that if one of these people were to survive, the child could be traced.[129]

As they searched for potential rescuers, some parents were willing to promise anything if only the rescuer would consent to take their children. Still, they found it difficult to accept the fact that their child, the only surviving vestige of their family, would not remember the family; that is, to all intents and purposes, that the family would cease to exist. Often, however,

---

125 Shmuel Krakowski, "Relations Between Jews and Poles during the Holocaust: New and Old Approaches in Polish Historiography," in *Yad Vashem Studies,* 19 (1989), pp. 317–340.

126 Ringelblum, *Polish-Jewish Relations,* pp. 197–198; Gutman, "Jews of Poland in the Holocaust," p. 493; testimony Yeshayahu Drucker, YVA, O.3/3249.

127 Memoirs Elżbieta Miszczyk; testimony Reuven, in Küchler, *We Accuse,* pp. 149–156; story of Avigdor Baranowicz with Vered Berman (stage director and producer), "Wanda's Lists," Israel Television, Channel 1, November 22, 1994 (Hebrew).

128 Testimony Bella Choter, YVA, O.3/5708; Berman, "Wanda's Lists."

129 Kahana, *After the Deluge,* p. 16; Leiberman, "The Heartbreak of a Jewish Mother"; child card of Jozio (Yosef Aizik) Szrajber.

the opposite occurred: a framework of contacts and dependency between the rescuer and the rescued took shape.[130] After the end of the war, such a framework could help in the child's rehabilitation and eventual return to the Jewish people.

If neither the child's relatives nor any of the confidants survived the war, the only way to discover a hidden child was if the rescuer reported it willingly or delivered the youngster to one of the Jewish institutions that were established after the war ended. Obviously, it was easiest to remove Jewish children from Gentile homes when the children themselves eagerly anticipated the moment of liberation in order to shed their false identities and seek out fellow Jews. This, however, was not the usual situation. Most of the children remained with their rescuers, making it necessary to devise creative searching methods.[131]

This, then, was the background of the phenomenon of Jewish children hiding in Polish non-Jewish homes at the end of the war. It was under these circumstances that the efforts to locate the children and bring them back to the Jewish people began.

130 Testimony Reuven, in Küchler, *We Accuse*, p. 152; Neshamit, "The Koordynacja for the Redemption of Children in Liberated Poland," p. 134; Fogelman, *Conscience and Courage*, p. 141.

131 Kahana, *After the Deluge*, p. 16; S. L. Sznajderman, "A Jewish Mother Fights for Her Daughter," in Moshe Tamari, ed., *Węgrow Memorial Book* (Tel Aviv: Former Residents of Węgrow in Israel, together with former residents of Węgrow in Argentina, 1961, Hebrew), pp. 71–72. Article reproduced in *Davar*, November 13, 1957; Neshamit, "The Koordynacja for the Redemption of Children in Liberated Poland," pp. 136–137.

CHAPTER 2

Poland and Polish Jewry after the War

"The Jews are like photos on display in a show window
All together in different heights, living and dead
Grooms and brides, bar-mitzva boys with babies
And pictures reconstructed from old yellowed photographs.

Sometimes people come by and shatter the window
And burn the pictures, then they start
To photograph all over again and develop again
And display them again, aching and smiling."

Yehuda Amichai[1]

With the end of the war, Poland began to rehabilitate itself. The events during the years that immediately followed would have an effect, both social and political, on the few Jews who had survived the Holocaust. The actions to locate the children who had been concealed and move them to Jewish institutions also depended largely on the events of the time and the setting. In order to discuss them, a survey of the prevailing background events is necessary.

Poland after Liberation

In July 1944, Soviet forces crossed the River Bug and entered the area that constitutes present-day Poland. By late January 1945, the Red Army had reached the western boundary of Poland between the first and second world wars.

---

1 Yehuda Amichai, *The Fist Was Once an Open Hand and Fingers, Too* (Jerusalem and Tel Aviv: Schocken, 1989, Hebrew), p. 135.

The process of liberating Polish Jews who were living in Belarus, western Ukraine, and western Lithuania began as early as January 1944, when the Soviet forces crossed the pre-war frontier between the USSR and Poland. The Soviet offensive reached the eastern bank of the River Wisła in early August and halted there for several months. The offensive resumed only in January 1945, when the Soviets crossed the river and continued to advance westward.[2]

The devastation in the liberated areas was enormous. The retreating German forces had left scorched earth behind them and indulged in widespread looting. The fighting had caused such damage to transport systems that food and other daily needs could not be provided regularly. Financial resources for repairs were lacking.[3]

Jews who were liberated on Polish soil east of the Wisła were inclined to return to their homes, believing that they would be able to reinhabit them and anxious to search for acquaintances and relatives. At this time Jews had not yet suffered the consequences of antisemitism; it was even widely rumored that the Soviets had placed the Jews under their patronage and would exact revenge against anyone who harmed them.[4] However, the returnees realized very quickly that they could not remain in their pre-war places of residence. Only a few found surviving relatives, and a sense of emptiness and disillusionment took over. In most cases, their homes had been occupied by Polish families that were not prepared to relinquish them. Furthermore, if the Jews thought that their former neighbors would respect them for having managed to survive, they were mistaken; many of the latter merely uttered insulting and sarcastic remarks of amazement over the very fact of their survival. Under such conditions, it was hard to contemplate beginning a new life and to find housing and sources of livelihood.[5]

If this were not enough, the Jews faced genuine physical danger. From the very beginning of the liberation of Jews on Polish soil, many were attacked

---

2 Gutman, *The Jews in Poland*, p. 11; Engel, *Between Liberation and Escape*, p. 41.
3 Engel, *Between Liberation and Escape*, p. 48; Samet, *When I Came the Day After*, pp. 28–44; report Anton Mara, a member of the Jewish Brigade who visited Poland, returned to Palestine, and presented a detailed account of his impressions to the Hano'ar Hatzioni Executive Committee on February 6, 1946, Massuah Archives, Testimonies, 25/27; interview by author with Ita Kowalska, August 1994.
4 Shlomi, "Initial Organization," pp. 299–300.
5 Ibid., pp. 300–301; Engel, *Between Liberation and Escape*, pp. 46–48; Fogelman, *Conscience and Courage*, pp. 273–274; for an account of how many survivors there were, see Gutman, *The Jews in Poland*, pp. 12–13.

as they traveled to their old homes.[6] This happened for several reasons, including the internal struggle in Poland over the future of the country and the regime that would govern it.[7] On July 21, 1944, as the Red Army crossed the border of today's Poland, pro-Soviet elements established the Polish National Liberation Committee (*Polski Komitet Wyzwolenia Narodowego* — PKWN) as the provisional institution of executive authority in Poland.[8] As this committee was being set up, a delegation of the National Liberation Council (*Krajowa Rada Narodowa* — KRN)[9] was present in Moscow, and a decision was made to install Eduard Osóbka-Morawski, a member of the radical wing of the Polish Socialist Movement, as chairman of the PKWN. The new body agreed to shift the Soviet–Polish border to the west, that is, it acquiesced in the annexation to the USSR of territories that had belonged to eastern Poland before the war.[10] In late December 1944, the Provisional Polish Government (*Tymczasowy Rząd Polski*) succeeded the PKWN as the executive authority,[11] and after the liberation of the areas west of the Wisła, the government moved to Warsaw.

6   Yisrael Gutman, "Polish Jews from Liberation to Emigration, 1944–1946," in Pinkus, ed., *East European Jews Between Holocaust and Redemption*, p. 114; Fleiszer, "The Rescue of 24 Children," p. 300; testimony Moshe Kagan, in Dror (interviewer and ed.), *Pages of Testimony*, B, p. 454; interview by author with Yeshayahu Drucker; testimony of Binyamin Blustein, YVA, O.3/5058.

7   Gutman, *The Jews in Poland*, pp. 60–61; idem, "Polish Jews from Liberation to Emigration," pp. 114, 118. Gutman traces the anti-Jewish campaign that took place after the war to four factors: 1. traditional enmity, which not only persisted but may even have gathered strength during the Nazi occupation and Holocaust era; 2. demonstrative opposition to the return of the Jews to their jobs and sources of livelihood; 3. opposition to the restitution of Jewish property; 4. the claim that Jews were the main source of support for the new regime. Warhaftig identified another reason: fear among those who had collaborated with the Germans and denounced fugitives that their "secret" would be discovered. See Warhaftig, *Refugee and Survivor*, p. 381; Debora Zilber, an activist in the Koordynacja, attested to this from her personal experience. See testimony Debora Zilber (Marysia), Oral History Department of the Hebrew University of Jerusalem (OHD), 27(68). Lena Küchler proposed yet another reason: after the war, the Poles believed that the Jews, unlike them, had plenty of food and money. Therefore, jealousy was a motive for attacks on Jews. See Küchler-Silberman, *My Hundred Children*, p. 190 (Hebrew edition).

8   On the unfolding of events before this committee was established, see Gutman, *The Jews in Poland*, pp. 15–17; Engel, *Between Liberation and Escape*, pp. 49–50; Shlomi, "Initial Organization," p. 295.

9   Established in 1943.

10   Gutman, *The Jews in Poland*, pp. 17–18.

11   Engel, *Between Liberation and Escape*, p. 58; on the parties of which this government was composed, see Samet, *When I Came the Day After*, pp. 46–47.

Most of the Polish population regarded these events as acts of coercion and feared that the communists were about to take over the country. In various locations, armed operations began against the new regime and those thought to be its supporters. The Jews were again characterized as communists. Antisemitic remarks once again began to be heard and the anti-communist struggle of the resistance was also manifested in action against the Jews. Within a few months after liberation, Polish underground gangs murdered hundreds of Jews who were returning to their home towns or migrating along the roads.[12]

Several Jews were members of the KRN and the PKWN that had come into being with the establishment of the new Polish regime in late July 1944. The most prominent of them was Emil Zommerstein, a former member of the Polish *Sejm* (parliament) whom the PKWN placed in charge of its war compensation office. On August 8, 1944, the PKWN established a relief affairs department for the Jewish population, headed by Szlomo Herszenhorn, a physician and veteran Bund activist from Lublin. In late August, a committee was established in Lublin to deal with Jewish survivors; most of its members were members of Zionist parties. In November 1944, an institution for Jewish children was established in Lublin; its first wards were children who had been rescued from the Majdanek death camp and others who had reached Lublin in their wanderings.[13]

12 Yehuda Bauer, *Flight and Rescue: The Brichah* (New York: Random House, 1970) pp. 113–114; Yitzchak (Antek) Zuckerman, *A Surplus of Memory: Chronicle of the Warsaw Ghetto Uprising* (Berkeley, Los Angeles: University of California Press, 1993) p. 629; Engel, *Between Liberation and Escape*, pp. 50–51; Gutman, *The Jews in Poland*, pp. 27–28. Polish underground gangs that operated after the war were composed of radical elements that had acted during the war under the National Armed Forces (*Naradowe Siły Zbrojne* — NSZ), members of the Freedom and Independence Movement (*Wolność i Niezawisłość* — WiN), and ultra-nationalists from the AK (*Armia Krajowa*).

13 Engel, *Between Liberation and Escape*, pp. 53–55; Boleslaw Drobiner represented the socialists as director for labor, welfare, and health affairs; Jan Stefan Haneman was inspector for economic affairs and the treasury. See Gutman, *The Jews in Poland*, pp. 18–19, 67; Shlomi, "Initial Organization," pp. 295, 303–307, 314. Zommerstein had represented the Jews in the Sejm for years before the war and had been imprisoned in the Soviet Union during the war; see also Gutman, "Polish Jews from Liberation to Emigration," p. 117; Engel, *Between Liberation and Escape*, p. 55. Engel claims that there are indications that this committee did not begin to operate until October 1.

The Survivors Organize on Polish Soil

As the number of survivors climbed, the need for a central institution that would handle all affairs related to Jews in their different places of residence became clear. Thus, the Provisional Central Committee was officially established in November 1944, and twelve local committees were formed in places east of the Wisła where Jews were congregating.[14] In January 1945, with the liberation of Warsaw, the Committee moved its headquarters to the capital. Zommerstein was elected chairman and its members included representatives of several Zionist factions,[15] Jewish communists, Bundists, Jewish partisans, and Jewish democrats.[16] In February, the committee changed its status from "provisional" to "permanent" and was henceforth called the "Central Committee of the Jews of Poland," or the "Central Committee." At the end of April, the Committee's presidium was informed that the Polish government had recognized it as the official representative body of Polish Jewry.[17] From the start, the government provided the Central Committee with financial support, albeit not enough to cover all its needs.[18] As Jewish institutions

14 Shlomi, "Initial Organization," pp. 308–313.

15 Engel, *Between Liberation and Escape*, p. 80. The membership of the Central Committee included Zivia Lubetkin representing Hehalutz, Yisrael Shaklar representing Hashomer Hatza'ir, Josef Sak representing Po'alei Zion, CS, and Stefan Grajek representing the erstwhile Organization of Jewish Partisans. See Zuckerman, *A Surplus of Memory*, pp. 564–572; Sarid, "Initial Deployment," p. 274; testimony Zvi Shner, in Dror (interviewer and ed.), *Pages of Testimony*, D, pp. 1417–1418.

16 Kahana, *After the Deluge*, p. 27; Gutman, *The Jews in Poland*, p. 20. The Central Committee and its executive arm, the presidium, were never chosen in general elections; instead, they were assembled on the basis of an intra-party agreement. In late 1945, the committee had twenty members and the presidium eight. Although the presidium was balanced — four leftist members and four Zionists — Zommerstein's status as chairman gave the Zionists something of an edge. In early 1946, the committee and its presidium were reorganized. In its new configuration, the committee had twenty-five members: thirteen Zionists and twelve PPR members and Bundists. See Gutman, ibid., p. 81; on the committee and its departments in the second half of 1946, see Record of Actions of the Central Committee, January 1–June 30, 1946, ŻIH; "The Bund" is the abbreviated title of the *Yiddisher Arbeter-Bund in Russland, Liteh un Poiln* (League of Jewish workers in Russia, Lithuania, and Poland), a Jewish socialist labor party founded in Vilna in 1897 that vehemently rejected Zionism, Hebrew culture, and the Hebrew language. The Bund aspired to equal rights for Jews within the framework of a socialist and democratic state in which the Jewish public could enjoy cultural autonomy equal to that of all the other peoples that inhabited the country. See "Bund," in *Encyclopedia of the Holocaust*, pp. 272ff.

17 Shlomi, "Organization of the Jewish Survivors," p. 536; idem, "Activity of Polish Jewry," p. 214.

18 Samet, *When I Came the Day After*, p. 60.

came into being and began to operate, they probed the authorities' stance toward them, and the communists and Zionists conducted an open debate concerning the future of the remnant of Polish Jewry that had survived the war. Both camps realized that as the governing system concluded its phase of provisional organization, the Jews would need to define their own organization in clear terms.[19]

Another entity was the Council of Jewish Religious Communities in Poland (*Komitet Organiszacyjny Żydówskich Kongergacji Wyznaniowych w Polsce*). This was established in February 1945 at the initiative of the Polish government in order to provide orthodox Jews with basic religious services. The council was chaired by Rabbi David Kahana, who had also served as chief Jewish chaplain of the Polish Army from November 1944. Two religious parties that did not align themselves under the Central Committee — Agudath Israel and Mizrachi — operated under the aegis of this body. The Council of Religious Communities dealt with the full range of religious and welfare services needed by the survivors. In 1946, according to the Council's report after its first year of activity, eighty-three religious communities were affiliated with the rabbinical center in Warsaw, part of the Council of Religious Communities, and in the larger cities, twenty rabbis operated with the authorities' approval.[20] Relations between the two bodies were tense, the Central Committee viewing the reestablishment of religious communities as an attempt "to revive the dead by electric shock." In November 1944, orthodox leaders had suggested that the survivors' religious needs be provided by the local committees, but the latter refused to allow the orthodox to influence the shaping of the new Jewish collective in Poland and even sought to thwart such influence. Conversely, the Council of Religious Communities did not wish to be allied with the Central Committee. It was facing pressure from abroad, from the Religious Affairs Department of the Ministry of the Interior, from the Jewish Affairs Department of the Foreign Ministry, and also from

19 Shlomi, "Initial Organization," p. 299.
20 Kahana, *After the Deluge*, pp. 22–25, 35, 44–46, 103. According to Kahana, he received his appointment as representative of all Jewish religious communities in Poland from the Office of Public Administration. From November 25, 1945, the Council of Holy Communities in Poland (the phrasing "Religious Communities" was a translation of the council's name in Polish) was recognized as a religious institution under the law. See Gutman, *The Jews in Poland*, pp. 20, 78; idem, "Polish Jewry from Liberation to Emigration," p. 117; Engel, *Between Liberation and Escape*, pp. 87–88.

Szymon Zachariasz, head of the Jewish department of the Polish Communist Party.[21] A World Jewish Congress delegation (Segal, Margoshes, and Warhaftig) that visited Poland in early 1946, tried to persuade the Central Committee to expand by coopting representatives of the Mizrachi movement and Agudath Israel, but to no avail.[22] Since the Polish government did not support the operations of the Council of Religious Communities,[23] the council had to arrange funding from alternative Jewish sources.

Polish Jews first established contact with the Jewish world abroad even before the Central Committee was officially constituted. In August 1944, Zommerstein cabled the JDC and the Jewish Agency in Palestine with his requests. These bodies accepted his requests in principle but since the transfer of relief funds was complicated as they had to be channeled via Moscow, it was only later in the year that substantial assistance began to arrive.[24]

Attacks on Jews

After the first survivors who returned to their old homes were assaulted by members of the Polish population, most Jews who came later avoided their former places of residence. Although the law entitled the Jews to sue for restitution of property that had been taken over by non-Jews, in fact, restitution was seldom made. The demands of the Jews merely fed the enmity of the Polish population. Therefore, the Jews had to bolster their economic rehabilitation by their own initiative with the help of financing agencies, foremost among them, JDC. The assistance obtained from these agencies was helpful but also caused an escalation in anti-Jewish sentiment.[25] In contrast to the

21 Kahana, *After the Deluge*, pp. 102–106. According to Kahana, the pressure from Zachariasz was the most important because it was he who "pulled the strings" in all political and social decisions of the Central Committee.
22 Warhaftig, *Refugee and Survivor*, p. 390.
23 Engel, *Between Liberation and Escape*, p. 88
24 Shlomi, "Initial Organization," pp. 309–312.
25 Gutman, *The Jews in Poland*, pp. 60–61. The journalist Samet claimed that when he interviewed the Polish Minister of Justice, Henryk Świętowski, concerning the anti-Jewish attacks, the minister recommended that the Jews move to the cities where their safety could more easily be assured, since in small localities they were difficult to protect. See Samet, *When I Came the Day After*, pp. 116, 120–121.

hostility of most of the Polish population, the official attitude of the new government of Poland toward the Jews and their problems was sympathetic. The government did what it could to suppress the wave of antisemitism that swept the population,[26] but it was not enough to prevent attacks on Jews.

In August 1945, a pogrom took place in Kraków as an enraged, incited mob vented its spleen against the Jews, causing casualties and property damage.[27] The pogrom took place a day before 170 survivors from a children's home in Kraków were to be moved to convalescent homes in the Zakopane Mountains, and the events generated a great deal of tension and fear. The fear was well founded: in the autumn, after the children had already settled in their new homes in Rabka and Zakopane, gangs of rioters attacked them.[28]

The reports about the attacks on survivors reached Palestine and were widely reported in the local press. As for the motives behind the attacks, one article said, "The Jewish problem is but an excuse for war against the new Poland."[29] Members of the Histadrut executive committee brought up the topic for discussion at a meeting with Polish government representatives who were visiting Palestine. The guests insisted that the government was fighting the forces of reaction doggedly, and added:

> Despite [what happened], we have already accomplished something. There are no pogroms in the accepted sense of the word. Apart from the Kraków pogrom, there have been no mass actions against Jews, just a few lowly, underhand assaults.... I can promise on behalf of my government that within a few months we will arrive at a situation where no one will dare to raise a hand against a political functionary, against a worker, against a Jew.[30]

26 Gutman, "Polish Jews from Liberation to Emigration," pp. 113, 118; Bracha Habas, "Report from Visitors to Poland," in *Davar*, August 28, 1945, p. 2. Members of the Jewish Brigade visited Poland in July 1945.

27 Engel, *Between Liberation and Escape*, p. 62. The headline of a leaflet that was distributed on the day of the pogrom stated that Jews had murdered Polish children. Below it sent a warning to segments of Polish society that were spreading "Russian democracy," "profiteering on the word 'freedom,'" and "desecrating the holy word 'Poland.'" At the bottom of the leaflet, the two — the Jew and the Bolshevik — were linked.

28 Küchler-Silberman, *My Hundred Children*, pp. 101, 142–145.

29 Press clipping, *Haboker*, April 17, 1945, CZA, J 25/100; see also article in *Al Hamishmar*, April 22, 1945, ibid.

30 Report of meeting at the Histadrut Executive Committee with representatives of the Polish government, January 11, 1946, Labor and Hehalutz Archives, Lavon Institute, IV–209–4–364.

The Polish Refugee Committee in Palestine also expressed sorrow over the attacks on Jews but offered different explanations: "The Polish Diaspora turns to the Jewish public and its representatives and urges them to realize that the Polish people is not fully in charge of its plans at present and cannot truly assume responsibility for everything that is done at the behest of foreign entities in Poland."[31] As these remarks suggest, each side expressed sorrow over the attacks on the Jews but viewed differently the circumstances that had led to the attacks. The attitude of each side was determined by their outlook and beliefs about the future of Poland.

Political Activity among the Jews

Among those elements in the Polish intelligentsia that favored "people's democracy" (communist rule) and among political leaders, it was widely believed that Poland should devise its own path to socialism. Amid the nascent realities in Poland, there seemed to be some likelihood of fulfilling these expectations. In the initial period of post-war Polish life up to 1948, a pluralistic approach was envisaged, despite a commitment to socialist principles. The situation left its mark on the Jewish sector as well. The regime had to be especially careful in its attitude toward the Jews, since the world regarded this as a litmus test of the regime's socio-political intentions. Thus, the Zionist parties were allowed to exist on a basis of almost total equality with the communists and the Bund, and separate and nationally distinct Jewish institutions and organizations existed without opposition. Many pre-war parties and youth movements were allowed to resume their activities. The Revisionists, who were not authorized to resume activities and did not have representation on the Central Committee, reorganized despite their lack of official status. An atmosphere of political rivalry among the parties prevailed almost from the outset.[32]

In August 1944, Ichud, an alliance of several Zionist parties, was established in Lublin, and the slogan of unity among all surviving Jews on

---

31 Resolutions adopted at a protest rally, August 29, 1945, sponsored by all Polish Diaspora organizations in Tel Aviv. The report was submitted on October 10, 1945. Ibid., IV–208–1–3802.

32 Engel, *Between Liberation and Escape*, p. 71; Gutman, *The Jews in Poland*, pp. 20, 87; Gutman, "Polish Jews from Liberation to Emigration,"1944–1946, pp. 115–117; Sarid, "Initial Deployment," p. 274.

the basis of a broad Zionist platform was proclaimed. The founders of Ichud, who were affiliated with the Jewish committee in Lublin, considered themselves to be the sole legitimate leaders of the resurgent Zionist camp. Three youth movements — Akiva, Hanoar Hatzioni and Gordonia — considered themselves affiliated with Ichud, at least in its first few months of existence. The Dror movement of Po'alei Zion and Hashomer Hatza'ir did not align with Ichud and in April 1945, they established an umbrella organization called the League for a Labor Palestine. The youth movement members who convened in Lublin in January 1945 and established the *Bricha* (underground rescue) organization in Poland did not coordinate their actions with the heads of Ichud, to the severe displeasure of the latter's activists. Nevertheless, from its outset, Ichud competed with the pioneering youth movements that had formed the League for Zionist Supremacy among the Jewish survivors. In March 1945, another Zionist party, Po'alei Zion Left, began to reorganize (under Adolf Berman) and did not join any of the existing groups.[33]

Two additional, non-Zionist Jewish movements were active — the socialist Bund and the Jewish division of the PPR (*Polska Partia Robotnicza*, the Communist Party). The Bund resumed its activity in November 1944, preaching the strengthening of socialist class consciousness among Holocaust survivors. The Jewish division of the PPR believed that close relations could be established with the new national regime in order better to serve Jewish interests.[34]

The Jewish communists began to operate within branches of the Central Committee in order to participate in contacts with survivors and to help them organize and find housing and work. In contrast, the Zionists operated in two areas. First, they assisted in public work with survivors under the auspices of the committees.[35] The resulting foot in the door was important for their official status vis-à-vis the other organizations that were competing for leadership of the survivor community, since it gave them access to the Central Committee's sources of assistance and influence[36] and to information

---

33 Sarid, "Initial Deployment," pp. 292–295; Engel, *Between Liberation and Escape*, p. 72; Samet, *When I Came the Day After*, p. 195.

34 As implied by the draft ideological platform of the Jewish activists in the PPR from August 1945; Yishai, *In the Shadow of the Holocaust*, p. 101; Engel, *Between Liberation and Escape*, pp. 72–73.

35 Engel, *Between Liberation and Escape*, pp. 74, 81.

36 Ibid., p. 80; Zuckerman, *A Surplus of Memory*, pp. 572–574; Sarid, "Initial Deployment," p. 274; testimony Zvi Shner, in Dror (interviewer and ed.), *Pages of Testimony*, D, pp. 1417–1418.

about the survivors.[37] Secondly, they organized groups of survivors into training communes that remained in Poland for a short period before leaving for
Palestine. Due to their membership in the Central Committee, the Zionists
were able to place workers in positions in committee-sponsored schools
and children's homes, where they could influence pupils by providing them
with nationalist content and persuading them to leave Poland — in contrast
to the views that their non-Zionist educators were instilling in them.[38] The
joint activity on the Central Committee did not thwart disagreements that
originated in differences in worldview; each of the entities regarded the central body as an instrument with which they could influence the survivors.
Nevertheless, even though the Zionists worked in tandem with the non-
Zionists on the Central Committee, their activists sensed that it was the communists who determined the nature of the Committee and believed that the
communists were hampering their activities.[39] The emissaries from Palestine
felt the same way; they sensed that their presence was not well received, as
opposed to the warm welcome given to the American Jews who brought
funding for survivors' care. The reason, so the Zionists believed, was that the
communists hoped to gain control of these funds in order to finance the Central Committee's revitalization activities.[40]

Emigration from Poland

In response to the sense of anxiety and rootlessness, Jews began to emigrate
from Poland en masse in the second half of 1945 in an illegal outflux that
the Polish government did nothing to stop. Most of the emigrants availed
themselves of the Bricha organization, which at first had focused on helping people leave Poland for Palestine but now expanded its operations to

37 Interview by author with Sarah Shner-Neshamit, November 1993. For example, Sarah
   Shner-Neshamit told about a member of Hehalutz, Yosef Bundajew, who worked for the
   District Committee in Warsaw and forwarded information to the Zionist Koordynacja;
   see testimony of Devora Zilber, OHD 27(68); Koryski, "The Zionist Koordynacja for the
   Redemption of Jewish Children in Poland," p. 25.
38 Engel, *Between Liberation and Escape*, pp. 77–78, 81–82.
39 Testimony Yeshayahu Drucker, YVA, O.3/3249; Kahana, *After the Deluge*, p. 27; Samet,
   When I Came the Day After, p. 78.
40 Yishai, *In the Shadow of the Holocaust*, p. 74; letter Yishai to Moshe Shertok, Jerusalem,
   February 24, 1946, published in *Yediot* (internal Jewish Agency bulletin) 4, CZA, S25/5262;
   see also report Moshe Yishai, emissary of the Jewish Agency, March 12, 1946, published in
   Jewish Agency Bulletin (June 1946), ibid.

encompass anyone who wished to leave Poland, in the belief that they too, would eventually choose Palestine as their destination.[41] The number of Jews who still remained in Poland by the end of 1945, after the emigration wave, is estimated at between 80,000–90,000.[42]

The struggle between the non-Zionists and the Zionists within the Polish Central Committee was an ideological one between those who favored the integration of the Jews into the nascent modern egalitarian state as a minority with an autonomous cultural life of its own, and a Zionist national outlook, which aspired to resettle the Holocaust survivors in Palestine. Even within the non-Zionist Left, however, views were not unanimous: most Bundists looked askance at the Soviet regime and even Jewish communists held different opinions and attitudes. The Zionist camp was also not of one mind; its left flank expressed unreserved support for the regime, whereas the General Zionists supported it de facto but withheld ideological commitment. The pace of emigration to Palestine was also a bone of contention in the Zionist camp. Some Zionists expressed the view that all Jews should leave as quickly as possible; others believed that those who wished to depart should do so, but that those who chose to remain in Poland should also be looked after. This, they said, would strengthen Jewish bonds and would educate the Jews and their children in nationhood and eventual settlement in Palestine.[43]

Representatives of the Zionist movement in Poland and the Yishuv did not establish direct contact until early August 1945, at the European convention of the World Zionist Organization in London. The convention took place so that the Zionist movement could take stock generally and review its political options in the aftermath of the Holocaust.[44] At this time, the prevailing climate among the Polish Zionist movements favored unification, and sought to put paid to the phenomenon of partisanship. In reality, however, things were different; in their encounter with the delegates from Palestine, the Polish Zionists realized that the winds of factionalism were blowing from Pal-

41 Engel, *Between Liberation and Escape*, pp. 64–70; the Bricha began its activities on former Polish soil in the first half of 1944. See Bauer, *Out of the Ashes*, pp. 74–75. Bauer notes that the Polish government knew about the Bricha's operations but created no real obstacles.
42 Engel, *Between Liberation and Escape*, p. 60.
43 Gutman, *The Jews in Poland*, pp. 80–81; idem, "Polish Jews from Liberation to Emigration," pp. 116–117; See also letter Yishai to Moshe Shertok, February 24, Yishai report, CZA, *Yediot*, June 1946, S25/5262.
44 Engel, *Between Liberation and Escape*, p. 92.

estine. After they returned from London, the two components of Hehalutz, Dror and Hashomer Hatza'ir, parted ways.[45] Yitzchak (Antek) Zuckerman of Dror and Chaike Grossman of Hashomer Hatza'ir pleaded with the Yishuv leaders to send special emissaries to Polish Jewry in order to strengthen the sense of connection and give them encouragement. The first such emissary, Isser Ben-Zvi, was dispatched a short time later, on August 20, 1945, and two others followed: Yohanan Cohen and Zvi Melnizer. Their mission was surreptitious; they came under the auspices of the *Mossad leAliya Bet*, the clandestine organization that orchestrated illegal immigration to Palestine from the European countries. They were followed by movement emissaries[46] and, in March 1946, by a joint mission of the Yishuv.[47]

In early September 1945, the socialist Zionist youth movement Gordonia and its parent party, Hitahdut (both of which were strongly related to the Mapai Party in Palestine), seceded from the Ichud Party after having joined it a few months before, and joined Hehalutz and the League for a Labor Palestine. Within this framework, Gordonia also began to establish collectives of its own.[48]

American Jewish Joint Distribution Committee — (the "Joint")

In the first months of 1945, the director of JDC-Poland, David Guzik, managed to receive funds that had been forwarded to him from the west, with the assistance of Bricha officials, via Bucharest. However, JDC did not resume its official activities in Poland until July 1945.[49] Almost all aid sent that year

45 Zuckerman, *A Surplus of Memory*, p. 596–604; report "Gordonia — Young Maccabi," Łódź, November 6, 1946, Lavon Institute, IV–209–4–364; Sarid, "Initial Deployment," p. 298. Before the war, the name *Hehalutz* referred to an umbrella organization of Jewish youth, some but not all of whom were associated with youth movements and who were planning to move to Palestine and join the Labor Movement's settlement enterprise. After the war, it denoted a framework for cooperation between Dror and Hashomer Hatza'ir (and from September 1945, Gordonia as well) for the education of youth in the spirit of socialist Zionism. See Engel, *Between Liberation and Escape*, p. 196, n. 121.
46 Engel, *Between Liberation and Escape*, p. 92. The emissaries were Natan Belizowski, Uri Janowski, and Leibl Goldberg of Hakibbutz Hameuhad; Shaike Weiner of Hashomer Hatza'ir; and Shmuel Gavish-Padnowski of Gordonia. See Sarid, "Initial Deployment," p. 275.
47 Letter Yishai, Jewish Agency emissary, June 1946, CZA, S25/5262.
48 Engel, *Between Liberation and Escape*, p. 94.
49 Gutman, *The Jews in Poland*, p. 20.

was in goods; only in late 1945 did Poland acquire banking services through which foreign currency could be legally used.[50] After lengthy negotiations with the Polish government over the exchange rate, JDC received better conditions than any other organization in converting the dollars that it brought into the country.[51]

JDC played an immensely significant part in relations between the Central Committee and the Zionist movements. The topics that it intended to deal with — children, the elderly, youth, and emigration — were taken up in an initial meeting on September 18, 1945, between Josef Schwartz, director of JDC-Europe, and the Central Committee members. Schwartz made a condition that the transfer of money would involve the extension of the Central Committee's patronage to all operations undertaken; otherwise, JDC would finance its activities directly. Thus, if the Committee wished to exert control over the distribution of JDC money in Poland, it would have to reconcile its priorities with that of the funding organization. Since the PPR and the Bund favored the rehabilitation of the survivors in a new democratic Poland, they found it difficult to accept the subsidization of emigration to Palestine which JDC favored.[52] In October 1945, after each of the sides had discussed the issue at length, the sweeping objection to emigration was lifted but it was decided to oppose the organized Bricha and its Zionist operators. In January 1946, a resolution was adopted at the initiative of the communists to establish a special department of the Central Committee for the handling of affairs related to legal emigration.[53]

By adopting this resolution, the Committee seems to have attempted to neutralize the exclusivity of the Bricha operatives in emigration affairs and to make survivors who wished to emigrate feel that it was easier and safer to emigrate officially, with the Committee's assistance. Thus the Committee also signaled to JDC that it was playing a role in emigration and that accordingly, JDC should not withhold special financial support for this cause.[54]

---

50 Yosef Litvak, "The JDC's Contribution to the Rehabilitation of the Jewish Survivors in Poland, 1944-1949," in Pinkus, ed., *East European Jews between Holocaust and Resurrection* (Sde Boker: Ben Gurion University, 1987, Hebrew), pp. 340–341; Engel, *Between Liberation and Escape*, pp. 83–84.

51 Engel, *Between Liberation and Escape*, p. 137. The government agreed to a rate of 140 zlotys per dollar and, some time later, 170, as against the official rate of only 100. Ibid., p. 241, n. 203; see also Litvak, "JDC's Contribution," pp. 341–342.

52 Bauer, *Out of the Ashes*, pp. XVII-XVIII.

53 Engel, *Between Liberation and Escape*, pp. 101–102; Yishai report. CZA, *Yediot*, June 1946, S25/5262.

54 Engel, *Between Liberation and Escape*, pp. 101–102.

The rivalry over the emigration issue became more complex in early January 1946, when Moshe Yishai arrived in Poland as the official emissary of the Jewish Agency in Jerusalem in order to open a Palestine office that would concern itself with legal emigration from Poland to Palestine.[55] The day after he arrived, Yishai visited the Committee's offices but was not received for an official meeting. In subsequent days, too, Yishai was unable to confer with Committee members and came away with the feeling that they preferred not to grant him recognition as an emissary of the Jewish Agency[56] — as opposed to the Polish government which authorized the opening of the Palestine Office in mid-February 1946.[57] In January, a World Jewish Congress delegation visited Poland[58] and met with Committee members and representatives of the Zionist movements. To the Committee's surprise, the delegation members took a Zionist stance in regard to emigration, both in their talks with the Committee and with the government officials who hosted them.[59]

Internal Political Struggles and the Economic Crisis in Poland

Great Britain, the seat of the Polish government in exile,[60] recognized the national unity government that was established in late June 1945 as a provisional government only, meant to serve only until free elections could be held. By August 1945, however, it was widely believed at the British Foreign Office that the communists in Poland wished to establish a Soviet-type regime and had no intention of allowing elections to take place. The Polish government,

---

55 Ibid., p. 102; Yishai, *In the Shadow of the Holocaust,* pp. 96–102; Sarid, "Initial Deployment," p. 310.

56 Yishai report. CZA, *Yediot,* June 1946, S25/5262.

57 Yishai, *In the Shadow of the Holocaust,* p. 102. The government approved this step on three conditions: it should be called the "Palestine Office"; it should deal with immigration affairs only and not in other Zionist activities; and it should be opened without public fanfare and with no inaugural events. In a letter to Shertok, titled "Absolutely Secret," however, Yishai spelled out slightly different conditions: there was no agreement about using the term "Palestine" in the name of the office; therefore, it would be called "The Emigration Office of the Jewish Agency in Palestine"; the office would engage solely in affairs related to immigration based on "certificates" (entrance visas); the agreement was secret and not to be disclosed; and there was concern about the British response to the opening of the office. See letter Yishai to Shertok, February 24, 1946.

58 Engel, *Between Liberation and Escape,* p. 118; Sarid, "Initial Deployment," p. 308.

59 Yishai report. CZA, *Yediot,* June 1946, S25/5262.

60 See "Polish Government in Exile," in *Encyclopedia of the Holocaust,* pp. 1177–1178, and "Delegatura," ibid., pp. 356–357.

in turn, had several demands of the British, including the disbanding of the Polish Home Army units that were stationed in Scotland and Italy. Their commander, General Władisław Anders, remained loyal to the anti-communist government in exile and served as a focal point of identification and authority for many underground groups that were fighting the new regime. The Polish government also sought the dissolution of the government in exile, which still existed in Britain, and carried out propaganda against the government in Warsaw.[61] On the one hand, the government in exile regarded Stanisław Mikołajczyk as its emissary to the coalition in Poland, it being his function to look into the possibility of joining it; on the other, it encouraged gangs to make the soil of Poland "quake" and sow fear in the country so as to prove that the leftist government was too weak to maintain order and assure the population's safety. At a press conference called by the minister of defense of the Polish government, which was attended by the Jewish Agency emissary, evidence of the support of the Polish forces in Britain for the actions of the gangs in Poland was presented.[62] In view of the struggle against the government in exile in London and against the domestic enemies — the traditional and the far right — the new government of Poland had a political interest in maintaining good relations with the highly influential Jewish entities, which, in their opinion, could be of assistance.[63]

A bout of hyperinflation swept Poland in late 1945 and early 1946. Against this background, the government began to tighten its supervision of organizations that were receiving money from abroad, in order to make sure, among other things, that the funds would be converted at the official rate of exchange, which was much lower than that on the open market. The resulting situation hindered the operations of the Zionist movements, since the money they were receiving from the Jewish Agency, which covered most expenses for the collectives, was in sterling — a currency that was worth less

---

61 Engel, *Between Liberation and Escape*, pp. 107–108. According to the accords concluded in Yalta between the USSR, the United States and Great Britain in February 1945, the national unity government that would come into being in Poland would have to conduct free elections on the basis of universal and secret franchise at the earliest date possible. Only after such elections, the USA and the UK believed, could the government of Poland be recognized as permanent. The Soviets were opposed to the idea of free elections and ultimately torpedoed the scheme. In June 1946, a plebiscite over the method of governance took place and in January 1947, elections were held. Both the plebiscite and the elections, however, were conducted against the background of a communist campaign of intimidation and repression. See ibid., pp. 181–182, n. 223.

62 Yishai, *In the Shadow of the Holocaust*, pp. 54, 60.

63 Sarid, "Initial Deployment," pp. 301–309.

than the dollar at the time. This thwarted the expansion of activities such as establishing new collectives and opening Hebrew-language schools, soldiers' residences, etc. In the meantime, it was increasingly believed that the winner in the struggle for influence over the survivors would be the organization that had the most funds available for the recruitment of survivors.[64]

From August 1945 on, there seemed to be some likelihood of viable life in the former German areas in the west that had been placed under Polish civil administration at the end of the war. In the wake of the repatriation agreement concluded between the Polish and Soviet governments on July 6, 1945, an indefinite number of Jews — estimated by various sources at between 125,000, 150,000, or even 170,000 — were to return. The first group of repatriates arrived on February 8, 1946, paving the way for others who followed. In view of the large numbers of Polish and Jewish returnees, coupled with infrastructure and housing problems, the Polish government decided to encourage the repatriates to settle in the "new"- formerly German — territories. The Central Committee also began to encourage survivors to move to these areas, which, it seemed, would be receptive to the creation of large Jewish centers and subsequent economic renewal.[65] In view of the new opportunities, the non-Zionists on the Central Committee attempted to earn the government's sympathies and defeat the emigration plans of the Zionists. They focused on two matters that, in their opinion, justified the rehabilitation of the Jews in Poland itself: the attitude of the Yishuv toward Poland (as adduced from reports from Palestine that criticized the situation in Poland), and reports from refugees saying that they had fled from Poland due to persecution, thereby besmirching Poland's good name.[66] In view of the non-Zionist critical attitude and the escalating competition for the hearts of the remaining Jews in Poland, the Zionists found it easier to discuss matters that were related to their Zionist activities and that entailed official assistance with non-Jewish communists rather than with Jewish communists — whom, the Zionists felt, were being incited against them.[67]

64 Engel, *Between Liberation and Escape*, pp. 110–111; letter Mizrachi Committee in Kraków to Torah Va'avoda World Alliance in Palestine, September 6, 1946, RZRI, S.20IV.
65 Engel, *Between Liberation and Escape*, pp. 112, 114, 120; Gutman, *The Jews in Poland*, p. 13.
66 Yishai report.
67 Anton Mara report; Bauer, *Flight and Rescue: The Brichah*, pp. 113–114.

1946: Deterioration of the Political Situation in Poland, Changing Attitude toward the Jews and the Pogrom in Kielce

In late February 1946, relations between the PPR and the largest non-com-munist party in Poland, the Polish Peasants' Party (*Polskie Stronnictwo Ludowe* — PSL), took a turn for the worse. Until then, the two parties had been negotiating over the presentation of a united list in the general elec-tions that were due to take place according to the Yalta accords. After the inter-party talks ran aground and the PPR became concerned about the growing influence on the masses of the anti-communist opposition, the authorities launched a campaign of repression against the Peasants' Party — in accordance with which the anti-communist underground forces stepped up their attacks on those identified with the government, including the Jews. The Central Committee convened for an emergency debate, in which the fear of an escalation in attacks on Jews was expressed. Indeed, the situation deteriorated during the ensuing two months. In early May, the government announced a plebiscite to take place on June 30, in which the electorate would be presented with three motions. The announcement aggravated the political tension, since the communists favored all three motions, whereas the deputy prime minister, Stanisław Mikołajczyk — head of the Peasants' Party and the key individual in the anti-communist opposition — called for a vote against the first motion, the abolition of the Senate. The Polish public construed the electoral campaign that preceded the plebiscite as the definitive contest over the future of the Polish state.[68]

After the plebiscite was announced, the situation of Polish Jewry deteriorated further as the anti-communist forces used the Jewish community as a target for violence. Furthermore, the Central Committee announced the support of the Jewish public for all three motions in the plebiscite,[69] thereby taking a stand that was interpreted as siding with the PPR. The sense that the

68 Engel, *Between Liberation and Escape*, pp. 128–129; the three motions were the following: 1. to abolish the Senate (the upper house of the Polish parliament); 2. to introduce agrarian reform and nationalize large industrial enterprises; 3. to fully annex Lower Silesia and the Szczecin area. See Samet, *When I Came the Day After*, pp. 48–49.

69 Engel, *Between Liberation and Escape*, p. 128; for descriptions of the state of antisemitism in Poland in 1946, see also Yishai, *In the Shadow of the Holocaust*, pp. 37, 68–69; Levi Arieh Sarid, "Remarks about the Koordynacja," in Bornstein, ed., *Redemption of Jewish Chil-dren,* p. 16; report from Bein, director of JDC-Poland, to JDC-New York, October 24, 1946, microfilm from Poland, JDC Archives, HZ/46/1133.

authorities were relying on the Jews merely elevated the existing antisemitism to new heights.[70]

Senior government officials, foremost among them, the president and the prime minister, issued unequivocal public condemnations of the attacks on Jews and promised to take any action needed to uproot the phenomenon from Polish society. This rhetoric, however, did nothing to restrain the attacks and did not even calm the Jewish community.

On July 4, 1946, forty-two Jews were killed and many others wounded in a pogrom in the town of Kielce. The onslaught, perpetrated in broad daylight in a district capital in the middle of the country, coupled with the behavior of the police and the momentum gathered by the incident as a result of which attacks on Jews in other localities took place that day,[71] reinforced the feeling that the Polish–Jewish relationship was extremely fragile and might have been irreparably damaged.

Yitzchak Zuckerman feared that the situation in Poland would prompt more and more prospective emigrants to take action by means of the Bricha, forcing the government to stop it. Thus, immediately after the pogrom in Kielce, he initiated contacts with the Polish defense system in order to obtain its consent for opening the borders. In late July 1946, following contacts between the Zionists and the Polish deputy defense minister, General Marian Spychalski, a secret agreement was worked out in which, under certain circumstances, the Polish border would be opened for the departure of Jewish groups under the auspices of the Bricha.[72] The accord made it easier for the Bricha to absorb the rising tide of would-be emigrants and to get them out of the country.

Even earlier, on April 20, 1946, the Central Committee had sent a delegation to the United States to obtain assistance for the absorption of the emigrants. At the end of a large rally on June 11, Zommerstein, the keynote speaker at the rally, collapsed. The delegation carried on and returned to

---

70 Report Shmuel Epstein, member of Palestine mission in Poland, to the Jewish Agency, Jerusalem, May 30, 1946, CZA, S25/5262.
71 Engel, *Between Liberation and Escape*, pp. 129, 131; Gutman, *The Jews in Poland*, pp. 60–61, idem, "Polish Jews from Liberation to Emigration," pp. 114, 118.
72 Engel, *Between Liberation and Escape*, p. 134. The agreement imposed three conditions: 1. the crossing would be coordinated with Polish security officials; 2. the Bricha personnel would prevent non-Jews from emigrating (especially enemies of the regime who might exploit the freedom that was available in order to cross the borders) and would thwart the removal of national assets such as foreign currency; 3. the existence of the accord would not be divulged.

Poland after the pogrom in Kielce without Zommerstein, who had to stay in the United States due to illness.[73]

Stabilization of the Regime and the Situation of the Jews from Early 1947

In the general elections held on January 19, 1947, which were marked by marked tension and strong suspicion of fraud, 80.1 percent of votes were cast for the PPR-led Democratic Front (*Stronnictwo Demokratyczne* — SD).[74] By this time, the socialist wing had merged with the communists and several of the most prominent socialists were ousted from the party after having greeted the imposed merger unenthusiastically. Among those expelled were Osóbka-Morawski, the first post-war prime minister of Poland, and several Jews who had been leaders of the socialist left.[75] Although the political developments were not universally accepted, nearly all the unrest ended and no murders of Jews were reported in the following months.[76]

In early 1947, when the government sealed the country's borders, following the mass emigration, only about 80,000 Jews remained in Poland.[77] The Zionists among them focused mainly on education for young people in the Jewish localities[78] and withstood the heavy pressure that was brought against them.[79] The Jewish communists wished to stem the exodus and maintain the few Jewish centers that remained. The anti-emigration propaganda was fueled by reports about difficulties that Polish Jews were encountering in

---

73 Shlomi, "Organization of the Jewish Survivors," p. 533. Gutman claims that Zommerstein went to the US in February 1947 and did not return. However, he evidently left before the pogrom in Kielce and was not in Poland when it took place.

74 Shlomi, "Organization of the Jewish Survivors," p. 537; Engel, *Between Liberation and Escape*, pp. 181–182, n. 223; Kahana, *After the Deluge*, p. 93.

75 Gutman, *The Jews in Poland*, p. 96; Daniel Blatman, *For Our Freedom and Yours: The Jewish Labour Bund in Poland, 1939–1949* (London: Vallentine Mitchell, 2003), p. 210. In October 1948, the self-eradication of the Bund in Poland and its merger with the United Polish Labor Party was virtually complete. See ibid., pp. 200–201, 213.

76 Letter Gonjondzki, Mizrachi Federation, Poland, to Dr. M.A. Kurtz, Youth Department, Mizrachi World Federation, Tel Aviv, April, RZRI, S.21IV; letter J. Majus, member of Hashomer Hatza'ir executive, to E. Dobkin, the Jewish Agency, December 8, 1947, CZA, S86/73

77 Gutman, "Polish Jews from Liberation to Emigration," p. 119; letter Gonjondzki to Dr. M.A. Kurtz, April 1947.

78 Shlomi, "Organization of the Jewish Survivors," p. 546.

79 Letter Majus, December 8. 1947, CZA, S86/73.

displaced persons camps in Germany and the many complaints from those who had reached Palestine and were disappointed by what they found there.[80]

The Central Committee's school system was unable to surmount the provisional arrangements and to cope with the hardships and develop efficiently. Following the elections in January 1947, the Committee began negotiations with the Polish Ministry of Education over economic assistance for the Jewish educational institutions. The matter was handled swiftly, resulting in the nationalization of the Jewish system and the merger of its curriculum with the general one.

In March 1947, after the chair of the Central Committee had been vacant for some time, Adolf Berman was appointed as Zommerstein's successor. Its presidium was reconfigured when Hirsch Smolar was added as a seventh member, representing the partisans; Smolar, a veteran communist, tipped the scales in the Committee in favor of the communists. At a conference of Jewish committees that took place that month, there was talk about the need to reorganize the supreme institution of Polish Jewry. All agreed that the Committee was not functioning well and that it could not continue to operate under the inter-party agreement drawn up in Lublin in 1944. The Central Committee, its constituent members believed, should reflect the state of the Jews in 1947, that is, it should base its authority on general elections. But no such elections were held then. Only in the wake of changes in the Jewish wing of the Communist Party in 1948 did elections for the Central Committee take place — in February 1949.[81]

In the spring of 1947, the PPR conducted internal talks concerning the party's attitude toward the Jewish communists and the relationships to Jewish organizational efforts in Poland. According to motions tabled at the time, the Jewish sector was to play a role in the changes that were about to take place in Poland as a result of government centralization, by means of the reorganization of the Jewish institutions. The change took place that summer. A very large number of Jewish organizations and unions came into being, each focusing on a specific field and the Jewish communists made sure to staff the key positions in these bodies with their comrades. The organizational actions of the Jews were increasingly seen as a reflection of Jewish culture and not as a political factor. In November 1947, it was decided to establish a "National

---

80 Shlomi, "Organization of the Jewish Survivors," p. 541; Gutman, "Polish Jews from Liberation to Emigration," p. 119; letter Gonjondzki to Dr. M.A. Kurtz, April 1947.
81 Shlomi, "Organization of the Jewish Survivors," pp. 537, 539, 542, 544; Gutman, *The Jews in Poland*, pp. 68, 81.

Culture Association," and as this body gained in stature and depth, so did the Central Committee decline.[82]

In the first half of 1947, the members of the Council of Religious Communities again came under pressure to join the Central Committee. The Mizrachi and Agudath Israel parties, which were members of the Council, had been operating illegally until then because they had not received government recognition. In September, Rabbi Kahana met with Szymon Zachariasz, the Communist Party's official for Jewish affairs. In their encounter, Zachariasz told the rabbi that if the Council merged with the Central Committee, the pressure on the religious parties would stop. Previously, in June 1947, the idea of joining the Committee had been debated at the sixth general conference of the Council of Communities, which decided that, although the Council agreed in principle, the act of joining should be made conditional on several measures, including observance of the Sabbath as an official day of rest and observance of the Jewish dietary laws in the Committee's kitchens. From June to November, when representatives of the Committee and the Council met several times, it became clear that the Central Committee would not accede to the Council's religious demands. On November 15, 1947, the Council convened again, together with the Rabbinical Council, and resolved to stand firm with regard to the Sabbath. In March 1948, at a joint conference of the Central Committee and the Council of Religious Communities, the former announced its rejection of Sabbath observance and the dietary demands and added a demand of its own: that it take over the management of the Council's children's home. Despite the discord, the two entities decided to merge but agreed that the Council of Religious Communities would maintain its autonomy within the Committee.[83]

Two events at this time attracted the attention of Polish Jews and influenced their thinking: the transition of governance in Poland from a relatively moderate people's democracy to rigid, Soviet-style communism; and developments in the international arena and the Eastern Bloc with regard to Palestine preceding the establishment of the State of Israel in May 1948. The chairs of the Jewish committees in Poland convened in February 1947 and resolved to support the struggle for the establishment of the Jewish state. When, on November 29, 1947, the United Nations voted in favor of the partition of Palestine into two states, the Jewish collective in Poland responded with elation. The Central Committee, realizing that it could not staunch these

82 Shlomi, "Organization of the Jewish Survivors," pp. 538, 542.
83 Ibid., p. 536; Kahana, *After the Deluge*, pp. 35, 104–106.

feelings, issued a statement of fervent support for the UN resolution.[84] In the summer of 1948, after the independence of Israel had been proclaimed, an Israeli consular staff arrived in Poland under Yisrael Barzilai, whom the Jews in Poland knew from previous missions.[85]

Even after the Central Committee held its general elections in February 1949, Berman continued as chairman, although most members of the Committee's institutions came from the non-Zionist left. Two months later, a decision was made to unseat him[86] and to appoint Hirsch Smolar, a member of the presidium, as his successor.[87]

A turning point in the attitude toward the Zionist entities took place in late 1948, although it was neither acute nor accompanied with sanctions and arrests. However, this changed in late 1949, when the Zionist bodies were ordered to disband. The dissolution order was preceded by an announcement from the government that any Jew who wished to emigrate to Israel would be allowed to do so within a fixed period of time. The statement stressed that there was no place for Zionism in Poland, since any Zionist who regarded Israel as his or her homeland was welcome to leave the country. The Zionist activists greeted this decision bitterly and even weighed the possibility of carrying on in the underground. At this time, the process of communist takeover was taking place all over the country.[88]

As Poland moved ahead in its disengagement from the West, the Central Committee institutions resolved, in April 1949, to cease cooperation with the Joint Distribution Committee. In September, the director of JDC-Poland, William Bein, was summoned to Minister of the Interior Wolski, who informed him that JDC must close its office by the end of the year. With the closure of the JDC office, all the Jewish relief institutions collapsed.[89]

---

84 Shlomi, "Organization of the Jewish Survivors," pp. 537, 543–544.

85 Gutman, *The Jews in Poland*, p. 90.

86 Shlomi, "Organization of the Jewish Survivors," p. 545; Gutman claims that Berman was unseated as chairman of the Central Committee in 1948 (*The Jews in Poland*, p. 84) but reports elsewhere (p. 81) suggest that this happened in 1949.

87 Gutman, *The Jews in Poland*, p. 81.

88 Ibid., pp. 81–82, 86, 90–91; idem., "Polish Jews from Liberation to Emigration," p. 121. According to Gutman, the order to expel the Zionists from Poland was part of a general and comprehensive process and not a specifically anti-Jewish political policy. Shlomi claimed that the demand to oust the Zionists and give them exit visas was spearheaded by Zachariasz, who believed that the Zionists were causing harm to the Jewish population and to Poland. See Shlomi, *Organization of the Jewish Survivors*, p. 546; Litvak, "JDC's Contribution," p. 379.

89 Shlomi, "Organization of the Jewish Survivors," p. 545; Litvak, "JDC's Contribution," p. 379; Gutman, "Polish Jews from Liberation to Emigration," p. 121.

In November 1950, the Central Committee in its previous configuration was abolished and integrated into the National Association for Culture, which was reorganized as the Jewish Association for Culture and Society in Poland (*Towarzystwo Społeczno-Kulturalne Żydów w Polsce*).[90]

1944–1950: Overview

The first six years after the war were ones of constant upheaval. The Polish state underwent various processes of rehabilitation, reorganization, redrawing of borders, population transfer, and reorientation toward the Soviet Union. The Jewish survivors, battered by their suffering and losses, attempted to claw their way back to life. Existential and ideological needs drove the Jews to form institutions, political parties, and organizations. They also established contact with world Jewry and the Yishuv in Palestine, and, after independence, with the State of Israel. Paths of assistance in rehabilitation and emigration were created.

The Polish–Jewish relationship was emotionally charged and complex due to the general attitude of the Poles toward Jews and ideological conflicts that came about within their own society.

The achievements and activities of Polish Jewry in the initial postwar years paint an impressive picture in their extent and their many facets. Although they were aided by massive support from JDC and western Jewry, the initiatives came from the grassroots, originating in the liberated territories and powered by local activists.

90 Shlomi, "Organization of the Jewish Survivors," p. 545; Gutman, "Polish Jews from Liberation to Emigration."

CHAPTER 3

First Efforts to Locate Concealed Children:
The Establishment of Institutions
and Organizations

"God calls, always and everywhere:
"Man, where are you?"
Where are you in your world –

How many years have passed over you
And what did you do with your years?"

Menachem Mendel Schneerson[1]

After Liberation

Jewish soldiers served in the Red Army units that advanced from the east into Poland. Some were integral members of the fighting forces; others enlisted and joined various units as new areas were liberated.[2] As they progressed, these fighters became aware of the immensity of the devastation that had befallen the Jewish communities. Large Jewish populations in some localities had been eradicated and the reports on the ways and means of extermination were unendurably horrific. The reality of the situation shattered all the Jewish fighters' hopes of finding survivors in their communities. The stronger their sense of loss, the greater was their excitement when they encountered Jews by chance, and even more so when

---

1   Arye Ben-Gurion, ed., *Return to Yourself: The Life of Man between Birth and Old-Age — Collection from the Sources and from Modern Hebrew Poetry* (Tel Aviv: Hakibbutz Hameuhad, 1998, Hebrew), p. 18.
2   Shlomi, "Initial Organization," p. 303; Neshamit, "The Koordynacja for the Redemption of Children in Liberated Poland," p. 118.

they encountered a Jewish child or received information concerning a child who had survived and was living with rescuers.[3]

The battles were still raging; the front shifting eastward and westward until final liberation. Despite the fighting, there were Jewish soldiers who responded to requests for help in removing a child and some even did so at their own initiative. The stories that follow attest to the nature of such encounters. Jakob was twelve years old when Soviet forces approached the village where he was working and in which German units were still present. Accurately sizing up the economic situation and the value of livestock, the boy fled to the Soviet soldiers, taking a cow with him. A Jewish officer encountered him and, evidently because he was unable to take him along, placed him in an orphanage.[4] A Jewish girl had a similar experience: in late 1944, an army unit entered Giełczew, a village in Lublin District. In every location that they liberated, the Jewish commander of the unit made inquiries about the possible presence of Jewish children. In Giełczew he turned to the mayor who referred him to the Falk family. The girl related:

> They came, the officer and the mayor. I saw them coming closer, they were speaking with the master. I saw them looking at me. The officer tried to approach me, to give [me] a piece of candy, to ask something, to speak Yiddish. But I continued to deny it all because I was afraid. He continued to talk with the Pole who was looking after me. He apparently promised him some money; he wanted to take me to Lublin when he left with his soldiers. He didn't know when he'd be leaving and he had to hide me from his soldiers. His heart didn't allow him to leave a Jewish girl behind — who knew when she'd return to Judaism? He spoke with the goy and told him to tell [me] that maybe I'd meet up with my parents. This began to have an effect on me, and when he came again, I already made gestures showing that I understood Yiddish. Finally, he hid me in the trunk of his car and we drove away.

The Jewish officer brought the girl to Lublin, where reorganization of Jewish life had begun, hoping that she would encounter someone who knew what had become of her family. Then he continued onward with his unit. "And I didn't even know who he was," the girl testified years later.[5]

---

3   Shlomi, "Initial Organization," pp. 303–304; Gutman, *Jews in Poland*, p. 32; interview by author with Yeshayahu Drucker.
4   Testimony Jakob Lutner, MA, A.402; autobiography Jakob Litner (Lutner), in Tenenboim, *One of a City and Two of a Family*, pp. 97–98.
5   Recorded memoirs of Haviva Barak-Owiec; Dekel, *Remnants of the Sword*, p. 644.

In these examples and in other accounts, the Jewish soldier concentrated on the act of removing the child from his or her surroundings and not necessarily on the institution to which he would hand over his charge. He wished to remove the child from the influence of the environment as quickly as possible, perhaps because of an inner conviction that the child had to be removed, or because he was afraid that the youngster would be ill treated. The following story is indicative of the latter. A Jewish soldier serving with the First Polish Division encamped in a village near Góra-Kalwaria located three Jewish brothers in various houses in the village. The soldier tells the story:

> We'd been encamped in the village for three days and we had to move on. What should we do? How could we make sure they'd be safe? The war was drawing to a close but the times were not quiet and there were various kinds of people in the village. Who knew what a peasant would do if something scared him? There were two other Jews in the battalion, and the three of us consulted each other. We wrote out a certificate in the name of the goy with whom two of the boys had been hiding: 'I, so-and-so — I provided a first name and a family name — undertake to take care of the three children... ; if something bad happens to any of them, I will be responsible and face prosecution.' We forced him to sign and we took the certificate with us...[6]

In some cases, Jewish soldiers who reached the areas of their own homes, discovered that their families were no longer alive and began to search in nearby villages in hopes of discovering child relatives. If such a child was indeed found, the encounter may have had a definitive effect on the soldier's continued participation in the fighting. For some soldiers, the sense of responsibility for the child survivor transcended any prior commitments.[7]

As the army advanced and liberated the country area after area, the local population began to prepare for a life free of the German occupier's yoke and became somewhat fearful about the intentions of the liberating army. Jews who had spent the past two or three years concealed in various hideouts, set out for nearby localities, mostly with no material basis on which to build a new life and in poor physical and emotional condition. Although by then

---

6   Nessia Orlowicz-Reznik, *Mommy, May I Cry Now?* (Merhavia: Moreshet and Sifriat Poalim, 1965, Hebrew), pp. 222–224. The author directed the Hashomer Hatza'ir children's home in Ludwikowo. For another example of soldiers' inability to take a child whom they encountered during the battles, see 1946 autobiography of Shmuel Kroll, in Tenenboim, *One of a City and Two of a Family*, pp. 64–68.
7   Testimony Moshe Kuruc, YVA, O.3/4290.

most of them knew about the extermination of the Jews, their encounter with the emptiness was traumatic because it revealed the full extent of the catastrophe. As the last vestiges of extended families, the survivors carried the memories of those no longer alive. Unbearably lonely, each survivor felt like the last Jew on earth.[8] Although some had been saved by non-Jewish acquaintances, many survivors were angry at the Polish population, be it due to a bad personal experience, or due to the conviction that the Poles had done nothing as the extermination took place or, worse still, were pro-German collaborators.[9] Some survivors, disregarding their physical, psychological, or economic situation, gathered up a Jewish child whom they encountered on the road, even if the youngster was unrelated to them and they had not known the child's family[10] — evidently prompted by the desire to gather together any surviving Jews and to rebuild a life.

For survivors who had placed a child with non-Jews during the war, trying to locate the child was, of course, the first priority. Some found their children and had emotional reunions.[11] For others, the attempt ended differently due to several circumstances: the time that had elapsed; the child's surroundings; and the way the child had been brought up. The situation was complex for both sides and all hopes of reunion and healing were sometimes dashed. Parents faced children who did not recognize them and refused to go with them.[12] The nature of such an encounter depended on whether the child remembered the family and whether the rescuers helped to facilitate the reunion.

In most cases, the parents did not survive, but relatives who did made supreme efforts to obtain any shred of information about the fate of their families. Sometimes relatives knew about a family member who had been

---

8   Yitzchak (Antek) Zuckerman, *Exodus Poland: On the Bricha and the Revitalization of the Pioneering Movement* (Tel Aviv: Ghetto Fighters' House and Hakibbutz Hameuhad, 1988, Hebrew), p. 28; Shlomi, "Organization of the Jewish Survivors," pp. 523–524; Engel, *Between Liberation and Escape*, pp. 39–40.

9   Berman, *From the Days of the Resistance*, p. 188; interview by author with Moshe Tuchendler; Gutman, *Jews in Poland*, p. 32.

10 Yishai, *In the Shadow of the Holocaust*, p. 179; autobiography of Arik Holder, in Tenenboim, *One of a City and Two of a Family*, pp. 95–96; testimony Jakob Lutner, MA, A.402; testimony Arye Lindenbaum, YVA, O.3/5112.

11 Testimony Aviva Brawer, YVA, O.3/4509. Aviva was born in 1937; Śliwowska, *Dzieci Holocaustu Mówią...*, "Hanka Grynberżanka," pp. 156–164. Hannah (Hanka) was born in 1933; Grynberg, *Księga Sprawiedliwych*, "Honorata Skowrońska," p. 491.

12 Dekel, *Along the Paths of the Bricha*, p. 432; Frederbahr-Salz, *And the Sun Rose*, p. 167; Yerushalmi, *Children of the Holocaust*, p. 89. In most cases, the parents did not give up; they removed their children later on.

handed over; on other occasions they came upon the information as they searched. The need to rebuild the family and preserve the memory of the relatives, as well as a sense of responsibility, prompted them in most cases to take in the children.[13] For the children and rescuers alike, the advent of relatives was different from the reappearance of a parent. Sometimes children did not recognize relatives who suddenly burst into their lives, and even if they did recognize them, it did not necessarily mean that they had been particularly close before the war. Rescuers, too, did not always accept the entitlement of a relative to a child who had lived with them for so long and had become an integral part of their family. To remove children from rescuers' homes, the consent of all parties was needed. The case of twelve-year-old Moshe is a case in point. Moshe occasionally set out from the home of the peasant with whom he lived to sell merchandise. On his way, he repeatedly encountered Jews who attempted to persuade him to join them, but each time he refused and returned to the village. When his uncle discovered that the boy was alive, he searched and found him, but the encounter was not a success. Moshe related: "I'd made up my mind. I didn't want to be Jewish any more and I didn't want to recognize him as my uncle. I got up and ran away from him. He ambushed me a few days later..."[14]

Relatives who failed to remove children had two options: to stay in the vicinity and try to contact the child again, hoping that time would have an effect, or to turn to other parties for assistance. In the early liberation period, before the war ended, relatives turned to anyone whom they thought could force rescuers to return the children to a Jewish milieu: Jewish soldiers in the Red Army, Jewish partisans, or the police. This course of action was chosen, for example, by one woman who knew that her brother had handed his young daughter to a peasant woman and wanted to reclaim her. When the peasant refused to return the child and vehemently refused to negotiate with the aunt over the situation, the Jewish woman turned to Jewish partisans and the NKVD, the Soviet secret police, who removed the girl from the Polish woman's custody. The Jewish woman concluded her story as follows: "I was lucky that her husband wasn't home and that the goyish woman didn't know what to do. She was afraid both of Jews and Russians after the war."[15] Moshe, the

---

13 Frederbahr-Salz, *And the Sun Rose*, p. 171; Grynberg, *Księga Sprawiedliwych*, p. 171; testimony Rivka Lustigman, YVA, O.3/4152; testimony Binyamin Blustein, YVA, O.3/5058; Frank, *To Survive and to Testify*, p. 81; interview by author with Haim Edelstein.

14 Frank, *To Survive and to Testify*; testimony Rivka Lustigman, YVA, O.3/4152.

15 Testimony Rivka Lustigman, YVA, O.3/4152; Yerushalmi, *Children of the Holocaust*, p. 3.

boy who refused to join his uncle, also related: "When [my uncle eventually] discovered me, he came this time with a Jewish officer from the Red Army. The two of them made me go with them; they didn't let me go back and see the peasant again...".[16]

Immediately after the liberation, the survivors wandered, mostly vagrant and penniless. The roads were dangerous and in most cases, the population was hostile. Under these conditions, information received about a child did not always lead to his or her removal. Sometimes relatives made do with merely visiting the child,[17] perhaps feeling that the child was safest where he or she was, for the time being or even permanently. The story of Haim and his brother is a case in point. Haim, born in 1931, had been placed with a Ukrainian family in Stryj (a Ukrainian town that was part of Poland in the interwar period), whereas his brother, born in 1938, was left in the home of the family's former maid who lived in the same town. During the war, the children were allowed to meet several times. After liberation, Haim, about thirteen years old, spent hours wandering the streets. Thus he happened to encounter a cousin of his father, whose family comprised three people. The cousin wanted Haim to accompany him; the Ukrainian family also wanted him to leave. "I went to live with this uncle," Haim related. "It was tough, there was nothing to eat; there was no way to make a living." The cousin knew the whereabouts of Haim's younger brother and even visited the former maid's home in order to reclaim possessions that the boys' father had left with her. When the maid asked them to take the boy, the cousin refused, claiming that he could not do so because he had nothing to live on. Haim also asked him to take his brother and received the same answer. "I must have asked again," Haim recounted, "because he told me he'd gone there but by then the goyish woman refused to hand him over." In the spring of 1945, the family moved to Poland. "I didn't want to go without my brother, but he [his father's cousin] promised to go back for him after we'd settle down in Kraków." The maid came to the railroad station with Haim's little brother in order to say goodbye — and that was the last time the brothers saw each other.[18] This story illustrates the

---

16 Frank, *To Survive and to Testify*, p. 81.
17 Interview by author with Haim Edelstein; Śliwowska, *Dzieci Holocaustu Mówią...*, "Hanka Grynberżanka," pp. 156–164; letter Sarah Goldberg of Rishon Lezion to Rabbi Herzog, January 21, 1947, RZA, Rescue Files.
18 Interview by author with Haim Edelstein. Haim's brother still lives in the town where the two were born and works there as a psychiatrist. All of Haim's attempts to reestablish contact with him were rejected.

indecision that beset family members: some spared no effort to reclaim a child relative, irrespective of the difficulties. However, postponing the removal to a more propitious time seemed at that time to be no less logical.

Getting Organized: The First Steps

The first stage in tracking down the children was inevitably individual and impromptu. Within a short time, however, the situation changed. In several liberated areas, groups of survivors began to organize and establish rendezvous points which people visited every day in search of relatives and acquaintances.[19] In several places, the survivors began to act in order to locate and gather together Jewish children in villages in the vicinity. For example, a group of Jewish partisans with the Red Army, under Eliezer Lidowski, entered the town of Równe in 1944 and broke away from the army afterwards. Before they left the forests, the Jews decided that if they were privileged to survive, they would act on behalf of other Jews. Indeed, one of the first actions they took was to search for Jewish children and try to transfer them to appropriate settings. The same thing happened in Vilnius; after the city was liberated in July 1944, a group of partisans led by Abba Kovner, established a children's home and took children in.[20] The group used the services of a Professor Rawelski, a Jew and chief physician on the staff of the liberator of Vilnius, General Czernychowski, and founder of the military hospital in the city, to obtain a building that could serve as an institution for children. Rawelski used his army connections so that, whenever information was received about a Jewish child whose rescuers refused to hand him over, soldiers were sent to accompany the removal operatives. Some twenty children were placed in the home shortly after these operations began, and more arrived as other children heard about it and went there independently.[21]

Actions of these types were undertaken by local committees that formed in the centers of survivors when local initiatives were taken. In Kaunas, a pub-

---

19 Gutman, *Jews in Poland*, p. 13.
20 Sarid, "Initial Deployment," p. 276; idem, "Remarks about the Koordynacja," p. 17; in Lidowski's estimation, they gathered 50–60 children. See Sarid, *Ruin and Deliverance*, B, pp. 15, 17–18.
21 Testimony Cyla Wildstajn, MA, A.485; Sarid, *Ruin and Deliverance*, pp. 25–26; Yerushalmi, testimony of a child-removal operative, in *Children of the Holocaust*, pp. 92–94; autobiography of the boy Shmuel Kroll, in Tenenboim, *One of a City and Two of a Family*, pp. 64–68.

lic committee established a children's home to which non-Jews could bring children whom they had been hiding; at the same time, it began to search for children from the surroundings. The same thing happened in Łuck, Białystok, and Lwów.[22]

The searchers circulated in villages and towns, asking questions and making inquiries. When there was no information about a specific child, the searchers based themselves on a general feeling about the presence of hidden children. Sometimes these children had no memory at all about their Jewish origins; others did remember but were afraid to abandon familiar people for unfamiliar ones. Rachel's testimony is an example:

> Shortly after we were liberated, two Jews whom no one knew wandered around in our village and asked for information about Jewish children. The neighbors' children came to warn me: Look, they've come to take you away for Passover *matza* [i.e., to use her blood for the baking of matza, as in the finest tradition of the historic blood libel]. Of course, I went into hiding so they wouldn't find me and no one from the village told them where the Jewish girl was.[23]

However, the search for Rachel and others like her ultimately succeeded. Rachel continues: "As time passed, the story about the Jews began to stick in my mind. So one Sunday, out of curiosity or for some other reason, instead of going to Mass I decided to go into town [to look for Jews]." In other cases, however, children preferred to remain in the villages.

In the early post-liberation period, some rescuers turned to a Jewish center at their own initiative and delivered a child whom they had been sheltering — as if to turn in an object that had been held on deposit[24] — and asked for neither payment nor compensation for having concealed the youngster in their home. If the rescuers did ask for remuneration, the Jews organized spontaneously and handed over whatever sum of money they managed to raise. This kind of removal entirely depended on the rescuer's goodwill.

22 Kahana, *After the Deluge*, p. 15; testimony Yehoshua Olshin, in David Kranzler and Gertrude Hirschler, eds., *Solomon Schonfeld: His Page in History: Recollections of Individuals Saved by an Extraordinary Orthodox Jewish Rescue Hero during the Holocaust Era* (New York: Judaica Press, 1982), p. 157; Shner-Neshamit, *I Did Not Come to Rest*, pp. 184–186; testimony Mordechai Müller, YVA, O.3/3653; testimony Miriam Nakric, YVA, O.3/3921.
23 Interview by author with Rachel Wolf-Wajnsztok.
24 Autobiography of Arik Holder (b. 1935), in Tenenboim, *One of a City and Two of a Family*, pp. 95–96; testimony Naftali Packer, aged fourteen at the time of the liberation; testimony Arye Lindenbaum, YVA, O.3/5112.

When information about children existed but rescuers refused to surrender them, removal operatives could not appeal to the legal system and coerce rescuers into surrendering the youngsters. Turning to the police was not always effective. Rabbi David Kahana, chairman of the Jewish committee in Lwów, recounted his discovery of the whereabouts of Rabbi Halberstam's daughter. When his request for custody went unanswered, he went to the police. The Soviet chief of police, however, informed him that under Soviet law a child's mother might not necessarily be the child's biological mother, and anyway, since the girl's biological mother was not alive, why should she be removed from her adoptive mother? Some time later, the adoptive family left Lwów and traces of the girl were lost.[25]

The upshot of these accounts is that the removal actions were local if not random, and depended upon the survivors' character, power, and sense of mission. All actions on behalf of Jewish children depended on the human factor — the survivors' willingness to gather, receive, or search for children, and the rescuers' willingness to hand over to the Jews children whom they had sheltered during the war.

Any formal Jewish organizational action after the war would probably have included a department for the care of child survivors. The testimonies, however, suggest that the institutionalization of these operations was dictated by the situation in the field as the need for more comprehensive solutions came about. Even though each case demanded a unique solution, instrumentalities of some kind had to be created — methods of tracking and searching, referral of requests to non-Jews, relations with the institutions of the newly reorganized Polish state, locating relatives, and so on.

Organized Institutional Steps

The Child Care Department of the Central Jewish Committee

The first children to reach the Jewish center in Lublin were survivors from the adjoining Majdanek extermination camp. Others arrived on their own or were brought to the center by Jews who had encountered them on the way or by their rescuers. Initially, the youngsters were housed together with adult survivors in "Peretz House," an overcrowded facility that was made available

---

25 Kahana, *After the Deluge*, pp. 15–16.

to the Central Jewish Committee from August 1944.[26] A girl who had been taken to the home relates: "When we came to Lublin, [a Jewish officer] took me to his friend... She brought me to the Jewish Committee and I was shocked by the Jews who were there. I didn't want to stay so she arranged a place for me with a Jewish family."[27] Although she does not describe the reasons for her shock, her remarks imply that the encounter with the survivors and the facility left her horrified.

In the autumn of 1944, as the number of children increased, the first children's home was established at 60, Krakowskie Przedmieście Street in Lublin. No deliberate initiatives to search for children were taken at first, but as more and more gathered at the home, the staff began to believe that there must be additional children in Polish homes and that an attempt to track them down should be made. At the initiative of one of the staff members, notices were posted around town stating that anyone who had a Jewish child in their custody and delivered them to the Committee would receive an award. The gambit paid off: the number of children increased and eventually three children's homes were established in the city. A fourth was set up in Przemyśl, on the San River, in southern Poland.[28]

Upon the establishment of the Provisional Central Jewish Committee in Lublin in November 1944, a child care department (*Wydział Opieki nad Dzieckiem*) was set up under Dr. Szlomo Herszenhorn, a Bundist who had been a major in the Polish Army during the war and from August 1944 had headed the Jewish Relief Affairs Department of the PKWN.[29]

After the liberation of territories west of the River Wisła in January 1945, the provisional government of Poland moved to Warsaw and the Provisional Jewish Central Committee moved with it. The Child Care Department established an additional children's home in Otwock, south of Warsaw, and afterwards another in Helenówek, near Łódź. Over time, it became necessary to set up children's homes in Kraków, Częstochowa, Bielsko-Biała, Chorzów, Piotrolesie, Zatrzebie, and Legnica, as well as two homes in Śródborów. Sev-

26 Shlomi, "Initial Organization," p. 314; interview by author with Ita Kowalska, 1993. Shlomi states that eight children came from Majdanek; Kowalska speaks of three. See also Gutman, *Jews in Poland*, p. 67, and Engel, *Between Liberation and Escape*, p. 55.
27 Recorded interview with Haviva Barak-Owiec.
28 Interview by author with Rachel Frank-Friedberg, March 1996; interview by author with Ita Kowalska, 1993.
29 Pamphlet documenting the actions of the Central Committee of Polish Jews for January 1–June 30, 1946, p. 5, ŻIH; see also interview by author with Ita Kowalska, 1993; Shlomi, "Initial Organization," p. 314; Engel, *Between Liberation and Escape*, pp. 54–55.

eral such institutions were established in the former German areas of western Poland, and the children in the homes in Lublin and Przemyśl, on the eastern border, were transferred there.[30] By the end of 1946, the department in charge of children's affairs was being referred to as the Child Care Department; afterwards it merged with the Schools Department (*Wydział Szkolny*) and was named the Education Department (*Wydział Oświaty*).[31] Its duties expanded to include matters related to Jewish children in non-Jews' homes. The Department maintained relations with various Jewish organizations such as the World Jewish Congress, JDC, and HIAS (Hebrew Immigrant Aid Society), to name a few, and responded to their requests to track down children.[32]

The Central Jewish Committee had severely limited financial resources during this initial phase. Most of its funding came from the provisional government, which itself struggled to carry out its many tasks with very sparse resources.[33] The financial pressure also affected the actions taken with regard to the children. Some Poles delivered children whom they had been hiding and asked the Committee to reimburse them for expenses they had incurred during the war — and the Committee had no money to pay them.[34] Furthermore, as a staff member of the first children's home in Kraków attested, the allocation for the home was not enough to keep the children sufficiently fed. As a result: "I would spend all day running around town… in order to get flour, sugar, oil, medicines, soap and so on for the children… to my disgrace, I had great success in being a beggar."[35]

30 Engel, *Between Liberation and Escape*, pp. 54–55. For a list of children's homes of the Central Committee and other organizations that operated in Poland, including addresses and the number of children enrolled, see ŻIH Archives, Education Department files. The children's home in Kraków was initially located on the top floor of the Jewish Committee building on Długa Street. However, as its population of children increased and the conditions became unsuitable, the children were moved to a separate building on Augustiańska Street. The name Piotrolesie was a literal translation from the German of Peterswalden, Silesia. Today the town is known as Pieszyce.

31 Pamphlet documenting the actions of the Central Committee of Polish Jews for January 1–June 30, 1946, pp. 5, 21.

32 Interview by author with Ita Kowalska, August 1995; letters Education Department to World Jewish Congress, December 7, 1946; response in the matter of G.; to UNRRA, December 4, 1946, response in the matter of G.; to HIAS, July 24, 1947, in the matter of K.; letter JDC-Poland to Central Committee, May 27, 1946, in the matter of K.; ŻIH, Education Department, File 638.

33 Engel, *Between Liberation and Escape*, pp. 55, 118, 223 n. 11.

34 Recorded interview with Haviva Barak-Owiec. She had been staying with her rescuers while her parents were alive and in hiding in a nearby forest. When her parents were captured and murdered, she remained with the family until liberation.

35 Küchler-Silberman, *My Hundred Children*, p. 196.

Until the middle of 1945, if not later, the Central Committee received no meaningful assistance from Jewish organizations in the West.[36] Although the Committee had been established at Jewish initiative, the government of Poland approved of its activities and even provided it with an operating budget,[37] thereby strengthening its status. After JDC institutionalized its operations, it also provided the Committee with funds.[38] Thus, in October–November 1945, Dr. Josef Schwartz, director of JDC-Europe, concluded an agreement with the Polish Ministry of Finance whereby the latter would provide a subsidy against each dollar spent by JDC through the offices of the Central Committee.[39] From then on, most JDC assistance in goods and cash would be routed via the Committee. Even though the subsidies were now institutionalized, the needs outweighed the resources available. Nevertheless, the very fact that the Child Care Department received a regular financial allocation from the Central Committee's exchequer and did not have to raise funds by itself, assured the continuity of its activities.

The Department received many requests in Poland and from abroad urging it to search for Jewish children in non-Jewish homes and remove them. Sometimes the Department responded by contacting rescuers directly; in other cases it forwarded the request to the attention of the local committee closest to the child's location. Usually its initial communication in this matter was made in writing and phrased in a laconic and official tone.[40] After the communication had been sent, staff members of the local committees visited the homes of the rescuers, conducted the negotiations, and drew up

---

36 Gutman, *Jews in Poland*, pp. 19–20; Shlomi, "Initial Organization," pp. 309–312.
37 Shlomi, "Initial Organization," pp. 307–308; Samet, *When I Came the Day After*, p. 60; Engel, *Between Liberation and Escape*, pp. 58–59.
38 Samet, *When I Came the Day After*, pp. 68, 70; Engel, *Between Liberation and Escape*, pp. 85–86, 96–97.
39 Litvak, "JDC's Contribution," pp. 341–342; Engel, *Between Liberation and Escape*, pp. 137, 241 n. 203; Bauer, *Out of the Ashes*, p. 118.
40 Letters Education Department to Ostrów Mazowiecki committee in the matter of M.G., undated; to citizen Joskowitz, January 24, 1947, in the matter of A.J.; to Gdańsk committee, 1947, in the matter of Z.G.; to Bielsko-Biała committee, 1946, in the matter of L.J. See ŻIH, Education Department, File 638. A typical phrasing follows: "The Education Department of the Central Committee of Jews of Poland turns to the committee of Bydgoszcz, in the vicinity of which Dulewicz lives on 51 Gdańsk Street in Bydgoszcz, with a request to negotiate in regard to the child H.K.... so that he may be removed to relatives in America. Awaiting [your] response in respect to the deliberations." Letter Education Department to Jewish committee in Bydgoszcz, December 23, 1946, ibid.

preliminary agreements.[41] Whenever it was feared that rescuers would object to handing the child over to a Jewish organization, the committee staffers tried to outwit them. For example, in the draft of a letter to a woman rescuer, intended to find out the terms she was demanding for the surrender of a girl who was in her care, the expression "Send envelope without letterhead" (that is, without noting the name of the Central Jewish Committee was written in the margin as an instruction to the sender).[42] The senders may have believed that omitting the committee's name would make the negotiations and the removal easier. The Department spared no effort to locate children and availed itself of other organizations active in Poland, such as the Polish Red Cross and the office that took care of repatriates.[43] When making inquiries about children who had been in eastern Poland before the war, the Department availed itself of the Polish Embassy in Moscow.[44] Notably, when relatives asked other organizations that dealt with the removal of children to search for children across the border, these organizations replied that they were unable to operate across the new borders.

Routine negotiations for the return of a child included discussions about the amount of financial compensation that the rescuers would receive for the time that the child had spent in hiding with them. It was obvious to all that no sum could adequately compensate rescuers for the risks they had taken during the war. Nevertheless, it was considered clear that they should be paid

---

41 Letter JDC-Warsaw to Kolbuszowa committee, September 18, 1946 (unsorted material in ŻIH Archives that I received from Sarah Kadosh, archives director for JDC-Jerusalem in a microfilm from Poland); letter Education Department to Przemyśl committee, April 10, 1947, in the matter of H.K., ŻIH, Education Department, File 638. In this case, an order to remove the girl urgently was issued. The letter was phrased as follows: "On June 5, the District Committee approved a payment for the redemption of H.G.... . The boy has been placed in our children's home. 50,500 zlotys was paid for him. It is true that we should have sought approval but the pressure and the conditions made this impossible. An agreement for the return of the child is attached herewith." Letter Przemyśl committee to Education Department, May 15, 1947, ibid.
42 Letter Education Department to Justina Budnicka of Zielona Góra, November 6, 1947, in the matter of K.K., ibid.
43 Letters Education Department to Polish Red Cross, October 13, 1947, in the matter of L.J.; and to Łódź committee, 1946, in the matter of R.H., ibid. In the second letter, the Łódź committee was asked to contact the Polish State Authority for Care of Repatriates (Państwowy Urząd Repatriacyjny — PUR), which had been set up to deal with the housing and rehabilitation of Poles who had returned to Poland under agreements pertaining to the return of the population in areas not included in post-war Poland.
44 Letter Polish Embassy in Moscow to Education Department, April 9, 1948, in the matter of D.H., ibid.

something, as an expression of appreciation and as genuine assistance at a time of general deprivation. The committee determined a standard sum that seemed reasonable and within its means; in most cases, it was approximately 20,000 zlotys.[45] In negotiations with rescuers on the terms for returning a child, it was made clear to the rescuer, in writing, that compensation would be set "at the accepted price for similar problems in our country."[46] This convinced rescuers that there was a norm in such circumstances, which they accepted, unless they had been exposed to offers from other organizations. However, if a local committee that did the field work encountered a problem in a specific case, because of which it was feared that the child could not be removed later on, it overrode the standard procedure.[47] Once the negotiations were concluded, the Department had to obtain the approval of the Central Committee presidium in order to release the money.[48] After the child was placed in one of the Central Committee's children's homes, the rescuers received a letter of appreciation expressing gratitude for the humanitarian act they had performed during the war.[49] It is noteworthy that the Depart-

45 As for the problem of calculating the zloty exchange rate at any point in time, see Appendix, "The Value of the Zloty."

46 Letter Education Department to Katowice committee, June 13, 1947, ŻIH, Education Department, File 638.

47 Letter Katowice committee to Education Department, March 21, 1947, in the matter of G.G., ibid. In this case, the rescuer demanded 250,000 zlotys. The child's mother, who had survived the war, managed to raise 100,000 zlotys and the Committee agreed to make up the rest. There was concern that unless they acted quickly, the rescuer would abscond with the girl because she "changes addresses often"; Wasserstein-Blanker, "After the Holocaust I Didn't Want to Return to Judaism," p. 335.

48 Letters Education Department to Central Committee presidium, October 30, 1946, in the matter of E.G.; to Central Committee presidium, October 8, 1947, in the matter of Z.G.; to Central Committee presidium, September 24, 1946, in the matter of C.H. A typical phrasing of the letters was: "The Child Care Department of the Central Committee of Jews in Poland wishes to approve [the payment of] 20,000 zlotys to citizen Strzalecki, who during the occupation rescued two children, G.... and G...., and took care of them. The children have been claimed by their aunt, who has sent them abroad." Letter Child Care Department to Central Committee presidium, September 16, 1946, ŻIH, Education Department, File 638.

49 Examples of the wording of such letters follow: "The Education Department of the Central Committee confirms that during the war, for no [personal] interest, the couple Leon and Felicija Szostakow took care of the Jewish girl T... J..., twelve years old, until May 1945" — certification from Central Committee, January 31, 1947; "Letter of appreciation to a citizen who undertook to protect and take care of the Jewish girl. You did the duty of a civilian in democratic Poland. We ask you to visit our offices in order to discuss a certain matter." Letter Education Department to citizen Wicchowski, September 18, 1946, in the matter of K., ibid. The Committee paid the rescuer 10,000 zlotys.

ment undertook to pay rescuers even in cases where it had helped a relative to remove the child, even if the child did not remain afterwards in a Committee-sponsored children's home, and even when the child's relatives[50] or another Jewish organization had failed to pay the rescuer the entire sum that had been promised.[51] This behavior may be viewed as the assumption of Jewish public responsibility, since the committee's motive in making such payments was to protect the Jews' reputation and avert future difficulties in removing children.

At the same time, the operatives dealt with children who were being sought by others. Attempts were made, by publishing lists of names and identifying particulars of the children in the Jewish press, to locate relatives of children who were still in the homes of rescuers[52] and others who had been removed but had no known relatives.[53] At the other end of the inquiries, an alphabetized record of requests for assistance in searching for children was kept, and information about the children was registered.[54] Aware of the grave economic situation prevailing in Poland, the Department published notices in the press inviting Polish families that were still sheltering Jewish children to come forward and receive aid, it being assumed that such an offer might persuade them to give up the children. Inquirers were required to sign in at the Central Committee offices and provide details about the children in their custody. The Department then sent agents to try to persuade the families to surrender the children to the Central Committee's children's homes.[55]

The Committee's legal department also helped to trace children and remove them from the custody of non-Jews. Staff members collected depositions from Poles who volunteered information about Jewish children the

50 Letter Child Care Department to Central Committee presidium, July 2, 1946, in the matter of J.K., ibid. The mother removed her child in April 1945 and the Central Committee wished to complete the payment in accordance with its undertaking a year and a half after the child had been removed.

51 Letter Katowice committee to Education Department, March 21, 1947, in the matter of G.G. The girl was removed by members of the Zionist Koordynacja and the Central Committee undertook to assume the payment pledge that had not been honored.

52 Letter Education Department to Kraków Committee, undated, in the matter of E.H., ibid.

53 Page from the newspaper *Dos Naye Lebn*, 60 (168), ibid., file 437.

54 Alphabetized central record of inquiries from Jewish families searching for children whose fate was unknown, ibid., File 68.

55 Testimony Sabina Halperin, MA, A.201, aged four and a half at the beginning of the war: "A few days later, a woman came to talk me into returning to Judaism and going to the Jews, and I refused. She came every week to talk with me for two hours and I always refused."

whereabouts of whom they knew, and on the basis of this testimony requests for the children were delivered.[56] Rescuers who refused to surrender a Jewish child were invited to meetings[57] where attempts were made to conclude some form of settlement.

When a child was turned over to the Committee, the rescuers were in most cases asked to prepare a written account of the child's history from the moment they had received the youngster until the end of the war. These testimonies served two purposes: backing for the payment that the rescuer received and a source of information about the child in case someone would search for him or her.[58] A succinct account of the child's story as told by him or herself was also recorded. Most such testimonies were taken from children who had been born in the early 1930s. Only a few were taken from children born shortly before the beginning of the war or during it; obviously such children could neither know nor remember many details, if any.[59]

Because it was an official body that operated under governmental auspices, survivors perceived the Central Committee as omnipotent. In fact, however, the Committee was limited for this very reason; it had to act strictly within the limits of the law in order to exhaust all legal options available. Its administrative procedures, communications, correspondence, and exploration of various possibilities were time-consuming, as were problems that sometimes occurred in the middle of its operations. Thus, a gap developed between the expectations of relatives and the Department's ability to meet them. For example, a Jewish woman who struggled at length to reclaim her daughter wrote a letter of complaint to the Department:

> It's moving ahead so slowly with you. What's the reason? Is it the situation, or is it my luck? ...I hope and understand that you are doing everything you can, you have lots of work to do with the Jews in Poland, but I am also one of those who is suffering a great deal... Have pity on me, help me, at this time only you can help me with something that you will be proud of. As Jews who deal with public affairs, you have the great duty of returning a child to its mother, a Jewish child to the Jewish people...[60]

56 Records (depositions) to Legal Department adviser, ŻIH, Legal Department.
57 Record of Jopowicz deposition at Jewish Central Committee, May 8, 1947, in the matter of L.H., ŻIH, Education Department, File 638. Since Jopowicz refused to sign the deposition, which included the demands that he had presented, witnesses signed it in his presence.
58 Testimony Halina Sachocka in the matter of H.K, ŻIH, 301/5192.
59 Notebook containing handwritten autobiography, ŻIH, Education Department, File 636.
60 Letter Rachel Igenfeld-Besserman, Canada, to Central Committee Legal Department, June 27, 1949, in the matter of I.I., ŻIH, Legal Department.

The following appeared in a similar letter: "I have no way and no intention of complaining to anyone, but just the same, it gives me such heartache to hear that the Jewish community of Zamość cannot to this day find any possibility of rescuing this tender girl from the talons of strangers."[61]

The Department stayed in regular contact with those who had appealed to it to remove children and kept them abreast of what was being done, that is, the child's living conditions, the rescuers' demands, and the likelihood of being able to remove the child. If several correspondents asked the Department to investigate and remove a certain child, the report was forwarded to all of them. In a certain sense, the Department acted in the role of go-between.[62]

The working patterns that took shape at the Department indicate that it did not pursue legal action aggressively. Its tools were patience, forbearance, and an attempt to avoid confrontation with rescuers. The Committee also disapproved of other organizations' entanglements with the authorities with regard to the removal of children,[63] realizing that such actions might enrage the population and irritate the institutions of the new government. Its attitude also reflected respect for the rescuers and appreciation of the humane act they had performed. Thus, the process of handling cases was sometimes lengthy; and children continued to live with their rescuers even after a request to remove them had been submitted. Reports about such cases from Department staff members suggest that they had come to accept this reality.[64]

The Department continued to stay in touch with Polish families that refused to return children. It offered them economic aid and instituted regular

---

61 Letter D. Strauss, Haifa, to Rabbi Herzog, October 20, 1946, RZA, Rescue Files. The phrasing of the letter presents the rabbi's staff with a challenge, in contrast to the impotence of the Central Committee. It is evident, however, that the correspondents neither knew nor understood how the Central Committee went about its work.

62 Letter Education Department to Haar, Tel Aviv, August 23, 1947, in the matter of A.M., ŻIH Education Department, File 638; letter Education Department to HIAS, Warsaw, March 1946, in the matter of P. ibid., File 643. Treatment of the matter began in March 1946 and the girl was removed in January 1947. A similarly phrased letter on the same topic was also sent to the World Jewish Congress.

63 Testimony Arye (Leibl) Koryski, OHD, 15(68).

64 Documents received by the author from Erella Hilferding-Goldschmidt, Shadmot Devora, originating with the ŻIH. The documents, which deal with the child herself (under her Polish name, Irena Dąbrowska) show that the first report about her being with Janina Trybus appears on lists from 1945. There were also requests from JDC-Warsaw to take up her case, on behalf of a relative in the United States who wished to remove her, and correspondence with Trybus. Ultimately, the Koordynacja removed the girl in 1947 in conjunction with the Central Committee; letter Education Department, addressee indecipherable, in the matter of C.G., undated, ŻIH, Education Department, File 638.

home visits, thereby leaving the door open for eventual action. An example is the family with whom Krystina was living: from March 1945, the family received 2,000 zlotys a month in aid from the committee, Krystina attended the Jewish school in Warsaw, a Department representative stayed in touch with the family, and home visits occasionally took place. In April 1947, Krystina was still with the family. A report on a home visit to her in March 1946 stated: "Her living conditions are harsh, she looks bad, she [is living] in a cold cellar, is physically underdeveloped and neglected, and would like to get out of there. However, the family converted her to Christianity after the war. We have contacted [them] several times but they are utterly unwilling to hand her over." About a year later, in April 1947, the report on another home visit noted that the family was living in a cellar, seven people in one room, and that the landlady and her sister were the only breadwinners.[65]

Cases such as these left staff members with a feeling of helplessness. Although they maintained contact with the children and were able to provide supervision, there was no internal policy directive that could force rescuers to surrender them. Obviously they could not act until such a policy was decided upon. The resulting sense of frustration was especially acute in cases where there was a prima facie basis for a demand to remove the child from a family. A letter from the local committee in Warsaw to the Child Care Department reflects the sense of helplessness clearly:

> Many of the children under our wing are in Christian hands... Many guardians are not keeping [the children] in a morally and economically good atmosphere. [The children] are being baptized into the Church and are being taught to hate Jews in the spirit of the Catholic faith. They have even been led out of the faith [*shmad*]... Therefore, we ask the Child Care Department to give us guidelines about what we should do. In what ways can the center help us? We would appreciate a very quick reply because this has been going on for more than a year.[66]

---

65   Letters Warsaw Committee to Education Department, March 23, 1946, and April 25, 1947, in the matter of K.F., ibid. The girl K.F. was taken in by Mrs. Kolak in 1943 as the three-year-old wandered about near the fence of the Łęczna ghetto after the ghetto had been liquidated. Kolak had known her parents, who had been murdered together with the girl's older sister. After she took the child in, the Kolaks moved to Warsaw and the girl survived the war in their home.

66   Letter Warsaw Committee to Education Department, March 23, 1946, in the matter of K.F., M.L., ibid.

A letter from the Education Department to the Warsaw committee more than a year after an earlier letter shows that there was no policy stipulating the removal of a child even when it could be proved that the family or the child was in dire straits: "In response to your letter of July 7 [1947], we wish to inform you that our representative visited the location and confirmed that five-year-old Zisla Jadowska is living under conditions of severe poverty. The Department has decided to look for [a way] to improve the girl's conditions."[67] By implication, this was to be done in the home of her rescuers.

Sometimes all possibilities were exhausted and, for various reasons (especially due to outside pressure), the Department workers recommended that action be taken to remove a child. Only then was the case handed over to the Central Committee legal department and to attorneys operating under guidance of the district committees.[68] Most such requests were made on behalf of relatives, some in Poland and some abroad.[69] The Department also responded to requests for legal action from other organizations that were involved in removing children,[70] since only the Department, due to its status, could appear as a party in litigation.

The Committee adopted a policy that saw legal action as a last resort, since it knew that there was obviously no guarantee of success. In two letters containing updates about negotiations over the removal of a child, relatives who had requested the Committee's action received a detailed report about the rescuer's demands, accompanied with the following observation: "We can refer the problem to the court in order to demand the girl, but a hundred percent likelihood of success is not assured because the Jopowiczes are giving the girl excellent care and they love her. If Jopowicz wins the trial, you will not

---

67 Letter Education Department to Warsaw Committee, July 28, 1947, in the matter of Z.J., ibid.
68 Letter Education Department to Attorney Hoffer, via Rzeszów Committee, July 28, 1947, in the matter of E.M.H., ibid.
69 Letters Legal Department to court in Łódź, March 15, 1947, in the matter of R.E.; to court recorder in Wrocław, May 19, 1947, in the matter of P.A.; to court in Staszów, May 17, 1947, in the matter of S.H., ŻIH, Legal Department.
70 Decision of Łódź municipal court, Judge A. Dakowska. The trial began on December 28, 1946; the final ruling was handed down on January 13, 1947, File 37/46, in the matter of E.R., a.k.a. T. Zamarowna, ibid. In this instance, the Jewish committee in Łódź appeared as a litigant in the case of a girl who had been removed by the Koordynacja and whose rescuer subsequently asked the court to appoint her as the girl's legal guardian. In its ruling, the Court decided that the girl should be transferred to the children's home of the Jewish committee in Łódź and that guardianship should be divided between the rescuer and the head of the child care department of the Łódź committee.

be able to remove her until [she becomes] eighteen."[71] In a letter to another addressee in regard to the same girl, the following appears: "The Committee cannot remove a child against the will of the adoptive parents. A suit has to be brought, and the court's decision is not always in favor of the Committee."[72] Thus, some of the factors that made it difficult to remove a child from a rescuer's home were rooted in the nature of the relationship that had developed between the rescuer and the rescued. From the legal standpoint, this relationship was a weighty consideration: good relations and an emotional bond between child and rescuer made it more difficult to remove the child.[73] This relationship was treated as supremely important in the pre-removal inquiries made about children who had been found with their rescuers.[74]

An attempt to oppose the handling of a case by means of legal action might take place for several reasons. First, the Department staff might well believe that such a method should not be used against people who had performed a humanitarian act and where they suspected that legal action might worsen relations with the rescuers. Second, the Department staff might believe that the child would be better off remaining with the rescuers, with whom he or she had spent several years and a strong emotional bond had been created. The third reason (at least for several Central Committee policy-makers) was rooted in an ideological belief with regard to the place of the Jews in the formative Polish state and the belief that religion should not be accorded special importance. The fourth reason was the difficulty that might arise if legal action were the path chosen.

One cannot state absolutely that all Department staff members shared the first three reasons and crafted a consistent policy about them, since in some cases the Committee took all possible measures after trying lengthy negotiations and various methods of persuasion in order to remove a child from his or her rescuers' home. In other cases, in contrast, the Committee does not seem to have taken all possible measures, even when factors that might have made the action easier were present.

---

71 Letter Education Department to Kornwasser, Detroit, May 16, 1947, in the matter of L.H., ŻIH, Education Department, File 638.
72 Letter Education Department to Bini Rybak, Lódź, May 23, 1947, in the matter of L.H., ibid.
73 Ruling of district court in Lódź, File 37/46, in the matter of E.R.
74 Letter Education Department to Katowice committee, June 13, 1947, in the matter of O.K.; letter Częstochowa committee to Central Committee, July 3, 1946, in the matter of S., ŻIH, Legal Department.

As for the reasoning related to the difficulties that litigation would involve, a document produced by the legal department, apparently in the second half of 1946, is illuminating. The document, which suggests possible ways of taking action, was prepared on the basis of pre-war laws and on several court rulings handed down after the war[75] that do not yet relate clearly to the special situations brought about by the war. The document was needed since, as stated in its preamble, the Committee regarded the issue of the children as "one of the community's most difficult problems." The document was circulated among all departments, institutions, and local committees that dealt with children in order to help them wade through the morass of legal material.[76]

The document elucidated the difficulty and complexity that typically surfaced in the removal of children from the homes of rescuers. It also explains, at least to some extent, the Committee's modus operandi: use of a set of correspondence procedures, attempts at persuasion, lengthy negotiations with rescuers, application of gentle pressure, waiting, and patience, which were aimed at exhausting all possibilities before turning to the legal authorities. This was done, of course, only if the Committee staff were convinced that the child should be removed from a rescuer's home. The clause that discusses the fitness of a rescuer to care for a child or relations with the child explains the system of home visits that the Child Care Department introduced — a system that allowed the Department to gather data for possible use as court-admissible evidence with regard to the rescuers' economic and moral situation.[77] However, when the evidence gathered proved that the rescuers had formed a healthy relationship with the child and were sufficiently affluent, the Department staff understood readily that this would hinder the legal proceedings and preferred to negotiate a settlement with the rescuers.[78]

---

75 Legal document in the matter of Jewish children in the custody of non-Jews, distant relatives, and children's institutions, guidelines of the Central Jewish Committee Legal Department, ŻIH, Legal Department. Although undated, the document must have been written in the second half of 1946 at the earliest, since it bases itself on Polish laws and court rulings from 1945 and 1946. It was prepared on the basis of the Family Law, the Fostership Law, the Marriage Law, and a court ruling handed down on January 22, 1946, Dz. U, no. 6, of March 4, 1946; court ruling of September 25, 1945, Dz. U, no. 48, of November 7, 1945; ruling on May 14, 1946, Dz. U, no. 20, of May 24, 1946; ruling on May 21, 1946, Dz. U, no. 22, 1946.

76 For a detailed account of the provisions of the document, see "Involvement of the Polish Judiciary in Regard to Jewish Children," See chapter 5.

77 See, for example, letter Warsaw Committee to Education Department, March 23, 1946, in the matter of K.F., M.L.

78 Letter Legal Department to Częstochowa committee in the matter of S., ŻIH, Legal Department.

The very fact that these legal guidelines, describing the law with regard to fostership and entitlement of Jewish children, were written two years after the liberation of most of Poland, shows that the entitlement of parents or relatives was not always self-evident.

Children who had been removed from rescuers' homes or taken to a Committee branch office but not claimed by relatives were placed in children's homes. During the lifetime of the Central Committee's homes, from the second half of 1944 until 1948, 427 orphans who had been removed from non-Jewish homes spent some time in these facilities. Together with them were children who had been removed from convents and Polish orphanages, children who had come to Poland from the Soviet Union under the repatriation arrangement, and children whose parents or relatives handed them over for a temporary period.[79]

From the Department's first days, it was headed, as stated, by Dr. Shlomo Herszenhorn, a Bundist, and many members of the children's home staff belonged to this movement. The leaders of the Bund urged Jews to develop a healthy relationship with the Polish state, to be loyal to it, to identify with its values, and to demonstrate an interest in taking part in life together with other Polish citizens.[80] This outlook also had an influence on the education provided in the children's homes.

The Palestinian journalist, Shimon Samet, visiting Poland for the newspaper *Ha'aretz* in January–March 1946, met with the heads of the Child Care Department and was given a presentation on the principles of education at the children's homes: (a) instilling a sense of human dignity, developing an understanding of pan-human democratic ideas, progress, fraternity of nations, and "a connection with the nation that works and fights in the war of public liberation;" (b) instilling a positive and warm attitude toward, and a strong bond with, the new democratic Poland; (c) inculcating recognition of national honor, universal love of one's fellow Jews, and, in particular, of the progressive democratic players who are fighting the war of national and public liberation of the Jewish masses; (d) instilling a favorable and warm attitude toward the Soviet Union and its achievements in all areas of life; (e) assimilating the fundamentals of public ethics, responsibility for one's actions and words, collective solidarity, and altruism.[81]

---

79 The number was obtained from summaries and tables produced by Ita Kowalska, Warsaw, on the basis of the Central Committee's card catalogue of children, as part of a study on the topic. The study was not published and Mrs. Kowalska gave the material to the author.

80 Blatman, *For Our Freedom and Yours*, pp. 168–169, 174.

81 Samet, *When I Came the Day After*, p. 78.

These fundamental points leave no room for doubt concerning the worldview of the Central Committee members, whose opinions were those that mattered the most. However, at least in the first two years, the children's homes and the regional committees also had many staff members who belonged to Zionist movements; they too, did not conceal their beliefs. Irrespective of the general overt slant, the complexion of each individual children's home depended largely on its staff members. In Kraków, for example, the Child Care Department was headed by Miriam Marianska, who had operated under a false identity with an organization that helped Jews during the war. After liberation, she began to work for the Jewish committee in Kraków and ran it until 1948, when she moved to Israel. The goal she considered most important in the education of the children, she testified, was "to return them to Judaism, to implant in them a sense of national belonging"– even though she believed that this should be accomplished, not by coercion but slowly and indirectly.[82] In July 1945, three members of the Jewish Brigade visited Poland, including the children's home in Helenówek, near Łódź. They met with 240 orphaned children and, at the end of their visit, were given a letter written by a group of teachers and employees of the institution, pleading: "Do not forget us, help us to go to Palestine."[83] Another Brigade member gave a contrasting account after visiting children's homes of the Committee in February 1946. He found the conditions good but complained that the idea of remaining in Poland was being promulgated. When he asked a group of children whether they wished to go to Palestine, the teacher reprimanded him.[84] Moshe Kolodny (Kol) visited Poland in early 1946. When he returned to Palestine, he reported that during his mission he had visited the children's homes of the Central Committee and found that an anti-Zionist approach prevailed in most of them. He had also been told, he reported, that "the children have set up a Zionist underground and are very afraid that the fanatic Bundist director will find out about it." When he visited one of the Jewish Committee children's homes in Silesia, however, Kol came away impressed with the fervent love of Eretz Israel that he found and noted the way the children had prepared for his visit and rejoiced once he came. "In this place, all the educators are Zion-

---

82   Hochberg-Marianska, "I Cared For Child Survivors," pp. 12–13; Dekel, *Remnants of the Sword*, p. 170.

83   Habas, "Report from Visitors to Poland," p. 2.

84   Report Anton Mara, February 6, 1946, Massuah Archive, Testimonies, 25/27.

ists," he reported.[85] At a conference of directors of the Central Committee children's homes, one of them said that the children should be taught Hebrew and most of those present agreed. After she had spoken, the secretary of the Central Committee, Zielinski, passed her a note in which he asked her to come to his office and then reprimanded her and threatened to terminate her employment if she spoke about Hebrew studies. He added, "The Hebrew language means a return to fascism, to nationalism, to capitalism! I will fire you at once and bring you up on disciplinary trial!"[86]

As we have pointed out, the children's homes had different characteristics. Sometimes children in a home were susceptible to the influence of staff members with different ideologies. During the first year at least, the PPR and Bund-affiliated members of the Committee felt that most of the staff of the children's homes were Zionists and, therefore, exerted a powerful influence over the children.[87] As time passed, the possibilities of independent thinking diminished and the goal of organizing everything according to the educational policies of the Central Committee became dominant. After some Zionist staff members left Poland with the Bricha, the communist voice on the committees gathered strength. Those Zionists who remained in Poland were marginalized and most of the staff members of the homes were now Bundists and communists — people who had chosen to remain in Poland and whose declared educational principles corresponded to their personal ideology.[88]

From the standpoint of the Polish Ministry of Education, the Central Committee Education Department was a go-between that forwarded new laws and directives to the Jewish children's homes and education institutions, just as they were forwarded to the Polish education institutions. In early 1947, the ministry ordered all children's institutions in Poland to apply laws and directives that were not being enforced even though they had been established shortly after the end of the war. A letter from the Ministry of Public Administration in Warsaw to the Education Department in April 1947 stated

---

85 Moshe Kolodny, "Captive Children: Impressions of an Emissary," in *Dvar Hapo'elet*, August 12, 1946, Massuah Archive, A 3/75. Moshe Kolodny (Kol) was a founding member and leader of the Hano'ar Haoved Hatzioni Movement in Poland. He moved to Palestine in 1932, served on the board of Youth Aliyah and directed the organization after the death of Henrietta Szold. Kolodny visited Poland in April 1946 as a member of the Palestine mission.

86 Küchler-Silberman, *My Hundred Children*, p. 149. The English edition is a shortened version of the Hebrew, Hebrew edition, p. 348.

87 Engel, *Between Liberation and Escape*, p. 82.

88 Interview by author with Ita Kowalska.

that Law no. 2/63 (Law 272 from 1945), "concerning the determination of civil status in the giving of names and the determination of the approximate age of a child of unknown parentage," should be enforced. "The state will assume responsibility for this action," the letter noted. Local governing authorities "may determine only the approximate age of the child; [but] only higher echelons of the administration are authorized to determine other particulars of his parents." Furthermore, the Department was to provide the "Polish *monitor* [database]" with any information about children in its keeping so that it could be cross-referenced."[89] It is worth bearing in mind that Poland also had an orphan problem. Orphaned Polish children had been wandering the roads during and after the war and were being gathered into children's homes. The letter indicates that an attempt was being made to centralize all actions concerning the identity of orphans — Jewish and Polish — in order to prevent errors and to ensure that the identifying procedure would be performed professionally and in accordance with the law. An instruction to appoint a staff member of the children's home as the temporary guardian of children for whom a foster parent had not yet been found required court approval.[90] When an attempt was made to give an orphaned child an identity, a question of how to ascertain his or her identity occasionally resulted in problems and unpleasantness. For example, the director of the Committee's children's home in Chorzów, a Mrs. Szedler, wrote a letter to the Central Committee describing her visit together with a judge and a group of children, as an unpleasant encounter that had taken place in "loud tones." The judge, the director reported, did not accept her deposition affirming the Jewishness of two of the orphans and her observation that at least one of them had been circumcised. Instead, he had detained the children in an isolated room in order to examine them. Finally the judge named her the guardian of several of the children, but for the two whose Jewish identity had not been determined with certainty he appointed a professional guardian from the welfare bureau in Chorzów pending a final decision (evidently about their Jewishness). In the aftermath of Szedler's letter, the Central Committee contacted the Polish Ministry of Justice, on behalf of which the Inspector of Courts responded. The inspector claimed that the session had been conducted in this

---

89 Document Office of Public Administration to district chairs and the mayors of Warsaw and Łódź, April 30, 1947. The document originates with the ŻIH; I received it from Ita Kowalska.

90 Letter Polish Ministry of Education to Central Committee Education Department, May 27, 1947, concerning guardianship of orphans in children's homes. The document originates with the ŻIH; I received it from Ita Kowalska.

manner in order to ensure that all the tests that could determine the children's identity be performed, so that their identity would be ascertained irrevocably. Furthermore, "The court takes account of all events related to the children and assumes all liability for the legal aspects."[91]

Most Jewish children who had survived the war on the Aryan side had no birth certificate, this being a highly undesirable document under the circumstances of adopting a false identity. To solve the problem of the children's names, the Ministry of Education instructed all children's institutions (Jewish and Polish) to issue the youngsters with birth certificates from their places of birth or, where this was not possible, to do so through the courts. When a child's surname could not be ascertained in any way whatsoever, the ministry instructed the institutions to assign a surname with a Polish suffix such as *ak, ich, ik, cki,* or *ski.*[92]

Anything associated with the problem of the identity of Polish orphans was treated as a general problem; the question of Jewish orphans received no special attention despite the particular circumstances and the systematic extermination of most of Polish Jewry. Since the Central Committee was the official body that dealt with the problems of Jews in Poland, it had to obey the directives. The underlying principle that guided the Ministry of Education, as the letters indicate, was the "wellbeing of the child"; any further delay in dealing with the problem would leave the child with a vague identity. However, whenever there were no clear and agreed details about a child's identity, he or she was provided with personal particulars that were recorded in their papers lawfully, as required by the directives. It would not be possible for relations to identify such children at a later time. In 1947, however, the Education Department offices were still receiving many requests for assistance in locating Jewish children.

The Council of Religious Communities and the Mizrachi Movement

The Council of Religious Communities was established to meet the religious needs of Jews who had survived the war and were living in Poland. From the standpoint of the authorities, the council represented "Judaism," as opposed

91 Letter director of Chorzów local committee children's home to Central Committee Education Department, October 3, 1947; reply Inspector of Courts, January 5, 1948. The documents originate with the ŻIH; I received them from Ita Kowalska.
92 Circular Polish Ministry of Education to all children's institutions concerning certification of birth, July 18, 1947. The document originates with the ŻIH; I received it from Ita Kowalska.

to the Central Jewish Committee, which represented "the Jews." The two entities had different approaches to the question of "What is Jewish life?" — an issue that affected the removal and education of the children.

Rabbi David Kahana was liberated in Lwów in July 1944. After managing the Jewish library in that city, he moved to Lublin at Zommerstein's invitation and in late 1944, the Minister of Defense, General Michał Rola-Żymierski, named him Chief Jewish Chaplain of the Polish Army. Concurrently, the prime minister, at Zommerstein's recommendation, instructed him to begin organizational preparations for the regularization of Jewish religious affairs in Poland. Kahana established the Council of Religious Communities in February 1945 and was appointed its chairman. Before leaving Lwów, he had dealt with the cases of several Jewish children who had been living with their rescuers, and he also began to deal with the problem in his new capacity since this issue was an integral part of the Council's purview. Kahana claimed that the Religious Affairs Department of the Ministry of the Interior, regarded his actions with tacit consent even though they clearly overstepped the initial definition of the Council's functions.[93]

An initial manifesto that the Council published in the Polish-Jewish newspaper *Dos Naye Lebn* ("New Life") in Summer 1945, illustrates the importance that the rabbi attributed to the issue of the children: "Heaven forbid that we forget the youngest generation, our children, the thousands of children who rode out the *khurbn* [a Yiddish term for the Holocaust] in Christian homes... We must assure them a religious education worthy of the name. We must establish education centers for the young in every community...".[94] Since the Central Committee's children's homes were already functioning by this time, the manifesto presumably referred to separate children's homes that would stress religious education. According to Rabbi Kahana, the Central Committee and the local committees took a prejudiced view of the religious communities from the very outset of the latter's activities in the spring of 1945, due to clashes in outlooks and views. Therefore, he saw no possibility of collaboration.[95]

---

93 Kahana, *After the Deluge,* pp. 15–16, 22–25; 50; Gutman, *Jews in Poland,* p. 20; Engel, *Between Liberation and Escape,* p. 87.

94 Kahana, *After the Deluge,* pp. 41–43. The manifesto was signed by Rabbis David Kahana and Moshe Steinberg.

95 Ibid., p. 47. For further testimony about the nature of the relations, see Yehuda D., Report on Mission to Poland (November–December 1945), RZRI, S.21IV. The writer had gone on a mission from Belgium for the Jewish Legion as a representative of the religious soldiers. The report recounts the establishment of the Council of Religious Communities, the struggle between the Council and the Central Committee for the Jewish street, and the annoyance that the Council's activities caused the ruling party.

Rabbi Kahana's aides in the Polish Army were Aharon Beker, who was also responsible for liaison with the Mizrachi movement, and Yeshayahu Drucker, who dealt with the issue of Jewish children who had survived the Holocaust. Both men were given the rank of captain and the status of military chaplains.[96] The boundary between their functions in the chaplaincy and on the Council of Communities was vague and their responsibilities overlapped.

Drucker was a one-man operation who spent all his time locating and removing children — from receiving and checking information and up to decisions on what actions should be taken. Rabbi Kahana was also keenly interested in the issue; he shared his vacillations with Drucker and provided him with abundant support and assistance.[97]

The Council of Communities embraced, as a clear and open policy, the view that Jewish children should not be left with their rescuers, and that they should receive a Jewish education, and be sent out of Poland and placed in Jewish institutions, primarily in Palestine.[98] At the same time, the possibility of moving them to other countries was not ruled out. In 1946, for example, groups of children were taken to Britain.

Orthodox Jews referred to the removal of children from their rescuers as *pidyon shevuyim,* a term used in the Talmudic tractate *Hulin,* for example, to denote the redemption of captives. The very use of this term emphasizes the immense importance that the orthodox attributed to actions designed to leave no Jewish child "captive" in non-Jewish hands. The use of this rabbinical concept lent the act the status of a binding religious directive. As Kahana expressed it, "The *mitzva* [commandment] of redeeming children is one of the most important today. With so few Jews [remaining] in Poland and as every child torn from our midst faces assimilation and conversion [*shmad*], the matter is extremely important to us."[99] People who contacted the Council of Religious Communities for assistance adroitly stressed the sensitivity of Judaism to this matter and exploited the issue of redemption in their appeals. For example, the following was written in a letter to Rabbi Isaac Herzog, the chief rabbi of Palestine: "I beseech you, esteemed rabbi, to issue an order while you are in Poland and to rescue the girl, the last remnant of the

96 Interview by author with Yeshayahu Drucker. The team briefly had another member, a man named Steiglitz.

97 Ibid., Kahana, *After the Deluge,* p. 49; *The Rescue Voyage,* p. 61.

98 Warhaftig, *Refugee and Survivor,* p. 419.

99 Kahana, *After the Deluge,* pp. 49, 51; *The Rescue Voyage,* p. 61.

household of my late brother, who was murdered in Poland... I strongly hope that when your eminence reaches Poland, you will give thought even to this individual, small case of *pidyon shevuyim*."[100] After passing through several European countries, Rabbi Herzog visited Poland in August 1946 and was hosted by Rabbi Kahana, who accompanied him in meetings with the prime minister, the director-general of the Foreign Ministry, and the director of the department of Jewish affairs. In each of these meetings, the problem of Jewish children in non-Jewish hands was raised and Rabbi Herzog asked the officials to help assure their removal.[101]

The Jews — including the secular-minded — regarded the institution of the rabbinate as having both the authority and the right to remove Jewish children from non-Jewish custody. Thus, when it seemed that the efforts of other organizations were not succeeding, the rabbi was asked to invoke his status and contact everyone including Church officials,[102] in the belief that even Christian religious circles would honor his rabbinical authority.

The Council's offices, at 6 Twarda Street in Warsaw, became a destination of mass pilgrimage. Some visitors wanted a prayerbook, a *tallit* (prayer shawl), or *tefillin* (phylacteries); others came just for the experience of stepping through the portals of a Jewish institution; and there were those who came just to meet other Jews. Many arrived in Warsaw after visiting their pre-war homes, bringing information that they had received from a neighbor or acquaintance concerning Jewish children in the vicinity. In most cases, the details about the child derived from personal knowledge. The stories that these Jews brought were an initial source of information that Drucker used as a basis for the beginning of his search. He received further information from Poles who held public positions and thought it right to forward the information to the Council of Religious Communities specifically, believing that a Jewish child should receive a Jewish education. Drucker received so much information about children, he says, that he had no need to take any search initiatives of his own.[103]

100 Letter Bronka Cohen, Tel Aviv, to Rabbi Herzog, December 30, 1945, in the matter of R.K., RZA, Rescue Files.
101 Kahana, *After the Deluge*, p. 78; *The Rescue Voyage*, pp. 60–61.
102 Letters Canadian Federation for Polish Jews to Rabbi Kahana, Poland, September 22, 1948, in the matter of I.; letter to Rabbi Kahana, September 1949, in the matter of I. The phrasing of the letter suggests that its author was a friend. ŻIH, Legal Department; letter Attorney Ya'akov Etzioni to Friedman, Rabbi Herzog's bureau, Jerusalem, May 22, 1947, in the matter of Z.S., RZA, Rescue Files.
103 Interview by author with Yeshayahu Drucker; testimony Yeshayahu Drucker, YVA, O.3/3249.

Rabbi Herzog reached Poland armed with requests from Jews in Palestine for help in searching for child relatives. When it became known that the chief rabbi had been traveling in Europe and had taken action to remove 500 children from Poland by rail, the hopes of many families were rekindled and another wave of letters ensued. After his bureau became a well-known address for such appeals, requests that had been submitted to other organizations in Palestine were passed on to him, it being known that the rabbi took a personal interest in the issue.[104] All requests received by the rabbi or his bureau were sent on to Drucker in Poland, but as the tide of incoming letters grew, his staff saw no further point as serving as a go-between and suggested to the inquirers that they contact Drucker directly.[105] In view of the importance that the chief rabbi attributed to Drucker's activities and the appreciation that he felt for his work, a direct channel of communications was established between his bureau in Jerusalem and Drucker. Rabbi Herzog kept abreast of developments in the cases that he had referred to Drucker and sent Drucker letters of appreciation with encouragement for his successes.[106] This exchange of letters between Drucker and Rabbi Herzog's bureau is the main source of documentation on Drucker's activities and working methods. In addition, letters addressed to Rabbi Kahana due to his function and status, were handed on to Drucker for handling, and there was correspondence between the Council of Communities and JDC that attests to the extent of the Council's actions.

Since Drucker worked on his own, no working procedures were determined in advance; each case was handled on its merits and the nature of the actions taken reflected Drucker's personality and his ability to operate in the field. It was Drucker's practice to examine the information that he received, analyze the situation, and then choose the suitable modus operandi. Sometimes he had to visit the child's place of residence repeatedly in order to establish trust, make attempts to persuade, and negotiate.[107] When rescuers insisted on surrendering a child solely to his or her relatives, Drucker forwarded

104 Letters Jewish Agency Relative Tracing Department to Rabbi Herzog, October 6, 1946, RZA, Rescue Files; letter Rabbi Findling to Rabbi Herzog, December 13, 1946, ibid. The rescue files in this archive contain many letters sent to the rabbi with requests.

105 Letter Jechiel Goldman, Haifa, to Rabbi Herzog, June 22, 1947; letter Gwircman to Rabbi Herzog, April 2, 1946, RZA, Rescue Files; letter Nahman Har-Zahav, Tel Aviv, to Rabbi Herzog, November 5, 1946, ibid.

106 Letters Rabbi Herzog's secretary, M.A. Rakowski, to Drucker, Poland, June 28 and July 15, 1947; from Drucker to Rabbi Herzog, June 12, 1947, ibid. Additional letters are kept in the rescue files of the archive.

107 Interview by author with Yeshayahu Drucker.

details about the children to the Mizrachi movement's delegate to the World Jewish Congress, Dr. Zerach Warhaftig, so that Warhaftig would find or invent relatives for these children and send Drucker a power of attorney — real or fictitious — that would authorize him to remove the children.[108]

Drucker, as we have noted, operated under the auspices of two authorities: as an employee of the Council of Religious Communities and as a Polish military chaplain. This duality allowed him to visit rescuers' homes in the uniform of an army officer replete with insignia of rank. In the political situation prevailing in Poland, a uniform symbolized government and validated his demand for the surrender of a child. Drucker carried a Polish army rubber stamp that bore the words "Jewish Chaplaincy" in its bottom section; sometimes he stamped orders to remove a child with this stamp but imprinted only the upper part — concealing the lower part and the words "Jewish Chaplaincy" — knowing that rescuers would be afraid to disobey army orders. When the removal of a certain child seemed to run into difficulties that he could not surmount by himself, Drucker called in "reinforcements" — his office chauffeur, a Polish policeman whom he hired, or someone else — thereby lending greater authority to his actions. Even though in most cases he preferred to behave pleasantly, Drucker did not flinch from other means to attain his goal. It was his practice to give rescuers a sum of money as a sign of appreciation for what they had done and to help them cope with the hard times that followed the war. Afterwards, to validate the removal of the child, he made them sign a receipt confirming that they had received the money.[109]

The Council of Religious Communities prescribed religious education for the children and a practical, not only theoretical, return to Judaism. In the light of this, the Council decided to establish children's homes of its own. The first one was set up in Zabrze, Upper Silesia, and operated until 1949. Another home was established in Geszcze Pusta, Lower Silesia; it operated for a year and a half only, until the middle of 1947.[110] Even after the children's

108 Warhaftig, *Refugee and Survivor*, pp. 435–436. Warhaftig received a list with 125 names of children who were staying with non-Jews and in convents, together with an instruction to search for their relatives. His searches were aided by the Relative Tracing Department of the World Jewish Congress in New York.

109 Yeshayahu Drucker, "One Man's Actions in the Redemption of Children," in Bornstein, ed., *Redemption of Jewish Children*, p. 36; testimony Yeshayahu Drucker, OHD 28(68); Yishai, *In the Shadow of the Holocaust*, p. 78.

110 Kahana, *After the Deluge*, pp. 49, 51; Drucker, "One Man's Actions," p. 36. The lists of children's homes itemized by organizations, sent by the Central Committee to JDC-Poland, recorded an additional children's house of the Council of Communities, at 16 Smolenska Street in Bytom. This institution actually belonged to Agudath Israel. See JDC report

home in Zabrze was handed over to the management of the Mizrachi movement, the Council's patronage remained in effect. Drucker made a point of
staying in touch with the children whom he had delivered to the homes and
visited them regularly in his travels around the country. The education that the
homes provided, although religious, was typically tolerant and sensitive to the
children's needs. According to the educational concept prevalent in the homes,
the children were not to be force-fed religion and their feelings were not to
be ignored. Instead, they should be gradually inculcated with Jewish religious
content that would take the place of the Christian content to which they had
been exposed during the war.[111] Drucker acted in this spirit, even acceding
to children's requests to go to church with them on Sundays. The staff members of the children's homes were guided by the hope that time and education
would take effect and the power of Judaism would eventually prevail.[112]

Some orthodox delegates to the Council of Communities looked askance
at this educational tolerance. The disagreements arose not only among different religious currents; sometimes delegates from one movement argued over
different gradations of the religious outlook. Two Mizrachi delegates, for example, argued vehemently during deliberations over the allocation of funds
to the children's home in Zabrze. Their debates were influenced by the way
they perceived the kind of education that the institution was providing, one
delegate defining the children's home as "not religious enough" and the other
considering it "adequately religious."[113]

Although Drucker first began activities in the autumn of 1945, most of
his work took place in 1946–1947. During those two years, requests poured
in, information flowed, and the work was uninterrupted and intensive. Afterwards, the influx of requests subsided and the work became more difficult.
Drucker spoke of an additional and more important reason for the decline
in activity: resistance from the authorities, which no longer took a favorable
view of the activities of the Jewish organizations.[114]

---

on children's homes in Poland, late September 1948, JDC, microfilm from Poland; the
children's home in Zabrze was run by Dr. Geller. See Kahana, *After the Deluge*, p. 54; at
the children's home, they called Drucker *kindernaper dla idea* — someone who abducts
children in the service of an idea. See interview by author with Yeshayahu Drucker.

111 Kahana, *After the Deluge*; testimony Yeshayahu Drucker, YVA, O.3/3249; letter Gonjondzki,
Mizrachi Movement, Poland, to Dr. M.A. Kurtz, Youth Department, Mizrachi World
Organization, April 1947, RZRI, S.21IV.

112 Drucker, "One Man's Actions," p. 37; interview by author with Yeshayahu Drucker.

113 Interview by author with Yeshayahu Drucker. The disputants were Naftali Tuchfeld and
Leib Bialer.

114 Testimony Yeshayahu Drucker, YVA, O.3/3249.

Kahana left Poland in 1949 together with the last youngsters from the children's home in Zabrze. Since he was authorized to remove only the offspring of rabbis from Poland, the children were equipped with false papers fitting this description. Before the rabbi left, the Minister of the Interior promoted Drucker to the rank of major. By the end of 1949, the children's home of the Council of Religious Communities was no longer active and all that was left for Drucker to do was to maintain contact with children whose removal had not proved successful. In 1950, Major Drucker was discharged from the army and left Poland.[115]

It is hard to estimate how many children the Council of Religious Communities removed during its years of activity. The reports to JDC, the Mizrachi secretariat in Palestine, and the Youth Aliyah bureau in Paris do not sort the children by categories such as those removed from Gentile homes, those who came from the Soviet Union, and those liberated from convents. Nevertheless, data in my possession allow us to estimate the number of these children at several hundred at most.[116]

Most of the money that Drucker used to remove children was drawn from the exchequer of the Council of Religious Communities due to the vast importance that Rabbi Kahana ascribed to the issue. This source, however, was not a bottomless pit; after all, it also had to suffice for the establishment and rehabilitation of religious institutions and the religious needs of the

---

115 Interview by author with Yeshayahu Drucker; Kahana, *After the Deluge*, p. 136.

116 Letter Gonjondzki to Kurtz, April 1947; report Kaplinski, director of Youth Aliyah Poland, to Youth Aliyah Bureau Paris, December 22, 1947, CZA, L58/358; letters Council of Religious Communities to JDC-Warsaw, June 25, 1948, and from Council of Communities to JDC-Warsaw, September 28, 1948; report from late September 1948, JDC, microfilm from Poland; Litvak, "JDC's Contribution," p. 378; Warhaftig in *Refugee and Survivor*, claims that religious circles removed some 1,000 children but I found no support for this figure in any other source. Related to this is the debate over how many "Rabbi Herzog children" (as the children who left on the train organized by Rabbi Herzog were called) were from children's homes of the Council of Communities and the Mizrachi movement. Warhaftig quotes a bulletin published in Poland on the occasion of Rabbi Herzog's departure, stating that the rabbi's convoy had 250 "Mizrachi children" aboard. Thus, Warhaftig claims that most of the "rabbi's children," about 350 in number, were from Mizrachi-sponsored children's homes. See Warhaftig, *Refugee and Survivor*, p. 443; *The Rescue Voyage*, p. 80, concerning documentation of Rabbi Herzog's travels in Europe, states that Rachel Sternbuch of Agudath Israel delivered 350 children to the train station and that in all there were 500 children aboard the train; see Ella Mahler, "Redemption of Jewish Children from their Non-Jewish Rescuers," *Yad Vashem Bulletin*, 29 (July 1962), pp. 35–36 (Hebrew). She writes that the Council of Communities removed around 200 children. On the basis of the material that I examined, I consider this a reasonable number but a slightly higher estimate would also be plausible.

Jewish population. Since the government took the initiative to establish the Council but did not provide it with an operating budget, the quest for financial resources became one of Rabbi Kahana's duties.[117]

In early 1946, Rabbi Dr. Solomon Schonfeld, son-in-law of the British Chief Rabbi, Joseph H. Hertz, came to Poland to remove groups of children who had survived the war and bring them to Great Britain. After meeting with Schonfeld, the officials of the Council of Religious Communities twice placed groups of children in his custody, in return for which he gave them funds for the continuation of their removal operations. The Council received additional funding in early 1946 from a mission of the World Jewish Congress, and Rabbis Eliezer Silver and Wohlgelernter of the Rescue Committee of the American Orthodox Rabbis delivered some funds in 1946–1947.[118] During Rabbi Herzog's visit to Poland in the summer of 1946, he, too, gave the Council a grant of $5,000 so that it could continue to operate.[119] The Council of Communities stayed in contact with JDC-Poland and reported to it regarding children whom it had removed. According to the reports, JDC also provided financial aid. Apart from the official relationship between Drucker and Rabbi Kahana, on the one hand, and the director of JDC-Poland, William Bein, on the other, the three officials appreciated and trusted each other — a matter that was also reflected in financial assistance.[120]

When Youth Aliyah formalized its operations in Poland in 1946, it sent groups of children from the Council of Communities children's homes out of Poland en route to Palestine.[121]

---

117 Engel, *Between Liberation and Escape*, p. 88.
118 American rabbis established their Rescue Committee at the beginning of the war in order to assist rabbis and yeshiva students in Europe. At the end of the war, the Rescue Committee redirected its efforts to assistance for survivors. In the matter of children, the Rescue Committee operated through the offices of an institution called the Child Rescue Commission; in regard to the Rescue Committee, see Efraim Zuroff, "The Orthodox Public in the United States and the Destruction of European Jewry: The Rescue Committee of the American Orthodox Rabbis during the Holocaust 1939–1945," Ph.D. dissertation, The Hebrew University of Jerusalem, 1997 (Hebrew).
119 Interview by author with Yeshayahu Drucker; testimony Yeshayahu Drucker, OHD 28(68); Kahana, *After the Deluge*, pp. 50–77; Dekel, *Remnants of the Sword*, pp. 609–610; report in manuscript by Drucker on operations of the Council of Communities, September 22, 1947, CZA, S26/1424.
120 Report Council of Communities to JDC-Poland, September 28, 1948, JDC, microfilm from Poland; interview by author with Yeshayahu Drucker; in regard to JDC funding of the Council of Communities, see Bauer, *Out of the Ashes*, p. 77.
121 Interview by author with Yeshayahu Drucker; report Kaplinski, December 22, 1947; letter Gonjondzki to Dr. M.A. Kurtz, evidently early 1947, RZRI, S.21IV.

Although the Mizrachi and Torah va'Avoda movements were part of the Ichud party in Poland, they sought autonomy within the party in order to preserve their religious character. The movements, which worked together, held their first convention in Kraków in July 1945 and later that year, elected a six-member secretariat. Gonjondzki was elected chief secretary and two of Rabbi Kahana's aides were named to the secretariat as members: Aharon Beker as the Mizrachi delegate to the Ichud, and Yeshayahu Drucker as the director of the Culture Department. Reports from the Mizrachi movement in Poland to the Mizrachi administration in Palestine show that Drucker and Beker's dual roles made it hard for them to operate within the Movement.[122] Although all religious streams were represented on the Council of Communities, Mizrachi received special treatment and the domain of the two bodies sometimes overlapped.

Mizrachi established several collectives ("kibbutzim"), first in Łódź and later in Kraków, Sosnowiec, Gliwice, and Będzin. Presumably, the first children gathered up by movement members were placed in the movement's collectives and only afterwards were placed in their children's homes. The first of these institutions was set up in Kraków; others followed in Łódź, Reichbach, and Bytom. Furthermore, as stated, the movement directed the children's home of the Council of Religious Communities. After groups of children were sent out of Poland, the homes began to be closed down during 1947 and only one was still in operation in 1948.[123]

Mizrachi kept no records about its mechanism for the removal of children. Although various reports mention its children's homes and their population as of the date of the report, it is not possible to determine exactly how many children the movement removed from non-Jewish homes.[124]

---

122 Memorandum H. Besok, Poland, to Hapoel Hamizrachi, Tel Aviv, November 27, 1945, RZRI, S. 19IV; letter Gonjondzki, Mizrachi Organization Poland, to Mizrachi and Torah va'Avoda World Center, October 17, 1945, ibid. Reports Mizrachi secretariat-Poland to Mizrachi World Center, ibid., S. 20IV.

123 Rubinstein, "Reckoning of an Era," p. 182; the other movements, too, initially placed reclaimed children in their own collectives. See Sarid, *Ruin and Deliverance,* pp. 404–405; Yehuda D., report on mission to Poland, list of children's homes, October 14, 1948, report to Jewish Agency in Jerusalem, CZA, L58/516.

124 Testimony Baruch Kaplinski, OHD, 21 (68). The testimony cites figures from a survey that Kaplinski performed when he reached Poland in spring 1946; report of record of children's homes, itemized by movements, undated. I received the document, originally from the ŻIH, from Vered Berman of Jerusalem; report from Mizrachi and Torah va'Avoda Center, Poland, to World Mizrachi Center, March 12, 1946, with a detailed account of movement activities, RZRI, S. 20IV.

The movement in Poland maintained relations with its center in Palestine and with the administration of the World Alliance of Torah va'Avoda. In a report issued on November 13, 1946, it stated that up to that date reports had been forwarded about 513 children who had been removed by the movement.[125] This number includes children's homes of the Council of Communities and no distinction is made between children removed from rescuers' custody and others. Eliezer Rubinstein, the Mizrachi delegate to Youth Aliyah in Poland, termed the removal of children "the jewel in the crown of the Mizrachi and Torah va'Avoda movements in Poland. We established the redemption of children as one of the most important duties.... We have restored hundreds of children to our people and to God."[126]

However, this number should not be taken at face value: in an article in the Mizrachi newspaper, Rubinstein wrote about the children who were in the movement's institutions: "Nearly a thousand children — orphans and half-orphans –[. . .] including many who were redeemed and returned by our comrades — with exceptional devotion — to us." At the end of the article, describing the parting from the children, Rubinstein stressed the change that they had undergone and also mentioned "their Russian speech."[127] The choice of words shows that many of the children had come from the Soviet Union under the repatriation arrangement and others had relatives; thus Rubinstein used the concept of "removal" in a general way and applied it to them as well. Furthermore, since Mizrachi was responsible for education at the Council of Communities children's home in Zabrze, Rubinstein numbered Drucker among the removal operatives who acted on the movement's behalf. Although Rubinstein does not say so, one may surmise that along with members in the movement's collectives were others who acted on behalf of the movement to remove children from non-Jews' homes. It is noteworthy that the Council of Communities and the Mizrachi movement had the same ideological outlook on the duty of removing children from their rescuers and educating them and establishing their future in Palestine. They regarded religious education as the paramount principle and in this regard were distinct from other Zionist parties and movements that operated in Poland.[128]

125 Warhaftig, *Refugee and Survivor,* p. 436.
126 Rubinstein, "Reckoning of an Era," p. 185.
127 Idem, "Our Children"; the article appeared in Hebrew in *Mizrachi Movement Bulletin,* no. 21, published in Poland when Rabbi Herzog left Poland with the children. See Warhaftig, *Refugee and Survivor,* p. 442.
128 Letter Mizrachi and Torah va'Avoda secretariat, Poland, to Youth Aliyah-Poland, November 15, 1946, RZRI, S. 20IV.

The Zionist Youth Movements and the Establishment of the Koordynacja for the Redemption of Children

Young members of Zionist youth movements who had survived the war grouped together in Poland and established "training kibbutzim." These collective organizations attracted people who were looking to form a group for mutual support and also served as a channel for eventual emigration to Palestine. The first such kibbutz was established in Warsaw by members of Dror-Hehalutz and Hashomer Hatza'ir in the spring of 1945; additional youth movement collectives were established later that year.[129]

Always conscious of the small number of survivors in general and children in particular, the members spared no effort to locate and gather children. The children, who were of various ages, were housed in the dormitories of the collectives, which served them as a refuge but lacked an educational and caregiving infrastructure. The routine of kibbutz life left no room for child care and there was no permanent population of adult members.[130] Members of several kibbutzim even set out to places where Jews had gathered in order to collect the children who had been brought there or who had arrived by themselves. The act of deliberately searching for these children depended, of course, on the members' awareness that this was possible.[131] Dror-Hehalutz maintained offices and training collective at 38 Poznańska Street in Warsaw, and the first children whom its members gathered were brought there from Częstochowa. When additional children joined the collective and the quarters became overcrowded, they were transferred to the movement's first children's

129 Sarid, *Ruin and Deliverance,* pp. 197–198, 200–201; during that year, the Dror and Hashomer Hatza'ir movements jointly established another fifteen kibbutzim. In regard to the Ichud kibbutzim, see ibid., pp. 231–232; for those of Po'alei Zion CS and the Haoved movement, p. 262; the kibbutzim of Noar Borochov, Poalei Zion Left, p. 265; for those of Dror, p. 238; those of Hashomer Hatza'ir, pp. 292–293.
130 Ibid., pp. 197, 200–201; interview by author with Chasia Bielicki-Bornstein, May 1993; Shner-Neshamit, *I Did Not Come to Rest,* p. 190; Engel, *Between Liberation and Escape,* pp. 78–80.
131 Chasia Bielicki-Bornstein, "Back to the Bosom of Their People," in Dror Levy, ed., *The Hashomer Hatza'ir Book,* B (Merhavia: Sifriat Poalim, 1961, Hebrew), p. 318; testimony Arye Lindenbaum, YVA, O.3/5112; testimony Pinhas Krybus, OHD, 45(68); biography Hanna Pepperkorn, in Tenenboim, *One of a City and Two of a Family,* p. 202; Zuckerman, *A Surplus of Memory,* pp. 587–589; Dekel, *Remnants of the Sword,* p. 73; Neshamit, "The Koordynacja for the Redemption of Children in Liberated Poland," p. 120.

home, in Bytom, Upper Silesia.[132] Members of the Hashomer Hatza'ir collective in Łódź regularly visited the headquarters of the town's Jewish committee, which had established a public kitchen, and urged children who were eating there to join them.[133] At the Hashomer Hatza'ir collective in Sosnowiec, organized searching for children took place: two members of the collective visited towns and villages in the vicinity and returned each day with new children.[134] The first fifteen children were taken to the training collective itself, but again, as the numbers rose, they were placed in a children's home set up by the movement in Ludwikowo, Lower Silesia.[135] All the movements that had originally collected children and took them into their training collectives subsequently established kibbutzim made up of children and teenagers with staffs of educators and caregivers, providing such conditions as their resources allowed.[136] In late 1947, as the number of children declined, the number of children's homes also became less. The movements maintained children's homes until the autumn of 1949, when the Polish authorities terminated their activities and those of the political parties.[137]

In May 1946, Baruch Kaplinski came to Poland to direct the Youth Aliyah office. Upon his arrival, he contacted all the Zionist youth movements in order to estimate the number of children under their tutelage. From the reports that the movements provided, Kaplinski found that all of them had established children's homes. According to his records, 857 children and teenagers (including some born in 1929) were under the movements' care at

132 Engel, *Between Liberation and Escape*, p. 77 and notes 122–126; Zuckerman, *A Surplus of Memory*, 587–589; Sarah Shner-Neshamit, remarks about testimony of Arieh Sarid, January 1981, given to me by Shner-Neshamit; Yishai wrote that a group of forty Hashomer Hatza'ir children stayed in the sixth floor loft of the same building. One cannot tell from the account whether these were the same children or some other group. See Yishai, *In the Shadow of the Holocaust*, p. 167.
133 Interview by author with Chasia Bielicki-Bornstein.
134 Biography of Hanna Hessing, in Tenenboim, *One of a City and Two of a Family*, p. 216; Nessia Orlowicz-Reznik, "A 'Shomeric' Children's Home," in Dror, ed., *The Hashomer Hatza'ir Book*, B, p. 312; Engel, *Between Liberation and Escape*, p. 86.
135 Testimony Nessia Orlowicz-Reznik, MA, A.353; biography of Hanna Hessing, in Tenenboim, *One of a City and Two of a Family*, p. 216. Hannah, one of the two members who searched for Jewish children, recounted that the children were moved to Ludwikowa after their numbers had reached twenty-five.
136 Koryski, "The Zionist Koordynacja for the Redemption of Jewish Children in Poland," p. 24; on the Ichud children's collectives, see Sarid, *Ruin and Deliverance*, pp. 231–232; on children associated with Poalei Zion CS and Haoved, see ibid, p. 262; those of Noar Borochov: p. 265; those of Dror: p. 238; those of Hashomer Hatza'ir, pp. 292–293.
137 Litvak, "JDC's Contribution," p. 366; Kahana, *After the Deluge*, p. 136; Gutman, *Jews in Poland*, pp. 90–91.

the time and some of them still remained in the adults' collectives.[138] When the Youth Aliyah bureau in Poland began to operate, groups of children were removed from Poland under its auspices and were replaced in the homes by new children.[139]

The various Zionist political parties supported their own youth movements by means of emissaries from Palestine, visitors from other countries, and encounters of movement members from Poland at Jewish gatherings and conferences that took place after the war.[140] Although donations of money were intended for movement activities in general, each movement set aside some of the funds for the care of the children.[141] Later, most of the financial support came from the JDC.[142]

In autumn 1945, groups of emissaries from Palestine were sent by the Jewish Agency to Europe on the basis of party affiliation. Their task was to contact survivors and to help them organize in various ways. One of the members of the second group of emissaries, sent to Poland in October 1945, was Leibl Goldberg, a member of Kibbutz Yagur, representing the Mapai wing of the United Kibbutz Movement. Reaching Warsaw in mid-November 1945, Goldberg joined a Dror collective and from there set out on visits to

---

138 Testimony Baruch Kaplinski, OHD 21(68). This does not imply that all of these children had been removed from non-Jewish homes. Some had spent the war with partisans in the forests, migrated along the roads, worked in various places under false identities, or were in hiding. See Shner-Neshamit, *I Did Not Come to Rest,* p. 195.

139 List of children's homes, October 14, 1948; report late September 1948 about children's homes, JDC, microfilm from Poland; report Mata Planter, Youth Aliyah, Paris, March–April 1947, CZA, L58/810.

140 Sarid, "Initial Deployment," pp. 308–309, 311–312, 319; Pinhas Rashish, a Hehalutz leader who participated in the mission from Palestine, set out for Switzerland and France and came back with funds. See interview by author with Chasia Bielicki-Bornstein, who recounts that in January 1946 she attended the Hashomer Hatza'ir world convention in France and crossed Belgium and Switzerland on her way back. Chasia spoke at various encounters and raised money for the movement; Sarah Shner-Neshamit related that during her trip to Germany in spring 1946, she received $800 from a Dror coordinator in Munich, which she smuggled in a tube of toothpaste and delivered to the movement in Poland. See Shner-Neshamit, *I Did Not Come to Rest,* p. 198.

141 Interview by author with Arieh Sarid, November 1993; *Mission to the Diaspora, 1945–1948* (Tel Aviv: Yad Tabenkin, Ghetto Fighters' House, and Hakibbutz Hameuhad, 1989, Hebrew), p. 91; interview by author with Chasia Bielicki-Bornstein. The Zionist Congress took place in London in August 1945, the Hashomer Hatza'ir world convention in France in January 1946, and the World Zionist Congress in December 1946.

142 Testimony Leibl Koryski, OHD 15(68); Litvak, "JDC's Contribution," p. 352; Engel, *Between Liberation and Escape,* p. 118.

other kibbutzim, encountered members and participated in seminars across Poland. His comrades did the same.[143]

Shortly after he reached Poland, Goldberg visited the Dror collective in Kraków, where he asked the local Jewish committee to help the members of the collective. At the committee offices, Goldberg encountered a Polish woman who had a Jewish-looking child with her. When he asked her if the boy was her son, she replied that he was Jewish but he had been entrusted to her care; his parents had been murdered during the war and she was visiting the committee offices to receive the monthly relief payment. This random encounter evidently marked a watershed in Goldberg's activities, as he testified afterwards: "As a man of Eretz Israel, it did not seem right to me that a Jewish child who had survived the war still remained with non-Jews."[144]

Goldberg had $150 in his possession — the proceeds of the sale of two watches that he had sewn into his jacket lining before setting out on his mission to Poland — in case he needed cash to solve some problem. Since his trip had been uneventful, Goldberg sold the watches in Prague. After his encounter with the woman and child at the committee offices in Kraków, Goldberg contacted an acquaintance, told him about the money that he possessed, and asked him to use it as a payment to Poles who would agree to surrender a Jewish child who was in their custody. That very day, a girl of eight or nine years of age was brought to the Dror collective and Goldberg paid 25,000 zlotys for her. The girl's response taught Leibl Goldberg something about the emotional difficulties involved in the removal of children from their rescuers' homes: the girl gripped the door frame and refused to remain with the Jews. The deal went through anyway — with the rescuer's consent — and the girl remained at the Kraków collective. Goldberg returned to Warsaw but, still uneasy about the question of Jewish children, he decided to take up the issue with David Guzik, director of JDC-Poland in the hope of obtaining a sympathetic ear and advice. To Goldberg's surprise, at the JDC offices he again encountered Jewish children who had gone there to ask for money on behalf of their rescuers. He persuaded two of them to join him. The following day they arrived with

---

143 Sarid, "Initial Deployment," pp. 312–321, 275. Leib Goldberg later changed his name to Levi Arieh Sarid (Sarid is Hebrew for "survivor"). Engel, *Between Liberation and Escape,* pp. 117–118; interview Shlomo Bar-Gil with Arieh Sarid, July 1991; Sarid, "Remarks about the Koordynacja" p. 15.

144 Interview Bar-Gil with Arieh Sarid, July 1991; Sarid claimed that he had discussed the matter with the secretary of the Kraków committee, who told him that there was neither a program nor a budget for the rescue of these children. See his testimony in *Mission to the Diaspora,* p. 83; see Engel, *Between Liberation and Escape,* p. 117.

their rescuer and Goldberg remunerated her for the care she had provided the children during the war.[145]

Moved by the random encounter in Kraków, Goldberg pressed for the establishment of an organized body that would take up the entire issue of child survivors in a more focused manner. His decision was also colored by a personal aspect: due to tensions within the movement, Yitzhak Cukierman asked him not to deal with political affairs during his visits to the kibbutzim. This constraint made him ill at ease.[146] By tackling the problem of the Jewish children, he found a way to devote himself to something that was important and essentially uncontroversial.

Although the idea of an organized body had been Goldberg's, its implementation became possible due to a confluence of circumstances in which additional players were involved. In late December 1945, Sarah Dusznicka moved from Vilna to Warsaw. A leading Hehalutz member in Lithuania who dealt with education, in Vilna she had been involved in the removal of Jewish children from non-Jewish homes. Goldberg met with Dusznicka at Dror headquarters in Warsaw and shared with her the idea of establishing an organization. Sarah agreed to join — an important decision due to her status in

---

145 Interview Bar-Gil with Arieh Sarid; Sarid related that he had paid only 3,000 zlotys for the removal of the girl in Kraków; that he had received $240 for the watches, and that he approached the director of JDC-Poland in late November 1945. I believe, however, that the encounter took place at least one month later, since the date Sarid stated clashes with the sequence of events that he himself described: he says that this happened after Sarah Dusznicka (later Neshamit) reached Warsaw. See *Mission to the Diaspora*, p. 84. In my opinion, the remarks in *Mission to the Diaspora* reflect an attempt to report the onset of the Koordynacja's activities earlier than had actually occurred. As for the "buying" of children, in her article "The Koordynacja for the Redemption of Children in Liberated Poland," p. 118, Sarah Neshamit claims that it was she who removed the children in Warsaw and paid the Polish rescuer 15,000 zlotys, whereas in her book *I Did Not Come to Rest*, p. 192, she describes the same negotiations and writes that she eventually paid the rescuer 10,000 zlotys from the proceeds of the sale of Goldberg's watches; Goldberg himself claims that he personally paid 50,000 zlotys for the children in Warsaw. See *Mission to the Diaspora*, p. 84. Although one may blame the discrepancies among their recollections on the time that lapsed since the event, I tend to surmise — without derogating from the importance of their actions in principle — that the differences are based on personal pride.

146 Interview Bar-Gil with Arieh Sarid; Sarid, "Initial Deployment," pp. 320–321. According to Sarid, the emissaries who visited Poland on behalf of the Ahdut Ha'Avoda and Mapai parties operated in Poland under the auspices of Dror. In May 1946, the Noham movement (Noham — *No'ar Halutzi Meuhad,* United Pioneering Youth) came into being in Poland after having operated in displaced persons camps in Germany; henceforth the Mapai emissaries acted under its auspices.

the movement. After she presented the idea to members of the Dror central committee, it was agreed that the movement would take part in establishing this entity, which would deal exclusively in affairs concerning children.[147]

Concurrently, two visitors came from America: Louis Segal, secretary-general of the National Organization of Jewish Workers (in Yiddish, *Natsionaler Arbeter Farband*) and a leading figure in Poalei Zion in the United States, and Dr. Samuel Margoshes, editor of the Yiddish-language daily newspaper *Der Tog* ("The Day"). Goldberg met them when they visited the Hehalutz hostel to meet with Yitzhak Cukierman and Zivia Lubetkin (two of the leaders of the Warsaw Ghetto uprising). The next day, Goldberg brought two children who had been removed in Warsaw and took them to the Polonia Hotel, where the two visitors were staying, in order to present his idea and ask for financial support.[148] As Margoshes wrote in his newspaper after returning to the United States, they were very excited about both the meeting and the idea.[149] They gave Goldberg $5,000 and a promise of further support.[150]

Although the idea was still in its infancy and the organization had not yet come into being in any practical way, its progenitors began to remove children and place them in the Dror children's home in Bytom pending some other arrangement. Concurrently, an attempt was made to enlist the coop-

---

147   She is known today as Sarah Shner-Neshamit; interview Bar-Gil with Arieh Sarid; Shner-Neshamit, *I Did Not Come to Rest*, p. 189; ibid., notes on Sarid's testimony, Engel argues that the Koordynacja was established at a propitious time from the standpoint of the Zionist movements — just as it seemed that the momentum built up by the Bricha movement was abating and additional areas for action were needed. See Engel, *Between Liberation and Escape*, pp. 117–119.

148   Interview Bar-Gil with Sarid; *Mission to the Diaspora*, pp. 76–85. According to this source, Sarid claimed that Segal and Margoshes came in late November 1945; in another source ("Initial Deployment," p. 308), he dates their visit to late January and mid-February; Sarah Neshamit says that she decided to move from Lithuania to Poland in late December, that she met with Goldberg (Sarid) when she reached Warsaw, and that by the time Segal and Margoshes came she had already returned from a visit to the Dror kibbutz in Munich, in the spring of 1946. See Shner-Neshamit, *I Did Not Come to Rest*, p. 119; the Koordynacja newspaper, *Farn Yiddishn Kind* (File 798) reports on the event, stating that the first two children had been removed in Warsaw in mid-February. Comparison of the various events leads me to believe that Segal and Margoshes reached this location no earlier than mid-January; see also Engel, *Between Liberation and Escape*, pp. 118, 223, n. 15.

149   Samuel Margoshes, "How to Redeem Jewish Children in Poland," article in *Der Tog* (Yiddish), Apr. 4, 1946, p. 7.

150   *Mission to the Diaspora*, p. 85. Goldberg claims that the money came from the National Organization of Jewish Workers relief fund; see also Engel, *Between Liberation and Escape*, p. 223, n. 15.

eration of all Zionist movements, it being Goldberg's conviction that all the organizations, regardless of ideological disagreements, should unite behind an organization that would look after Jewish children who had survived the war. Sarah Neshamit maintains that cooperation was also essential because no one movement had the ability to establish on its own an organization that would deal exclusively with children; furthermore, Segal and Margoshes, who had been asked to support the operations, stated that in order to garner the publicity that it would need for fundraising, it had to be established as a joint enterprise of all the movements.[151]

From the moment the deliberations began, all the Zionist movements agreed on the need to establish an entity that would concentrate solely on the care of children and their restoration to Judaism, but they disagreed about the nature of the education that would be provided in the children's homes. Until then, each movement had educated "its" children in accordance with its own outlook and goals and regarded the children as its ideological reserve forces. But now, in contrast, an educational concept amenable to all factions had to be worked out. In meetings with the Ichud party and the Council of Religious Communities, representatives of Hehalutz insisted that the new organization be based on the principles of education in Zionism, Hebrew culture, and *aliya* (immigration to Eretz Israel). Ichud accepted these principles, but a common basis for cooperation could not be established with the Council of Religious Communities, which included Mizrachi and Agudath Israel. The members of these two organizations accepted the principles but demanded that the children should also receive religious education.[152]

The first meeting that discussed the formation of the organization took place in Warsaw in late January 1946. In subsequent meetings, the delegates discussed the formulation of a platform that would be acceptable to all the movements, determined the composition of the organization's institutions, devised its working methods, and acted for the establishment of joint children's homes. During the deliberations, it was decided to name the organiza-

---

151 *Mission to the Diaspora*, p. 85; interview Bar-Gil with Arieh Sarid; Shner-Neshamit, notes on Sarid's testimony; Sarid, "Remarks about the Koordynacja," p. 21; Shner-Neshamit, *I Did Not Come to Rest*, p. 191; idem., "The Koordynacja for the Redemption of Children in Liberated Poland," p. 120.

152 Shner-Neshamit, *I Did Not Come to Rest*, p. 191; interview by author with Arieh Sarid, November 1993. Although Mizrachi was part of the Ichud, due to the religious connection, it operated under the Council of Communities umbrella with regard to removing children.

tion, "the Zionist Koordynacja for the Redemption of Children."[153] On its letterhead, however, the following appeared in Hebrew: "Zionist Koordynacja for the Affairs of Children and Youth in Poland, 'Children's Emigration [to Palestine] Center.'" In Polish, the organization was labeled *Komisja Koordynacja dla spraw dzieci i młodzieży przy org. Ichud I Hechalutz-Pionier* (Ichud and Hehalutz Coordinating Committee for the Affairs of Children and Youth). The difference between the organization's official name and the one that all its constituents used may have originated in the heavy significance of the unofficial name and the more neutral tenor of the official name (which made no mention of "redemption") — especially in its Polish version, with the words "Children's Emigration Center" omitted. The thinking behind this, it seems, was that the omission might lessen the danger of opposition from Polish government bodies and Jewish communist rivals. The word "redemption" (*ge'ula* in Hebrew) denoted the "liberation" of the children from their rescuers and their restoration to the Jewish people, that is to say, it carried a subliminal national message. It also suggested liberation in the Zionist sense, which preached the binary opposite of "exile" versus "redemption." According to this, to achieve national liberation and renaissance, Jews must leave the Diaspora in order to redeem the nation on the soil of Eretz Israel (The Land of Israel). Thus, the very use of the word "redemption" also expressed an outlook on the children's future: liberation from their non-Jewish rescuers, a return to Judaism, and eventual immigration to Palestine.[154]

153 Mahler, "Redemption of Jewish Children from Their Non-Jewish Rescuers," p. 36; Sarid claims that delegates from Dror and Hashomer Hatza'ir were invited to the first meeting and the other movements were allowed to join only afterwards. See *Mission to the Diaspora*, p. 86; Sarid writes that there was a climate of merger attempts among the vestiges of the movements at the time and that they felt that fractiousness was ironic in view of the Holocaust. For this reason, the concept of Koordynacja (unity, coordinating committee) was widely invoked. Sarid, "Initial Deployment," pp. 295–296. In his interview with Bar-Gil in July 1991, Sarid claimed that this name for the organization was his suggestion; in *Mission to the Diaspora* (p. 86) he wrote that it was Ovadia Peled, an Ichud delegate, who had proposed it; according to Neshamit, the organization's full name was "The Hehalutz and Ichud Zionist Koordynacja for the Redemption of Children and Youth." See Neshamit, "The Koordynacja for the Redemption of Children in Liberated Poland," p. 116.

154 As this chapter has shown, various entities were active in removing children from non-Jewish hands. The first priority for each was to extricate the youngsters from the non-Jewish milieu in which they were living. Next, they aimed to educate the children in the most appropriate manner. In this sense, neither the movements nor the Koordynacja differed from other bodies. The question of whether the wish to "educate" the children in any particular manner prejudiced the efforts to remove them is discussed below.

The following movements took part in the Koordynacja: Dror, Hashomer Hatza'ir, Noar Borochov, Gordonia, Hanoar Hatzioni, and Akiva; they were joined by WIZO — the Womens' International Zionist Organization. Initially, the organization's governing committee was composed of the following members: Sarah Dusznicka of Dror (education coordinator), Leibl Arye Koryski of Hashomer Hatza'ir (child-removing mechanism and treasurer), Chasia Bielicki-Bornstein (director of the children's home), Ovadia Peled and Moshe Unger of Ichud (secretariat), Menahem Kunda of Ichud (education and finance), Pinhas Krybus of Noar Borochov (administration), Dr. Mella Mandelbaum of Gordonia (director of the children's home in Łódź), and Alicia Kyle and Bella Peszpjorka of WIZO (inspection of the children's homes).[155] Goldberg, who sired the idea of setting up the organization, served as its "foreign minister;" his activities were to focus on establishing relations with various bodies in Poland and abroad so as to advertise the nature and uniqueness of the organization and raise funds. His actions enabled the organization to operate and earned him a great deal of respect among the other Zionist activists.[156]

The goals of the Koordynacja were laid down during the discussions that preceded its establishment. The goals were fourfold; (a) the removal of Jewish children from non-Jewish custody; (b) the establishment of "children's kibbutzim" for those aged 3–13; (c) receiving orphaned and repatriated *ge'ulim* (the Koordynacja's term for "redeemed" children) up to age thirteen whose parents agreed to have them emigrate to Palestine; (d) providing the children with a Zionist pioneering education.[157]

The decision to keep children up to the age of thirteen in the Koordynacja children's homes stemmed from the belief that young children needed, before anything else, personal rehabilitation and the construction of a general "national affiliation." It would not be right, they thought, to burden them with various movement ideologies, as was being done with older adolescents.[158]

---

155 Sarid, "Initial Deployment," p. 315; Koryski, "The Zionist Koordynacja for the Redemption of Jewish Children in Poland," p. 24. People who worked for the movements usually received a salary from the Koordynacja. See testimony Leibl Koryski, OHD 15(68).

156 Testimony Leibl Koryski, OHD 15(68). In his testimony, Koryski praised Goldberg lavishly for his loyalty, sincerity, honesty, and boundless devotion; Dr. Margoshes, writing in *Der Tog*, described Goldberg's personality and actions at length and expressed much appreciation for the man and his actions. See Margoshes, "How to Redeem Jewish Children in Poland"; interview with Arieh Sarid.

157 *Farn Yiddishn Kind*; Koryski, "The Zionist Koordynacja for the Redemption of Jewish Children in Poland," p. 25.

158 Testimony Leibl Koryski, OHD 15(68); *Mission to the Diaspora*, p. 86.

However, occasionally one heard allegations about "certain activists" who were "buying souls" for their movements among the younger children as well. Koordynacja operatives also removed children over age thirteen from the homes of non-Jews but placed most of them in the individual movements' children's homes.[159] A minority of older children who were sent to the Koordynacja's children's homes were placed there for personal reasons.[160] Similarly, some children below the age of thirteen stayed in the children's homes of the movements.[161] One of the Hashomer Hatza'ir groups, for example, had some twenty children under the age of seven; this violation of the agreement among the movements attracted criticism.[162] One of the JDC reports about the children's homes contains the following remark: "In the case of Ichud, we would like to have the young children handed over to the Koordynacja."[163] Although this suggests that the policy was applied flexibly and the agreement was not always honored, generally it may be said that the movements cooperated fruitfully.[164]

As we have pointed out, the idea of establishing the Koordynacja was inspired by the wish to reclaim Jewish children who had spent the war in Polish homes and convents. Once established, however, the Koordynacja broadened its activities to include children who had been repatriated from the Soviet Union either as orphans or with their parents. All the movements regarded the issue of the children as the primary educational mission.

---

159 *Mission to the Diaspora*, p. 93; interview by author with Chasia Bielicki-Bornstein, May 1993; Sarah Neshamit relates that Hashomer Hatza'ir provided the first counselors, since even before the war this movement had alumni who had been trained in working with children and teenagers. Some claimed that its influence was too strong. Neshamit, a member of Dror, protested these allegations and praised the counselors' work. See Shner-Neshamit, remarks on Sarid's testimony.

160 Examples are the following catalogue cards: No. 4, M. Gersenwald; No. 16, A. Rosner; No. 56, Batya Goldstein; No. 96, S. Kessler. See Koordynacja card catalogue of children, GFHA, File 800; see also David Schirman, "Management of Redeemed Children's Homes," in Bornstein, ed., *Redemption of Jewish Children*, p. 40; testimony Leibl Koryski, OHD 15(68).

161 Report Kaplinski, director of Youth Aliyah Poland, to Youth Aliyah Bureau Paris, 1948, CZA, L58/358.

162 Transcript of telephone conversation Akiva Lewinsky, Youth Aliyah Paris, to Baruch Kaplinski, Youth Aliyah Poland, February 24, 1947, Section 7, CZA, L58/595; see also letter Mata Planter, Youth Aliyah Paris, to Dr. Landauer, Jerusalem, January 30, 1948, ibid., L58/382. Reporting on groups of children that reached France, Planter noted most of the Dror children were aged 5–18 and two children were even younger.

163 JDC report on children's homes in Poland, late September 1948.

164 Testimony Pinhas Krybus, OHD 45(68).

When it came to removing children from non-Jewish caregivers, the Koordynacja considered itself an agent of the children's parents, as it explained in its newspaper:

> They wanted the children to know who they are and why they lost them [their parents.].... We must take stronger actions to redeem the children. We will not desist until we redeem the last Jewish child and restore him to the [Jewish] people. We must carry out the testament of the fathers and mothers who were annihilated.... We are tying together the Jewish child, the fate of the Jewish people, and a happier future.[165]

The Koordynacja resolved that it would not flinch from any action that might redeem the children. Although it derived its legitimacy from the movements' measures to rehabilitate the youngsters and not from the authorities, its activists believed that the authorities knew what they were engaged in.[166] The immense appreciation of the rescue and the rescuers was part of the belief that these children represented the future of a reborn Jewish people. The movement activists knew that they were treading on thin ice and that crossing a line might bring their activities to a halt.[167] However, with Poland going through an uncertain period and the authorities preoccupied with their own problems, the activists did not hesitate to act in ways that clashed with accepted norms.

As the Koordynacja was being organized, an intelligence bureau was set up to determine the whereabouts of Jewish children. Private individuals provided the bureau with information; as did members of Zionist parties who worked for the Central Committee. These people perused the Committee's lists and extracted the names of rescuers who had contacted the Committee for financial support. The intention was that the movements should preempt the Committee by removing the children concerned. At the same time, deliberate action to search for children began as operatives were sent out to the countryside and bounties were promised to Poles who would provide information concerning the whereabouts of a Jewish child.[168]

165 "All the Children Must Return to Their People," *Farn Yiddishn Kind.*
166 Interview by author with Sarah Shner-Neshamit. Articles in the Koordynacja newspaper *For the Jewish Child* made the same point.
167 Testimony Leibl Koryski, OHD 15(68); Shner-Neshamit, *I Did Not Come to Rest,* p. 204; Dekel, *Remnants of the Sword,* p. 13; testimony Yehuda Bronstein, OHD 25(68).
168 Testimony Yehuda Bronstein, OHD 25(68); Shner-Neshamit, *I Did Not Come to Rest,* pp. 191, 208; interview by author with Sarah Shner-Neshamit; Sarid, "Initial Deployment," p. 315; *Mission to the Diaspora,* p. 86; Koryski, "The Zionist Koordynacja for the Redemption of Jewish Children in Poland," p. 25; testimony Genia Düstenfeld, March 1970, given to me by Tami Lavie and in my possession.

Devorah Fleiszer, who operated under the pseudonym Maria Dobrzyńska and the nickname Marysia, was the first person whom Goldberg recruited as a removal operative.[169] Marysia chose to work in the Lublin area, where she had been born and where she herself had been concealed during the war. Shortly before she began her activities, she was introduced to the treasurer of the Koordynacja. Her description of the meeting follows:

> Koryski came to me (they didn't have an office yet). He asked me how much I wanted for this work but I refused to take money. When he said that I had to make a living, I told him 2,000 zlotys. He said that I should be paid by head count. I asked him, "What am I, a German?" He said I would do better to work that way. I told him he was wrong.[170]

To understand the nature of this exchange, one needs to understand the division of roles at the Koordynacja. The organization's officers represented the movements; the people recruited for search and removal missions were those who were found to be suitable for this type of work,[171] and sometimes they were initially treated with suspicion. On occasion, however, operatives on behalf of the Koordynacja or the movements were sent on special one-time removal operations.[172]

The Koordynacja established its offices at 17/18 Zawadzka Street in Łódź and set up its first two children's homes in that city. One of the homes, on Narutowicze Street, was for children aged 7–13 and was run by Chasia Bornstein. The other, run by Hella Lenman, was on Piotrkowska Street and accommodated children under school age.[173]

Although the movements had promised to furnish the Koordynacja with counselors and caregivers who were experienced in working with children and knowledgeable in Hebrew culture, this did not happen. The Hashomer Hatza'ir movement provided the first counselors but they were not enough. None of the movements had enough counselors, even for their own youth

---

169 Sarid, "Remarks about the Koordynacja," p. 21; Neshamit, "The 'Koordynacja for the Redemption of Children' in Liberated Poland," p. 122; Shner-Neshamit, *I Did Not Come to Rest*, p. 208.

170 Testimony Devorah Zilber — none other than Devorah Fleiszer, "Marysia," OHD 27(68).

171 Testimony Pinhas Krybus, OHD 45(68).

172 Interview by author with Sarah Shner-Neshamit; interview by author with David (Jurek) Plonski, November 1996; testimony Leibl Koryski, OHD 15(68). One of the activists who were sent occasionally to remove a child was Jakob Gises, a former soldier.

173 Testimony Leibl Koryski, OHD 15(68); Neshamit, "The Koordynacja for the Redemption of Children in Liberated Poland," p. 123; Bielicki-Bornstein, "Back to the Bosom of Their People," p. 319.

collectives. To solve the problem, the Koordynacja decided in spring 1946 to open an intensive counseling seminar at which education, child psychology, Hebrew, history of the Zionist Movement, and problems of settlement in Palestine would be taught. The twenty teenagers who finished the first seminar were immediately hired to work in the children's homes.[174]

The first children whom Marysia brought in were housed with friends of hers; shortly afterwards, in March 1946, they were transferred to Chasia's children's home. The home accommodated twelve children by the end of its first week[175] and forty by the end of the month. Chasia kept a personal notebook in which she recorded details that each of the children had told about themselves, their families, and what had happened to them during the war.[176] As the pace of repatriation from the Soviet Union increased, two additional children's homes were opened in Silesia (in areas from which the Germans had been evicted), one in Piotrolesie and the other in Kamieniec.[177]

The Koordynacja established a policy of not leaving the children in Poland. Since legal emigration to Palestine was not possible at the time and there was no wish to endanger the children by using clandestine immigration routes, they were removed from Poland group by group and transferred to children's homes in Germany and France. Chasia set out with the first group, in July 1946, and was replaced at the children's home by Mordechai Benczuk, also of Hashomer Hatza'ir.[178] The Koordynacja operated intensively from 1946 to the middle of 1947 but its children's homes closed down progressively as the possibility of receiving new children diminished. By 1948, only the home in Łódź was still open.[179]

In late 1946, in the midst of the Koordynacja's operations, Goldberg left Poland for Germany. His move was preceded by ideological disagreements between him and his comrades in view of his resignation in July from the Dror movement and his participation in the establishment of the Noah (*Noar*

---

174 Shner-Neshamit, notes on Sarid's testimony; idem, *I Did Not Come to Rest*, pp. 191–192; Koryski, "The Zionist Koordynacja for the Redemption of Jewish Children in Poland," p. 31.

175 Ibid.; Bielicki-Bornstein, "Back to the Bosom of Their People," p. 319; interview by author with Chasia Bielicki-Bornstein.

176 Entries in Chasia Bielicki-Bornstein's personal notebook; given to me by Bielicki-Bornstein and in my possession.

177 Shner-Neshamit, *I Did Not Come to Rest*, p. 199; testimony Leibl Koryski, OHD 15(68).

178 Interview by author with Chasia Bielicki-Bornstein.

179 List of children's homes, October 14, 1948; JDC report on children's homes in Poland from September 1948. According to this report, there were thirty-six children in the Koordynacja's children's home at the time.

Halutzi, Pioneering Youth) movement.[180] During his first few months with the Koordynacja, he had acted vigorously to institutionalize the organization, reinforce its status, and obtain funds for its operations. Once he moved to Silesia with his colleagues, however, his relationship with the organization weakened steadily.[181] After he left, Abraham Berensohn, an emissary from Palestine and a member of Kibbutz Kfar Giladi, was named head of the Koordynacja, and Shaike Zszukowski, a member of Kibbutz Galil Yam, and Menahem Kunda, the Ichud Party delegate to the Koordynacja, served with him on the presidium. The appointment of an emissary from Palestine as Goldberg's successor was evidently based on the belief that the organization was part of a system that would develop relations with Palestine — Eretz Israel. From the standpoint of the local operatives, this gave the Koordynacja a degree of respect and connection with the Zionist movements in Palestine.[182] It also established a continuity of sorts; after all, the initiative for the establishment of the Koordynacja had come originally from an emissary from Palestine and not from local members.

The Koordynacja office in Łódź maintained a card catalogue with personal details on each child and his or her removal.[183] Some of the cards lacked many details; others contained errors due to vague information or confusion between the child's birth name and the false name that had been used during the war. This problem was especially acute with regard to children who were too young to furnish details about themselves and whose rescuers were no better informed.[184]

In November 1946, the Koordynacja issued the sole edition of a newspaper called *Farn Yiddishn Kind* ("For the Jewish Child"), in order to publi-

---

180 *Mission to the Diaspora,* pp. 80–81; interview Bar-Gil with Arieh Sarid. Afterwards, the movement was named Noham (*No'ar Halutzi Meuhad,* United Pioneering Youth). In an interview with Bar-Gil, Goldberg (Sarid) told his side of the departure story, claiming that he had been forced to leave because during one of his visits to the Polonia Hotel in Warsaw, where he received guests from abroad and where the Polish Security Police (*Ugrad Bezpieczenstwa*) were active, he had heard that people were talking about him. Since his documents were not in order, he felt that he might be in danger and decided to leave.
181 Shner-Neshamit, remarks about testimony of Arieh Sarid.
182 Interview by author with Menahem Kunda, a member of the Koordynacja presidium from spring 1946 to the end of December 1947, July 1997.
183 Shner-Neshamit, *I Did Not Come to Rest,* p. 209; Koordynacja card catalogue of children.
184 Catalogue card of Lucia Woleniak, given to me by its owner, Iko (Leah) Simhai of Kibbutz Hagoshrim. Only recently did Simhai discover that her birth name was Rachel Wolisz; catalogue card of Irena Dombrowska, given to me by its owner, Erella Hilferding-Goldschmidt of Shadmot Devora. Her correct name, Irena Wajnrat, was discovered recently. Source of cards: GFHA, catalogue of Koordynacja children.

cize its activities in Jewish centers across Poland and, by so doing, to obtain support, assistance, and new information. The articles in the paper carried headlines such as "All Jewish Children Should Return to Their People," "This Is How We Began," "These Are Our Children: Facts, Episodes, Pictures;" and "One Story among Many." The paper also published pictures and capsule stories as well as a list of children in the Koordynacja's children's homes.[185]

Some removal operatives were recruited by members of the Koordynacja; others enlisted at their own initiative. If they were to carry out their mission loyally and use all methods of persuasion and pressures to attain the goal, they had to believe in the justice of the cause. They were given no training in how to operate but the general intent was obvious and each operative followed the dictates of his or her personality and nature. At one point, there was an attempt to recruit a Christian Polish woman as a removal operative. However, even though in theory she understood the nature of the task and was willing to undertake it, her perseverance flagged; and after removing two children she refused to continue.[186] This may point to the sine qua non of belief in the need to remove the children from non-Jews' homes; that is, those who lacked this belief could not do the job successfully. None of the operatives worked throughout the entire history of the Koordynacja — some left Poland when they themselves obtained emigration visas and others did so when they felt the ground burning under their feet.[187] Either way, it was hard to operate for a lengthy period of time because their actions were sometimes dangerous and caused emotional burnout, making it necessary to recruit new operatives from time to time.[188] Usually, the permanent operatives, those who worked for some time, were paid a monthly salary apart from the reimbursement of

185 Neshamit, "The Koordynacja for the Redemption of Children in Liberated Poland," p. 123; *Farn Yiddishn Kind* — the newspaper consisted of eight pages; testimony Leibl Koryski, OHD 15(68). Koryski said that the list also contained names of children who had come from Russia. Sarah Shner-Neshamit terms the list "the list of the redeemed." See Shner-Neshamit, remarks about testimony of Arieh Sarid. Actually, the concept of "redeemed" children is used inclusively here, not referring only to those removed from the homes of non-Jews.

186 Interview by author with Menahem Kunda.

187 Interview by author with Yosef Haezrahi-Bürger, November 1993. Bürger worked for the Security Police and, concurrently, as a removal agent for the Koordynacja; interview by author with Yehuda Bronstein, May 1997; Fleiszer, "The Rescue of 24 Children," pp. 300–304.

188 Interviews by author with Yosef Haezrahi-Bürger and Yehuda Bronstein; Fleiszer, "The Rescue of 24 Children," pp. 300–304; testimony Yehuda Bronstein, OHD 25(68); interview by author with David Plonski, 1996.

their expenses — unlike operatives who set out on nonrecurrent tasks.[189] The operatives were equipped with a letter of appointment from the Koordynacja, confirming that their bearers were acting on their behalf.[190] To make their operations look official, after each mission the agents would provide the secretariat with an up-to-date report about the operation and its results.[191]

Due to the reputation that the Koordynacja acquired by virtue of its perseverance, various bodies as well as relatives turned to it. Success, however, was not assured, and in the case of operations which did not produce the desired results, the Koordynacja asked the Central Committee for assistance in turning to the courts.[192] Notably however, and contrary to its image, whenever the complexity of a given issue seemed to compromise the existence of the organization, the Koordynacja suspended negotiations.[193] Even then, it did not abandon the case altogether, but kept lists of these children so that further attempts to establish contact and remove them could be made. The lists were forwarded to the Youth Aliyah office in Poland so that action could be made to locate the children's families.[194] Due to the reputation that the

189 Interview by author with Menahem Kunda; testimony Leibl Koryski, OHD 15(68).
190 Letter of appointment confirming that Akiva Gerszater is a Koordynacja operative, GFHA, Correspondence File, 788–790; testimony Devorah Zilber, OHD 27(68); Neshamit, "The Koordynacja for the Redemption of Children in Liberated Poland," pp. 143–144.
191 Working report by Teofilia Goldman, GFHA, Correspondence File, 788–790; testimony Devorah Zilber, OHD 27(68); Neshamit, "The Koordynacja for the Redemption of Children in Liberated Poland," pp. 143–144.
192 Letter Bein, Poland, December 18, 1947, to Koordynacja, Ichud, and Hehalutz, Łódź, JDC, microfilm from Poland; Dekel, *Remnants of the Sword*, pp. 645–651; Neshamit, "The Koordynacja for the Redemption of Children in Liberated Poland," pp. 124–125; testimony Devorah Zilber, OHD 27(68); letter Hirsch Isaac Kurc, Melbourne, Australia, to Koordynacja in Łódź, September 28, 1947, in the matter of R.D. GFHA, Correspondence File, 788–790; letter Koordynacja Secretariat, Łódź, to JDC-Warsaw, May 12, 1947, in response to letter May 6, 1947, JDC, microfilm from Poland; testimony of Leibl Koryski, OHD 15(68); minutes of Kolbuszowa municipal court, Mark P3345, September 12, 1946, concerning an agreement concluded in Niepołomice municipal court, in the matter of Maria Anna Sknydlewski, R.K. GFHA, Correspondence File, 788–790; decision of Tarnów district court, File OP16/46 (Icz361/46), in the matter of C.Z. and S.Z., known as Hubel, February 24, 1947, ibid.; appeal at decision of Nowa Ruda court, submitted by Helena Fuchsberg to the court in Kłodzko, case mOP1/46, May 5, 1948, in the matter of L.F., who also appears as Jacques Grzegorczyk, GFHA, Correspondence File, 788–790; decision of Łódź municipal court, File 37/46, in the matter of E.R.
193 *Mission to the Diaspora*, p. 89; testimony Yehuda Bronstein, OHD 25(68).
194 Lists of children who remained in non-Jewish homes and should be removed, GFHA, Correspondence File, 788–790; Kaplinski report, December 2, 1947. The list also contains the addresses of Poles with whom children of vague identity were staying. Most of these children were aged 6–12; two were aged 20; testimony Leibl Koryski, OHD 15(68).

organization had acquired as a body with an interest in Jewish children, more than once relatives and strangers exploited it for their personal needs.[195]

When the removal activities began, operatives who set out on missions received a sum of money to cover their expenses. A report submitted by one of these operatives itemizes the expenses as follows: "Our entire group reached the informant's home, where I paid the son of Jagiello [a peasant who had sheltered a child during the war] 100,000 zlotys. I gave the informant 10,000 guilders for her participation in the operation and paid the acting Chief of Police 5,000 guilders for cooperating and watching over the boys as far as Łódź."[196]

The Koordynacja was not always satisfied with the uses that removal operatives made of the money with which they had been provided. The main problem was the Koordynacja's financial problems and its concern that uncontrolled spending might thwart the removal of additional children. The Koordynacja leaders viewed matters from a wide perspective and lacked details about the minutiae of the situation facing the operative. Marysia described a case in which she removed a child but gave his mother, who remained with the rescuer, 5,000 zlotys in order to delude the rescuer into thinking that she would continue to stay with him. When she returned to Łódź and reported this, "They got angry about the money that I'd given, but I explained that otherwise there would be neither mother nor child. They understood. Ultimately they always understood."[197]

Later on, the method changed; operatives had to bring rescuers in person to the Koordynacja offices in order to hand over the child and receive the payment. There was an advantage in escorting the rescuers: it made the trip

195 Shner-Neshamit, *I Did Not Come to Rest*, p. 201. A man visited the Koordynacja offices together with a child, identified himself as a relative of the boy, and asked for money in order to pay his rescuer for having taken care of him. Later on, he placed the boy in the children's home of the Koordynacja. After the youngster was taken to Germany, it was discovered that his mother (who was privy to the secret) demanded his return; in another case, the Koordynacja secretariat told about a Polish child who had fled from a Polish orphanage and informed an acquaintance that the Jews were paying for children. Then, as part of a plan that the two had concocted, the acquaintance "delivered" the boy to the Koordynacja and was paid for having "rescued" him. Only afterwards, when a suspicion arose that the boy was not Jewish, was he was handed over to the Polish Red Cross. See testimony Genia Düstenfeld.

196 Neshamit, pp. 143–144. The operative's report, dated February 2, 1947, states that the boys left the peasant's home where they had stayed during the war and moved in with another peasant. After they were taken to Łódź, they fled back to the village.

197 Testimony Devorah Zilber, OHD 27(68). The intention was to remove the child first, afterwards the mother would leave on her own.

easier for the children, who often refused to leave with the operatives, and it separated the operation from the children's and the rescuer's surroundings.[198] When this could not be done, rescuers were forced to sign, in the presence of witnesses, a document confirming the voluntary and uncoerced surrender of the child and the receipt of payment. At the bottom of the document, a legal-sounding clause appeared, such as the following: "We hereby state that we shall present no further financial, moral, and legal claims on account of the rescue, education, care, and board of the Jewish child. We have no such claims and will have none in the future."[199] Changes in modus operandi were usually prompted by incidents and occurrences during operations and constituted attempts to respond to and plug possible breaches. However, some rescuers turned to the courts and demanded the return of the children on the basis of various arguments even after they had signed the certification.[200]

The sum of money that the Koordynacja paid for the removal of a child varied with circumstances and the demands of the rescuer. The Koordynacja reports show that the level of payment changed perceptibly during 1946, the first year of activity, from 15,000 zlotys on average at the beginning of the operations to around 50,000 zlotys by year's end. The average payout climbed to 100,000 zlotys in early 1947 and surpassed 200,000 zlotys by the middle of that year.[201] In a report from the Koordynacja to JDC, not before 1948, most of the sums were in the region of 100,000 zlotys but amounts of 200,000 and 300,000 zlotys were also paid. A million zlotys was paid for one girl and 1,952,000 zlotys for another.[202] During the Koordynacja's years of activity, it made no decision about the level of payment that would be made for a child[203] and insisted vehemently that no child would be left with rescuers because of the payment requested. In practice, however, negotiations were sometimes

198 Testimony Yehuda Bronstein, OHD 25(68); testimony Genia Düstenfeld; nevertheless, children were sometimes taken from rescuers' homes even after the policy change. See certification given by Bronstein to Natalia Roztropowicz, October 11, 1948, ŻIH, documents with interim marking, May 23, 1998, RSLF.
199 Statement signed by Michelina Smolczyńska and Władysława Polubińska, September 25, 1948, GFHA, Correspondence File, 788–790.
200 Decision of Łódź municipal court, File 37/46, in the matter of E.R.
201 Koordynacja income and expenditure report to Jewish Agency Rescue Committee, March 1946–August 1947, CZA, S26/1424.
202 Report Koordynacja to JDC-Poland, JDC, microfilm from Poland. The report carries the names of thirty-four children. It was probably not written before the second half of 1948, since it includes the names of M.S. and S.S., who were removed at that time after lengthy negotiations.
203 Interview by author with Menahem Kunda.

broken off after rescuers demanded a sum that the Koordynacja could not then afford.[204]

Considerable sums of money were expended on related expenses such as travel, gifts and bribes; these claimed a large portion of the Koordynacja's budget. In 1946, for example, 239 children were removed at a total expenditure of 4,491,000 zlotys, including 1,455,500 zlotys in related expenses. By August 1947, seventy additional children had been removed for a total of 9,028,500 zlotys, including 1,989,600 zlotys in related expenses.[205] Thus, the related expenses for the removal of children escalated over time and became disproportionately inflated.

As early as January 1946, Goldberg cabled to Palestine with an urgent request for financial aid: "800 children living with non-Jews. Immediate danger of *shmad*. Must establish child-redemption fund. Send immediately advance of 10,000 *stefans* [dollars], otherwise [will be too] late."[206] The urgency expressed in this request was typical of subsequent requests as well; throughout its term of activity the Koordynacja was pervaded by a sense of opportunities being lost for lack of funds. The rumors that swept Poland regarding world Jewish support for survivors encouraged rescuers to raise their financial demands. However, the belief that the unification of the movements under the Koordynacja umbrella would inspire Jewish bodies and institutions, both in the Diaspora and in Palestine, to allocate large sums of money for child-removal operations did not fully come about. Goldberg believes that in January–May 1946[207] the Koordynacja had no more than $10,000 available — half from Segal and half from donations — with a market value of 4,000,000–5,000,000 zlotys. In February–March, after around 100 children had been removed, funds ran out. Goldberg claims that his requests to the Jewish Agency

---

204 Testimony Yehuda Bronstein, OHD 25(68).
205 Koordynacja expenditure report.
206 Cable Ben Asher, Hadash, Zivia, written by Goldberg, to Golda Meyerson (Meir) at the Histadrut (General Federation of Jewish Labor in Palestine), Tel Aviv, CZA, S26/1317. The date marked on the cable as the date of reception — January 13, 1945 — does not stand to reason because the Koordynacja was not established until about a year later. The cable was probably received in January 1946; see also *Mission to the Diaspora*, pp. 91–92.
207 Officially, the Koordynacja was established in late March 1946. When Goldberg speaks about the organization's activities, he includes the period preceding its official establishment. At that time, removed children were transferred to the Dror children's collective in Bytom. In a letter to the Jewish Agency Rescue Committee in Paris, members of the Koordynacja presidium described the organization's activities and stated that it had been set up in April 1946. See letter Koordynacja presidium to Jewish Agency Rescue Committee, August 10, 1947, Paris, CZA, S26/1424.

and the Histadrut executive were not honored, and in the meantime the organization borrowed a modest sum of money from various Jews in Poland. In
March, Dobkin sent $15,000 on behalf of the Jewish Agency. Although most
of this allocation was used to repay debts, it also sufficed for the continuation
of the work. In late July, Segal sent another $10,000, as he had promised when
on a visit to Poland.[208] Goldberg's remarks on different occasions contradict
each other as to the sums available to the Koordynacja in the first half year
of activity.[209] The reason may be based not on the facts but on his frustration
about the many possibilities for action that existed but could not be acted
upon due to lack of funds.

According to the Koordynacja income statement for 1946, $8,000 was
received from Segal at the beginning of the operations[210] and $10,000 and
$2,000 in September, bringing Segal's contribution to $20,000. Various Jews
donated $14,000 in April–August and the Hashomer Hatza'ir emissary from
Palestine delivered $2,000 in April. From June to December, JDC forwarded
8,940,200 zlotys ($23,300) for the upkeep of children's homes and the
removal of children, and in December a Mrs. Epstein handed over $3,750
from the Hadassah Women's Organization.[211]

After receiving Segal's first sum, the Koordynacja expected a strong flow
of donations and the formalization of support as activities got under way.
However, the inflow to the Koordynacja's exchequer proved to be irregular.
Long-term planning of operations could not be performed based on abstract
and uncertain sums that might or might not reach the organization's coffers.[212]
Frustration increased as it became clear that the operations entailed a much
larger financial investment than was available. Everyone who knew about the
Koordynacja's activities acknowledged the direct connection between its abil-
ity to act and the means at its disposal. Moshe Kolodny (Kol), visiting Poland

208 *Mission to the Diaspora*, pp. 91–92; in his article "Remarks about the Koordynacja," p. 21,
    Goldberg wrote that the organization was not short of funds at the time, and $35,000–
    $40,000 was collected, in addition to funds from the general budget and the clothing re-
    ceived from JDC; see also Engel, *Between Liberation and Escape*, p. 118.
209 See Sarid's comments in *Mission to the Diaspora*, p. 91; letter Leibl (judging by the con-
    tents — Leibl Goldberg) to Hans Beit, Youth Aliyah-Warsaw, July 18, 1946, CZA, L58/
    595.
210 In contrast to the sum of $5,000 that Sarid mentioned in interviews and in written
    sources. See interview by author with Arieh Sarid; Bar-Gil interview with Arieh Sarid;
    Mission to the Diaspora, p. 85.
211 Koordynacja income and expenditure report, March 1946–October 1947.
212 *Mission to the Diaspora*, p. 92.

in the spring of 1946, published an article on his return to Palestine entitled "Children in Captivity," in which he explained what the Koordynacja was doing to redeem children and the special fund that was earmarked for the purpose. An excerpt follows:

> The Christians must be paid for having kept and supported the children during the war. The fund needs additional money *with the greatest urgency* [emphasis in the original]. Often during my month in Poland, Christian women who had come to offer up Jewish children stayed at my hotel. Each child is a shocking chapter in life...[213]

Although articles such as this had some influence, they were unable to elicit the strong inflow of funds for which the Koordynacja had hoped.

In the first half of 1946, the activists believed that it was a propitious time for the removal of children. The Polish government was busy fighting right-wing forces in the country that were attempting to overthrow it and tended to overlook deviations from official policy where Jews were concerned. Much of the Polish population believed that the Jews wielded power and influence over the regime — and many rescuers were afraid that they would not be allowed to keep the Jewish children who were in their custody. Thus, the activists assumed that for a decent consideration children could be removed without special difficulties. At that time, too, copious information about children in various places across Poland was being received.[214]

In late 1946, Kunda complained that operations were becoming increasingly difficult and dangerous. Furthermore, "Christians who came to their senses have decided to speculate in Jewish children, and the more time passes, the more money they demand. Working under these conditions is becoming more difficult with each passing day." The letter ended with an urgent request: "Every opportunity that we lose because of money will never recur." To illustrate the urgency of the matter, a list of children awaiting removal was attached to the letter.[215]

Amid the efforts to recruit organizations that might help the Koordynacja with funding, on August 8. 1946, Goldberg took part in a meeting of the Youth Aliyah staff in Poland and proposed to merge the Koordynacja with Youth Aliyah. "In our times," he argued, "there is no room for two institutions

---

213 Kolodny, "Captive Children."
214 *Mission to the Diaspora*, pp. 91–92.
215 Letter Koordynacja presidium to Bein, director of JDC-Poland, November 15, 1946, JDC, microfilm from Poland.

that operate in the same field and that draw on the same financial sources."[216] Four days later, Kaplinski, director of Youth Aliyah-Poland, reported this idea to Youth Aliyah headquarters in Geneva and asked for its officials' opinion about a merger.[217] Akiva Lewinsky, head of Youth Aliyah-Europe, responded disapprovingly: "Youth Aliyah has no available funds for operations in the Diaspora and I do not know where to raise them."[218] After it became clear that Youth Aliyah had no budget for child-removal operations and that the merger would not benefit the financial situation as was hoped, the idea was discarded.

The Koordynacja's financial situation worsened even more in 1947. In August, it informed the Jewish Agency Rescue Committee in Paris that many children remained who could be removed; negotiations were taking place for 200 of them and many others were waiting. However,

> We have totally exhausted our financial resources and due to the constraints we are now forced to cut back on the holy labors. It is hard for us to accept the idea that Jewish children will not be able to return to their people because of financial limitations. It was certainly the final goal of their parents, who died in the sanctification of God's name, that their children should return to Judaism.[219]

The Rescue Committee may not have been well informed about how the child-removal operations were being conducted and which organizations were active and on behalf of whom. Even though the Koordynacja had been operating for more than a year, it was told in response to its request that there would be an inquiry about the value of its activities in regard to children, by comparison to that of the Ichud party (which the Rescue Committee had been financing until then) and that the findings would determine sub-

216 Copy of minutes from Youth Aliyah High Committee meeting, August 8, 1946, CZA, L58/595; see also testimony Baruch Kaplinski, OHD 21(68); in regard to Youth Aliyah's activities in Poland, see Shlomo Bar-Gil, *Looking for a Home, Finding a Homeland: Youth Aliyah in Educating and Rehabilitating Holocaust Survivors, 1945–1955* (Jerusalem: Yad Yitzhak Ben-Zvi, 1999, Hebrew), pp. 47–81. Bar-Gil's study is very important for understanding the activities of Youth Aliyah. However, since it does not focus on the activities of the Jewish organizations engaged in removing children from rescuers' homes, his presentation of these organizations is marked with inaccuracies and non-factual information.
217 Letter Kaplinski, Youth Aliyah Poland, to Youth Aliyah Geneva, August 12, 1946, CZA, L58/595.
218 Letter Akiva Lewinsky to Goldberg, August 18, 1946, ibid.
219 Letter Koordynacja presidium, Abraham Berensohn, Shaike Zszukowski, and Menahem Kunda, to Jewish Agency Rescue Committee, Paris, August 10, 1947, CZA, S26/1424.

sequent actions. However, the letter from the Koordynacja had some effect: the organization received 5,000 Palestine pounds until the matter could be investigated.[220]

The cooperation agreement among the constituent movements of the Koordynacja did not require them to take part in its financing. The founders of the Koordynacja believed that their cause would capture the hearts of sympathetic Jews and that funding would not be lacking. In practice, however, the leaders of the organization had to make strenuous efforts to find sources of funds. After Goldberg left, Koryski took over responsibility for fund-raising. As the activities wound down in spring 1948, Krybus assumed this role[221] with assistance from members of the presidium. Throughout its years of activity, the Koordynacja never enjoyed a sense of economic well-being. Nevertheless, it remained active in removing children and running the children's homes.

From 1947 onward, Jewish communist opposition and government pressure against the Zionist youth movements was felt more intensively; and the Koordynacja also suffered from it.[222] The organization came under the watchful eye of the Security Police (*Urząd Bezpieczeństwa* — UB), and Jewish and non-Jewish communists paid inspection visits to the children's homes and the offices of the organization. Fewer new addresses of Jewish children made their way to the Koordynacja and even where information existed, the operatives found it difficult to act as they had before and had to make greater efforts to pursue the cases that were being dealt with. Since most Zionist staff members had left the district committees, information that had previously been forwarded via these workers was now also withheld.[223] Nevertheless, in certain cases the Koordynacja and the Central Committee did cooperate, the

---

220 Jewish Agency Rescue Committee budget report, from Gruenbaum, Sheffer, and Barlas, May 4, 1947, CZA, S26/1410.

221 Testimony Pinhas Krybus, OHD 45(68).

222 Ibid.; Shner-Neshamit, *I Did Not Come to Rest*, p. 210; testimony Leibl Koryski, OHD 15(68); Sarid, *Ruin and Deliverance*, pp. 421–424, 433–434; contrary to the opinion of the activists that the pressure was already perceptible in 1947, Gutman claims that the turning point in the government's attitude took place in late 1949. See Gutman, *Jews in Poland*, p. 90. Shlomi presents the same argument. See Shlomi, "Initial Organization," p. 546. The disagreements may trace to different perspectives: the scholars analyzed the information from an overview on the authorities and their actions vis-à-vis Jewish issues at large, while in the field various local individuals and interested parties were applying pressure.

223 Testimony Leibl Koryski, OHD 15(68) and Pinhas Krybus, OHD 45(68).

local committee using operatives of the Koordynacja[224] and the Koordynacja using the legal department of the Central Committee.

In late 1947, Sarah Dusznicka-Shner and Menahem Kunda, two of the founders of the Koordynacja, left Poland. Fearing that the authorities would search the offices and seize documentary material, it was decided to exploit the departure of the members from Poland by moving the documentary material to Palestine. The material was divided up among three emigrants but, for various reasons related to the hardships of the trip, only two-thirds of it reached its destination.[225]

When the authorities realized that their inspection visits and warnings were not bringing the activity to an end, officials of the security police visited the Koordynacja office in March 1948 and arrested Koryski. The investigation focused on the way children were leaving Poland. They ordered Koryski to admit in writing that the children were being removed illegally, even though by then they were leaving on official passports. After his release, Koryski also left Poland.[226]

After Koryski's departure, the organization carried on with a reduced staff composed largely of members of Ichud. Among the members of this vestigial staff, only Krybus had been with the Koordynacja from the beginning until the end. Gerszater continued to work as a removal operative and Yehuda Bronstein was recruited for this purpose in summer 1948. During his eight months of activity, Bronstein managed to remove only seven chil-

---

224 Letter Warsaw Committee to Central Committee, April 25, 1947, in the matter of K.F., ŻIH, Education Department, File 638. A Koordynacja operative visited the rescuer's home and submitted a report to the Central Committee Education Department about the family's situation; see testimony Sabina Halperin, MA, A.201: a representative of the Central Committee visited the girl regularly in an attempt to persuade her to leave the family but she refused. Eventually, she was removed by an operative of the Koordynacja.

225 Sarah left Poland in December 1947. She did not work continuously for the Koordynacja during this, the second year of Koordynacja activity. Occasionally she set out on missions for her movement in Poland and elsewhere and was on pregnancy leave shortly before she left. See Shner-Neshamit, *I Did Not Come to Rest*, pp. 210, 217–219; interview by author with Sarah Shner-Neshamit.

226 Koryski, "The Zionist Koordynacja for the Redemption of Jewish Children in Poland," p. 32; testimony Leibl Koryski, OHD 15(68). In the course of his interrogation, Koryski realized that the authorities had discovered that the Koordynacja had recorded the name of a child in its children's home on a passport that had belonged to a child who had been sent out via the Bricha. Koryski worked with the Koordynacja from March 1946 to April 1948; Krybus recalls that people unknown to them began to visit and inspect the office. "Their policy was to step on [our] toes and not allow [us] to operate." See testimony Pinhas Krybus, OHD 45(68).

dren — most of whose rescuers had refused to surrender them previously. His efforts in regard to five other children did not succeed and he dropped their cases due to fear of entanglement with the legal authorities.[227]

In official and unofficial meetings with Jewish communists, Krybus was told that the efforts to remove children from non-Jewish homes had to cease and if it transpired that they were indeed removing children, they would have to surrender them to the children's homes of the Central Committee. The heads of the Koordynacja refused to accept the edict; they realized from the way the issues were phrased that the communists did not object to the mere removal of the children from non-Jewish homes, but rather, to the children's emigration to Palestine. In March 1949 or so, Krybus was summoned to the offices of the security police, where he was interrogated about the Koordynacja's sources of funding and its relations with foreign organizations that were helping them spirit the children out of the country. Dr. Adolf Berman of the Central Committee arranged his release from detention but there was a condition attached. Krybus was to close the organization's offices and surrender the eighteen children in the Koordynacja's custody to the children's home of the Central Committee. The directive was forwarded to representatives of the movements, who decided not to comply. The Koordynacja refused to close its offices of its own volition and suggested that the authorities close the offices themselves if they insisted on terminating its activities. Indeed, in the summer of 1949 the authorities closed down the offices of the Koordynacja, confiscated its documents, shut down the last children's home in Łódź, and transferred the children to the educational institutions of the Central Committee. Krybus spent six months in prison; by the time he was released, the

---

227 Interview by author with Yehuda Bronstein, 1997; testimony Yehuda Bronstein, OHD 25(68). Bronstein reached Łódź in 1948 after having been released from a Soviet prison and thought of this town as a way station en route to Palestine. In Łódź, Bronstein encountered David Meller of Ichud, who enlisted him for work with the Koordynacja. Gerszater, according to the secretary of the Koordynacja, was about sixty years old when he went to work full-time for the Koordynacja. Financially independent, he refused to accept a salary and received only reimbursement of travel expenses. See testimony Genia Düstenfeld.

228 Testimony Pinhas Krybus, OHD 45(68); Koryski, "The Zionist Koordynacja for the Redemption of Jewish Children in Poland," p. 32; according to the Koordynacja secretary, the Central Committee was more interested than the authorities in shutting down the Koordynacja because it opposed the removal of children to destinations abroad. According to her version of events, she was summoned to an interrogation in July 1949, and when it was over she returned to the office and placed various documents with neighbors so they would not be discovered. Five people searched the office; three from the Jewish Central

Koordynacja had ceased to exist.[228] At the time of its discontinuation, the organization still had a list of children whom it had not managed to remove.[229]

Despite the economic hardships, the largest number of removals was accomplished in 1946, since at that time, many children were available for removal and it was easier to negotiate with rescuers. In fact, most of the children about whom the Koordynacja had information were removed that year.[230] In August 1947, the Jewish Agency Rescue Committee in Paris was informed that 230 children had been removed from the homes of non-Jews in 1946 and sixty-three others had been removed during the first half of 1947.[231] According to lists in Koryski's possession, 968 children had passed through the Koordynacja's children's homes by April 1948, and 191 of them had been reclaimed from the custody of non-Jews.[232] During the organization's remaining year of activity, additional children were removed but there were no more than twenty in all.

The various movements housed many more youngsters in their children's homes than the Koordynacja did in its homes, although we cannot know how many of these children had been removed or taken away from the homes of non-Jews or had left such homes on their own. The importance of

Committee and two from the police. The same day, they transferred the children to the children's home of the Central Committee. See testimony Genia Düstenfeld; according to Sarah Neshamit, the Koordynacja was closed down in 1948. See Shner-Neshamit, remarks about testimony of Arieh Sarid. The reason that she made this claim, it seems, is because many founding members of the Koordynacja from Dror and Hashomer Hatza'ir had already left Poland by then. Nevertheless, the organization and the children's home continued to be run by a skeleton staff composed largely of members of Ichud. As for the regime's policy toward the Jews in 1949, see Gutman, *Jews in Poland*, pp. 90–91.

229 Testimony Leibl Koryski, OHD 15(68).
230 Neshamit, "The Koordynacja for the Redemption of Children in Liberated Poland," pp. 122–123, claimed that the Koordynacja had removed about 250 children by the end of that year. The concept of "removal" was used inclusively and was not limited to children removed from non-Jewish families for payment.
231 Letter Koordynacja presidium to Jewish Agency Rescue Committee, August 10, 1947, CZA S26/1424; Koordynacja expenditure report signed by Kunda and Koryski, ibid. The report states that 239 children were removed in 1946 and 70 others by August. It seems that this number includes children who were not removed from the homes of non-Jews.
232 Koryski, "The Zionist Koordynacja for the Redemption of Jewish Children in Poland," p. 32. Of the total, 530 were repatriation children and the others, about 430 in number, were divided as follows: 191 children removed from non-Jewish custody, 164 removed from Polish children's homes; 63 who had been in ghettos; 14 who had survived in the forests with partisans or in hideouts; and six from concentration camps; in *Mission to the Diaspora* (p. 93), Goldberg stated that the Koordynacja had removed 400 children from Polish homes, convents, and institutions. Sarid in "Initial Deployment," p. 316, places the number of children who were removed from Polish homes, convents, and children's homes at 380.

the Koordynacja, however, lies in the fact that it was the only organization in Poland that had been established solely for the purpose of action regarding Jewish children. Some believed that the Koordynacja also enhanced the reputation of Zionist youth movements among Jews in Poland and elsewhere by proving that they had the ability to tackle a problem caused by the war, just as the momentum built up by the Bricha seemed to have ebbed slightly.[233]

Agudath Israel

Although the organized ultra-orthodox religious camp in post-war Poland went by the name of *Po'alei Agudath Israel* (Agudath Israel Workers — PAI), it was not politically aligned with Agudath Israel. The name was adopted for the entire ultra-orthodox movement because survivors felt that the newly-organized regime in Poland was socialist and anti-religious in outlook. By attaching the word *Po'alei* (Workers), they hoped to earn the government's acceptance of organizational efforts by orthodox Jews.[234] However, this did not happen; the government did not recognize PAI and the party operated under the patronage of the Council of Religious Communities. Nevertheless, it developed ramified illegal activities for the sustenance of religious life in Poland.[235]

In summer 1945, PAI opened its main office at 66 Zachodnia Street in Łódź, the largest Jewish center after the war. Szymon Cukier was elected chairman and Jechiel Granatstein as secretary.[236] In various towns across Poland, ultra-orthodox Jews gathered together in "kibbutzim" that the headquarters in Łódź funded.[237] Children who were found nearby or in searches instigated by members were placed in these collectives.[238] From the outset of

---

233 This was Engel's belief. See Engel, *Between Liberation and Escape*, p. 119.

234 Interview by author with Jechiel Granatstein, 1993; Jechiel Granatstein, *Days of Genesis* (Bnei Brak: Pe'er, 1997, Hebrew), p. 160.

235 Kahana, *After the Deluge*, pp. 104–105.

236 Interview by author with Jechiel Granatstein, 1993. Granatstein had arrived from the east in the late winter of 1945 as a repatriate. See Granatstein, *Days of Genesis*, pp. 133, 135, 152, 163. The Palestine PAI newspaper *She'arim*, September 13, 1945, reported about the reestablishment of the PAI movement in Poland, ibid., photocopy on p. 276; memorandum, H. Basok, A. Beker, and S. Stern, Mizrachi, Poland, to World Alliance of Torah va'Avoda, July 27, 1945, RZRI, S. 19IV.

237 Granatstein, *Days of Genesis*, p. 137; PAI established kibbutzim in Łódź, Sosnowiec, Będzin, Częstochowa, Kraków, and Tarnów. See ibid., p. 278, photocopy of article in *She'arim*, November 11, 1945.

238 Interview by author with Rina Finkelstein, May 1997.

the operations, severe financial difficulties apparently impaired the organization's ability to gather additional children. A letter sent on October 4, 1945, from PAI in Łódź to the movement in Palestine, printed in the party newspaper *She'arim*, contained the following plea: "We turn to you with a cry of alarm; help us to save our children... Were it not for a few members who have pledged themselves fully to the cause, who knows where we would be heading. So help us, and again help us — both materially and in matters relating to emigration to Palestine."[239]

Two Jewish removal operatives acted on behalf of the headquarters in Łódź: the elderly Abraham Dziadek and Leibl Zamość, a young man. PAI maintained two children's homes: one in Łódź, where most children found by Zamość were sent, and one in Bytom. Although the homes provided religious education, the children were not abruptly forced to change their previous way of life. As at the religious children's homes of the Council of Communities, children who wished to go to church on Sundays were allowed to do so, it being thought that eventually the new religious content would slowly displace behavior previously acquired.[240] The children did not remain in Poland for long and were removed from the country in groups. Although the extent of activity tapered off in 1948, both children's homes continued to operate and searches for more children continued.[241]

No written documentation about PAI operations has been preserved. According to Granatstein, the party secretary, it did not keep a systematic card catalogue with details about children who had been removed. Even if the rescuer had provided some information about a child when the youngster was removed, it was not recorded systematically. Since most of the children spent only a short time in children's homes before emigrating, some were still referred to by their wartime false names. As the years passed, the activists realized their inability to help some children search for information about their identity.[242]

---

239 Granatstein, *Days of Genesis*, p. 277, photocopy of article in *She'arim*, October 4, 1945.
240 Granatstein, *Days of Genesis*, pp. 118–125, 123; idem, *A Double Life* (Bnei Brak: Pe'er, 1991, Hebrew), pp. 11–14.
241 List of children's homes, October 14, 1948; letter Mata Planter, Youth Aliyah Paris, to Dr. Landauer, Jerusalem, December 18, 1947, ibid., L58/382; Granatstein, *Days of Genesis*, p. 129.
242 Interview by author with Granatstein, October, 1993; Granatstein, *Days of Genesis*. Granatstein relates that years after the war, while in Israel, he received inquiries from former children who now asked him for help in tracing their identities, and he was unable to help them.

The children's home in Bytom was operated by Rachel (Recha) Stern-buch of Switzerland, who represented the Rescue Committee of American Orthodox Rabbis and subsequently represented Agudath Israel on the Jewish Agency Rescue Committee.²⁴³ Sternbuch first came to Poland in early 1946 and contacted the PAI secretariat in Łódź,²⁴⁴ under the auspices of which she coordinated the first year of relief activities for Jewish survivors. In 1947, after having arranged the emigration of groups of children, she moved her activi-ties to Katowice, in southwestern Poland, closer to the Czech border, so that emigration would be easier. Sternbuch was able to tap funds that had been given to her by the Committee of Rabbis in the United States, and she spent the money at her discretion on relief operations, emigration, and the removal of children from non-Jewish custody. During her intermittent stays in Poland, Sternbuch established relations with government bodies in order to obtain legal emigration visas²⁴⁵ and concurrently organized illegal emigration.

The first residents of the children's home in Bytom were gathered up by various Agudath Israel activists. Sarah Lederman worked as a caregiver at this institution and was supposed to set out in July 1946 by train with a group of children that Rabbi Herzog had organized during his visit to Poland. At the border control, police arrested her and removed her from the train on the charge of "possessing a counterfeit passport." Lederman claimed that Stern-buch had engineered her arrest and removal from the train; furthermore, she was not the only person who carried a fake passport (which Sternbuch had given her). "Mrs. Sternbuch," she explained, "wanted the children's home to continue to operate and understood that she would be out of business if I left." Lederman returned to the children's home but not as a caregiver. She began to work as a removal operative and received addresses and funding for this purpose from Sternbuch.²⁴⁶

243 Testimony Sarah Lederman, OHD, (68)50; Joseph Fridenson and David Kranzler, eds., *Heroine of Rescue: The Incredible Story of Recha Sternbuch, who Saved Thousands from the Holocaust* (New York: Mesorah, 1984), pp. 161–164; letter Shragai to Shertok (Sharett), April 30, 1947, CZA, S25/5241; in regard to the Rescue Committee, see below, "Relations and Support among the Organizations."
244 Interview by author with Jechiel Granatstein, 1993; Warhaftig, *Refugee and Survivor*; Fridenson and Kranzler, eds., *Heroine of Rescue*, p. 163.
245 Fridenson and Kranzler, eds., *Heroine of Rescue*, pp. 160–162, 166–167. Ibid., pp. 172–173, notes that Sternbuch visited Poland in January-February. 1946, in mid and late 1946, at least three times in early 1947, and in the autumn of 1947; see also interview by author with Jechiel Granatstein, 1993.
246 Testimony Sarah Lederman, OHD 50(68). According to her testimony, she worked with-out receipts and no one knew how much she actually paid for various children; see also Warhaftig, *Refugee and Survivor*, p. 429.

Convinced that the communists should not be allowed to preside over the education of Jewish children, Lederman was prepared to operate for the Jewish Committee's children's homes as well, in an attempt to persuade children to move to the Agudath Israel (Sternbuch's) institutions. After one case in which a girl was removed from the Central Committee children's home in Bielsko-Biała, the police searched the home in Bytom and arrested Lederman. The girl was not found; Lederman insisted that she had nothing to do with the affair and was released some time later. After this, the local Jewish committee seems to have stepped up its supervision of the Agudath Israel children's home. Lederman was ordered to shut it down and move the children to a Central Committee home, on the grounds that she was not a certified caregiver. Realizing that these conditions would mean that she would not be able to continue to operate, Lederman tried to find a way to avoid handing over the children. Of the forty-five youngsters who were in the home, she placed some with families that were about to leave Poland; twenty-five youngsters who remained in the group were to slip out of Poland illegally with one of the teachers. As they waited at a hotel near the border before attempting to cross, the children aroused the suspicions of the security police and the teacher was detained. Lederman, who had come to the location to help arrange the crossing, was also arrested. Unfortunately for her, the security police had amassed a great deal of evidence about her illegal activities and she faced severe punishment. However, a Jewish friend who had been in touch with her arranged the "disappearance" of some documents in the investigation file; ultimately she was sentenced to fourteen months in prison (which she served from late 1948 to early 1950).[247]

The removal of children from the Central Committee's children's home was not a one-off event. At least in one case when children were taken out of the home in spring 1946, Sternbuch handled the entire process personally: arranging false passports, transportation, setting up the crossing point, bribing the guards, and financing the entire operation. Thus, an entire children's home of the Committee, complete with its educational staff, crossed into Slovakia. From there they continued to Prague, where local Agudath Israel operatives took over.[248]

The Agudath Israel operatives in Poland who dealt with child survivors disagreed as to whether Palestine should be regarded as a destination.

247 Testimony Sarah Lederman, OHD 50(68).
248 Küchler-Silberman, *My Hundred Children*, pp. 166–176, 186–189; Lena Küchler-Silberman, *The Hundred [Children] to Their Border* (Jerusalem and Tel Aviv: Schocken, 1969, Hebrew), p. 13

One reason for Sternbuch's involvement was to deny the Bricha organization, which moved children to Youth Aliyah institutions in Europe, a monopoly on removing children from Poland. Bricha, she maintained, brainwashed the young people with anti-religious propaganda, raised them in Zionist ideology, and prepared them spiritually for settlement in Eretz Israel. Since these ideas were contrary to her ideology, she felt it important to establish an alternative. Therefore, she recruited orthodox institutions and families in western countries that would rear the youngsters in a religious atmosphere.[249]

Rabbi Solomon Schonfeld, a British Agudath Israel emissary who delivered groups of children and adolescents from Poland to Britain, was also anti-Zionist by conviction.[250] However, Marcus Retter, a member of the rabbi's staff, claimed that the allegations about Schonfeld's rejection of Palestine as a destination due to his worldview were incorrect. Rabbi Schonfeld's reason for transferring children to Britain, Retter says, was rooted in the belief that, in view of the prevailing political situation and the British refusal to open the gates of Palestine to refugees, the rescue of the children and their departure from Poland had first priority. He considered the transfer of the children to Britain purely as an interim solution — until emigration to Palestine would become feasible.[251]

Jechiel Granatstein, secretary of Po'alei Agudath Israel in Poland, recounted that at an Agudath Israel conference held in the summer of 1946 in Antwerp, Benjamin Mintz, the Agudath Israel delegate to the Jewish Agency Rescue Committee, spoke specifically about the necessity of aliya. Granatstein elaborates:

> Benjamin Mintz had quite a war on his hands with some people from certain overseas circles who tried, albeit for humanitarian reasons, to remove children who had been redeemed from Gentiles in Europe to the United States, so that they could be adopted by ultra-orthodox families — in other words, to replant the living saplings in the countries of the Gentiles. He allowed himself neither rest nor quiet for this cause. He raised a tumult and sounded an alarm; he fought like a lion.[252]

249 Fridenson and Kranzler, eds., *Heroine of Rescue*, p. 162.
250 Meir Sompolinski, "The Anglo-Jewish Leadership: The British Government and the Holocaust," Ph.D. dissertation, Bar-Ilan University, 1977 (Hebrew), p. 1987. For Schonfeld's views on Zionism, see ibid., pp. 17–20.
251 Kranzler and Hirschler, eds., *Solomon Schonfeld*, "Marcus Retter," pp. 52–53.
252 Granatstein, *Days of Genesis*, pp. 192–193.

The stance of Agudath Israel in Poland, as articulated at the conference mentioned above, was unequivocal: Palestine should be the sole destination of those leaving the Diaspora (in this case, Poland).[253] This stance, however, was theoretical only. In practice, the Agudath Israel operatives in Poland cooperated during this time with anyone who would help them get the children out of the country, whether they were Zionists or non-Zionists: Sternbuch,[254] Rabbi Schonfeld,[255] or Youth Aliyah.[256]

Most of the regular subventions for PAI in Łódź were provided by JDC via the Council of Religious Communities. PAI received additional funding from the Rescue Committee in the United States and from the world headquarters of Agudath Israel. These sources, however, were irregular; although they helped to keep the activity going, they could not be a reliable basis for action.[257]

It is difficult to estimate the number of children removed by Agudath Israel from the custody of non-Jews. The operations undertaken by Zamość, Dziadek, and others were undocumented. Lederman claims that Sternbuch deserves credit for having removed 150 children personally but her testimony suggests that not all these children had been taken from non-Jewish homes.[258] Notably, however, Lederman did not begin to work as a removal operative until the late summer of 1946. According to the testimony of a member of Rabbi Herzog's mission, Sternbuch placed 350 Agudath Israel children aboard the "Rabbi's Children" train and delivered them to the station. Some of them must have spent the war in the homes of non-Jews.[259]

Disagreements and Rivalries among the Organizations

Each organization that acted on behalf of children in Poland knew about the activities of the others. Due to differences in their respective *Weltanschauung*, their relations often involved disagreements, mutual criticism, and rivalry.

Criticism of the Central Committee

The criticism that various organizations leveled against the Central Jewish Committee focused mainly on the issue of the children's education and their

253 Ibid., p. 201; interview by author with Rina Finkelstein.
254 Testimony Sarah Lederman, OHD 50(68).
255 Kranzler and Hirschler, eds., *Solomon Schonfeld*, pp. 48–49; letter Drucker to JDC-Warsaw, December 6, 1946, JDC, microfilm from Poland, Granatstein, *Days of Genesis*, p. 152.

future. The Zionist organizations, believing Jewish life was possible only in Palestine, regarded the attitude of the Committee — which supported staying in Poland — as a betrayal of Judaism. Some alleged that the children's homes of the Central Committee were providing anti-Zionist and anti-Jewish education that would lead to assimilation.[260] The journalist Shimon Samet, visiting Poland for the newspaper *Ha'aretz*, summed up his impressions following a talk with the heads of the Committee: "The Central Committee stalwarts really did take care of everything but they happened to forget the name of Eretz Israel and overlooked the act of settling the Land of Israel. Zionism? Perish the thought. A Jewish homeland? 'Whatever country you settle in.'"[261] A letter from a member of the Palestine mission to Poland was no less dramatic:

> In the children's home supervised? — by the Jewish committees, are they raising Jews there? I doubt it, or more correctly, I'm sure they're not! These [institutions] are controlled mainly by [Jewish] members of the PPR [the Communist Party] and the Bund, and their specific wish is to make the children into good and loyal Poles without teaching them even how to speak Yiddish.[262]

The Youth Aliyah staff also complained about the Central Committee: not only did it not cooperate with them, they alleged, it even barred them from its children's institutions.[263]

256 List of children's homes, October 14, 1948; letter Mata Planter to Dr. Landauer, December 18, 1947.
257 Letter Bein, JDC-Poland, to JDC-Paris, May 24, 1948, JDC 12B C–61.023; interview by author with Jechiel Granatstein, 1993; Granatstein, *Days of Genesis*, p. 200. The response of the leaders of world Agudath Israel in London to the announcement about the establishment of PAI in Poland appears on p. 274.
258 Testimony Sarah Lederman, OHD 50(68).
259 *The Rescue Voyage*, p. 80.
260 Internal report by Meir Schwartz, October 1946, CZA, S86/73: The report states, "The children are receiving anti-Zionist and assimilationist education there"; see also Shner-Neshamit, *I Did Not Come to Rest*, p. 190. Sarah Neshamit alleged that "The educational tendency of these institutions led to assimilation and caused the children to forget their Jewish identity."
261 Samet, *When I Came the Day After*, p. 78.
262 Letter Epstein, member of Palestine mission, to Jewish Agency, Jerusalem, May 30, 1946, CZA, S25/5262. The letter was defined as "secret."
263 Report Lewinsky, Director of Youth Aliyah Europe, February 3, 1947, CZA, L58/578; final working report by Kaplinski, Director of Youth Aliyah-Poland, October 30, 1947, ibid., L58/428; in a telephone conversation, in contrast, between Lewinsky and Kaplinski that month, the following was said: "Youth Aliyah also removes groups of the *Tsentral* [the Central Committee]." See transcript of telephone call Lewinsky to Kaplinski, February 24, 1947, Paragraph 5.

These dramatic and moving testimonies illustrate, more than anything else, the sense of ideological rivalry and loss that the Zionist personnel felt with regard to the children who were in the Central Committee's institutions. They could not accept the idea that these children would remain in Poland and would not emigrate to Eretz Israel. This sense was not exclusive to the Zionists; the Agudath Israel activists also believed, although not for Zionist reasons, that leaving the children in the hands of the Central Committee was tantamount to forfeiting their Jewish identity.[264]

The Committee actually gave the Zionists reasons to feel as they did and engaged them in both covert and overt confrontations. the operations of the Zionist movements threatened its hegemony and undermined its desire to ensure that the Jews in Poland adhere to its views.[265] The director of one of the Committee-sponsored children's homes, wishing to get the children out of Poland, was reprimanded: "Who has the right to run away from democratic Poland? Where in the world could it be better for children than here with us?"[266] A proposal to establish a tripartite committee (Central Committee, JDC, and the Jewish Agency) to deal with the emigration of children from Poland fell through due to the resistance of the Committee.[267] As it happened, as soon as Poland had been liberated, the Central Committee turned to different Jewish communities around the world and asked them to accept children from its children's homes.[268] Thus it is clear that the Committee did not consider Palestine to be the preferred destination and the propaganda and efforts of the Zionists merely sharpened the dispute.

Plans proposed by individuals considered Zionists were not accepted. Zerach Warhaftig, for example, devised a "One Thousand Plan," that is, the

---

264 Testimony Sarah Lederman, OHD 50(68).
265 Engel, *Between Liberation and Escape*, pp. 83, 117–118.
266 Küchler-Silberman, *My Hundred Children*, p. 158 in Hebrew edition.
267 Report Akiva Lewinsky, February 3, 1947, CZA, L58/578.
268 Letter Australian Minister of Immigration, Arthur Calwell, August 28, 1946; letter Immigration Department, Canberra, to Central Committee, February 24, 1946. I received both from Ita Kowalska, Poland; they originated with the ŻIH. The letter from the Minister of Immigration concerns permission to transfer 100 children to Australia; and the Immigration Department letter deals with approval of the entry of 300 children aged 7–14; testimonies of children who stayed in the Central Committee children's homes about the attempt to transfer them to other countries, see interview by author with Zwi Ksiazenicki-Harel, August 1997 — The destination was South Africa"; see also Haran, ed., *What We Remembered to Tell*, p. 38; Zahava Glaz-Wolfeiler stated in her testimony that they had wanted to move her to Mexico. In regard to emigration of Jews to Australia during these years, see Michael Blakeney, *Australia and the Jewish Refugees 1933–1948* (Sydney: Croom Helm, 1985).

transfer of 1,000 children to Sweden, and in March 1946, in coordination with Rabbi Kahana, he broached the idea to the Central Committee. The Committee rejected it outright and explained its stance by handing Warhaftig a document setting forth a previous decision, adopted in January, about a World Jewish Congress proposal to move fifty children to Finland — a decision that had been rejected on administrative grounds.[269]

During the Committee's years of activity, some of its members took action to limit or even thwart the operations of the Zionist children's homes. "They fought them," Rabbi Kahana stated,[270] and complained to the security police about illegal activity on the part of these institutions[271] so that the police would shut them down. With such tensions in the background, one may understand that even unpleasant directives that various government institutions handed to the Central Committee — for forwarding to all Jewish institutions — were seen to be directives from the Committee,[272] thereby souring relations even further. In 1948–1949, as organizations operating in Poland came under increasing official pressure and there was an inclination to force them to cease activities, Central Committee delegates (most of whom by then represented leftist parties) were involved in audits at offices and institutions and had a vested interest in closing them.[273] These actions enraged the Zionists. The war for the children's souls, however, masked a broader struggle over beliefs and views. One of the Koordynacja members explained the roots of the conflict astutely:

> When it came to the removal [of children], the committees, including their communist members, viewed the matter sympathetically because the Jews had suffered greatly and most of us had lost families. They knew it was important to get the children out, but the question, of course, was the meaning of getting them out. For the Jewish people, would it be to Palestine or Poland?[274]

269 Warhaftig, *Refugee and Survivor,* pp. 440–441.
270 Kahana, *After the Deluge,* pp. 47, 105–106; testimony Pinhas Krybus, OHD 45(68).
271 Interview by author with Yosef Haezrahi-Bürger.
272 "Civil Status for the Granting of Names," circular from Polish Ministry of Education to children's institutions in Poland, April 30, 1947 — the document originates with the ŻIH; I received it from Ita Kowalska; "Guardianship of Orphans in Children's Homes," circular from Public Administration Ministry in Warsaw to regional chairs and presidia in Warsaw and Łódź, May 27, 1947, ibid.; "Birth Certificates for Children," circular from Polish Ministry of Education to all children's institutions in Poland, July 18, 1947.
273 Testimony Düstenfeld, testimony Sarah Lederman, OHD 50(68).
274 Testimony Pinhas Krybus, OHD 45(68).

Questions of the children's education and concerns about their future led to sweeping criticism of the Central Committee's actions in general. To belittle the importance of the Committee's actions in removing children from non-Jewish homes, the Committee's rivals accused it of preferring to leave children with their rescuers. They also alleged that the children in its homes had been taken there at the initiative of Poles only and not due to actions undertaken by the Committee itself.[275] These charges, however vehemently expressed, were untrue. The testimonies of Zionist activists themselves show that, during its entire tenure, the Central Committee acted to remove children.[276]

As early as June 1945, Herszenhorn asked the Committee members to prepare for action so as to remove children from non-Jewish institutions and families. His demand encountered no ideological resistance but its implementation was impeded by the Committee's financial situation. For the same reason, Hirszenhorn's proposal to expand his staff in order to gather information about the children was defeated. During Segal and Margoshes' visit, a special session was called by the Central Committee in their honor and the topic was laid before them. When the two guests were asked about the World Jewish Congress relief programs, they said that, while the Congress was willing to finance a mechanism that would deal with Jewish children in the homes of non-Jews and to cover any related expenses, "The children belong to the Jewish community in Palestine." The Central Committee could not accept this condition.[277] Realizing that they would receive no assistance from the World Jewish Congress, the Committee officials carried on with the meager resources that were available. The Committee may not have adopted an explicit resolution about how and to what extent it would tackle the issue of the children, but practically speaking, due to the needs and the many requests that were being addressed to the Committee, with time, the Child Care Department expanded and became more active. In the field, the Zionist organizations and Jewish committees cooperated despite their disagreements.[278]

---

275 Warhaftig, *Refugee and Survivor,* pp. 428–429; testimony Yeshayahu Drucker, YVA, O.3/3249; testimony Devorah Zilber, OHD 27(68); testimony Leibl Koryski, OHD 15(68); Kahana, *After the Deluge,* pp. 54–55.

276 Testimony Yehuda Bronstein, OHD 25(68); Sarid, "Remarks about the Koordynacja" p. 17.

277 Engel, *Between Liberation and Escape,* pp. 118, 223, notes 11–14.

278 Letter Hirszenhorn, Director of Central Committee Education Department, to Lublin Committee, July 3, 1949, in the matter of I.I. ŻIH, Legal Department. Although Kahana held power of attorney, the Central Committee took care of the legal aspects; Ruling of Lublin district court, panel of judges J. Policzkiewicz (presiding), P. Gnoiński, and H. Cieślik, February 7, 1947, in the matter of J.K. (S.R.), GFHA, Correspondence File, 788–

The testimonies hardly reflect this, but they do provide elaborate descriptions about events that illustrate the tense relations that prevailed between the sides.[279]

Apart from the differences over the children's education, there was also a difference in modus operandi. The Committee's operations with regard to families that accommodated Jewish children stayed within the legal limitations. The Committee did not act to remove children at any cost, it did not impose its views on Poles who refused to surrender children, and did not "invent" relatives for children in order to get them out. This approach originated in the Committee's conviction that there was no call to remove a child who was being well looked after in the rescuer's home and was not being sought by a relative. Furthermore, as an official legal body operating under government auspices, the Central Committee was subject to the constraints of the law. In determining its modus operandi, the Committee had to consider the possibility that coercive actions against non-Jews might result in restrictions and prevent the removal of other children. Samet, the *Ha'aretz* correspondent in Poland, described the outcome of this thinking: "The Committee uses legal and practical measures to return children to Jewish homes and institutions... The operation should be done slowly and lovingly."[280] The key words were "legal and practical." All the other organizations considered this a concession of sorts and reasoned that the Committee's worldview ruled out a firm and unequivocal stance on removing children from the homes of non-Jews. The other organizations did take a clear and tough stance in this issue, but it was in theory only. In practice, they, too, sometimes allowed children to remain in non-Jewish homes — although they allowed themselves greater latitude than did the Committee.

790; working report by Teofilia Goldman; testimony Leibl Koryski, OHD 15(68). Koryski described a case in which the Central Committee represented the Koordynacja in a suit against a Polish woman who demanded the return of a child whom the Koordynacja had removed. Although it had been agreed that the child would stay at the Central Committee children's home and that the Polish woman would visit her, the girl continued to reside at the Koordynacja's children's home and was removed from Poland notwithstanding the agreement.

279 Shner-Neshamit, *I Did Not Come to Rest*, p. 205; Fleiszer, "The Rescue of 24 Children," p. 304; Neshamit, "The Koordynacja for the Redemption of Children in Liberated Poland," p. 122; testimony Sarah Lederman, OHD 50(68).
280 Samet, *When I Came the Day After*, p. 75.

The Zionist Movements and the Koordynacja, the Council of Religious Communities, and the Mizrachi Movement

When the Zionist movements discussed the establishment of the Koordynacja in early 1946, Mizrachi and the Council of Religious Communities seemed to have been left out and each side had a different reason for the exclusion. In a letter to Youth Aliyah, Goldberg noted that all the pioneering movements except for Mizrachi were participating in the Koordynacja. Mizrachi, he continued, was guided by the principle of the "indivisibility of the Jewish religion"– even though the Koordynacja made efforts to sustain the connection with the Jewish tradition in its homes. Later in the letter, Goldberg claimed, "The religious association is receiving huge sums of money from various rabbis and institutions and all our efforts to draw them into the general enterprise have been in vain."[281] In testimony given later, Goldberg said that he had opposed such a merger from the outset because he foresaw disagreements regarding the children's education and the nature of the children's homes, even though the two institutions did not disagree about the child-removal operations themselves. "My simple common sense," he said, "tells me that it is impossible to place religious and non-religious children in one institution."[282] Elsewhere, as he explained in more picturesque wording, "I knew that you can't hitch a horse and a donkey to the same cart."[283] In contrast, Sarah Neshamit claimed, "The negotiations with them fell through because some of them were non-Zionist and hostile to the Labor Movement... . The stories that are being published now, alleging that we refused to cooperate, are utterly false."[284] Even if this testimony does not indicate the phase of the negotiations to which Neshamit was referring, one may infer from it that the disagreements were the deciding issue.

Indeed, the Council of Religious Communities was not composed solely of Mizrachi members; the entire religious spectrum was represented, all sharing the conviction that the children should receive a religious education. Rabbi Kahana claimed that the Koordynacja "refused to tolerate a religious children's home under its umbrella,"[285] Drucker regarded the prospects of unifying the ranks as condemned from the outset.[286]

---

281 Letter Goldberg to Beit and Lewinsky, Youth Aliyah, April 10, 1946, CZA, L58/578.
282 Interview Bar-Gil with Arieh Sarid.
283 Interview by author with Arieh Sarid.
284 Shner-Neshamit, *I Did Not Come to Rest*, p. 191.
285 Kahana, *After the Deluge*, p. 54.
286 Testimony Yeshayahu Drucker, YVA, O.3/3249.

That being the case, cooperation was ruled out by the ideological disagreements over the question of how to educate the children. Initial feelers towards cooperation seem to have been made, but failed early on. Jewish individuals and bodies outside Poland did apply intermittent pressure, arguing that it would be easier to raise funds for the operations if they could be undertaken jointly. For them, the issue was neither ideological unanimity nor finding ways to bridge the disagreements for the common cause, but rather merely a marriage of economic convenience.[287]

The pressure did not work, at least at first, and Goldberg even used the expression "I didn't surrender" in describing the meetings.[288] To justify the lack of cooperation, albeit after the fact, Neshamit alleged that some children never made their way to Palestine: "Later I found out that some of the children who had been redeemed by organizations or people from the religious bloc did not reach Palestine at all; instead, they were put up for adoption in England and the United States."[289] By making this claim, she attempted to place all the orthodox movements within a homogeneous non-Zionist framework. Although everyone knew that ultra-orthodox groups were moving children to countries in the Diaspora, Neshamit was evidently alluding to a group of youngsters that Drucker had removed from the Council of Religious Communities children's home and that had set out with Rabbi Schonfeld to Britain. Drucker claims that these children were transported to Britain because of financial distress and that in return the Council received funding for the continuation of its activities. "The thinking was that the operation would run aground unless money could be found, and what good was information about children if we couldn't redeem them?!"[290]

After Hans Beith, director of Youth Aliyah and coordinator of Youth Aliyah emissaries in Europe, and his deputy, Akiva Lewinsky, reached Poland in early July 1946, they brokered a cooperation agreement between the Koordynacja and the Council of Religious Communities. The signatories were Goldberg on behalf of the Koordynacja, Aharon Beker on behalf of Mizrachi, Dr. Kahana on behalf of the Council of Communities, and Beit on behalf of the Jewish Agency. In the five-section agreement, it was stipulated that the

---

287 Interview by author with Arieh Sarid; see also memorandum to Youth Aliyah in Paris, CZA, L58/358, written by Youth Aliyah staff in Warsaw or by the Koordynacja. Its place in the archive file suggests that it dates from late 1947.

288 Interview Bar-Gil with Arieh Sarid.

289 Shner-Neshamit, *I Did Not Come to Rest,* p. 191.

290 Interview by author with Yeshayahu Drucker.

project of redeeming children should be conducted jointly, that the funds should be placed in a joint exchequer, that half of the children would be placed in religious institutions and the other half handed over to the Koordynacja, and that the JDC money would be apportioned: thirty-five percent to the Council of Communities and sixty-five percent to the Koordynacja. It was also stipulated that the individual movements would retain funds they had received directly from their governing institutions.[291] Despite the stipulations, the agreement was not evident in work in the field.

More than a year later, after Itzhak Gruenbaum, president of the Jewish Agency Rescue Committee, visited Poland, the Rescue Committee presidium decided to extend its patronage to the operations of the Koordynacja. In a letter to the Koordynacja, the presidium stated that the committee had decided to approve the agreement that had been concluded with Mizrachi but recommended that a similar agreement be signed with Agudath Israel. It was also decided that a representative of Agudath Israel should be appointed to the Koordynacja.[292] By implication, the agreement with Mizrachi was presented to the Rescue Committee as a valid and ongoing arrangement. After the fact, the proposed idea of concluding an agreement with Agudath Israel seems to have been unworkable; after all, the Koordynacja and Mizrachi were unable to put their cooperation agreement into effect even though both shared the Zionist ideology.

The conflicting testimonies about cooperation between the Council of Communities and the Koordynacja despite the absence of a written agreement are of interest. Koordynacja activists spoke about working relations and even about permanent — and to some extent institutionalized — cooperation with Drucker.[293] In contrast, Drucker's statements on the top-

---

291 Letter Mizrahi secretariat, Poland, to Warhaftig and Greenberg, U.S., July 9, 1946, RZRI, S. 20IV. After the agreement was concluded, the Mizrachi people forwarded it to the movement leadership for its approval. Hans Beith and Landauer served as co-directors.

292 Letter Gruenbaum and Sheffer, Jewish Agency Rescue Committee, to Koordynacja, Łódź, November 3, 1947, with copy to B. Mintz, PAI, Tel Aviv, CZA, S26/1317.

293 Memorandum to Youth Aliyah-Paris (probably at the end of 1947), CZA, L58/358. The memo states that after Gruenbaum's visit, close cooperation prevailed between the Koordynacja and Drucker, who headed the religious child-redemption project; see also testimony Leibl Koryski, OHD 15(68). Koryski claims that Drucker worked for them at some stage; see also testimony Pinhas Krybus, OHD 45(68), who mentioned "exchanges of information about addresses" and spoke about unofficial fortnightly meetings; Genia Düstenfeld, the Koordynacja secretary, said that Drucker had worked briefly for the Koordynacja but did not receive a salary. See testimony Genia Düstenfeld.

ic are vague and his interviews and testimonies contain irreconcilable differences.[294]

The differences may be accounted for, among other things, by the way matters seemed after the fact and the way each of the principals — personally or speaking on behalf of one of the bodies — was concerned as to how the matters would be viewed. The answer may lie in Drucker's own remarks: "There was no coordination at all; there was even rivalry. I must make it clear that we did not think about ideology at the day-to-day level... It was more a matter of succeeding, even personal prestige. Wherever he failed — I would succeed."[295]

Whatever cooperation may have occurred, be it under an agreement or in the field, it was not enough to affect or prevent the debate over the children's education. When Rabbi Wohlgelernter, the Mizrachi delegate to the Rescue Committee of the Orthodox Rabbis in the USA, visited Poland, he asked Goldberg to surrender to the Mizrachi institutions in Poland those children whose parents had observed Jewish tradition. Goldberg replied, sarcastically, that he was willing to do this "but the children don't remember at all how their parents behaved."[296] The Mizrachi secretariat then demanded that Youth Aliyah transfer to it children from religious families so that they could be removed from Poland and placed with religious institutions. The children in Poland, the secretariat reasoned, were staying in movement-affiliated children's homes due to the special conditions that prevailed in the country, and also:

294 Kurek-Lesik, "*Udzial Żeńkich.*" Drucker testified that he had cooperated with the Koordynacja in 1945 or 1946 — when Gruenbaum, president of the Jewish Agency Rescue Committee, came on a visit. (The Koordynacja was not yet active in 1945; Gruenbaum visited Poland in 1947 — E.N.G.). He describes this cooperation, however, as short-lived because the money that Gruenbaum had promised never materialized. In his testimony (OHD, 68[28]), Drucker claimed that an agreement had been signed under the influence of the Jewish Agency Rescue Committee because the money that the Agency transferred to Poland belonged to the Jewish people as a whole, but the agreement was never implemented. Elsewhere, Drucker stated that the cooperation took place in a late phase of the activities, by which time operating had become difficult. See Drucker, "One Man's Actions," p. 36. Drucker described the nature of relations as cooperation based on a personal relationship with Akiva Gerszater, a removal operative of the Koordynacja; at the end of the period of activity he said, they helped each other in cases where it was difficult to operate. See interview by the author with Yeshayahu Drucker; see also testimony Yeshayahu Drucker, YVA, O.3/3249; in his testimony, however, Drucker claimed that he had worked with the Koordynacja on a salaried basis during the final months (testimony Yeshayahu Drucker, OHD, 68[28]).
295 Interview by author with Yeshayahu Drucker.
296 This account was related by Goldberg (Sarid); see Sarid, "Initial Deployment," p. 309.

...because religious education was unavailable in one town or another.... Furthermore, there are plenty of children for whom nothing about their origin can be determined; therefore, they should... receive a religious education. The [mere] presence of these children in non-religious institutions does not entitle the owners of these homes (the Koordynacja or the political parties) to keep them in their institutions and deny them the possibility of religious education even after they leave Poland.[297]

The letter disregards the fact that the children in the care of the Koordynacja had actually been gathered from all over Poland irrespective of the locations of the homes or the question of whether religious education was available in one town or another. It also makes no mention of the inter-movement rivalries that had been raging during the period when the search for children had begun.

The education debate made its way to the Zionist Congress in Basel in late 1946. In a discussion about Youth Aliyah, Bezalel Birzinski, a Mizrachi delegate, brought up the issue and asked:

Does anyone have the right to deny these orphaned children the same kinds of education and content that their parents would certainly have provided them had they survived? — a thorough education in belief in the God of Israel and efforts to follow the paths of Jewish tradition?... The question is, is it moral to force children to lead non-religious lives, to rob them of their faith? Some people think that dealing with the rescue of the children also gives them a claim to the child's soul... Let them continue to be educated in the spirit that their parents would have wished.

In response, Pinchas Lubianiker (Lavon) of the Zionist Labor Movement said, "I would like Comrade Birzinski not to indulge in a contest over parents who were put to death. They were the parents of us all. We were all brought up in Jewish families and no one has a monopoly over the parents' wishes." He added that after seven years of war, and considering the way of life that the children had practiced during the war, for some it would be an act of coercion "to force them into accepting an education that they do not want."[298]

297 Letter Mizrachi and Torah va'Avoda secretariat, Poland, signed by Atlas, Beker, Gonjondzki, Drucker, and two others whose signatures are not clear, to Warhaftig and Greenberg, May 23, 1946, RZRI, S. 20IV.
298 XXII Zionist Congress, Basel, December 9–24, 1946: transcript of minutes, Zionist Organization Executive, Jerusalem (1947?), Session 23, pp. 474–476 (Hebrew).

The dispute persisted; the report of the debate in the budget and finance committee of the Congress contains a resolution to the effect that the following motion should be handed on to the executive for discussion and decision: "All orphans up to age fifteen who are in the care of Youth Aliyah should receive religious education."[299]

Mizrachi and Agudath Israel — Religious Education

Since both Mizrachi and Agudath Israel wished to provide the surviving Jewish children with a religious education, in late 1945, they decided to establish a joint entity as a branch of the Rescue Committee of the Orthodox Rabbis in the USA that would remove children from non-Jewish homes. The committee that was formed for this purpose allocated 10,000 zlotys for the rescue of each child. The new organization attracted criticism from the outset, and by the end of 1945, even before it was fully established, various voices in Mizrachi were demanding that their movement secede from the initiative.[300] Although in theory the committee continued to operate, Mizrachi officials repeatedly expressed the wish to leave[301] due to dissatisfaction with the ways in which the resources for the operations were being apportioned. Sternbuch, to whom the Rescue Committee had entrusted its money, favored the Agudath Israel officials and withheld funds from Mizrachi. Furthermore, during her visit to Poland, Sternbuch refrained from meeting with members of the Council of Religious Communities and Mizrachi. The latter complained about this to the Rescue Committee: "Tell us, our scholars and rabbis! Is this what our mentors and rabbis taught us? Is it right that the Rescue Committee in the United States has authorized Mrs. Sternbuch to give the Committee's money only to the Aguda[th Israel] people? And if this is the case, what should we do [with the kibbutzim and the children's homes]?"[302] More than two months later, as Sternbuch's approach remained the same, another letter of grievance was written on the same topic: "Rescue Committee, Mrs. Sternbuch has 'ascended the stage' again. She came here this week and surely she will again spend

---

299 Report of Budget and Finance Committee, ibid., p. 598.
300 Yehuda D., report on mission to Poland This emissary represented the Mizrachi movement on behalf of the Rescue Committee of the Orthodox Rabbis in London and the USA.
301 Letter Mizrachi and Torah va'Avoda Federation, Poland, to Warhaftig and Greenberg, May 23, 1946.
302 Letter Mizrachi secretariat, Poland, Atlas, Beker, and another unclear signature, to Rescue Committee of the American Orthodox Rabbis, February 18, 1946, RZRI, S. 20IV.

huge amounts of rescue funds on the Aguda's needs."[303] Rabbi Herzog also received complaints on this issue while in France. He convened the officials of Agudath Israel, PAI, and Mizrachi in order to find a solution,[304] but to no practical effect.

Although Mizrachi and Agudath Israel were both Orthodox, this was not enough to bridge over their ideological differences, which found expression in the debate over the future of the children. Mizrachi was a Zionist movement that collaborated with Youth Aliyah and intended to send "its" children to Palestine. Sternbuch and Schonfeld, in contrast, were interested in arranging the transfer of children to ultra-Orthodox communities in the west.[305] Notably, however, Agudath Israel was not cut of one cloth and PAI in Poland acted in a different spirit, seeking to deliver its children to Palestine. Warhaftig of Mizrachi described Sternbuch in subsequent testimony as an extreme Agudist who was hostile to national-religious education and opposed emigration to Palestine, believing that Jewish life should be rebuilt in the Diaspora. The Mizrachi members spent a great deal of time complaining about Sternbuch and her actions to the members of the Rescue Committee, insisting that the children should be taken to Palestine.[306] However, the complaints did not change the nature of her activities.

The rivalry that developed surrounding the children's intended destination spilled outside the borders of Poland. In a letter to Mizrachi, Dr. Joseph Burg and Aharon Beker complained that Sternbuch had lodged a grievance against the Zionist organizations with the French Foreign Ministry — which had forwarded her letter to the police. Sternbuch alleged that Zionist counselors at a children's home in France, had prevented her from removing children and delivering them to Belgium because they wished to take them to

---

303 Letter Moshe Jung to Mizrachi Center, Jerusalem, June 23, 1946, ibid. In a previous letter to Warhaftig and Greenberg of the Mizrachi secretariat in Poland, great anger was expressed about Sternbuch and her methods. The letter contains many cynical expressions describing her activities, such as "the famous activist," "this woman of valor," and "her astounding feats." After describing her condescending attitude, the writer requested, "Please cut this woman's hands off... ," presumably wishing to have her powers reduced. See letter Mizrachi and Torah va'Avoda secretariat to Warhaftig and Greenberg, May 23, 1946.

304 *The Rescue Voyage*, p. 30.

305 Kranzler and Hirschler, eds., *Solomon Schonfeld*. Retter, a member of Rabbi Schonfeld's team, claims that the rabbi thought it important to find an immediate place for the refugees, whereas the Zionist movements considered it more important to build the Jewish state.

306 Warhaftig, *Refugee and Survivor*, p. 443.

Palestine illegally. The police responded to this information by seeking to arrest four counselors. Burg and Beker protested this and warned that Sternbuch was "using denunciation methods to thwart emigration in any way she could."[307]

All Together and Each for Himself

The ideological and political disagreements among the organizations splintered the forces in the field, leaving the Koordynacja as the only body with which all the different ideological movements cooperated. Although there was no lack of tension among its constituents, the Koordynacja continued to operate by dint of its broad common denominator. It is to the credit of the Koordynacja that even if Ichud and the League for Labor Palestine cooperated in other matters on the agenda, they did not interfere with the work of the Koordynacja in the tracking down of Jewish children.

Each of the organizations labored strenuously in locating the children. Although all had their welfare in mind, each had a different notion as to what this entailed. But even if not stated in so many words, all of them, without exception, wanted the children for their own organization or movement and wanted the youngsters to swell their ranks.[308] For this reason, they often com-

---

307 Letter Dr. Joseph Burg and Aharon Beker to Mizrachi, June 9, 1947, YVA, P-20/8; in the prologue to his book, Grodzinski expressed his opinion about the need to separate the subjective writer from the objective material. See Joseph Grodzinski, *In the Shadow of the Holocaust; the Struggle Between Jews and Zionists in the Aftermath of World War II* (Monro, Maine: Common Courage Press, 2004), see prologue in the Hebrew edition only (Tel Aviv: Hed Artzi, 1988, Hebrew), p. 23. Nevertheless, in chapter four, which deals with the children, Grodzinski provides a one-sided portrayal of Rachel Sternbuch, describing her as a person whose concern for the children was prompted by a "national Jewish" perspective (as opposed to the "Zionist Jewish" outlook). See ibid., pp. 82–86. Without belittling her contribution to the cause of the child survivors, one should bear in mind that Rachel Sternbuch represented her worldview exactly as did all the other principals. Sternbuch herself was aware of the severe criticism that was being leveled against her and responded to it in the following way: "I will do as [God] wishes, and if you don't like it, you may complain about me to the Rescue Committee in America." See letter Mizrachi and Torah va'Avoda secretariat, Poland, to Warhaftig and Greenberg, May 23, 1946.

308 Thus Yishai states in a report to the Jewish Agency, "Young people who have no place anywhere else go to the Central Committee institutions — and that's a long way from being ours. [The Central Committee] is fighting us in invisible ways." See Engel, *Between Liberation and Escape*, p. 111; on the way the Central Committee fought the Zionist movements in order to thwart the removal of children from Poland, see Gutman, *Jews in Poland*, pp. 54–59; in a letter to the World Alliance of Torah va'Avoda, Gonjondzki, from the Kraków branch of the Mizrachi Movement, wrote about children from their branch who had de-

peted for the same children and did not hesitate to act even when they knew that another organization was handling the same case. Each organization's belief in the correctness of its way caused it to rule out all other ways so vehemently as to create a free-for-all anarchic situation. One Mizrachi emissary reported a case in which a member of his movement had worked out a "redemption" sum with a Polish rescuer but "when Agudath Israel got word of it, they immediately offered the Gentile twice as much and took the child away." The emissary added, "This is an example of how Aguda[th Israel] works.... It's a great pity about those fine young people who will be lost to ultra-orthodoxy unless we transfer them to ourselves." Later, the emissary expressed another concern: "the danger is that they will fall into the hands of the secularists."[309] Moshe Yishai, a Jewish Agency emissary, reported the following:

> A scandal is brewing in this matter of taking children out of non-Jewish homes. An agent named Wohlgelernter, a rabbi in a little American town, came from the Rescue Committee in New York. He came and proclaimed that he pays for children in dollars. The "price" rose by a factor of four or five right away.[310]

In a letter to the directors of Youth Aliyah immediately after the Koordynacja was founded, Goldberg described how the Zionist movements were competing for children:

> We are witnessing a strange phenomenon that has never been encountered in the history of our youth projects: each youth movement sets up homes for children and youth aged 8–15, makes the little ones pledge allegiance, and pastes labels and emblems on them. We are witnessing a struggle for the children's souls.

parted on Rabbi Herzog's train, and added: "This gives us a guarantee that in the future, too, the children will be educated in our way." See letter Gonjondzki, Mizrachi and Torah va'Avoda, Poland, to World Alliance of Torah va'Avoda, Tel Aviv, September 6, 1946, RZRI, S. 20IV. The issue was not the removal of children from non-Jewish homes — an act that was perceived as their personal rescue — but rather their future and that of Judaism. As we have seen, Agudath Israel and the Mizrachi movement determined their decision-making on the basis of this issue but had no doubts about removing children from non-Jews' homes; see Dan Michman, ed., *Holocaust Historiography, A Jewish Perspective; Conceptualizations, Terminology, Approaches and Fundamental Issues* (London: Vallentine Mitchell, 2003), pp. 396; *Historiography and Interpretation* (Jerusalem: Yad Vashem, 2003).
309 Yehuda D., report on mission to Poland.
310 Report Moshe Yishai, Jewish Agency emissary, March 12, 1946, *Jewish Agency News* (June 1946, Hebrew), CZA, S25/5262.

Goldberg then asked the Jewish Agency to intervene by raising the following argument:

> Jewish children should be together in the Youth Aliyah homes of the [Jewish] Agency, and no movement has the right to apply its movement tag to a child who gets off the train or has been removed from a non-Jew... . Is the absolute fragmentation that is taking place all across Europe today [i.e., ideological fragmentation among the Zionist parties] preying on the souls of toddlers and children?... The bitter meaning of this is that the holiest rescue enterprise of all is being totally fragmented and divided up. Is it history's verdict that a child who survived from this or that city should regard his counterpart as a rival and someone to hate? Can there possibly be a division today between "our" and "their" children? Speak out![311]

If this were not enough, the various organizations did not hesitate to belittle the importance and extent of each other's operations so as to stress their own importance and success and claim primacy. Even related bodies that seemingly had no reason to do so, indulged in such conduct. For example, Drucker claimed that Mizrachi and the Council of Religious Communities should be separated because the former only maintained children's homes, but was not involved in removing children.[312] Mizrachi members, in turn, said that people acting on their behalf circulated in the villages in "mortal danger" and gathered up children with a sense of "holy labor," as Drucker presumably knew. Drucker rationalized the absence of cooperation between the Council and the Koordynacja: "Maybe... unification did not come about because the Council of Communities managed to remove the largest number of children from the goyim [non-Jews]. Therefore, it might not have been worth its while to go into the matter together with the Koordynacja."[313] Success was measured in terms of how many children each organization brought in to its own ranks. The youth movements vied with each other no less vigorously,[314]

311 Letter Goldberg to Beit and Lewinsky, April 10, 1946. The melodramatic tenor of these remarks is tendentious. Goldberg wanted his correspondents to decide that Youth Aliyah should centralize all operations under Jewish Agency patronage; if this were done, he would be heralded as the man whose initiative brought the movements together under the Koordynacja and confirmed as the official responsible for the operations.
312 Interview by author with Yeshayahu Drucker.
313 See testimony Yeshayahu Drucker, YVA, O.3/3249; according to Warhaftig, "The religious circles have been spearheading the operation with ongoing consistency." See Warhaftig, *Refugee and Survivor*, p. 419.
314 Testimony Baruch Kaplinski, OHD 21(68).

viewing the future in the same way but disagreeing on the issue of education. A memorandum from the Koordynacja to Youth Aliyah, for example, claimed that sums of money that had been sent to Poland to remove children remained in the hands of Hashomer Hatza'ir, "which doesn't have any children's homes"[315] — even though everyone knew that Hashomer Hatza'ir, like the other movements, did indeed have children's homes.

Apart from the differences in worldviews and ideologies, the scarcity of and competition for financial resources helped exacerbate the fragmentation and rivalry. In a letter to Youth Aliyah, Goldberg complained that the orthodox were obtaining huge sums of money from American rabbis.[316] Drucker, in contrast, claimed that the Jewish Agency was disbursing enormous sums to the Zionist movements but not to him.[317] The many complaints of Mizrachi against Agudath Israel were also almost all related to the money that the Rescue Committee was providing. Mizrachi accused Agudath Israel (that is, Rachel Sternbuch) of using the resources to compete with it and proposed that it "pull out of the Rescue Committee–Agudath Israel partnership and send the money directly to our movement." The people in the field felt a harsh sense of discrimination in the apportioning of funds and noted in disgust that an "overnight guest (a Mizrachi official who was visiting them) didn't notice the fraud,"[318] thereby playing into the hands of the others.

Rivalry as a By-Product

Jewish families and organizations that wished to find children sometimes sent requests to each of the organizations involved,[319] in the hope that at least one of them would succeed or that heightened pressure would bring the desired

315 Memorandum to Youth Aliyah-Paris.
316 Letter Goldberg to Beit and Lewinsky, April 10, 1946.
317 Testimony Yeshayahu Drucker, OHD 28(68).
318 Yehuda D., report on mission to Poland. The "overnight guest" who failed to notice the fraud was Warhaftig.
319 See letter Chief Rabbinate, Tel Aviv, to Rabbi Herzog, January 20, 1946, in the matter of C.H., RZA, Rescue Files. The writer also turned to the Central Committee in Poland; see letter Organization of Jews from Opoczno to Rabbi Herzog, March 31, 1946, in the matter of R., RZA, Rescue Files. Writers also petitioned Youth Aliyah; see copy of letter Kurt Grossman to Rabbi Kahana, September 8, 1949, ŻIH, Legal Department. A copy was sent to the Jewish Committee together with a request for action on its part as well; see also letter Bein to Koordynacja, August 12, 1947, JDC, microfilm from Poland; letter Drucker to JDC (in response to letter from JDC asking him to deal with several cases), Warsaw, April 17, 1947, ibid.

result. Consequently, sometimes different organizations dealt with the same cases simultaneously and competed with each other. A letter from a lawyer in Lublin who was active in one of these cases provides an indication of the difficulties this caused:

> Thus far, I have given detailed information about this matter to (1) the District Committee in Lublin, (2) JDC in Warsaw, (3) the Koordynacja for Children's Affairs in Łódź, [and] (4) a special emissary from Łódź who contacted me in March this year... Since additional organizations are always taking an interest in the matter and asking me to provide them with information, I now understand who is authorized to contact me in the matter.[320]

The tone of the letter suggests that the lawyer was exasperated by the many requests and the need to give information to all of them. In this case, the lawyer served as a gatekeeper of sorts in discussions over who was to receive a child. In other instances, however, different organizations approached the rescuers and presented them with a deluge of uncoordinated offers. Sometimes one bidder did not know about the others' existence. It also happened that an emissary who visited a rescuer to negotiate over a child found that another organization had already removed the youngster[321] and that the journey and investment in time and money were wasted.

"Stealing" Children

The criticism over education in the children's homes of the Central Committee was, as we have seen, almost the only common denominator among the Zionist and non-Zionist organizations operating in Poland. Since the differences in ideologies could not be bridged and each organization considered its path the correct one, the various organizations arrogated to themselves the right to "steal" children from the Central Committee's homes. Removal

---

320 Letter Attorney Jan Stalinski, Lublin, to Central Committee, April 10, 1949, in the matter of R. Besserman (mother of I.I.), ŻIH, Legal Department. Notably, since this case was pursued unsuccessfully for five years, the mother filed requests for aid to every possible source. It is interesting that the correspondent does not list the Council of Religious Communities as one of the principals, since the mother in Canada had conferred power of attorney on Rabbi Kahana, the chairman of the Council.
321 Letter Drucker to Rabbi Herzog, January 28, 1947, in the matter of J., RZA, Rescue Files; letter Central Committee to Jewish Congress, December 7, 1946, in the matter of S.M.G., ŻIH, Education Department, File 638.

operatives contacted children in the Committee's homes and arranged their "escape" to their own homes. They did this uninhibitedly, using all emotional, historical, and material tactics.[322] From the standpoint of the operatives, the ends justified any means.

Some children who were housed by Jewish committees testified that different organizations had contacted them and that they were able to choose between them. One girl related:

> Lots of people from the movements came and they would talk us into leaving the children's home and moving to them. A few children disappeared each time; they'd go away with somebody from the movements. One group left with somebody from Hashomer Hatza'ir. I wanted to go with them as well but they didn't want me because I was too young. There were so many emissaries that we could decide on the basis of how well we liked them. Once we almost went with someone from the orthodox. Eventually we left with someone from Dror.[323]

Sometimes the escape was arranged not by an emissary from outside but by a counselor at the children's home who belonged to one of the movements; when this happened, the counselor left together with the children.[324]

The disappearance of children from the Central Committee homes began in summer 1945 and coincided with the establishment of the movements' children's collectives. Whenever this happened, the district Jewish committees — not to mention the PPR and Bund delegates to the Central Committee — were outraged. Several meetings were called to discuss the events, protests were lodged, and practical conclusions were drawn. Nevertheless, the children continued to disappear and it was clear that they were being taken to the children's homes of the movements.[325]

---

322 Testimony Leibl Koryski, OHD 15(68); Yishai, *In the Shadow of the Holocaust*, p. 172; Neshamit, "The Koordynacja for the Redemption of Children in Liberated Poland," p. 122; Shner-Neshamit, *I Did Not Come to Rest*, p. 205; a boy was asked to form a group of friends for the purpose of running away and was told that it would not be worth his while to be raised as a Pole and distance himself from Judaism in the location where his parents had perished; Lederman, an Agudath Israel removal operative, visited children's homes of the Central Committee, introduced herself as someone representing America, and promised the children the wonders of the western world. See testimony Sarah Lederman, OHD 50(68).

323 Interview by author with Haviva Barak-Oweic, January 1996. See also testimony of Sukha Shmueli, MA, A.217; interview by author with Lucia Milch-Rosenzweig; Lidya Armoni, "Testimony," in Bornstein, ed., *Redemption of Jewish Children*, pp. 64–68.

324 Interview by author with Zvi Ksiazenicki-Harel, 1997.

325 Engel, *Between Liberation and Escape*, pp. 82–83.

In September 1946, the Kraków committee called a meeting with representatives of all the movements and organizations that were involved with the rescue of children. At the meeting, a statement from the director of one home concerning the disappearance of children from his institution was read out and the attendees were asked to decide how the phenomenon could be stopped. After a lengthy debate, they "condemned the action that had been taken and resolved not to undertake operations that clashed with their ideological principles," that is to say, the "stealing" of children. It was resolved to take steps to prevent similar incidents and "discover who was responsible."[326] One may call the resolution no more than lip-service; indeed, after it was adopted, all the officials who had voiced objections to the ways of the Central Committee continued to move groups of children to their own institutions.

A Means or an End?

The discussion thus far raises the question of whether the seemingly inevitable rivalry advanced or retarded the cause.

The operatives were of two minds. Some spoke in favor of the rivalry, describing it as an impetus and stating that it spurred them to greater efforts to remove the children.[327] Some also claimed that a comprehensive operation organized under one roof would have attracted attention and that the government could then not have refrained from intervening. Furthermore, "An organized entity cannot do things like kidnapping or grabbing; they'd have to be more solid."[328] This, in fact, is how the Central Committee behaved. By implication, the very proliferation of organizations, with its wide spectrum of operating methods, was crucial in this point of view.

Other arguments, however — some expressed by the same people — decried the competition, especially because the visits of different emissaries to one rescuer resulted in escalation of the price and inefficiency.[329] One of the

---

326 Minutes of meeting at the Kraków Committee, sent to Central Committee, September 19, 1946. In attendance: representatives of the district committee, Agudath Israel, Mizrachi, Hitahdut, Dror, Gordonia, Haoved, and Poalei Zion. Absent although invited were representatives of Ichud, Hashomer Hatza'ir, and Hehalutz. In an addendum, it was explained that the minutes would be completed as soon as the Ichud people explained their absence. See ŻIH, Education Department.

327 Shner-Neshamit, notes on Sarid's testimony.

328 Interview by author with Yeshayahu Drucker. By implication, Drucker realized that the Central Committee's limitations originated in its official status.

329 Testimony Yeshayahu Drucker, OHD 28(68); testimony Yeshayahu Drucker, YVA, O.3/3249; testimony Pinhas Krybus, OHD 45(68); see also Yehuda D., report on mission to Poland; Yishai report.

activists expressed this argument when he described the case of a girl whose removal was dealt with by different organizations: "Mrs. Goldfarb of Biały Kamień, Poland, the Jewish Committee, Ichud, Mizrachi, HIAS, and now ourselves as well. It only harms the cause to have several institutions chasing one girl."[330]

Conclusion

The differences in beliefs among the organizations engaged in removing children from non-Jewish homes in Poland seem to have been unbridgeable. One might even state that sensitivity to the interests of the children merely sharpened the disagreements, exacerbated the criticism, and created the rivalries.

All those who acted on behalf of children did so, above all, for the sake of the children or, to be more precise, for what they understood to be the best interests of the children at the time.[331] The question is whether a person could consider the basic information from other points of view, understand other ideologies, and test his or her actions in the light of different perspectives. The foregoing remarks indicate that none of the organizations did this: the individual and his or her outlooks, beliefs, and actions are indivisible. Moreover, real life is not a theoretical exercise.

The competition that took place did lead to profiteering, but also heightened the movements' efforts. Like many events in history, the rivalry had both good and bad aspects at one and the same time.

Relations and Support among the Organizations

As soon as the eastern parts of Poland were liberated, initial attempts were made to establish relations between the survivors and various Jewish organizations. In August 1944, Zommerstein, then a senior PKWN official who had the authority to deal with the needs of the Jewish survivors,[332] cabled JDC in the United States and the Jewish Agency in Palestine and asked for urgent relief for some 10,000 persons. Jewish newspapers in the United States and

---

330 Letter Kaplinski, Youth Aliyah, Poland, to Youth Aliyah, Paris, March 14, 1947, in the matter of E. and J.F., CZA, L58/748; Moshe Yishai wrote about another case in his book. See Yishai, *In the Shadow of the Holocaust*, p. 78.

331 With regard to examining these matters in view of the era in question, see Michman, *Holocaust Historiography: A Jewish Perspective*, p. 398.

332 Engel, *Between Liberation and Escape*, p. 54.

Palestine carried articles about the survivors, interviews with Zommerstein, and general information about the Central Committee that had been established in Lublin. It took some time to organize the project and the first relief shipments did not arrive until late 1944. Concurrently, JDC tried to obtain authorization to provide relief in the liberated areas, but to no avail.[333] Only in October 1945, about five months after the end of the war and three months after a national unity government had been established in Poland with Western recognition, did Dr. Josef Schwartz, director of JDC-Europe, manage to visit Poland. Schwartz entered Poland, not as a representative of JDC, but as a member of the advisory staff of Earl Harrison, the special envoy of the American President Harry S Truman who was sent to Europe to examine the state of the displaced persons in the American occupation zone. In the same visit he also visited Poland.

Once in Poland, Schwartz was given a very respectful reception. Various meetings were arranged for him and he was able to establish initial relief arrangements. However, until the end of 1945, relief was provided only in the form of goods. Such goods could not be obtained locally due to the economic situation prevailing in Poland. Moreover, the new regime was impeding the organization of free trade, and the government was laggard in establishing national-level means of production, supply, and marketing. Only in late 1945 did banking services begin to operate; until then, foreign currency could not be brought in and used legally. In July 1945, David Guzik was named director of the JDC office in Poland after having served before the war as assistant director, and Gittler-Barsky, another veteran JDC staffer, was appointed as his deputy. Schwartz visited Poland again in May 1946,[334] and he and the government concluded lengthy negotiations that gave JDC a higher exchange rate than the official one for the funds it would be bringing into Poland.[335]

JDC underwrote welfare projects and institutions in Poland while doing the same for Bricha. This approach was compatible with the outlook that had evolved among American Jews. The lessons of the war and the Holocaust had convinced the JDC leadership that it was their duty to support crucial operations even if carried out clandestinely.[336]

---

333 Gutman, *Jews in Poland*, p. 19; Litvak, "JDC's Contribution," p. 337.

334 Litvak, "JDC's Contribution," p. 338, 340–341; Engel, *Between Liberation and Escape*, pp. 85, 125; Gutman, *Jews in Poland*, p. 20.

335 Bauer, *Out of the Ashes*, p. 118.

336 Gutman, *The Jews of Poland from Liberation to Emigration*, pp. 120–121; on JDC's contribution to Aliya Bet (clandestine immigration to Palestine), see Bauer, *Out of the Ashes*, pp. 256–260.

Now that the war was over, Jewish organizations and political parties from the Yishuv could send envoys to Poland, meet with survivors and assess their needs, and establish bodies that would provide material relief and spiritual and ideological support. Among the first to visit were soldiers from the Jewish Brigade who had been serving in Europe and visited Poland at their own initiative or as part of a mission. All of them encountered child survivors during their travels and recorded their impressions.[337]

In late 1945 and early 1946, missions and delegates from Jewish communities both in the west and the Yishuv poured into Poland[338] and some encountered Jewish children who had survived the Holocaust. The operatives in Poland, as well as the visitors, considered the children supremely important and made this clear in their reports. The operatives also saw this as a way to get the visitors involved and make them ambassadors for financial support so that the relief operations could continue.[339] Akiva Lewinsky, director of the Youth Aliyah office in Europe, expressed the thinking aptly:

> We didn't understand exactly what was happening in Europe when the war ended, we wanted information, we didn't understand it yet.... Henrietta Szold told me a month before she died, "Bring the children who survived home" [to Palestine]. It seemed such an obvious thing to do but I didn't realize yet that they had to be redeemed. We didn't understand the complexity of the problem in the field, and even if we had known, we didn't grasp the significance... The first time I encountered the problem of redeeming the children was when friends from the youth movement came to me in Warsaw in Polish army uniform and told me, "We've got to redeem the children," and suddenly I understood. The realization came as a shock to the Yishuv emissaries, plus the shock over having to search for the children, and the searching was no simple matter.[340]

337 Habas, "Report from Visitors to Poland," p. 2, based on a report by Corporal Margalit; report Anton Mara; Sarid, "Initial Deployment," pp. 303–304; Yehuda D., report on mission to Poland.

338 Yehuda D., report on mission to Poland; Sarid, "Initial Deployment," pp. 307–311; Warhaftig, *Refugee and Survivor*, p. 370; Granatstein, *Days of Genesis*, p. 152; Moshe Kolodny, "Captive Children"; Yishai report; Margoshes, "How to Redeem Jewish Children in Poland," p. 7.

339 Report Anton Mara; Moshe Kolodny, "Amidst Polish Jewry [Report on a Visit to Poland]," *BaHistadrut* (June–July 1946), pp. 28–31, Massuah Archive A 36/16; idem, "Captive Children," Engel, *Between Liberation and Escape*, p. 224, n. 19; Leib Shpiesman, "New Marranos in Poland," *Der Tog*, April 7, 1946.

340 Akiva Lewinsky, "Redeemed Children as Part of Youth Aliyah," in Bornstein, ed., *Redemption of Jewish Children*, pp. 102–104.

The visits and reports had their effect. Some of the visitors, already aware of the issue of the children and the need for their rescue, had brought money for their own operations and to support the existing organizations.[341]

As mentioned, in mid-January 1946, Dr. Margoshes, editor of the American Jewish newspaper *Der Tog*, and Louis Segal, secretary-general of the National Organization of Jewish Workers, visited Poland as emissaries of the World Jewish Congress. A third member of the mission, Zerach Warhaftig, reached Poland in the middle of February.[342] The arrival of Segal and Margoshes provided the removal operations with vital assistance. The guests were given a warm welcome by government ruling circles and the Central Committee, and as emissaries of the World Jewish Congress they raised expectations that more assistance would arrive from the west.[343] Segal disbursed money that he had brought with him to the Gordonia and Dror movements, with which he had political party relations. However, he also honored the requests of Goldberg, the Koordynacja official, by giving him an initial sum of money for operations. Furthermore, as he had promised, he continued to support the Koordynacja operations even after the mission returned to the United States.[344] In 1946, the WJC formalized the operations for which the three emissaries had set out, and expanded its support to include institutions of the Central Committee and Mizrachi as well as the children's homes of the Ichud party.[345]

From late August 1945 onward, emissaries from the Jewish Agency began to fan across Europe and several headed for Poland. Upon arrival, they

341 Granatstein, *Days of Genesis*, p. 152; Sarid, "Initial Deployment," pp. 308–309; interview by author with Arieh Sarid.
342 Sarid, "Initial Deployment," p. 308; Warhaftig, *Refugee and Survivor*, pp. 365, 370, 393– 395. Warhaftig claimed that Margoshes returned to the U.S. immediately after his arrival and that Segal stayed on another two weeks or so. Warhaftig himself remained in Poland for about five weeks; Moshe Yishai, head of the Palestine office in Poland, said that Segal was the first to return to the U.S. and that Margoshes remained in Poland. Yishai wrote the following about Warhaftig's arrival: "Warhaftig was shrouded in secrecy. No one knew on whose behalf he had come to Poland. People from his party always trailed behind him. He left as suddenly as he had appeared and no one knew what he was up to." See Yishai, *In the Shadow of the Holocaust*, pp. 82–83.
343 Engel, *Between Liberation and Escape*, p. 118; Report Yishai; in regard to the World Jewish Congress, see Shmuel Frimerman, "Activities of the World Jewish Congress in 1938– 1946," MA thesis, Bar-Ilan University (Hebrew), 1995.
344 Sarid, "Initial Deployment," p. 308; idem, *Mission to the Diaspora*, pp. 91–92; Koryski, "The Zionist Koordynacja for the Redemption of Jewish Children in Poland," p. 25; testimony Leibl Koryski, OHD 15(68).
345 World Jewish Congress Report, Relief and Rehabilitation Department, Child Care Division, December 1945–October 1946, CZA, C/6.

established contact with the Zionist movements and began to help with their operations. In early January 1946, the Jewish Agency sent Moshe Yishai to inaugurate an Eretz Israel office in Poland. The first Yishuv mission arrived in March; the second one in April. Members of both missions met with Jews in various locations and consulted with members of the movements in order to assess their needs and familiarize themselves with the problems.[346]

Some of the bodies that funded actions to remove and educate children who had been staying in non-Jewish homes gave money only to organizations that were affiliated to them and shared their educational doctrine. Other organizations, however, responded to the requests of various bodies that were ideologically unrelated to them.

Most of the money that the Rescue Committee of the Orthodox Rabbis in the USA had collected and earmarked for child survivors in Europe was transferred, as we have seen, to Rachel Sternbuch, the Rescue Committee representative who visited Poland repeatedly from her home in Switzerland.[347] Even though she could have operated under the auspices of the rescue committee that had been established in Łódź, with the participation of representatives of Agudath Israel and Mizrachi, she preferred to operate on her own.[348]

Although envoys on behalf of the Rescue Committee caused the Religious Zionist people much displeasure,[349] the Council of Religious Communities, under which umbrella the Mizrachi delegates operated, also received lavish support from the Rescue Committee.[350] Rabbi Schonfeld, representing the Chief Rabbi's Religious Emergency Council in Britain, also helped the Council of Communities,[351] but at the same time, donated directly to Mizrachi[352] and Agudath Israel.[353]

---

346 Sarid, "Initial Deployment," pp. 275, 307; interview by author with Arieh Sarid; Yishai, *In the Shadow of the Holocaust*, p. 12.

347 Fridenson and Kranzler, eds., *Heroine of Rescue*, pp. 163–164, 166–167; As early as March 1945, the U.S. government allowed the Rescue Committee to transfer $937,000 to Switzerland and deposit it in a special account in the names of Sternbuch and McLilland, the agent of the "Committee for Refugees in Switzerland." See Haim Barlas, *Rescue during the Holocaust* (Tel Aviv: Ghetto Fighters' House and Hakibbutz Hameuchad, 1975, Hebrew), p. 92.

348 Fridenson and Kranzler, eds., *Heroine of Rescue*, p. 166; letter Mizrachi secretariat to Rescue Committee of the Orthodox Rabbis in USA, February 17, 1946, RZRI, S IV20.

349 Memorandum H. Besok to Hapoel Hamizrachi; Yehuda D., report on mission to Poland.

350 Kahana, *After the Deluge*, p. 54; interview by author with Yeshayahu Drucker; testimony Yeshayahu Drucker, OHD 28(68).

351 Kahana, *After the Deluge*, pp. 54, 77; testimony Yeshayahu Drucker, YVA, O.3/3249.

352 Memorandum H. Besok to Hapoel Hamizrachi, November 27, 1945, RZRI, S IV20.

353 Interview by author with Jechiel Granatstein, 1993.

When Warhaftig arrived in Poland early in 1946, he gave Mizrachi some relief by leaving them with a sum of money and continued to help them afterwards because of the rapport that had been established. Some of the money came from the Rescue Committee; the rest originated in donations that Warhaftig had received from various institutions and organizations.[354] These funds, however, did not suffice to improve the financial situation of the Mizrachi operatives for long. In April 1947, the Kraków branch of Mizrachi complained of the movement's financial woes in a letter to the director of the Youth Department of the Mizrachi World Alliance: "[. . .] Our financial condition has become much worse. First we lost 2,500 st [*stefans* — dollars] from Rabbi Wohlgelernter, who gave us checks a year ago. We received cash for them but now they haven't cleared and we have to clear them."[355] These remarks give us an idea of the financial manipulations that took place after the war.

On his second trip to Europe, Rabbi Herzog reached Poland in August 1946[356] and upon his arrival met with Rabbi Kahana, representatives of various Jewish groups, and Jewish officials in the Polish government. Then, accompanied by Rabbi Kahana, he met with Prime Minister Osóbka-Morawski, to whom he presented three demands. One of them was "to pass a law requiring the registration of Jewish children who are in non-Jewish hands."[357] The chief rabbi repeated this request in France,[358] reasoning that by so doing he would make it easier for them to locate the children. Among the three demands, however, it was precisely on this that the rabbi refrained from applying pressure "in view of the vague and unstable situation in the country, which has diminished the practical utility of passing laws in any case."[359] While in

354 Warhaftig, *Refugee and Survivor*, pp. 431–432, 349.
355 Letter Gonjondzki to M.A. Kurtz, April 1947, RZRI, S IV20.
356 *The Rescue Voyage*, p. 60; Kahana, *After the Deluge*, p. 78. Kahana writes mistakenly that Rabbi Herzog made his visit in July. Rabbi Herzog's first trip to Europe after the war began in February 1946 and focused on Italy, where he met with the Pope, toured the south of the country, and returned to Palestine to appear before the Anglo-American Commission. In May 1946, he returned to Europe and visited France, London, France again, Czechoslovakia, and Poland.
357 *The Rescue Voyage*, p. 60. The other two demands were "(a) to facilitate the emigration of Jews from Poland and (b) to provide stronger security for the Jews of Poland, over whom the sword of the terror of death looms relentlessly."
358 Ibid., p. 26.
359 Ibid., p. 60; Kahana, *After the Deluge*, p. 78. According to Kahana, Rabbi Herzog was told at this meeting that a socialist government could not look after such matters. His interlocutors hinted that they knew about the removal of children by the Council of Communities and the Zionist Organization but considered it an internal Jewish affair.

Poland, Rabbi Herzog took a special interest in the issue of child survivors and even brought new search requests with him.[360] Among other actions, he met with representatives of the Zionist groups involved in the operations and left money — some from the Jewish Agency and some from a fundraising drive that he had initiated in London — with them so that they could carry on with their activities.[361]

For security reasons, Rabbi Herzog had to leave Poland on August 13, 1946, but he returned several days later in order to meet Fiorello La Guardia, the chief executive of UNRRA. Immediately after the meeting the rabbi flew to Katowice, where a train meant to remove Jewish children from Poland was waiting for him. The possibility of effecting emigration in this manner came about because the rabbi had brought French entry visas with him. Aboard the train were 500 youngsters who had been gathered up from children's homes throughout Poland.[362]

Upon his return to Palestine, Rabbi Herzog appealed to "every Jewish home" to help with the important work of "rescuing Jewish children." Only limited actions had been taken up to that time, he stated emphatically, noting that action was still called for because thousands of children who were still living with non-Jews could be removed with the help of money. "In all countries," the rabbi said, "committees are dealing with the rescue of children but are hampered by lack of resources and disinterest in their work."[363] Even before he went to Poland, Rabbi Herzog dealt extensively with the matter of child Holocaust survivors and this was one of the main topics that he tackled during his trip. His impressions from his encounter with the child survivors and the operatives prompted him to turn to the Yishuv at large and urge it to become emotionally and financially involved.

Some time after he returned to Palestine, Rabbi Herzog received a re-

360 Letters to Rabbi Herzog from Mizrachi Organization, Palestine, Immigrant Care Department, January 15, 1946, from Bronka Cohen, Tel Aviv, December 30, 1945; from Gwircman, Tel Aviv, December 11, 1945, in the matter of Z.S., RZA, Rescue Files.
361 *The Rescue Voyage*, pp. 23, 54, 61; report aid and rescue project, October 1946–1947, expenditure line, CZA, S26/1410; report on expenditures in various countries from Rabbi Herzog to Jewish Agency Rescue Committee, April 20, 1947, ibid., S26/1266; Report Drucker about Council of Communities operations. Drucker claimed that he received no money from the Jewish Agency Rescue Committee, but this report indicates that at least some of the money that Rabbi Herzog gave him originated with the Committee.
362 *The Rescue Voyage*, pp. 60–80. Rachel Sternbuch had handed over 350 of these children. The train was supposed to have carried 750 children but 250 failed to reach the departure point in time.
363 Ibid., p. 100.

quest from Rabbi Schonfeld for assistance in paying for the care of the children he had brought from Poland to Britain, by means of the money that Rabbi Herzog had collected in London. Replying two months later, Rabbi Herzog noted that little of this money remained because the emissaries who were busy removing children from the homes of non-Jews needed more funds than he was in a position to offer. Furthermore, he stated, it had been decided in advance that this money would be earmarked for the removal of children and not for their upkeep. Rabbi Herzog thanked Rabbi Schonfeld for having helped him while he was in London but advised him to turn to JDC and other organizations.[364]

At the Twenty-Second Zionist Congress, convened in Basel in December 1946, one of the topics on the agenda was the removal of Jewish children from non-Jewish custody.[365] The Palestine delegation presented the presidium with a photo album of Koordynacja children and attached a letter noting that thousands of Jewish children were still in non-Jewish hands and must be returned to their Jewish heritage. The letter concluded: "With this album, the [children] issue a heart-rending outcry: Bring us home! [cf. *Jeremiah,* 31:17 '...and your children shall come back to their own country.'] Immigration to Palestine and redemption for our orphans, our parentless and forlorn Jewish children!"[366] The presentation of the album was an act of propaganda that focused attention on the children by showing their young faces peering out from its pages. The activists hoped that when Congress delegates "met" the children face to face in the pages of the album, they would redouble their efforts in support of the rescue effort.

Most operations of the Zionist youth movements were funded by their parent movements and parties. They received the money in various European countries and from emissaries visiting Poland.[367] The ideological glue held firmly; even when the members visited within the framework of a national delegation, their principal commitment was to their comrades.[368]

---

364 Letter Rabbi Schonfeld, London, to Rabbi Herzog, December 2, 1946; reply Rabbi Herzog to Rabbi Schonfeld, May 3, 1947, RZA, Rescue Files.

365 Remarks by Moshe Kolodny, 22nd Zionist Congress, Session 24, p. 507.

366 Ibid., Session 21, Excerpts from letter attached to the album, pp. 414–415. The album was submitted by the Palestine delegation, and since it was described as having come from Kibbutz Yagur, it was evidently the property of Goldberg, a member of that kibbutz.

367 Interview by author with Chasia Bielicki-Bornstein; Shner-Neshamit, *I Did Not Come to Rest,* p. 198; interview by author with Sarah Shner-Neshamit; interview by author with Arieh Sarid.

368 Warhaftig, *Refugee and Survivor,* p. 333.

The Koordynacja, as stated, was a new star in the constellation of Jewish movements and parties in Poland, and even though it had been established by and composed of their representatives, it had no permanent major organization behind it. Thus, its activists had to navigate in uncharted waters. The founders of the Koordynacja presumed that a unified entity with a goal that was so clear, focused, and sensitive for the Jewish people would attract the interest of various institutions and benefit from their funding. Reality, however, was different: since, the first priority of the movements was to direct the children into their own ranks.[369]

At the end of the war, the Jewish Agency Rescue Committee was in dire financial straits: it had a huge deficit, new fundraising drives had not yet begun, and the predictions for 1946 were grim. Eliyahu Dobkin, a member of the Committee, summed up the situation: "What we want to do is one thing; what we're actually doing is another — the problem is financial."[370] It was then that all the rehabilitation actions began to take on institutional form; the needs were immense, and all the Zionist bodies operating in Poland viewed the Rescue Committee as the organization that should fund the rescue and rehabilitation activities.[371]

When Yishai, the Jewish Agency emissary, reached Poland and became aware of the enormous number of operations that needed funding, he sent a request for aid to Palestine: "In my report to the Immigration Department, I wrote, 'Send money.' Now again I cannot conclude with anything but a call to scrape up money. Send as much money as you can, because nothing else matters." Later in the report, Yishai drew a connection between the need for funds and the removal of children from non-Jewish homes.[372]

In March 1946, Levita, a member of the Palestine mission, delivered $15,000 to the Koordynacja from Dobkin. Most of this money, however, was needed to repay debts and it was exhausted very quickly.[373] Shortly before set-

---

369 Memorandum to Youth Aliyah-Paris. During 1946, the Koordynacja managed to raise some $40,000 from various organizations and around $10,000 from individual Jews. See Koordynacja Income and Expenditure Report, March 1946–October 1947; *Mission to the Diaspora*, pp. 91–92; Sarid, "Initial Deployment," p. 315; testimony Leibl Koryski, OHD 15(68).

370 Letter Eliyahu Dobkin to Gruenbaum, Jewish Agency Rescue Committee, late 1945, CZA, S26/1266.

371 Cable World Jewish Congress, Stockholm, to Dobkin, Jewish Agency Rescue Committee, November 4, 1945, S 26/1317; on the situation of the Rescue Committee, see Barlas, *Rescue during the Holocaust*, pp. 106–107.

372 Yishai, *In the Shadow of the Holocaust*, p. 73; report Yishai.

373 *Mission to the Diaspora*, p. 92.

ting out on his second trip to Europe, Rabbi Herzog appeared before a joint assembly of the presidia of the Jewish Agency Rescue Committee and the Jewish fundraising organizations and described the nature of his itinerary. After the meeting, he was given 10,000 Palestine pounds[374] from the 90,000 pound budget that the Jewish Agency had allocated to the Rescue Committee that year.[375] Although this was a substantial sum — one-ninth of the Rescue Committee's annual budget — Rabbi Herzog's report, submitted about a year later at the request of the Rescue Committee, indicated that it had sufficed to cover only a small portion of his expenditures for rescue purposes.[376] The Rescue Committee's financial distress and the allocation of such a large portion of its budget to Rabbi Herzog may have created tension between the Committee and the rabbi and fomented criticism of the latter's activities. In a report that Rabbi Herzog received from his bureau during his stay in Europe, members of his entourage were asked to report to the bureau in Jerusalem as to what they had been doing about the rescue of Jewish children. The writer from Jerusalem related the following:

> At a press conference held together with Mr. Dobkin, a journalist asked him about the esteemed Chief Rabbi's involvement and role in the rescue of children. At first he chose not to answer at all and at the end of the assembly he asked the journalists not to publish his reply. Then he answered, "*Nothing.*" [emphasis in the original.] After all, they themselves should understand that the rescue of children is not a matter for the rabbinate... It is the job of the [Jewish] Agency and its operatives.

The writer added: "We have to brace ourselves for criticism, especially if the Agency has been providing the finances."[377]

It is possible that through poor communications on one hand, and the numerous requests for assistance that the Jewish Agency Rescue Committee had been receiving from various bodies in Poland on the other, the Jewish

374 *The Rescue Voyage*, pp. 23–24; Barlas, *Rescue during the Holocaust*, p. 106.
375 Letters Toparski to Shapiro and Mofarski in regard to the allocation of funds, March 25, 1946, CZA, S26/1266.
376 Letter Gruenbaum and Toparski, Jewish Agency Rescue Committee, to Chief Rabbi Herzog, March 30, 1947; letter Rabbi Herzog's office to Jewish Agency Rescue Committee, April 20, 1947, ibid.
377 Letter Rabbi Herzog's secretary, Bureau of the Chief Rabbi in Jerusalem, to Rabbi Herzog (received during the rabbi's trip), May 12, 1946, RZA, Rescue Files; in regard to the Chief Rabbinate's dependence on the national institutions, see Shulamit Eliash, "Relations between the Chief Rabbinate of Palestine and the Mandate Government (1936-1945)," doctoral dissertation, Bar-Ilan University, 1979 (Hebrew), pp. 83–90.

Agency Rescue Committee may not have known exactly which forces were active in regard to children in Poland and whom they represented. In early 1947, Gruenbaum visited Poland, met with representatives of the various Zionist groups, and even asked them to find a way to induce the Koordynacja and the Council of Religious Communities to cooperate.[378] Nevertheless, in response to a letter that the Koordynacja had sent him in June 1947 with a request for assistance, Gruenbaum noted in puzzlement and sadness, that although he was interested in the subject, "No one from your institution contacted me [during my visit to Poland] and I knew absolutely nothing about your operations." He gave this response even though the Rescue Committee had given the Koordynacja a sum of money in early 1946. It is possible that the Koordynacja had been described to Gruenbaum, during his stay in Poland, as a united entity that acted on behalf of the movements and not as an independent body that arranged its own sources of funding. The question has not been fully resolved. However, despite his amazement, Gruenbaum wished to be apprised of the Koordynacja's needs so that he could help them.[379]

Pursuant to this letter, the Rescue Committee received a detailed report about the Koordynacja's activity, coupled with an urgent request for money and an emphatic comment to the effect that the lack of funds was hampering the child-rescue efforts.[380] At that time — July 1947 — the Rescue Committee contacted the World Jewish Congress and tried to arrange its cooperation in removing children, and a meeting between the two organizations was set up. The WJC complained about its own financial problems and said that it could not help. But then it proposed an entirely different course of action: that of presenting the matter to the Economic and Social Council of the

378 Interview by author with Yeshayahu Drucker; memorandum to Youth Aliyah-Paris.
379 Letter Gruenbaum, Jewish Agency Rescue Committee, to Koordynacja, Łódź, July 21, 1947, CZA, S26/1317; earlier, the Rescue Committee had decided that "Comrade Barlas should determine the value of the operations of the 'Koordynacja Committee' and of Mrs. Kosovar [Ichud] and should prepare proposals for the future." See Rescue Committee budget report. Notably, Gruenbaum spent the period from early September 1945 to May 1946 in Paris in an attempt to help his son, who was suspected of having aided the Nazis while a prisoner in Auschwitz. During his stay in Paris, Gruenbaum decided not to visit the DP camps and Poland, lest his absence cause his son harm. Shortly after he returned to Palestine together with his son, on the "Black Sabbath" of 29 June, 1946, Gruenbaum was arrested and imprisoned in Latrun. See Roman Frister, *Without Compromise* (Tel Aviv: Zmora Bitan, 1987, Hebrew), pp. 291–300. Against this background, one may surmise that Gruenbaum did not know about the money that Dobkin had handed over to the Koordynacja. This may also explain why he was not fully aware of the identity of the people who were involved in the operations in Poland.
380 Letter Koordynacja presidium to Jewish Agency Rescue Committee, August 10, 1947.

United Nations. The author of the WJC's response also related that members of the WJC had launched discussions with members of the Council so that the issue would be debated by it and the UN secretariat for the purpose of forcing non-Jews to surrender Jewish children to Jewish institutions. However, he expressed concern about the difficulties that might ensue if this essentially religious issue was indeed taken up for discussion; therefore, he indicated that the situation would be reviewed and an attempt would be made to determine what the response was likely to be.[381]

The WJC reply did not dissuade the Rescue Committee. In November 1947, despite its financial plight, the Committee sent the Koordynacja a report stating that the presidium had resolved to extend the Committee's patronage over the Koordynacja's actions; henceforth, the Koordynacja would be the executive body of the Rescue Committee, which would operate in accordance with its instructions. The Koordynacja, in turn, was asked to promise to stop accepting funds from other institutions and to cooperate with Mizrachi and Agudath Israel. Finally, the Committee would allot the Koordynacja the sum of 3,000 Palestine pounds per month (less sums already given over by other institutions).[382] In December 1947, due to difficulties in transferring funds to Poland, the Rescue Committee turned to the main office of the Jewish National Fund and asked it to forward the money to the Koordynacja via its Warsaw branch for the purpose of "redeeming" children.[383] In January 1948, the Koordynacja sent Gruenbaum a letter alleging that the Rescue Committee had not met its undertakings and even though the Koordynacja had submitted an income and expense report, as required, and had severed all relations with other sources of revenue, the Rescue Committee money had not been received and the situation was catastrophic.[384] Nevertheless, the Rescue Committee advised the JNF in Jerusalem that unless it had already forwarded

381 Letter Gruenbaum, Jewish Agency Rescue Committee, to World Jewish Congress, July 1, 1947, CZA, S26/1317; report Jewish Agency Palestine Office, September 6, 1947, ibid., C6/113; letter Dr. Stein, World Jewish Congress, to Gruenbaum, Jewish Agency Rescue Committee, July 21, 1947, ibid., S26/1317.

382 Letter Gruenbaum and Sheffer, November 3, 1947. The letter began by stating that the articles of the agreement would be determined on the basis of the agreement that had been concluded with Gruenbaum during his stay in Poland. Concurrently, the Rescue Committee instructed the Jewish Agency Finance Department to forward the sum to the Koordynacja; see letter Rescue Committee to Jewish Agency Finance Committee, expenditure report, November 3, 1947, ibid., S26/1410.

383 Letter to Jewish National Fund head office, December 1947, unsigned, ibid., S26/1424.

384 Letter Koordynacja, Łódź, to Gruenbaum, Jewish Agency Rescue Committee, January 2, 1948, ibid.

the money to the Koordynacja, the Committee's previous request that this be done should be considered void.[385]

The World Mizrachi Organization also sent Gruenbaum a request for aid. Attached to its request were excerpts from a letter from Drucker, in which he expressed despair over the financial situation of the child-removal project. Drucker wrote that even though children who could be removed still remained and that accurate addresses were available, "Money for this purpose has almost run out and I do not see anyone in our great world taking an interest in this problem; evidently they've already made peace [with the situation...]. Unfortunately, I have no money left and do not know how to carry on with the work. Unless they come to [our] assistance, we will have to call off the project..."

Gruenbaum, apparently moved by this message, issued an order, in handwriting, on the letter he had received, to instruct Kosovar (of Ichud) by cable that he should enter into discussions with Drucker in order to help him.[386] However, according to Drucker, no money was sent either in response to this letter or pursuant to other agreements.[387]

The Rescue Committee was interested in aiding the organizations that were active on behalf of children in Poland but it was in serious financial straits. Its correspondence with Jewish fundraising mechanisms in countries that donated to it provides yet another indication of its financial distress. In a letter to the South African Jewish Appeal, Gruenbaum reported that it had been decided that the Koordynacja would operate under Rescue Committee auspices and had therefore been granted a monthly budget, in the hope that thus it would be able to act more vigorously for the removal of children.[388] However, even if the fundraising organizations were interested in funding these activities, they themselves were financially embarrassed after having spent much of their budget on the care of refugees and children who had

385 Letter Jewish Agency Rescue Committee to JNF head office, Jerusalem, March 10, 1948, ibid. Paragraph H of the budget report for the first five months of 1948, starting March 2,1948, states that 3,000 Palestine pounds per month had been allocated for the removal of children in Europe — i.e., 15,000 pounds out of a budget of 40,437 pounds. See ibid., S26/1410. In 1948, a way to transfer the allocated sums to the Koordynacja through channels other than the JNF may have been found.
386 Letter Birzinski, World Mizrachi Organization, to Gruenbaum, Jewish Agency Rescue Committee, Jerusalem, May 21, 1947, ibid., S26/1317.
387 Interview by author with Yeshayahu Drucker.
388 Letter Jewish Agency Rescue Committee to South African Jewish Appeal, part of a report on the use of South African Appeal money, November 24, 1947, CZA, S26/1291.

reached their countries after the war.[389] In view of this correspondence, a letter sent to the Koordynacja by an Australian Jew, asking the Koordynacja to deal with the case of his niece, should be viewed ironically. After expressing his wish, the writer added, "Obviously you don't have to think about money because you've already got connections with the Jewish fund in Melbourne."[390]

Thus, there was a gap between the wish of the WJC to help and its ability to do so. During the course of a WJC mission to Poland in early 1946, its members (Segal, Margoshes, and Warhaftig) gave the Zionist movements $5,000 for the removal of children. Warhaftig had raised this sum by taking out a personal loan, believing that the WJC would cover the expenses. More than a year later, he had not been repaid, and since he had signed the loan personally, Segal helped him get the money from the WJC. Over a four-month period, the sides corresponded at length in search of a way to repay the money. During this time, the sum was divided up and the Poalei Zion Executive Committee for Relief and Rehabilitation in the United States eventually paid some of it. Warhaftig had taken out the loan in early 1946 and, after various calculations and reductions, he should have received it back in September 1947.[391]

After JDC organized its operations in Poland, it funded all the Zionist and non-Zionist organizations that were engaged in removing children and maintaining them in children's homes. JDC channeled 70–80 percent of the money to its destination via institutions of the Central Committee but forwarded some amounts directly to other entities.[392]

389 Letter United Jewish Overseas Relief Fund, Melbourne, to Gruenbaum, Jewish Agency Rescue Committee, July 29, 1947, ibid., S26/1317.

390 Letter Hirsch Yitzhak Kurtz to Koordynacja in the matter of R.D., September 28, 1947.

391 Letter Louis Segal, secretary-general of National Organization of Jewish Workers, to Dr. Kubowitzki, World Jewish Congress, April 3, 1947, YVA, P-20/8; letter Segal to Dr. Kubowitzki, 28, 1947, ibid.; letter Segal to Dr. Baumgold, secretary of Poalei Zion Executive Committee for Relief and Rehabilitation, May 3, 1947, ibid.; letter Segal to Dr. Warhaftig, World Jewish Congress, May 22, 1947, ibid.; letter Leon Kubowitzki to Dr. Stein, June 18, 1947, ibid. Copies were sent to Dr. Marcus, Folderman, and Warhaftig. Letter Louis Segal to Dr. Warhaftig, June 20, 1947, ibid.; letter Baumgold to Dr. Warhaftig, July 11, 1947, ibid.

392 Litvak, "JDC's Contribution," pp. 341–342, 346–347; Gutman, *Jews in Poland,* p. 61; interview by author with Jechiel Granatstein, December 1996; Kahana, *After the Deluge,* p. 54; Dr. Schwartz, director of JDC-Europe, met with Rabbi Herzog in London before the rabbi set out for Poland and gave him $25,000 to use for rescue actions as he saw fit; see *The Rescue Voyage,* p. 55; Goldberg stood by his claim that JDC did not provide the Koordynacja with funds for the redemption of children. As he puts it, all his appeals to Guzik, director of JDC-Poland, and Schwartz, director of JDC-Europe, went unanswered.

A memorandum submitted by JDC in 1946 to the Anglo-American Committee of Enquiry Regarding the Problems of European Jewry and Palestine attests to the importance that JDC attributed to the cause of child survivors. The first part of the memorandum deals with the "fate of Jewish children," describes the appalling plight of children who had been in hiding and in camps, and stressed the need for comprehensive action.[393] JDC applied this thinking at the practical level: its mission in Poland was involved both directly and indirectly in negotiations over children who were living with non-Jews and in liaison between private individuals and various organizations around the world and the various entities that operated in Poland.[394] Thus, at the request of relatives, the JDC's relative-tracing department located sixty children.[395]

In spring 1946, the official JDC allocation for the removal of a child from a rescuer's home was 5,000 zlotys; later on, it was raised to 10,000 zlotys.[396] In practice, however, much larger sums were needed. Sometimes JDC made up the difference but its exchequer was not a bottomless pit. In its first year of activity, JDC spent 603,000 zlotys for the discovery of children. In fact, JDC disbursed larger sums for this activity than did any other organization, until its operations were halted at about the time that those of all Zionist entities in Poland met the same fate.[397]

Although every group that took action in Poland to remove Jewish children from the homes of non-Jews homes managed to raise funds for its

See Bar-Gil interview with Arieh Sarid, July 1991; Sarid, "Remarks about the Koordynacja," p. 21; *Mission to the Diaspora*, p. 91. Guzik held this office until March 1946, when he was killed in an accident, and was succeeded by William Bein. Goldberg left Poland in September 1946, but before doing so he moved to Silesia under the auspices of Noham and became less active in Koordynacja affairs. JDC may have come around to the policy of funding child-redemption operations during the first few months of 1946. In practice, it forwarded money to the Koordynacja for redemption purposes. See JDC 1946 financial statements, November 1946, JDC, microfilm from Poland, VIII; testimony Leibl Koryski, OHD 15(68).

393 Azriel Carlebach, ed., *The Anglo-American Committee of Enquiry Regarding the Problems of European Jewry and Palestine*, B (Tel Aviv: Leitzmann, 1946, Hebrew, JDC memorandum), p. 645.

394 List of twenty-five children in non-Jews' homes, undated; letter Drucker to JDC-Warsaw, with detailed account of handling in cases that JDC had referred to him, September 23, 1948; letter Koordynacja presidium to Bein, director of JDC-Poland, November 15, 1946. The documents were given to me by Sarah Kadosh, archives director for JDC-Israel.

395 Litvak, "JDC's Contribution," p. 371.

396 Report Yishai; Yishai, *In the Shadow of the Holocaust*, p. 80.

397 Litvak, "JDC's Contribution," pp. 352, 376; JDC expenditure report, October 1945–September 1946, p. 15, JDC, microfilm from Poland.

activities, money was always in short supply. Indeed, the shortage of funds impeded the activity more than any other factor. The search and locate operations were hard to perform and demanded creative methods of action. The sense of mission that typified the organizations that did the work — each with its own beliefs and motives — prompted them to keep going, but the financial hardship caused frustration, disillusionment, and tensions both internally and between them and the organizations from which they expected support. As Goldberg wrote to Hans Beith of Youth Aliyah, "I cry out to you from the depths of my heart: either make it easier for me to operate by obtaining resources or send someone who can accomplish more than I can and relieve me of this entire burden, which is literally driving me to physical collapse. I cry out to you: *resources, resources, right now!*" [emphasis in the original.][398] The recurrent appeals for larger subventions, however, did not always have the expected results.

On the other side of the divide, the world Jewish and Yishuv entities had limited maneuvering room. After the war, they had to help the Holocaust survivors and finance the needs of the Yishuv. Although they wished to take action and valued supremely the cause of removing children from non-Jewish custody, they were unable to raise the amounts of money that were needed, and were requested by the operatives in the field. Like a blanket that is simply not wide enough to cover the bed, its size remained unchanged no matter how hard it was pulled.

398 Letter Leibl to Hans Beith, July 18, 1946.

CHAPTER 4

Working Methods: Searching, Locating, and Negotiating for the Removal of Children

"Captives shall not be redeemed for more than they are worth, so that the world shall remain sound. And captives are not smuggled away, so that the world shall remain sound. Rabban Shimon b. Gamliel says, so that captives will be treated properly."

Mishna, Gittin 4:6 [1]

The Operatives

When Jewish organizations began to search for Jewish children in the homes of non-Jews across Poland, they had constantly to bear in mind the internal problems of post-war and post-Holocaust Poland, the development of relations within Polish society, and the attitude of Polish society towards the Jewish population.

The Central Jewish Committee, as we have seen in the previous chapter, chose to deal with the removal of children via the Child Care Depart-

---

1   Pinchas Kehati, *Mishnayot mevua'rot* (Jerusalem: Heikhal Shlomo, 1977, Hebrew). Rabbi Kehati interprets the passage thus: *"'Captives shall not be redeemed for more than they are worth, so that the world shall remain sound'*– since if the Gentiles see that [Jews] are redeeming captives for more than they are worth, they will take captives prolifically. *And captives are not smuggled away* — no ruse shall be employed to allow captives to escape from their captors — *so that the world shall remain sound* — so that the Gentiles will not mistreat future captives. *Rabban Shimon b. Gamliel says, so that captives will be treated properly* — Rabban Gamliel is not concerned about the sound treatment of other captives who might fall into their hands at a later time but rather about the treatment of captives presently in their hands, for if one of them should escape, they will treat the remaining captives severely. Thus, if they are holding only one captive, he is smuggled away and the rule is not observed strictly."

ment and with the assistance of the district committees. Most of the work was centralized at the department offices; searches for children and relations with their rescuers were conducted by correspondence. At this stage, direct contact with families was established only when a home visit was required, in order to prepare a report concerning the child's situation in the rescuer's home. Once the rescuer agreed to surrender the child however, employees of the district committee nearest the locality in question were sent to remove him or her. Other organizations involved in child rescue acted differently; they employed removal operatives whose task was to travel around the country, collect information, track down children, and take action to remove them from their rescuers' homes.

From autumn 1945 until 1950, Yeshayahu Drucker operated alone as a removal operative for the Council of Religious Communities;[2] Abraham Dziadek and Leibl Zamość performed this duty for Po'alei Agudath Israel[3] and Sarah Lederman acted on behalf of Rachel Sternbuch, who represented Agudath Israel and the Rescue Committee of the Orthodox Rabbis of the

2 Interview by author with Yeshayahu Drucker; testimony Yeshayahu Drucker, OHD 28(68). Drucker fought in the ranks of the forces that liberated Poland. He advanced all the way to Berlin with his unit and returned to Poland at the end of the war. After hearing about what the Council of Religious Communities was doing to revive Jewish life, he wrote to Rabbi Kahana and asked to join the organization. Two weeks later he began to work for the Council of Communities and was placed in charge of the "Children's Portfolio." Drucker became the longest-serving removal operative of them all.

3 Interview by author with Jechiel Granatstein, 1996; Granatstein, *Double Life*, p. 11; idem., *Days of Genesis*, pp. 119–121. Dziadek was an elderly man; Zamość, a young man, was liberated from a labor camp in Częstochowa at the end of the war. Zamość looked Polish but with his short stature and emaciated features he posed as an unpredictable man whom people should treat warily — all of which helped him to attain his goal. He met Granatstein, secretary of PAI in Poland, when the two of them were helping to bury Torah scrolls that had been damaged in the Holocaust. In his book *Double Life* and in an interview with the author, Granatstein claimed that Zamość had been a Ger hasid before the war, whereas in his book *Days of Genesis* he says that Dziadek was the Ger hasid. According to Zamość's "survivor card," he was thirty years old in 1946. See Leibl Zamość, YVA, Arolsen card catalogue.

4 As she retells the story, Lederman (b. 1902) vowed during the war that if her two children survived, she would devote two years of her life to working with orphaned Jewish children. After her sister-in-law returned from the Soviet Union with her children, Lederman sent her elder son to a collective of the Dror movement and she, together with her eight-year-old daughter, began to work at the Agudath Israel children's home in Bytom. Lederman also used the name Safian; she had a second passport in this name which had been arranged for her through the Council of Communities. Lederman served as a removal operative from the summer of 1946 until 1948, when she was arrested. See testimony Sarah Lederman, OHD 50(68); interview by author with Yeshayahu Drucker.

USA.[4] The Koordynacja, in contrast, employed many operatives who worked for different periods. Its first operative was Marysia Fleiszer;[5] others joined over time: Moshe Jeruchamzon,[6] Akiva Gerszater,[7] Yosef Bürger,[8] Yehuda

5   Marysia's (Devorah Zilber Fleiszer) husband died of typhus during the war. She lost contact with her only son, aged seventeen, at the beginning of the war when he was in Białystok. She managed to leave the ghetto in her hometown of Szczebrzeszyn (near Zamość) on forged papers. In the first months after the war, Marysia went from town to town, searching for her son and other members of her family. Being unable to locate them, she based herself in Łódź and there met Goldberg at the home of friends; it was Goldberg who recruited her for the Koordynacja. Marysia was forced to leave Poland in November 1946 after an acquaintance told her that a directive to kill her had been issued in the town where she was living on the grounds that she was a communist. The directive was issued following a rumor about her relations with the new regime and fears that she would denounce persons whom she knew had collaborated with the Germans during the war. See testimony Devorah Zilber, OHD 27(68); Fleiszer, "The Rescue of 24 Children," pp. 300–304; Dekel, *Remnants of the Sword*, pp. 121–123.

6   Moshe Jeruchamzon worked as a removal operative under a non-Jewish name that he had assumed during the war, Mieczyslaw Jankowski. Jeruchamzon was a Polish army officer at the beginning of the war; after a stay in the ghetto, he escaped and was captured several times and was eventually interned as a Pole in a camp for Polish underground prisoners until the end of 1944 — at which time he and forty-nine others escaped, joined the partisans, and fought against the Germans. Jeruchamzon received a citation of valor and medals of excellence from the new Polish government. After the war, he found his twelve year-old son. See testimony Moshe Jeruchamzon, OHD, 44(68).

7   Gerszater, the oldest member of the group, at about sixty years old, worked from 1946 to the end of the Koordynacja's tenure in Poland. See interview by author with Yeshayahu Drucker; testimony Genia Düstenfeld (who worked in the offices of the Koordynacja secretariat); see also Koordynacja letter of appointment to the post of removal operative, GFHA, Correspondence File, 788–790; testimony Yehuda Bronstein, OHD, 25(68); testimony Devorah Zilber, OHD, 27(68).

8   At the beginning of the war, Bürger took part in the defense of Warsaw, was taken prisoner and transferred to a labor camp in Lublin, from where he escaped and joined the partisans. In March 1945, he enlisted in a special-duties detail and subsequently worked for the Polish security police and was stationed in Łódź. He stated that one day he noticed the Koordynacja sign on the front of its building and entered the organization's offices out of curiosity. When he asked what they were doing, the Koordynacja staff were initially frightened, because his uniform identified him as an employee of the security police, but were reassured when he identified himself as a Jew. After he learned about the Koordynacja operations, Bürger accepted their offer that he help in the removal of Jewish children. He worked from January 1, 1947, to May 20, 1948, while still serving with the security police. Bürger was forced to leave Poland after a Polish rescuer complained to the police that he had removed at gunpoint a Jewish girl who was staying in her home. After it was proved that his gun had indeed been used, Bürger was arrested. He claimed that he did not use the weapon in this particular case. Seventeen days later, the Koordynacja secured his release by paying 500,000 zlotys and promising the authorities that he would leave the country. Interview by author with Yosef Haezrahi-Bürger; Menahem Kunda, a member of the Koordynacja presidium, claims that Bürger began to work with the Koordynacja after a townsman of Kunda's brought him to the organization. See interview by author with Menahem Kunda.

Bronstein,[9] Teofilia Goldman,[10] someone called Grynszpan, a woman operative named A. Shejnjuk-Slucki, Sonia Margolit-Kaminski, Jakob Gises, and
others.[11] Additional people, usually members of movements, were recruited
for occasional tasks.

Although each operative had his or her own reasons for volunteering, all
shared a willingness to undertake the risks involved: traveling by rail at a time
when Jews were being removed from trains and shot; hitch-hiking among
villages and towns amid a population that was usually hostile; contending
with widespread rumors about the abduction of Christian children by Jews;
and concern about the behavior of the children themselves — since children
who wished to escape the operative's clutches might attract unwanted attention and have to be "bribed" by means of candies and gifts. To overcome all
these risks, the removal operatives had to be courageous, fluent in Polish,
and familiar with the ways of life and religious customs of the various groups
within the Polish population. "Good" (that is, "Aryan") facial features could
help them melt into the local population and improve their chances of not
attracting too much attention in their travels.[12]

Even though the organizations stood behind all their operatives, they
were on their own during the mission; their ability to contend with different
situations they encountered on the mission depended solely on their resource-

---

9   On the eve of the war, Bronstein was a student at the Lwów Polytechnicum. When the Ger-
    mans entered the town, he fled to the Soviet Union, joined the Red Army, and was wound-
    ed in action. Afterwards, he was accused of anti-Soviet propaganda and was sentenced to
    eight years in prison. Pursuant to the repatriation agreements, Bronstein was released from
    prison and taken to the Polish border in the summer of 1948. At the border checkpoint, he
    encountered representatives of the Zionist movements who were waiting for returnees and
    joined an Ichud collective. He was recruited for the Koordynacja by David Meller, an Ichud
    leader in Poland, who promised to use his services for only a limited period of time — until
    such a time that he could obtain an emigration visa in order to move to Israel and join
    the Israeli army. Bronstein worked as a removal operative for eight months — from sum-
    mer 1948 until spring 1949. See testimony Yehuda Bronstein, YVA, O.3/5130; testimony
    Yehuda Bronstein, OHD, 25(68); interview by author with Yehuda Bronstein, 1997; labor
    permit from Koordynacja in the name of Yehuda Bronstein, given to me by its owner and
    in my possession.
10 Working report Teofilia Goldman, November 1946, GFHA, Correspondence File, 788–
    790.
11 A man named Altman also worked for some time but was dismissed after he lied about
    his financial expenses. See testimony Leibl Koryski, OHD 15(68); Koryski, "The Zionist
    Koordynacja for the Redemption of Jewish Children in Poland," p. 26.
12 Testimony Devorah Zilber, OHD, 27(68); Granatstein, *Days of Genesis*, pp. 118–119; Nesh-
    amit, "The Koordynacja for the Redemption of Children in Liberated Poland," pp. 118–119,
    122; Mahler, "Redemption of Jewish Children from Their Non-Jewish Rescuers," p. 36.

fulness and intuition. They had to be proficient in sizing up people, predicting their responses, determining how to converse with them, and finding ad hoc solutions to unexpected problems.[13] The first removal operatives developed their working methods on the job; their successors received initial instruction from their predecessors and worked out the rest as time progressed in accordance with their own individual personalities.[14] Drucker, Jeruchamzon, Grynszpan, and Bürger, who had been in the army or had served in state police agencies in post-war Poland, were able to travel in uniform and exploit the authoritative and intimidating appearance thus projected[15] — even though due to attacks against and even murders of military personnel, whom some Poles regarded as collaborators with the new regime, appearing in uniform could also be dangerous.

Sources of Information and Difficulties in Tracing Children

All the organizations that dealt with children received information from Jewish survivors who, after returning to their home towns, found out about a Jewish child who was staying with a Polish family.[16] The organizations also received information from institutions and individuals outside Poland as well as relatives who had received information during or after the war — sometimes from the rescuers themselves — and passed it on to Jewish institutions in Palestine and elsewhere or even directly to the organizations

---

13 Mahler, "Redemption of Jewish Children from Their Non-Jewish Rescuers," p. 36.

14 Testimony Sarah Lederman, OHD 50(68); interview by author with Yeshayahu Drucker; interview by author with Yehuda Bronstein, 1997; testimony Devorah Zilber, OHD, 27(68).

15 Dekel, *Remnants of the Sword*, p. 158; interview by author with Yeshayahu Drucker; testimony Genia Düstenfeld; Koryski, "The Zionist Koordynacja for the Redemption of Jewish Children in Poland," p. 26.

16 Testimony Yeshayahu Drucker in the matter of T.W., YVA, O.3/3249; testimony Leibl Koryski, OHD 15(68); responses Tamar Jacobi to my questionnaire. Tamar's mother, who was living in Warsaw under false papers, encountered her husband's teacher from Kazimierz Dolny and told her where her daughter was staying. Afterwards, the mother was deported to Majdanek, never to return. The woman who received the information passed it on to the Koordynacja after the war.

17 Interview by author with Yeshayahu Drucker; testimony of Leibl Koryski, OHD 15(68); Warhaftig, *Refugee and Survivor*, p. 434; Shner-Neshamit, *I Did Not Come to Rest*, p. 198; letter Koordynacja secretariat, Łódź, to JDC-Warsaw, May 12, 1947, JDC, microfilm from Poland. The letter was written in response to a request from JDC to the Koordynacja that the latter see to the removal of specific children. Letter Israel Rosenberg to Youth Aliyah-Jerusalem, undated, in the matter of P.L., CZA, L58/748. Rosenberg received information about the girl from a Pole who asked him after the war to help him reclaim the expenses he had incurred,

in Poland.[17] In some cases, the information provided nothing more than a slender initial lead.[18] Sometimes information came from children who had been placed in children's homes and knew about the whereabouts of other children whom they had come across.[19] Polish citizens provided information for several reasons: appreciation of the Jewish organizations' efforts to rebuild a Jewish community;[20] the feeling that it was better for the child to return to his or her Jewish identity;[21] sorrow about the care that the children had received in their rescuers' homes;[22] quarrels among neighbors that ended with the denunciation of one by another in revenge, thereby striking the rival in the "soft underbelly";[23] or for remuneration.[24] There was also disinforma-

and, some time later, offered to surrender her for $1,200; letter organization of Jews from Opoczno to Rabbi Herzog, March 31, 1946, RZA, Rescue Files; letter Avramsky, Tel Aviv, to Rabbi Herzog, December 29, 1946. Avramsky wrote that he had heard from a woman from his town that his nephew was in a village near Grajewo. See RZA, Rescue Files.

18 Letter Sternlicht to Rabbi Herzog, December 17, 1946, RZA, Rescue Files. The correspondent was informed by a relative who had moved to Palestine that his sister, who had been with a relative in the labor camp in Sandomierz, had told him while they were in the ghetto, that she had surrendered her daughter to non-Jews in Opatów but refused to give more precise details. Sternlicht himself visited Poland in 1938 in an unsuccessful attempt to persuade his family to move to Palestine and encountered a Polish friend in their home. He wanted to find out whether his niece was living with this non-Jew or with members of his family; letter OSE in Mexico to TOZ (*Towarzystwo Ochrony Zdrowia* –Association for the Maintenance of the Health of the Jewish Population) in Łódź, April 22, 1947, in the matter of B.G., a document that I received from Ita Kowalska, Poland. A member of the organization in Mexico received information to the effect that his nephew was staying with the Błasik family in Częstochowa; he requested assistance in removing him.

19 Testimony Leibl Koryski, OHD 15(68); testimony Genia Düstenfeld.

20 Testimony Pinhas Krybus, OHD 45(68); testimony Yeshayahu Drucker, OHD 28(68). Drucker mentions assistance that he received from Irena Adamowicz, an employee of the Polish Ministry of Education after the war. Adamowicz had been a member of the Polish Scouts and during the war was active in the Polish resistance and aided the Zionist youth movements.

21 Biography of R.M., written on October 8, 1946, GFHA, Correspondence File, 788–790.

22 Deposition Pawel Milczuk, June 14, 1947, ibid. The deposition was given in the presence of counsel for the district Jewish committee and a representative of the Zamość police, about a Jewish boy who had been in the care of the Slagda family ever since his parents had placed him with them during the war. Milczuk accused the family of treating the boy poorly, forcing him to perform difficult jobs, and subjecting him to beatings by the woman of the home, even though he knew that the family had received goods from the boy's parents in return for his upkeep.

23 Shner-Neshamit, *I Did Not Come to Rest,* pp. 206, 208; testimony Pinhas Krybus, OHD 45(68).

24 Testimony Pinhas Krybus, OHD 45(68); Dekel, *Remnants of the Sword,* p. 197; Granatstein, *Double Life,* pp. 13–14. Zamość, for example, used various peasants as sources of information.

tion, especially when the informant's motive was related to money. For example, sometimes the child was not at the address provided or was not even Jewish.[25]

Even though the various sources provided a great deal of information, the Koordynacja and PAI did not content themselves with this alone. The receipt of information at the initiative of others actually spurred them to explore other ways of locating children. At the outset of its activity in 1946, for example, the Koordynacja placed a "shot in the dark" advertisement in the press on the possibility of receiving food parcels and payment for information about Jewish children.[26] Some of the travels of the operatives were undertaken for the purpose of gathering information through methods developed by each operative on his or her own. Drucker, for example, received information from concierges, who usually lived in one place for a lengthy period of time and knew the residents of the building in which they worked. Sometimes he would leave a sum of money with a concierge to encourage him or her to provide information and would then return at a later time to collect it.[27] Marysia circulated in the villages dressed as a peasant woman and, while selling haberdashery and candy on market days, established trusting and friendly relationships with various people, especially children. She probed, asked questions, interrogated, and navigated her conversations in directions that might reveal the whereabouts of Jewish children.[28] Zamość spent many hours in taverns, drinking vodka with other customers until the alcohol loosened his drinking partners' tongues, at which point he steered them into conversations about Jews in general and Jewish children in particular.[29] In fact, all the removal operatives used their time on the road to investigate, eavesdrop, initiate conversations, and elicit information.[30] It is ironic that despite the operatives' intentions and efforts, there was often something very random about the way information arrived or a Jewish child was located. In one example, a Polish woman in a train on her way back from the baptism of her son at a church in Częstochowa shared with another passenger the story of how the

25 Testimony Pinhas Krybus, OHD 45(68); working report Teofilia Goldman; Shner-Nesh-amit, *I Did Not Come to Rest,* p. 208.
26 Shner-Neshamit, *I Did Not Come to Rest,* p. 208; testimony Sabina Halperin, MA, A.201.
27 Interview by author with Yeshayahu Drucker.
28 Responses Fredzja Rothbard to my questionnaire, June 1993.
29 Granatstein, *Days of Genesis,* pp. 118–119.
30 Koryski, "The Zionist Koordynacja for the Redemption of Jewish Children in Poland," p. 25.

boy had come into her care during the war. One of the other passengers was a Jew; after overhearing her story he reported it to the Koordynacja.[31]

The operatives had no easy task. It would be wrong to assume that information could be obtained merely by initiating a search for it, since solid information about children's whereabouts was hard to come by. Moreover, in cases where information was available, and the operatives did not have to search for it, the question of how to remove the child from the rescuer's home remained unanswered. In view of the circumstances that had placed Jewish children into non-Jewish hands during the war, finding the point at which a search could begin was akin to groping in the darkness. Even if there was someone who knew where the child had first been handed over and had survived to tell about it, there was no assurance that the child would be found in the same place years later. He or she might have been handed over to a third party and then to a fourth, causing all traces to vanish.[32] Furthermore, since the children had been handed over secretly and rarely in the presence of witnesses, parents who had perished took the secret with them to the grave.[33] Other parents had

31 Child card of Eduard Radomski, no. 58, GFHA, catalogue of Koordynacja children's cards, File 800; see also interview by author with Erich Lichtman, May 1996. While serving as secretary of the Hanoar Hatzioni collective in Jelenia Góra, Lichtman encountered two Jewish officers — one of whom was a former schoolmate — and learned from them that two Jewish children were staying with their regiment commander after their parents had handed them over to him; see also Ferderber-Salz, *And the Sun Appeared*, p. 171. Ferderber-Salz relates that when she came to take away her brother-in-law's children, who had been given to their caregiver, she heard from the caregiver's sister that a Jewish child was also staying in her home.

32 Neshamit, "The Koordynacja for the Redemption of Children in Liberated Poland," pp. 124–125, in the matter of the girl Sarah-Maria; letter Education Department to Kobryner, undated, in the matter of R.G. The girl had been placed in the care of the Figurska family but was then passed on to someone else; see also letters to Wicek Listonosz, Chmielnik, July 3, year not noted, and to district committee in Kraków, July 8, year not noted, in the matter of A.G. The girl stayed with Wisław Jezierski until 1943, when her father sent her elsewhere. Her father was captured afterwards and all traces of the girl were lost. See ŻIH, Education Department, File 638; Sznajderman, "A Jewish Mother Fights for Her Daughter," pp. 71–72.

33 Story of Yosef Gorny (b. Warsaw, 1938), *Farn Yiddishn Kind*, pp. 4–5, GFHA, File 798; in interviews by author with Jan Kuder and correspondence with Pawel Cypryańsky, Poland, 1995, I was told that the mother of the baby Henia Wiszniewska was living with her under a false identity. The mother became friends with Pawel's mother, Mrs. Cypryanska, and visited the Cypryanskis frequently. One day, sensing that the Nazis were on her trail, she visited the Cypryanskis at home and left her daughter with them; see also Grynberg, *Księga Sprawiedliwych*, "Apolonia Ołdak," p. 387. In 1942, Apolonia found a girl crying near a place where Jews were being shot and took her in. She kept her after the war as well. When Apolonia's husband died in 1950, she moved to Israel and took the girl with her, see ibid.,

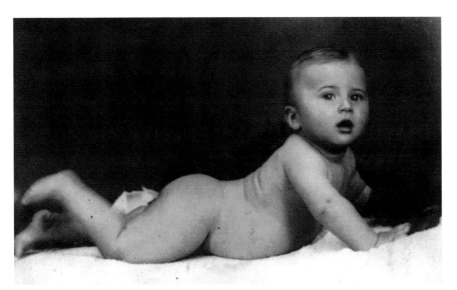

Elżbieta Kopel in the home of her rescuer, Stanisława Busold. Elżbieta was born in January, 1942 in the Warsw Ghetto and a few months later was removed from the Ghetto and given over to Stanisława for safekeeping.
(Courtesy: Elżbieta Ficowska-Kopel, Warsaw, Poland)

Teaspoon given by Elżbieta's grandfather to the baby's rescuer. The teaspoon is engraved with the name and date of birth: "Elżunia, 5.1.42."
(Courtesy: Elżbieta Ficowska-Kopel)

The girl, Irena Dąbrowska (Erella Goldschmidt), who was saved by the Trybus family from Zakopane, posing, together with her older "sister," Janina Trybus, during the war. (Courtesy: the late Erella Goldschmidt, Shadmot Dvora)

Irena Dąbrowska (Erella Goldschmidt) during the war. (Courtesy: the late Erella Goldschmidt)

Leonka (Ita-Leah) Igenfeld aged ten. Her Polish adoptive rescuers, the Pycz family, sent this photograph to the girl's mother in Canada in 1951. On the back of the photograph, the mother wrote, "This is a picture of my beloved daughter... who remains in the coarse hands of an antisemite to this day..." (Courtesy: Rina Rozin, Ramat Gan)

Rachel Igenfeld-Besserman and her daughter Ita-Leah in 1957, after the girl was sent by her adoptive rescuers in Poland to her mother in Canada. On the back of the photograph, the mother wrote, "I... together with my redeemed daughter after fifteen years of war and suffering... Imma Rachel." (Courtesy: Rina Rozin)

Zula (Hanita Leshem) together with her rescuers, the Wrarzej family from Lwów during the war. (Courtesy: Hanita Leshem, Jerusalem)

Rabbi David Kahana and his family after the war, when he served as chief chaplain of the Polish army and head of the Council of Jewish Religious Communities in Poland

Yehuda Bornstein, an activist for the "Zionist Koordynacja for the Redemption of Children," together with four girls whom he removed from the homes of their Polish rescuers in 1948. (Courtesy: Tami Lavie, Haifa)

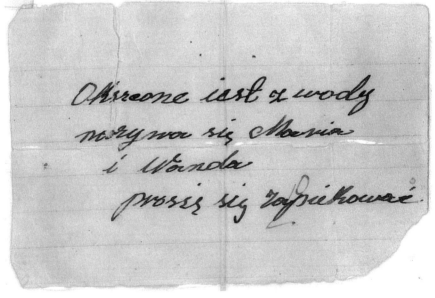

Pouch sewn into the inside of the velvet dress of the girl, Wanda Czarnecka (Tami Lavie), by a Polish friend of her mother. Inside the bag was a written note saying, "Baptized in [holy] water, pleading to look after her." The girl, wearing a crucifix round her neck, was left at a monastery near the town of Zamość. The pouch and the note were returned to Tami Lavie by the mother superior of the convent in 1988, when she visited Poland. (Courtesy: Tami Lavie)

Dnia 26 grudnia 1948 r. o godz. 10 w kościele Garnizonowym w Łodzi odbędzie się uroczystość zaślubin

Rózi Sobczyńskiej
z Jerzym Drudzkim

na którą mają zaszczyt prosić W. P.

Rodzice i Narzeczeni

Fictitious invitation to the wedding of Rózi Sobczyńska (Ruszka Gutmorgen) and Jerzy Drudzki (Yeshayahu Drucker, an activist on behalf of the Council of Jewish Religious Communities in Poland). The invitation was printed in order to achieve the release of Ruszka's younger sister, Hanka, after Hanka's rescuers refused to hand the girl over. (Courtesy: Ruszka Gutmorgen-Luster, Kiryat Ata)

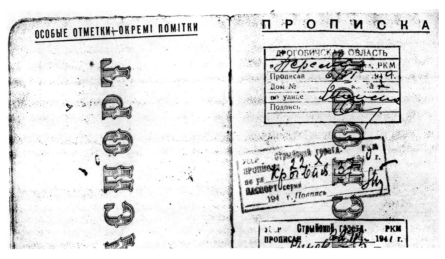

In 1943, Sheva Steigbeigel visited her son in the home of his rescuers. Knowing that she was being followed by the Germans, she left her leather handbag behind when they parted and they never met again. Later on the child was removed from the rescuing family and transferred to a different place. In the 1960s, Roma Jarska, daughter of the rescuers, found the bag and unstitched its lining. She discovered Sheva's passport and her son's birth certificate in a hidden pocket. The picture shows pages from the passport. (Courtesy: Roma Jarska, Kraków, Poland)

had to leave the ghetto under false papers[34] or they had abandoned children
at the doors of non-Jewish homes, leaving no information whatsoever.[35] As if
this was not enough, the children had to be given false names[36] by which they

Leokadia Statnik-Pessel, pp. 510–511. The girl whom Leokadia had rescued had been given
to her by her father, whose traces vanished afterwards; see child card of Juzio, Józef, ŻIH,
catalogue of children. The only detail that appears on the card is the boy's first name (and
there is no certainty that this was indeed his name).

34 Testimonies, documents, and papers concerning Erella Hilferding-Goldschmidt, given to
me by her and in my possession. While Erella was a baby, her mother fled with her from
Lwów to Zakopane, using false papers. After her mother was captured, Erella remained
with the owners of the hotel where her mother had been staying under a false name, Dombrowska.

35 Testimony Abraham Tsoref, in Dror (interviewer and editor), *Pages of Testimony*, A, p. 95.
Tsoref told the story of a friend who had been with him in a camp in Germany and wished
to return to Poland after the liberation in order to search for his son, whom his wife had left
on the steps of a convent while he was a baby; see also autobiography of fourteen-year-old
Sala Reiss in Tenenboim, *One of a City, Two of a Family*, pp. 98–99. Sala and her younger
sister were the sole survivors of her family. When Sala realized that she could not take care
of her sister, she left her at the door of a public kitchen and watched over her until someone took her in. She does not know where her sister was taken; see also Hellman, *Avenue
of the Righteous*, pp. 170–171, 226. In late 1942, the parents placed their baby daughter at
the edge of a forest and were unable to stay there. A Polish woman eventually found the
girl; Neshamit, "The Koordynacja for the Redemption of Children in Liberated Poland,"
p. 134, tells about a Jewish women who gave birth in August 1940 in the home of a midwife
in Radomsk, left the baby there, and returned to the ghetto. The midwife, afraid to keep
the infant in her home, had him placed at the entrance of the municipal hospital, where a
childless couple took him in; see also Grynberg, *Księga Sprawiedliwych*, "Pelagia Vogelgesang," pp. 590–591. Pelagia lived near Warsaw. One day in May 1943, she heard adult voices
and the crying of a child. Stepping outside, she did not see the adults but heard gunshots
and found a baby girl on her doorstep. She took the girl into her home and raised her; see
also letter World Jewish Congress to Central Committee, March 31, 1946, ŻIH, Education
Department, File 643. The letter was sent to the Committee on behalf of a mother who had
left her daughter on the steps of the Wisockis' home in Lubartów; letter Tenenbaum, Rome,
via Committee of Polish Jews in Italy, March 3, 1948, to Central Committee, ibid., File 638.
Tenenbaum reported that in 1942 he had led his granddaughter into a forest, where he
left her under an agreement with a man who was to place her in a Polish orphanage. The
grandfather did not know what had become of her.

36 Hellman, *Avenue of the Righteous*, p. 174. A woman who found a baby girl at the edge of
a forest named her Bŏgumiła — *bŏg* meaning God and *miło* meaning beloved; Neshamit,
"The Koordynacja for the Redemption of Children in Liberated Poland," p. 134, tells of a
baby who was found in a basket at the door of a hospital in Radomsk and whose name was
recorded as *Radomsky*, named after the city; letter Bozena Szaniewska, April 1995, in my
possession. A two-year-old Jewish girl was placed in the care of Szaniewska's mother during the war and was recorded under the name of Szaniewska's sister, who had died in 1939;
see also child card of Woleniak, given to me by the owner of the card, Iko Simchai, and in
my possession. Until recently, Iko did not know her true family name, Walisz; Grynberg,
Księga Sprawiedliwych, "Ksenia and Ignacy Madej," p. 319. The Madej family took in a

were raised — often without knowing, or having forgotten, their real name. When they were searched for after the war, the confusion of names made it uncertain that the child was Jewish at all.[37] If a parent or relative who knew the child's supposed whereabouts had survived, that could establish a point of departure that made the child easier to trace. Some survivors found the children in this manner[38] but others failed to do so because the trail along which they tried to reconstruct the children's movements was broken.[39]

Most of the children were baptized by their rescuers during the war — either for religious reasons or to make them "official" so that their presence in the family would be more plausible.[40] It was difficult to adopt a child during

girl named Halina Awerbuch and renamed her Karysia Winnicka; Koryski, "The Zionist Koordynacja for the Redemption of Jewish Children in Poland," pp. 29–30. Additional names that were given to children of whom nothing was known included *Niewidomski* ("unknown"), *Nicyes* (nothing), and *Bozanski* (Godly).

37 Letter Drucker to JDC (in response to letter JDC, asking him to take care of several cases), Warsaw, April 17, 1947, JDC, microfilm from Poland. Responding to JDC's inquiry about a girl in Dębice known as D.A., Drucker reported that he knew of a girl named D. Knie in Dębice and assumed it was the same one; letter Education Department to Bielsko-Biała Committee in the matter of L.J., who was staying with a family named Trybus — but the girl actually found with this family was named I.D. (in other documents, the name "Maria" appears) — her false name, taken from the forged papers that her mother had arranged. (Her real name was recently discovered to be Irena Hilferding-Weinrat. See ŻIH, Education Department, File 638.)

38 Working report Teofilia Goldman on the children B.R. and F.R.; interview by author with Rachel Mizoc-Gewing, March 1988. Rachel's sister claimed her from the house of the man with whom she had been left; Grynberg, *Księga Sprawiedliwych*, "Stefania Lipska," p. 308; ibid., Władysława and Bolesław Brejna, p. 59; Ferderber-Salz, *And the Sun Appeared*, p. 61.

39 Helman, *Avenue of Trees*, p. 157: The father searched for his daughter in the vicinity of the place where he had left her but was unable to find her. In his testimony, he related that in his despair he burst into tears and cried out, "Shifra, my baby girl, where are you?" After a number of fruitless investigations and inquiries, he left Poland for Rome en route to Palestine. After visiting a fortune teller in Rome, he returned to Poland and began to search again and found his daughter some time later; interview by author with Eugenia (Tova) Bein, January 1997, in the matter of J.S.: the boy's father returned to Kraków from a camp in Germany after the war in order to search for his son, whom he had left with his wife (who was subsequently captured) and could not find him. The father moved to the United States, remarried, and died about ten years ago. In 1995, after receiving a communication from Roma Jerska of Kraków (who was about five years old when the boy had been in their home), I met her and she gave me documents (birth certificate and passport) that the boy's mother had sewn into the lining of her handbag and that were found by chance years later. I took part in the search for the "boy" and our investigation showed that he had reached Palestine after the war as a member of Lena Küchler's group of children and only his first name was known. Due to the lack of details available about him, he was renamed in Palestine. He was recently introduced to relatives who live in Israel; see also Kempner, "Only the Baby," pp. 31, 33, 56.

40 Kempner, "Only the Baby," pp. 31, 33, 56; the village mayor contacted the woman with

the war because adoption entailed investigation and the production of proof that the youngster was a Polish orphan. However, if the child had been removed from a Polish orphanage and his or her origin was unknown or could not be proven, there was a chance that adoption could be arranged.[41] These actions, regardless of their motives, only strengthened the bonds that had formed between the children and their adoptive parents and reaffirmed the parents' intentions. Families that regarded the children whom they had taken in as members of their households took deliberate action to adopt them after the war, thereby making the arrangement official.[42] Obviously it was very difficult to locate these children.[43]

whom the baby girl had been placed and ordered her to surrender the infant to the police. The woman pleaded with the policemen to allow her to raise the girl. She had lost five children in infancy and had no other children. One of the policemen, taking pity on her, suggested that she have the girl baptized and promised that they would cease to harass her, and he kept his word; Grynberg, *Księga Sprawiedliwych,* "Zofia and Klemens Leszczyński," p. 305: the Leszczyńskis received the girl from acquaintances as a Polish orphan and only afterwards did they discover that she was Jewish. After consulting with a priest, the couple decided to have her baptized and to keep her in their home.

41 Grzywacz, "To the Bosom of My People," pp. 62–63. The Łukasiewiczes, staunch Catholics, removed the child from a Polish orphanage and wished to adopt him. After observing their devotion and love for him, he told them that he was Jewish. The Łukasiewiczes remained as warm towards him as they had been before and protected him even more zealously. They reported the situation to their priest, who knew him as a choirboy, and the priest baptized him with his consent; see also letter to author from Maria Bogumila Kordzikowska, Poland, April 1995: Maria's family had removed her from a Polish orphanage that had relocated from Warsaw to Wolbrom in the aftermath of the Polish uprising in 1944, and adopted her. Afterwards, they discovered that she was Jewish and had been found in the Warsaw Ghetto during the uprising with a band bearing her name around her neck. Maria grew up in Poland and lived as a Christian woman.

42 Mahler, "Redemption of Jewish Children from Their Non-Jewish Rescuers," pp. 37–38, describes how a removal operative sometimes had to turn back without the child she had intended to remove because the family refused to surrender him and threatened her. She returned with a police escort the following day, but the rescuer produced adoption papers carrying the date of the previous day; Amalia Argaman-Barnea, "Girl of War," *Yediot Aharonot,* Friday Supplement, June 11, 1993, pp. 84–85, 96: after the war, a Polish family removed a girl from a convent and adopted her; letter Warsaw committee to Child Care Department, March 23, 1946, in the matter of K.F. and M.L., ŻIH, Education Department, File 638: the letter notes with displeasure that the rescuers' practice of baptizing children was "de-Judaizing" the youngsters and making it hard to remove them; child card of Eduard Radomski. During the war, the rescuer wished to register the boy in her name but did not receive authorization to do so because his origin was in doubt, so the boy was baptized after the war; Grynberg, *Księga Sprawiedliwych,* "Blichert," p. 45: the girl whom the Blicherts adopted after the war continued to live with them until 1957, when she turned fifteen. At this point, Mrs. Blichert allowed her to join Jews who were leaving for Israel.

43 Yishai, *In the Shadow of the Holocaust,* p. 79; Neshamit, "The Koordynacja for the Redemption of Children in Liberated Poland," p. 130.

Another difficulty faced by the removal operatives had to do with changes of address by rescuers. Some moved during the war; others did so in the course of the population transfer that followed it.[44] Polish families that did not wish to part from the children in their custody and feared that the Jewish organizations would be able to trace them at their prior addresses, seized the opportunity to relocate and melt into new surroundings.[45]

Due to the many obstacles faced by the removal operatives, attempting to trace children was usually time-consuming. In some cases, even the initial information arrived belatedly.[46] Although much thought and labor were invested in the attempt to trace the children, success was not always achieved.

Methods of Removal

Even after the operatives had located Jewish children, they were in no rush to remove them. Experience had taught them that it was better to wait and gather as much information as possible concerning the rescuer family and the child's role within the family.[47] With this information, they might be able to obtain a broader picture that would subsequently facilitate the removal of the child. This factor did much to determine the timing of the operation.

The relatively copious information that accumulated in the first year of operations allowed the operatives to act intensively. Since travel was danger-

44 Letter Child Care Department to Łódź district committee, 1946, in the matter of R.H., ŻIH, Education Department, File 638: the department asked the committee to inquire with the Polish State Authority for Repatriation Affairs, in Łódź, about the whereabouts of citizen Woźniakowa, previously of Lwów; card no. 14 — Rama Tuczyńska, card no. 31 — Shoshana Tumim, GFHA, catalogue of Koordynacja children, File 800; Grynberg, *Księga Sprawiedliwych*, "Blichert," p. 45: the Blicherts moved from Lithuania to Lower Silesia; ibid., Władysława and Bolesław Brejna, p. 59: after the Polish uprising in Warsaw in 1944, the family, together with the girl, moved to Pruszków.

45 Letter Director of Legal Department, Adv. Gutmacher, to court registrar in Wrocław, May 19, 1947, in the matter of P.A., ŻIH, Legal Department; the father of the girl's rescuer was located and was known to have been in touch with his son. However, the father refused to reveal his son's address so that the girl's mother could not reclaim her; Neshamit, "The Koordynacja for the Redemption of Children in Liberated Poland," pp. 125, 130; Kahana, *After the Deluge*, p. 16, in the matter of the daughter of Halberstam, rabbi of Zaklików.

46 Letter David Igra, Tel Aviv, to Rabbi Herzog, February 1, 1947, RZA, Rescue Files; letter Moshe Goldberg, Rishon leZion, to Rabbi Herzog, January 21, 1947, ibid.

47 Interview by author with Yeshayahu Drucker; testimony Dvora Zilber, OHD, 27(68); testimony Yehuda Bronstein, OHD, 25(68); letter Education Department to Katowice Committee, June 13, 1947, in the matter of O.K., ŻIH, Education Department, File 638; letter Education Department to Rzeszów committee, April 1, 1946, in the matter of I.G., ibid.

ous, operatives tended to combine several cases in a given area into one journey — obviously, each case was in a different phase of treatment[48] — and used the time to search for and track down additional children.[49]

There was no single method of removal; one may even say that there were as many methods as there were children. The method had to be tailored to the situation, which varied from one family to the next. Several visits to one home were usually needed because the family, and the child, had to become accustomed to the idea. The first visits were calculated to improve the atmosphere and get acquainted; at this meeting, the operative attempted to gauge the family's willingness to hand over the child and tried to estimate the hardships that should be expected as a result. One should bear in mind that the Central Committee also used the exploratory technique in its first contact with the families. In some cases, several operatives from one organization dealt with the removal of a child in order to find just the right person, even if this meant that the case would take longer to resolve.[50]

The operatives had only one goal in the negotiating process: to convince the rescuers to surrender the child. Acutely convinced of the righteousness of their actions, the operatives did not hesitate to promise anything that would help to remove children from rescuers' hands. Numerous arguments were used in these persuasion sessions: the operatives claimed that it would have been the parents' wish;[51] that in view of their love for the child, the rescuers should realize that life in Poland would eventually lead the child into a confrontation with rampant antisemitism; that the Jewish state soon to be declared would give the children a country that would also be a home;[52] that the rescuers would receive the family's property in consideration of surrendering the child;[53] and that the child had relatives in the west and it would be in his or her best interests to join them. In one case, Lederman even falsely promised a rescuer who persisted in refusing that she would receive an American passport and could join the girl.[54]

---

48 Working report Teofilia Goldman.
49 Ibid.; testimony Yehuda Bronstein, OHD, 25(68); Marysia, in contrast, eschewed the combined itinerary and dealt with each case separately. See testimony Devorah Zilber, OHD, 27(68).
50 Testimony Leibl Koryski, OHD 15(68).
51 Dekel, *Remnants of the Sword*, pp. 122–133.
52 Testimony Yehuda Bronstein, OHD 25(68).
53 Dekel, *Remnants of the Sword*, pp. 206–213.
54 Testimony Sarah Lederman, OHD 50(68). When representatives of the Jewish committee contacted the rescuer, she told them that she preferred to surrender the child to the woman who had promised to take her as well. When the Committee people explained to her that

The promises given to the children may have been simpler. In the dire economic state of post-war Poland, many children and their rescuers lived in conditions of severe hardship. Therefore, the children could be enticed with trivial things: a train ride,[55] a piece of candy, a toy, new clothing,[56] and stories about Palestine, oranges, and sunshine.[57] Operatives sometimes introduced themselves to a child as family members — uncles or even parents — and showered them with all sorts of presents as "compensation for our years apart."[58]

There were no limits in the attempt to win a child's trust. When one boy told Lederman, the Agudath Israel operative, that he wished to live only with Christians, she said that she understood him well and that she herself used to be Jewish but was now Christian. When the boy asked her to buy him a crucifix, Lederman not only honored his request, but also even bought a crucifix and a Christian prayer book for herself.[59]

Sometimes operatives chose to outwit the children, the rescuers, or both. Bronstein, for example, testified about a girl who was living with her rescuer and had formed a strong bond with him: the man married after the war and his new bride pressured him to hand the girl over to a Jewish organization, but the rescuer and the girl were not easily convinced. Ultimately, the girl gave her consent but asked her "mother" to sew some money into the sleeve of her coat — so that if she regretted having left, she could escape and return to them. The stepmother did as asked but reported it to the operative,

she had been deceived, the rescuer responded by going to the children's home and abducting the girl. She was caught at a bus stop and taken to the police station on the grounds that she had signed a document making it clear that she had surrendered the girl of her own free will and had been reimbursed for her expenses incurred on the girl's account. The girl was returned to Lederman, who was discomfited by the incident and asked the police commander to release the rescuer from detention.

55 Testimony Yeshayahu Drucker, YVA, O.3/3249, on the subject of T.W.
56 Mahler, "Redemption of Jewish Children from Their Non-Jewish Rescuers," p. 36; letter Maria Madej, Poland, April 21, 1995. In the letter, Maria described how a Jewish family had enticed her sister, Zosia, by promising to buy her things that the rescuer family could not afford: "Helena pampered Zosia, gave her dresses to wear, gave her candy, did everything to attract the little one to her. My brothers, Zosia, and I wore wooden shoes. I remember the words that Mrs. Helena said: 'If you stay with me, you'll have pretty shoes.'"
57 Responses Tamar Jacobi to my questionnaire.
58 Berman, "Wanda's Lists;" testimony Shoshana Wajman, in *Conference of Koordynacja Children,* Kibbutz Lehavot Habashan, October 1985 (Hebrew), given to me by Chasia Bielicki-Bornstein. Marysia told her that she was her mother. The girl knew this was not true because she remembered her mother from her last visit with her in the village; testimony Sarah Lederman, OHD 50(68).
59 Testimony Sarah Lederman, OHD 50(68).

who removed the money from its hiding place[60] and in so doing destroyed the girl's chance of returning.

The operatives did not flinch from any measure that might help them attain their goal: they arranged fictitious powers of attorney,[61] dressed up as state employees,[62] had neighbors sign depositions stating that the child was being mistreated,[63] applied pressure by threatening to disclose relations with the Germans[64] or with the AK (the Polish nationalist underground),[65] or made any other threat that could be seen as relevant to the case at hand.[66] Sometimes an unforeseen situation came about that gave the operatives an opportunity to remove the child, and they exploited such opportunities to the limit. Once, for example, a Polish woman found a Jewish baby girl during the war and took her home, telling anyone who was curious that the girl was her daughter, born to her from a German friend who was visiting her and even helping her take care of the baby. After the war, her neighbors caused her much suffering by accusing her of having had "relations" with the Germans. One of the removal operatives discovered this and hurriedly exploited the woman's distress, providing her with a certificate for having rescued a Jewish girl, in return for her surrendering the girl to him.[67]

When all avenues of persuasion and pressure, including recourse to the courts, were exhausted and the conclusion of an agreement still proved impossible, the option of abducting children was not ruled out. For example,

---

60 Testimony Yehuda Bronstein, OHD 25(68). In my conversation with the child, now an adult, it transpired that she still believed that her stepmother had not kept her word and had not sewn the money into her coat.
61 Warhaftig, *Refugee and Survivor*, p. 435.
62 Interview by author with Sarah Shner-Neshamit; Dekel, *Remnants of the Sword*, pp. 60, 160; Jeruchamzon appeared in his uniform at a convent near Wrocław and introduced himself as an inspector from the Polish Koordynacja who had been sent to examine the conditions of maintenance of war orphans. In his "inspection," he noticed two Jewish children and suggested to the convent directors that they be transferred to a Jewish children's home so that the Jews would pay for their care. The ruse was discovered and he received a reprimand from the Deputy Minister of Welfare for the impersonation.
63 Testimony Moshe Jeruchamzon, OHD 44(68); deposition of a Polish citizen named Milczuk, GFHA, Correspondence File, 788–790; Dekel, *Remnants of the Sword*, p. 197.
64 Working report Teofilia Goldman.
65 Testimony Yeshayahu Drucker, OHD 28(68).
66 Granatstein, *Double Life*, p. 13. Granatstein testified that when Zamość encountered resistance, he stopped behaving pleasantly and went over to tough language, even making threats to get what he wanted; testimony Sabina Halperin, MA, A.201: the girl claimed that the men who came to take her behaved aggressively and threatened her rescuer with imprisonment if she interfered.
67 Kurek-Lesik, *"Udzial Żeńkich,"* p. 350.

a young man applied to Drucker and told him that he had not managed to convince his sisters to return to Judaism and that he had to leave Poland, as he had an immigration visa for Palestine. The older sister refused to leave the convent where she was staying unless her younger sister, who was living with her rescuer, agreed to come with her. When all Drucker's attempts to persuade the girl and the rescuer to part failed, the operative, in collaboration with the older sister, devised a subterfuge: they printed up invitations to their "wedding" at a church in Łódź and invited the rescuer to attend. In the meantime, they asked the rescuer to let them take the girl in order to buy her appropriate clothing for the wedding. The rescuer agreed; she suspected nothing and was actually pleased about the older sister's marriage to a Polish officer. In the nearest town, the two of them hired a taxi and drove to Łódź, where, despite the girl's protests, the two of them joined a collective in Silesia. When the rescuer went to Łódź on the day of the "wedding" she discovered that she had been tricked and that she would not see the girl again.[68] The operatives

---

68 Testimony Yeshayahu Drucker, OHD 28(68); interview by author with Chana Martynows-ki-Gutmorgen; the wedding invitation was given to me by Ruszka Gutmorgen-Luster and is in my possession. It is phrased as follows: "On December 26, 1948, the wedding of Rozi Sobczyńska (Ruszka Gutmorgen's false name) and Jerzy Drudzki (a Polish-sounding corruption of Yeshayahu Drucker's name) will take place at Garnizonów Church in Łódź. It is our pleasure to invite you as our esteemed guests. The family and sponsors." The girl had spent six years with her rescuer; I found further testimonies about acts of abduction only in regard to members of the Koordynacja and the Council of Religious Communities. See testimony Leibl Koryski, OHD 15(68); Kahana, *After the Deluge*, p. 53; testimony Yeshayahu Drucker, YVA, O.3/3249. Drucker recounted a case in which the aunt of a girl won a legal injunction but the rescuer, a peasant from a village near Skarżysko-Kamienna, refused to return her. Drucker visited the peasant's house with an escort but the peasant's wife mobilized the villagers and the operatives fled, pursued by a mob. Some time later, they returned to the village as part of a nine-member group and surrounded the house at 3:00 in the morning and took the girl even before the peasant and his wife realized what was happening; Dekel, *Remnants of the Sword*, pp. 81, 95, 203–213; the rescuer of two children demanded $3,000 for surrendering them. Since this sum could not be raised, the Koordynacja removed them by means of deception: two soldiers were sent to arrest the peasant and his wife, telling them that the reason for this action would be revealed at the police station. After they were taken to the police station, the children were removed from their home; interview by author with David Plonsky, 1996. Jorek related the story of a girl from Łódź whose rescuers refused to surrender her. After they found out where she went to school, the operatives visited the school and enticed her with candy to accompany them to an apartment nearby. Since the rescuer was a high-ranking Communist, the searches for the girl began that very day. Even trains leaving Łódź were searched on the assumption that the girl would be removed from the city. Only after the searches were called off was the girl removed from the apartment and taken to a children's home; see also Neshamit, "The Koordynacja for the Redemption of Children in Liberated Poland," pp. 123–124.

were ill at ease with behavior of this kind, although they felt that the rescuers' refusal left them no choice.[69] According to Drucker, the police probably knew about these cases after receiving complaints from Polish citizens but took no action.[70] Koryski, in contrast, says that police alerts were issued after abductions and that members of the organization were arrested. Notably, the Central Committee disapproved of this way of removing children, arguing that it was illegal and jeopardized the continuation of their activities.[71]

Older children did not have to be reminded of their Jewish identity; their years in non-Jewish homes may have blunted their memories but had not obliterated them. It was uncertain, however, how much remained; to what extent they knew about other Jews who had survived; and whether they were interested in leaving their rescuer families and society and returning to life among Jews. The answers to these questions depended on the situation of each child at the time. Some children, at the end of the war, asked to leave their host families and tried to contact Jews at their own initiative so as not to be on their own.[72] Mira, nine-and-a-half years old when the war ended, is a case in point. Mira had told the family with whom she stayed before liberation that she was a Polish orphan named Marysia Malinowska, the daughter of a Polish officer who had been taken prisoner by the Germans at the beginning of the war. When the war ended and the names of Polish prisoners of war began to be announced, the family delightedly told her about an officer of that name. For a while the girl lived in dread that her lie would be discovered. One evening, however, she heard members of the family conversing about a Jewish family from the same locality that had survived the war and returned. Mira went to her family to tell them that she was Jewish and, fearing that her rescuers would no longer be interested in her, falsely told them that her

---

69 Testimony Leibl Koryski, OHD 15(68); Dekel, *Remnants of the Sword*, pp. 206–213; interview by author with Yeshayahu Drucker.
70 Interview by author with Yeshayahu Drucker.
71 Testimony Leibl Koryski, OHD 15(68).
72 Letter G.M. to Koordynacja, October 22, 1947, GFHA, Correspondence File, 788–790. A fifteen-year-old boy wrote that he had heard about the Koordynacja and wanted to move into a children's home; letter B. to Koordynacja, undated, ibid. B., twenty years old, was working in a village near Malbork. While in town, he read in a newspaper about the Zionist Koordynacja and decided to contact it. He sent a letter describing his experiences up to that time, adding, "I am writing to you to ask you, please, don't leave me [here] so long. I am not giving [you] my personal address because I don't want to be discovered until the last moment." The boy gave a post office box number at which he could be contacted; testimony Sukha Shmueli, MA, A.217.

family had a great deal of property. The rescuers reported her presence to the Jewish committee in Kraków, which sent a staff member to claim her.[73]

Other children were in no hurry to identify themselves, electing instead to stay where they were under their false identities even though they knew that the war had ended. Only when the removal operatives came and persuaded them did they agree to leave.[74] Still others, in contrast, would not be persuaded and refused to return to the Jews.[75] The operatives, however, were not easily daunted and made an immense effort to persuade them. Although the children had grown up during the war and had often endured life-threatening ordeals, the operatives believed that the children's views were subjective and influenced by their experiences and that, consequently, their wishes should not be taken into consideration.[76] More than once, however, the operatives backed down after their many attempts at persuasion failed. A Koordynacja operative, for example, told the following story: in one of the trans-

---

73 Interview by author with Mira Erlich-Bramm, February 1995; testimony Mira Bramm. While at the children's home in Rabka, she received letters from her rescuers' family, describing their dire economic situation and asking her to help them — on the basis of the lie she had made up about her family's great wealth.

74 Testimony Chana Owrucki-Mandelberger, YVA, O.3/5773; testimony Avraham Friedman, MA, A.403; child card of Batya Goldstein, card no. 56, GFHA, catalogue of Koordynacja children, File 800.

75 Letter Drucker to Rabbi Herzog, June 12, 1947, in the matter of A.N., RZA, Rescue Files; Perlberger-Shmuel, *This Girl Is Jewish*, pp. 61, 63–65; Dekel, *Remnants of the Sword*, pp. 130–131, 194; letter Hirsh Yitzhak Kurz, Melbourne, to Koordynacja,. Łódź, September 28, 1947, GFHA, Correspondence File, 788–790: despite the operative's attempts to persuade her to leave, the girl decided to stay in the convent and to become a nun; clarification report by removal operative in the matter of Grandmother Cyngiser, February 23, 1947, GFHA, Correspondence File, 788–790. In fact, the report deals with two of her grandchildren. The boys left their rescuer after the war and worked for peasants in two different villages. When the operative first came, he did not manage to remove them. The second time, he came accompanied by two policemen. The seventeen-year-old was captured and taken away against his will but the fourteen-year-old escaped and stopped only after several gunshots were fired. Both boys were delivered to the Koordynacja in Łódź under police escort but fled three days later. In his report, the operative suggested waiting for two or three months and then trying to search for them again; list of twenty-five children whose cases were in progress, undated, JDC, microfilm from Poland; according to the list, one of the children had been removed by Agudath Israel and returned to his rescuers, who now refused to surrender him.

76 Dekel, *Remnants of the Sword*, p. 198; clarification report in the matter of Grandmother Cyngiser, February 23, 1947; biography R.M., October 8, 1946: in the biography, the eighteen year-old girl notes that after the war she joined a training institute for nuns and did not reveal her Jewish identity. The female operative whom the Koordynacja sent to visit her persuaded her to return to Judaism. GFHA, Correspondence File, 788–790; Neshamit, "The Koordynacja for the Redemption of Children in Liberated Poland," pp. 143–144.

ports, two siblings — a boy and a girl — were among the Jews in the wagons that reached the Treblinka village railroad station before they could be moved to the extermination camp. While they were waiting, the people in the wagon broke through the wooden floor and several escaped. The guards chased and fired at them but the two children managed to reach a house in the village and hide there, terrifying the owner, whose own children were playing in the yard. When she saw the guards pursuing them, the woman directed the guards to her own house. The guards shot the woman's children, assuming they were the fugitive Jewish youngsters who were hiding in the house. The terrified woman regained her composure quickly and decided that if this was her fate, she had no choice but to raise the Jewish youngsters. The operative did not know the source of the information about these children after the war but was told that emissaries had been sent to remove them several times, failing each time. In 1947, when he was asked to deal with their removal, the children were sixteen and seventeen years old. They knew they were Jewish but refused to leave their "mother," as they called their rescuer, since she had lost her own children and had saved them. The mother left the decision up to them: both persisted in their refusal and remained in the village.[77]

In some cases, the removal of youngsters to a children's home did not indicate the end of the case. Some children were removed more than once — either because their rescuers regretted their consent and reclaimed them,[78] or because the children themselves fled from the homes and returned to their rescuers.[79] In these cases, it was harder to go back and search for them, since neither the child nor the rescuers would cooperate. The children's homes had prepared for this possibility from the outset and took measures to thwart it, but could not prevent it altogether.[80]

77 Interview by author with Yosef Haezrahi-Bürger.
78 Testimony Sarah Lederman, OHD 50(68), Neshamit, "The Koordynacja for the Redemption of Children in Liberated Poland," p. 125.
79 Dekel, *Remnants of the Sword*, p. 197–198; Neshamit, "The Koordynacja for the Redemption of Children in Liberated Poland," pp. 143–144; clarification report in the matter of Grandmother Cyngiser, February 23, 1947; list of twenty-five children in non-Jews' homes, undated, JDC, microfilm from Poland.
80 Interview by author with Chasia Bielicki-Bornstein.

Negotiations with and Compensation for Rescuers

The operatives had no argument with the need to be grateful to rescuers and to compensate them for the hardships they had experienced during the war. While they could not assign a cash value to the risk that the act of rescue had involved, at least some rescuers had received consideration in cash or in kind from the children's parents when they were placed in hiding. In view of the severe economic straits in post-war Poland, however, compensation could help rescuers overcome their hardships.[81] The question that troubled all organizations that dealt with removing children was how to define "appropriate compensation," especially in view of their own limited resources.[82]

According to Krybus, the Jewish Agency Rescue Committee and JDC told the Koordynacja to pay rescuers any sum they demanded. This guideline, Krybus added, was consistent with the Koordynacja's understanding of the situation.[83] Drucker corroborated Krybus' remarks, stating that whenever there was a possibility of removing a child and the problem of funding came up, he turned directly to Guzik, the director of JDC-Poland, and was answered in the affirmative[84] even though officially the JDC subvention was limited to 5,000–10,000 zlotys per child.[85] The Koordynacja repeatedly debated the question of payment. At no time was an arbitrary decision made about the amount that would be paid for a child; the tendency was to consider each case on its own merits.[86] According to Lederman, Sternbuch imposed no

81 Interview by author with Yeshayahu Drucker; interview Bar-Gil with Arieh Sarid. Sarid related that in 1946 he paid 300,000 zlotys to a rescuer after she presented him with a document from the Gestapo attesting that her husband had been executed after being found to have hidden Jews; Kahana, *After the Deluge*, p. 15; Mahler, "Redemption of Jewish Children from Their Non-Jewish Rescuers," pp. 36–37; testimony Devorah Zilber, OHD, 27(68). Marysia mentioned an additional rationale for wishing to determine a level of compensation that would be appropriate and satisfactory to the rescuer: the fear that if rescuers felt dishonored, they might in their anger attack random Jews who were totally unrelated to the operations.

82 Yishai, *In the Shadow of the Holocaust*, p. 80. Yishai noted that in early 1946, JDC allocated 10,000 zlotys for the removal of a child whereas the religious councils (evidently the Council of Religious Communities) paid sums of 15,000–20,000 zlotys, if not more.

83 Testimony Pinhas Krybus, OHD 45(68). Since the guideline originated with the Jewish Agency Rescue Committee, it was presumably given in 1947. By then, everyone involved in the matter knew that families that still kept Jewish children had no intention of surrendering them. If negotiations fell through due to failure to agree on payment, such children would remain with their rescuers.

84 Interview by author with Yeshayahu Drucker.

85 Litvak, "JDC's Contribution," p. 352; Yishai, *In the Shadow of the Holocaust*, p. 80.

86 Interview by author with Menahem Kunda.

limits on the amounts to be paid out and left the decision to her.[87] However, aware that the funds were not bottomless, the removal operatives often bargained with rescuers in order to lower the "price" of a child.[88]

The negotiations were usually conducted, at least at first, between rescuers and representatives of the organizations without the child being consulted on the issue of whether he or she would be surrendered.[89] The result was a crisis in relations between the children and their rescuers. In some cases, children expressed their amazement and protested over the negotiations taking place in their presence. One nine year-old boy, for example, asked his rescuer after the sides bargained over his "price," "What, am I a calf that's being bought? You're selling me?"[90]

During the initial post-liberation period (up to the autumn of 1946), it was relatively easy to remove children. Some youngsters were handed over at the initiative of rescuers who were seeking a connection with the children's relatives[91] or had contacted the Jewish organizations that had been estab-

---

87 Testimony Sarah Lederman, OHD 50(68).

88 Testimony Yeshayahu Drucker, YVA, O.3/3249; testimony Yehuda Bronstein, OHD 25(68), in the matter of a girl that he removed from Gdynia. To avoid entering into unlimited negotiations, Bronstein usually told rescuers that the organization that had sent him would not allow him to exceed a certain sum. He knew that the financial possibilities were limited but feared that if rescuers knew from the ouset that they had no chance of getting what they wanted, they would not consider him an appropriate negotiating partner; Mahler, "Redemption of Jewish Children from Their Non-Jewish Rescuers," pp. 37–38: the rescuer demanded 100,000 zlotys for a boy and Marysia bargained him down to 40,000; Dekel, *Remnants of the Sword*, pp. 567–568: the rescuer demanded 100,000 zlotys and after negotiations received 50,000.

89 Dekel, *Remnants of the Sword*, pp. 567–568. Dekel describes negotiations for a certain girl as having been taken place dispassionately, as if ordinary merchandise was at issue. Even at the moment of parting, no special emotions were expressed — although the operatives knew that the rescuers had found the girl alone during the war and, at their initiative and without any prior acquaintance, took her in and gave her loving care; Küchler-Silberman, *My Hundred Children*, p. 88-90.

90 "That's How We Began," *Farn Yiddishn Kind*, p. 1; see also Neshamit, "The Koordynacja for the Redemption of Children in Liberated Poland," p. 131. Neshamit describes a case in which a boy was present during the negotiations over his surrender and asked his rescuers, "Why are you selling me?" When he was told that his father would have wanted him to live among Jews, he exclaimed, "With the Jews? If it's like that, you shouldn't have rescued me"; Granatstein, *Double Life*, pp. 13–14. Granatstein described the case of a boy who wandered around uneasily because he suspected that a "guest" who, whenever he visited, holed himself up with the rescuer as if the two of them were concluding a sale.

91 Shulamit Magen, "First and Last Memory," written in 1992 and given to me by her husband; testimony Yeshayahu Drucker, OHD 28(68). Drucker told the story of a girl who had spent the war living with a school principal, who treated her well and loved her dearly. When members of her family came to claim her, she refused to go with them even after the

lished after the war,[92] others were removed at the initiative of the organizations themselves. There were rescuers who surrendered children voluntarily, demanding no payment and refusing to accept sums that were offered them as a sign of gratitude for what they had done. Others, in contrast, were pleased to have an opportunity to ease their economic plight.[93] In certain cases, the children themselves, having personal knowledge of the dire financial circumstances of their host families, asked the operatives in gratitude to give them money in return for having looked after them.[94] The topic of money was not central in these cases and no special problems arose. Since the negotiations were brief, no tension developed between the organizations and the rescuers and no residual anger remained.

Whenever it contacted rescuers to probe their willingness to return children, the Central Committee expressed its intention to compensate them with the sum "accepted in our country under these circumstances" — without specifying an amount.[95] Ultimately, the sum dispensed was usually about 20,000 zlotys –irrespective of how long the child had stayed with the rescuers and irrespective of their material situation (with exceptions in unusual

rescuer tried to convince her. Finally, the man decided to make it easier for her to part with him by telling her in anguish that he no longer wanted her; Koryski, "The Zionist Koordynacja for the Redemption of Jewish Children in Poland," p. 26.

92 Grynberg, *Księga Sprawiedliwych,* Józef and Franciszka Kruriata, pp. 284–285. In one such case, rescuers took in a boy whom they had found in the forest and knew nothing about his family. After the war, they tried to look for his relatives but found none. In December 1946, they handed him over to the "rabbinate" (evidently the Council of Religious Communities); ibid., Jan and Janina Kosuth, p. 257: the couple contacted the Jewish committee in Praga, a suburb of Warsaw, at their own initiative in order to help the committee to search for relatives of a girl whom they had rescued; interview by author with Sabina Neuberg; the story of Michael, in Küchler, *We Accuse,* p. 164. Michael's caregiver wanted him to be Jewish like his parents when he grew up; autobiography Shoshana Wajman in Tenenboim, *One of a City and Two of a Family,* p. 218; Shner-Neshamit, *I Did Not Come to Rest,* pp. 136–137, 193.

93 Testimony Yeshayahu Drucker, OHD 28(68); Dekel, *Remnants of the Sword,* pp. 121–123, 132–133; Jacobi-Friedman, "Testimony," p. 58; the story of Marysia and Reuven, in Mahler, "Redemption of Jewish Children from Their Non-Jewish Rescuers," pp. 36–37; story of Izio and Pola Müller, in Sarid, "Remarks about the Koordynacja," p. 20; Grynberg, *Księga Sprawiedliwych,* Wanda Rachalska, pp. 446–447.

94 Interview by author with Sabina Neuberg; Lewinsky, "My Wanderings and My Rescuer," p. 22: in view of the antisemitism that spread in the area after the war, the rescuer was worried about the child and asked him to join the Jews. When the boy refused, the rescuer initiated a visit by a Jewish friend at his home in order to persuade him.

95 Letter Education Department to Justina Budnicka of Zielona Góra, November 6, 1947, ŻIH, Education Department, File 638.

cases).[96] All the other organizations visited rescuers at home to negotiate with them. Generally speaking, the Koordynacja, the Council of Religious Communities, and Agudath Israel paid much more than did the Central Committee. Although they matched the Committee's payments in the first months, before their financial sources stabilized during 1946, they were already paying out amounts that reached 100,000 zlotys and, in some cases, even more.[97] The Central Committee did not increase its own payments in response to the other organizations' levels. It is hard to know whether this impaired its ability to remove children, but the huge sums definitely created an incentive for rescuers. Once the possibility of getting larger sums of money arose, obviously the prices could only rise.

Sometimes the negotiations with rescuers were complex and difficult in both the emotional and the practical sense. Rescuers who expressed willingness to hand over children did so when the removal operations first began; it is clear that anybody who did not surrender children then did not wish to do so. In these cases, the negotiating difficulties first surfaced in the attempt to talk the rescuer into agreeing to part with the child, and indeed, to enter into negotiations at all. For example, Marysia's rescuer, who had a horse farm, refused to negotiate and blurted at the operative, "Take the horses but leave Marysia."[98] There were were cases in which the deliberations over the surrender of the child and the level of payment dragged on and on.[99] In at least some of these, the operatives felt that the rescuers were measuring their "love" of the child in terms of money and that the protests of inability to part with their

96 Letters Child Care Department to Central Committee presidium, ibid.; letter September 28, 1946, in the matter of H.K. H. Sachocka, who had cared for the child for three years, received 10,000 zlotys; letter September 28, 1946, in the matter of M.G. Stanisława Zawadka received 10,000 zlotys; letter August 24, 1946, in the matter of L.G. Kański who took care of a girl for four years and received 20,000 zlotys. The letter to him acknowledged the severe anguish that he had endured while the girl was in his custody during the war; letter July 2, 1946, in the matter of J.K. The letter itemizes 20,000 zlotys in payments that the rescuer Alexandra Nowakowska had received intermittently over a thirteen-month period.

97 In 1946, Marysia paid a manufacturer 125,000 zlotys for a girl whom she removed from his custody. See testimony Devorah Zilber, OHD, 27(68).

98 Interview by author with Yosef Haezrahi-Bürger in the matter of Marysia; Sarah Neshamit concurs. See interview by author with Sarah Shner-Neshamit.

99 Testimony Yehuda Bronstein, OHD 25(68). Bronstein described a case in which the argument about the surrender of a girl focused on the amount of money that the rescuer would get and not over the question of returning her. After three visits at different times, Bronstein paid 300,000 zlotys for her.

"beloved" little one were for bargaining purposes only. Wherever this happened, the sums demanded for the surrender of the child were steep.[100]

The relentless pressure by the organizations caused some rescuers to demand sums so large that they hoped the organizations could not possibly pay up, thereby allowing them to keep the children.[101] For example, one man, Jopowicz, had removed Leah from an orphanage during the war and adopted her. In 1947, when a relative of the girl found out that Leah was in his custody, she tried to claim the girl and, when Jopowicz refused to surrender her, turned to the Central Committee for assistance. After lengthy and exhausting negotiations, Jopowicz gave the Committee three options: arrange his and his wife's resettlement in the United States, give him $50,000, or give him title to the Hirszman family's house in Wierzbnik plus $10,000,[102] terms that seemed preposterous at the time.

Most of the sums demanded in 1947 and 1948 were immeasurably greater than those paid out in 1946.[103] There were several reasons for this: the families concerned were loath to part with the children and demanded large sums, as if to put the operatives to a test; the children in question had spent longer periods of time with their rescuers and had therefore incurred greater expenses for their care; and few children remained for the organizations to remove and the organizations competed fiercely for them, thereby also influencing the demands of the rescuers.

The organizations were of two minds about the involvement of relatives in removing children. Sometimes they felt that a child's relatives were not doing enough to help to remove him or her.[104] Conversely, they claimed that

---

100 Bielicka-Bornstein, "Back to the Bosom of Their People," p. 319; Granatstein, *Double Life*, pp. 13–14; Neshamit, "The Koordynacja for the Redemption of Children in Liberated Poland," p. 123.

101 Interview by author with Yosef Haezrahi-Bürger; Margoshes, "How to Redeem Jewish Children in Poland," p. 7; Hellman, *Avenue of the Righteous*, p. 238.

102 Record of Jopowicz deposition with Central Jewish Committee, May 8, 1947, in the matter of L.H., ŻIH, Education Department, file 638. Eventually the girl was abducted from her rescuer's home.

103 Income and expenditure statement for October 1947, sent to Jewish Agency Rescue Committee, Redemption of Children, CZA, S26/1924: for eleven children, 1,815,000 zlotys were paid out (not including payments made for information, travel expenses, board, operatives' wages, and office expenses); Neshamit, "The Koordynacja for the Redemption of Children in Liberated Poland," p. 122.

104 Letter Migration Services, United Service for New Americans, Inc., to JDC-Warsaw, September 8, 1948, JDC, microfilm from Poland. The letter discusses a delay in handling the matter of K.Z. and blamed it on the fact that an appeal to the girl's relatives in the U.S. had not been answered in a way that could advance the matter: one relative had not responded

relatives who requested assistance did not understand the nature of the work, were hysterical, and hindered the operations.[105] Relatives who negotiated with rescuers were usually willing to promise large sums and register family property in the rescuers' names. The organizations found it hard to compete with such promises. "The parents are promising to send the caregiver appropriate travel papers for her and the children," one of the operatives wrote. "Now that they have made this promise, our exertions are obviously futile."[106] Furthermore, when relatives who had initially acted on their own eventually turned to the organizations to assist in removing a child, the rescuers preferred not to cooperate with the organizations and preferred to continue negotiations with the relatives, confident that that would be to their financial advantage.[107]

Often rescuers exploited the situation: seeing the interest in the children as evidence of the vast amount of money that the Jews possessed, they raised their asking price.[108] Rescuers often asked Drucker to make several repeat visits in order to test the extent of his commitment — and raised their price according to the results.[109] Koordynacja officials summed up the matter in

to the request at all; another advised that he had sent penicillin to the Polish woman with whom the girl was living and could not help further; a third asserted that since he was only a distant relative he should not be contacted, even though he was willing to send the girl clothing and food via recognized organizations; letter Education Department to Bini Rybak, May 13, 1947, ŻIH, Education Department, File 638. The letter protests the fact that the addressee had not bothered to search for the girl herself and did not know anything about her until she had been informed, whereas now she expressed many complaints: "We are amazed that she waited two years for someone to run around in her stead"; Shner-Neshamit, *I Did Not Come to Rest*, p. 27; Sarah removed a girl at personal danger and at a high price. Some time later, a relative of the girl materialized and demanded custody. Since the girl had inherited a great deal of property, Sarah suspected that the relative's interest in her was only pecuniary.

105 Warhaftig, *Refugee and Survivor*, p. 437.
106 Letter Drucker to JDC, April 17, 1947.
107 Letter to Adv. Ya'akov Etzioni. The sender's name does not appear but the contents indicate that it was sent from Rabbi Herzog's office, July 8, 1947, RZA, Rescue Files; working report Teofilia Goldman in the matter of K.W. and E.R.; letter Education Department to Aher, Tel Aviv, August 23, 1947, in the matter of E.M., ŻIH, Education Department, File 638; letters Central Committee to Staszów committee, November 26, 1946; to Reingererc, Buenos Aires, January 8, 1947; to Weiblatt, UK, May 28, 1947, in the matter of S.H., ibid. The letters state that the girl's uncle in the United States had promised to arrange the rescuer's entry to America. The rescuer refused to surrender the girl even though Rabbi Schonfeld and a representative of Rabbi Kahana contacted him. The Central Committee offered to give him title to a house owned by the family, and he rejected this offer too. Ibid.
108 Margoshes, "How to Redeem Jewish Children in Poland," p. 7; working report Teofilia Goldman, in the matter of R.P.
109 Testimony Yeshayahu Drucker, YVA, O.3/3249.

a letter to JDC-Warsaw: "Christians who have become keenly aware of the situation are beginning to speculate in Jewish children; the more time passes, the more money they demand."[110] Some rescuers concealed information about children and conditioned providing it on a substantial payment.[111] The avarice of some rescuers even led to cases of fraud. While negotiating over a girl in his custody, for example, a Polish man said that the girl belonged to a certain wealthy family in his town — and demanded the family's property in return. The girl was removed under the name given but afterwards a neighbor identified her as belonging to a different family — an impoverished one.[112] In another case, a woman came to the offices of the Council of Religious Communities together with a girl and demanded 50,000 zlotys for her surrender. Drucker was surprised at the low price and quickly paid it, but several days later a municipal official visited his office with police escort and told him that the girl in question was a semi-orphaned Pole who was living in a municipal children's home. She occasionally visited the home of the woman who had delivered her to Drucker, and the latter decided to profiteer. The woman obtained the girl's consent by promising to have her moved to a better children's home. Drucker quickly gave the girl back.[113]

The issue of compensation became an emotional point in relations between organizations and rescuers, especially when rescuers recanted or denied having given their consent after receiving the agreed sum of money and surrendering the child. In response to such cases, the organizations began to make rescuers sign an affidavit in the presence of witnesses, confirming the details of the negotiations, forgoing future claims and confirming that they accepted the sum paid and considered it reasonable. In so doing, the organizations tried to protect themselves against additional demands and to give the removal operation validity in case of legal proceedings.[114]

---

110 Letter Koordynacja presidium to Bein, director of JDC-Poland, November 15, 1946, JDC, microfilm from Poland; see also Shner-Neshamit, *I Did Not Come to Rest,* p. 200; *Mission to the Diaspora*, p. 86; Dekel, *Remnants of the Sword*, p. 77.

111 Küchler-Silberman, *My Hundred Children*, p. 191.

112 Testimony Yeshayahu Drucker, OHD 28(68): the girl was removed under the family name of Klein whereas her real name was Hodes.

113 Testimony Yeshayahu Drucker, YVA, O.3/3249.

114 Records of Kolbuszowa municipal court, Mark P3345, September 12, 1946, about an agreement concluded in Niepolomice municipal court, before Judge Stepień, in the matter of Maria Anna Skrzydlewski, R.K., GFHA, Correspondence File, 788–790; affidavit signed by Michelina Smolczyńska and Władysława Polubińska, September 25, 1948, ibid.; testimony Yehuda Bronstein, OHD 25(68).

Vacillations about the amount of payment to be made were shared by all participants in the removal of children. The sums depended on many factors: financial limitations, the prevailing situation in Poland, the demands of the rescuers, and the nature and complexity of each individual rescue story. The contact with rescuers had various effects on the operatives. At first they appreciated and respected the rescuers, but as time went on and they had gained experience in situations of difficult bargaining, price-hiking, and peculiar demands, they became toughened and developed distrust and a great deal of anger toward the rescuers. They may actually have found it easier to bargain in such situations, as the erosion of their initial appreciation of the rescuers facilitated the process of negotiation.

Conclusion

An examination of how the various organizations prepared to search, locate, and remove Jewish children from the homes of rescuers, and study of the working methods developed, proves that they were determined to gather in as many children as possible. They invested a great deal of thought, time, and financial resources to the cause, sent into the field the people who seemed best suited for the tasks, and utilized the experience that accumulated as time went on. Nevertheless, the operatives did not always succeed; they often came away disappointed when their efforts, no matter how strenuous and costly, did not bring the desired results.

There were many reasons for the failures. Sometimes the information gathered was insufficient.[115] Sometimes the case was delayed for various reasons, as a result of which contact with the rescuers was severed and the child could no longer be found. In other cases, problems that came up during negotiations were never solved and the children remained with their rescuers. In one such example, a mother who tried to reclaim her son was threatened that harm would come to the boy if she continued to persevere. Valuing her son's life over her wish to reclaim him, she left Poland alone and turned down the movements' offers to intervene.[116] These cases left the operatives badly

---

115 Letter OCE to TOZ, April 22, 1947. On May 19, 1947, the following was handwritten on the letter: "The boy's fate cannot be clarified or determined."

116 Dekel, *Remnants of the Sword,* pp. 137–138; See also power of attorney sent by Rachel Igenfeld-Besserman of Canada to Rabbi Kahana, Warsaw, April 20, 1948, ŻIH, Legal Department.

dejected. In their testimonies, however, they did not refrain from noting their failures along with the successes.[117] The descriptions of the working methods, the doggedness, the decision to employ deception in difficult cases, the willingness to call in the police and even to abduct a youngster — give the impression that the operatives were prepared to let nothing stand in their way. However, the failures that occurred illustrate the limited nature of their abilities and their willingness to take far-reaching measures.

Time acted against the organizations. One need only peruse the Koordynacja lists from spring 1946 to summer 1947, which report the number of children who were placed in children's homes each month, to realize that more children were removed from rescuers' homes during each month of this period than in all of 1948.[118] It should be borne in mind that in contrast to the painful slowness that typified the work of tracing and removing children, political developments were succeeding each other apace: borders were sealed off, the Polish government stabilized, the children grew older, and the bonds between them and their new families became stronger. As the war receded in time, the pool of information became less and the detection of new children consequently became more difficult. The willingness of rescuers to surrender children also diminished, and the process of removing each child took longer.[119]

Occasionally the organizations drew up lists in which cases in progress were gathered and examined. A study of these lists illustrates the complexity of the difficulties and problems faced by the operatives. The efforts invested in removing the children were immensely disproportionate to the successes achieved, that is, the actual number of children removed from non-Jewish homes. A JDC list with data on the handling of twenty-five children illustrates this:

One boy was to be removed soon and sent to his father, who was in Hungary; with respect to two children, the rescuers were willing to hand them over but were waiting for the approval of relatives abroad; one child had been removed and was in a sanatorium in Otwock; the cases of six children were still in progress, the rescuers demanding huge sums (the list details the

---

117 Interview by author with Yehuda Bronstein, 1997. Bronstein recounts having removed two children from a family in Garwolin and later, when it turned out that the youngsters were born to a mixed couple, had to give them back; testimony Sarah Lederman, OHD 50(68).

118 Interview by author with Yehuda Bronstein, 1997. Bronstein worked from summer 1948 to spring 1949. He dealt with thirteen cases and removed seven children during this time.

119 Ibid.

demands in each case); the cases of two other children were in progress, the rescuers demanding the family's property; one child's case was in progress (there was no explanation of what this meant and how it differed from the other cases); one child was removed by Agudath Israel, he ran away and returned to his rescuers, who refused to surrender him; the cases of five children were in progress; the rescuers were refusing to hand them over for the time being; the matter of two other children were being dealt with in court; the caregivers of two children changed addresses often, making it hard to locate them; the rescuers of one child were hiding him; negotiations over one child were in progress.[120]

Our discussion of the working methods might make it appear as though the operatives acted without constraints and that their resolve and faith in the correctness of their actions made them insensitive to the bond that had formed between rescuers and children. This was not the case. In their testimonies, the operatives expressed the doubts that afflicted them regularly and their realization that, at least in some cases, they were treating rescuers unfairly. They admitted that they did not always take account of the emotional price that the children would pay and realized that they might be doing the children an injustice.[121] Although this did not prevent the work continuing, the operatives found it difficult because of the very fact of this awareness. The immense number of facets, the convoluted nature of fate, and the powerful effects of all this on the removal operative may be appreciated by the following story: During the war, a pregnant Jewish woman fled from the ghetto and while hiding in the forest gave birth to a boy. A Jew who was with her in hiding took the baby and placed him on a window sill of a house in the village of Radomyśl Wielki. The crying of the infant awakened the husband and wife, who hurriedly brought the baby in. Later on, the wife became pregnant and died in childbirth, leaving the peasant alone to deal with two infants. The Jewish mother survived the war and emigrated to the United States, oblivious to the whereabouts of her baby and uncertain about whether he was still

120 List of twenty-five children in non-Jewish homes, undated, document from JDC Department, ŻIH. The document, which I received from Sarah Kadosh, is organized by names but I rearranged it by topics to show how acute the problem was. The list contains names of children whom the author knows were removed in 1948. This indicates that the organizations did not give up and that, at least in some cases, their continued efforts were fruitful.
121 Mahler, "Redemption of Jewish Children from Their Non-Jewish Rescuers," pp. 36–37; testimony Devorah Zilber, OHD, 27(68); interview by author with Yeshayahu Drucker; Shner-Neshamit, *I Did Not Come to Rest*, p. 204.

alive. A letter she wrote to the Jewish institutions in Poland serendipitously reached the Jew who had left the baby infant at the peasant's home and he forwarded the letter to Drucker. Drucker contacted the peasant and asked him to return the boy to his mother. The peasant recounted the history of the event but refused to surrender the boy, claiming that he had formed an inseparable bond with him. When the peasant learned what the boy's mother had suffered during the war, he suggested that she return to Poland and that the two of them raise the children together. Drucker appreciated the humanity of the man and tried to persuade him to give up the boy in return for the family's property and a sum of money. When the peasant continued to refuse, Drucker turned to the local police for assistance. The police commander, before whom Drucker appeared in Polish officer's uniform, did not ask many questions and sent policemen to bring in the peasant and the boy. The boy was surrendered to Drucker, who deposited with the commander 1,200,000 zlotys for the peasant.[122] Although Drucker believed that he had made the right decisions at the time, there was a bitter taste in his mouth. To this day, in every testimony, interview, conversation, or discussion on the topic of the children, Drucker retells the story with a sense of agony and immense appreciation of the peasant's humane attitude.

---

122 Testimony Yeshayahu Drucker, YVA, O.3/3249; interview by author with Yeshayahu Drucker; Kurek-Lesik, *"Udzial Żeńkich,"* p. 351.

CHAPTER 5

Poland and the Question of Removing Jewish Children

Both Your Mothers

To Bieta[1]

Under a futile Torah
under an imprisoned star
your mother gave birth to you
you have proof of her
beyond doubt and death
the scar of the navel
the sign of parting for ever
which had no time to hurt you
this you know
[...]
And at once a chance
someone hastily

bustled about your sleep
and then stayed for long afterwards
and washed you of orphanhood
and swaddled you in love
and become the answer
to your first word
That was how
both your mothers taught you
not to be surprised at all
when you say
I am

Jerzy Ficowski[2]

---

1 Elżbieta (Bieta) was born in January 1942 and was handed over several months later to the midwife who had assisted in her mother's birth; this woman raised her as a mother. Only as a teenager did she discover by chance that she was Jewish. Elżbieta married the Polish poet Jerzy Ficowski, who wrote this poem as a gesture to his wife's two mothers: her birth mother and the woman who had raised her.
2 "Both Your Mothers," in Jerzy Ficowski, *A Reading of Ashes*, translated by Keith Bosley (London: Menard Press, 1981), pp. 30–31.

215

Official Attitudes Toward the Question of Jewish Children

*T*he first years after the liberation were difficult for Poland. The government was busy rebuilding the ruins, creating jobs, tackling security problems, struggling against the supporters of the Right, and attempting to quell the spirit of resistance that pulsed through the Polish population. The government faced daunting economic and social problems for which there were no ready solutions. Due to this state of affairs, the Zionist organizations were able to pursue their routine activities practically unhindered.[3] Other organizations, such as Agudath Israel, were able to do the same even though they were officially banned.

Visiting Poland in August 1946, Rabbi Isaac Halevy Herzog, the Ashkenazi Chief Rabbi of Palestine, met with the Polish Prime Minister, Edward Osóbka-Morawski, and asked him to ensure the passage of legislation which would require the registration of Jewish children who were living with gentiles. Rabbi Herzog's intention was twofold: to try to determine how many such children there were and to prevent their disappearance. Osóbka-Morawski promised to have his government discuss the request. The members of the rabbi's delegation, however, sensed that the passage of laws would be of little practical use in view of the vague and unstable situation prevailing in Poland. Therefore, no pressure was applied at this point.[4] Rabbi Kahana, Chief Jewish Chaplain of the Polish army and Chairman of the Council of Jewish Religious Communities in Poland, attended Rabbi Herzog's meetings. He put forth a contrasting claim: they had been told at meetings with officials that a socialist government could not deal with such problems. There were even hints, he said, that the Polish government was aware that the Council of Communities and the Zionist Organization were removing Jewish children but considered this to be an internal Jewish affair.[5] If this was indeed the situation, one could assume that the government would rather ignore the issue instead of adding it to the lengthy list of issues calling for its attention.[6] Until 1947, the activists

---

3   Interview by author with Ita Kowalska, 1995; report Anton Mara, February 6, 1946, Massuah Archive, Testimonies, 25/27; Engel, *Between Liberation and Escape*, pp. 70–71; interview by author with Yeshayahu Drucker, September 1997.

4   *The Rescue Voyage*, p. 60.

5   Kahana, *After the Deluge*, p. 78.

6   This claim was advanced by Ita Kowalska, a Jewish woman who was a communist activist. Drucker and Koryski had the same impression. See interview by author with Ita Kowalska, 1995, interview by author with Yeshayahu Drucker, 1997, and testimony Leibl Koryski, OHD 15(68). I found no governmental or research sources that mention the official stance of the Polish government concerning the removal of Jewish children from Gentile homes.

had the feeling that the government knew what they were doing but chose to ignore it. From that year on, however, they were increasingly convinced that they were under surveillance.

Indeed, the government did not pass legislation requiring the registration of Jewish children in the homes of Gentiles. A legal document issued by the Central Jewish Committee, however, drawn up on the basis of Polish laws and court rulings, stated that municipal councils, police, and other government bodies should help parents who were demanding the return of their children from rescuers who refused to return them.[7] The organizations that dealt with the children had been availing themselves of police help before the document was published, even in cases where the claimants were not the children's parents.[8] The inquiries were usually referred to the police station nearest the rescuers' home or were based on personal acquaintance with police personnel. The police helped by escorting the child-removal agent to the rescuers' home. By their presence, the police gave the demand to remove the child the mantle of state authority. Sometimes, to thwart resistance by rescuers or other problem that might arise during the mission, the agent and the child were escorted back to the children's home of the relevant organization. In most cases, the police were paid for their assistance.[9] Notably, however, the police played a double game: while helping the Jewish organizations, they also responded to calls from Poles who asked them to prevent the removal of a child. One of the Jews who tried to take action, for example, wrote to the

---

7 Document drawn up by the legal department of the Central Jewish Committee, in the matter of Jewish children in the custody of non-Jews, distant relatives, and children's institutions, ŻIH, Legal Department. The document is undated but was presumably written no earlier than the second half of 1946, since it was based on laws and rulings issued in Poland in 1945–1946. Notably, there is no such instruction in regard to sections dealing with the claims of relatives or the Jewish organizations. They had the option of turning to the courts.

8 Testimony Devorah Zilber, OHD, 27(68); autobiography of Withold Wajman, in Tenenboim, *One of a City and Two of a Family*, pp. 131–132; Dekel, *Remnants of the Sword*, pp. 130–131; working report Teofilia Goldman, November 1946, in the matter of R.P., Ghetto Fighters' House Archives (hereinafter: GFHA), Correspondence File, 788–790; clarification report by child-removal emissary in the matter of Grandmother Zingisser, February 23, 1947, ibid.

9 Testimony Devorah Zilber, OHD, 27(68); testimony Sarah Lederman, OHD 50(68); testimony Moshe Jeruchamzon, OHD 44(68); interview by author with Yosef Haezrahi-Bürger; testimony Yeshayahu Drucker, YVA, O.3/3249; interview by author with Yehuda Bornstein, 1997; Neshamit, "The Koordynacja for the Redemption of Children in Liberated Poland," p. 125; clarification report in the matter of Grandmother Zingisser, February 23, 1947; testimony Zipora Minc, MA, A.262.

prime minister, complaining that policemen had arrested and beaten him after he had located his niece and wanted to remove her. He alleged that the police representative had justified the policemen's behavior on the grounds that he had attempted to kidnap a Polish child.[10]

The Polish Population and the Rescuers

Now that the war was over, it seemed that the rescuers' role was also over. After all, the reason for which they had concealed the children no longer existed. It is true that in most cases there was a sense of emotional relief, but uncertainty about the continuance of the relationship made both sides uneasy — the rescuers, whose action had become an important part of their identity, and the children, whose ordeals during the war had transformed their lives.[11]

In the towns and villages both survivors and rescuers often encountered a lack of sympathy that made Poland after the war a hostile place for both sides. Groups of extremists sought out Jews and "Jew-lovers" with murderous intent and most rescuers knew that the downfall of Hitler did not spell the end of antisemitism.[12]

During the war, the surrounding atmosphere had harmed many rescuers. Because of the Germans' punitive policies, some claimed that the rescuers were endangering their neighbors. On other occasions, rescuers faced problems due to hatred of Jews and refusal to countenance their actions.[13] One child survivor, for example, expressed his astonishment about the neighbors' negative attitude toward the foster mother who had saved him. "I don't know why," the boy said. "Maybe it's because they thought a foster mother should love only Polish children."[14] This behavior, coupled with the need to

10 Letter M. Teller to Prime Minister Osóbka-Morawski, July 25, 1946, GFHA, Correspondence File, 788–790.
11 Fogelman, *Conscience and Courage*, p. 273.
12 Ibid., pp. 275, 277; letter of testament by Pola to her daughter Helena Guzala, whom she had rescued, dated March 1954, reached me via Janina Chryc, Poland. In the letter, the rescuer attempted to explain to her daughter why she had not revealed her Jewish identity to her and to others: "Jews are persecuted, even by our Poles."
13 Gutman, *Jews in Poland*, p. 32 Gutman claims that extremist Poles decried the rescue of Jews as an act not worthy of true Polish patriots; Donia Rosen, *The Forest, My Friend*, in Hebrew edition (Jerusalem: Yad Vashem, 1985), pp. 27–28, 43–46; testimony Leibl Koryski, OHD 15(68); Brunowski, *They Were Few*, pp. 159–162.
14 Testimony Reuven, in Küchler, *We Accuse*, pp. 157, 159. Reuven recalled that the neighbors were very angry with the foster mother who had taken care of him.

keep their actions secret, resulted in the social isolation of many rescuers. As the war neared the end and the front approached, there were even cases where rescuers were harassed by people who had attacked them during the war and now feared that the rescuers would testify against their assailants.[15] This persecution of rescuers continued after the war, indeed, some rescuers paid with their lives for what they had done.[16]

In this sense, the end of the war brought no relief. Many rescuers continued to suffer from their neighbors and society at large. They were still socially isolated because those around them, who had not acted as they had during the war, did not accept them once the war was over.[17] One rescuer, for example, related that his neighbors claimed that he had brought everlasting shame and disgrace upon the entire town by having rescued Jews. Polish society was composed of two ideological extremes, and the rescuers were caught in the middle. One extreme assailed them for having concealed Jewish children; while the other, nationalist religious fanatics, sometimes attacked people who had surrendered a Jewish child whom they had protected to Jews who came to remove him or her.[18]

Since rescue was not perceived as something to be proud of in postwar Poland, rescuers were circumspect about their actions. Poles who had rescued Jews asked the survivors not to divulge their whereabouts so as to avoid danger.[19] After the Jewish Historical Committee in the Kraków area decided to publish the names of Polish rescuers so as to express appreciation for their actions during the war, rescuers visited the Committee offices and complained that this had caused them harm and exposed them to abuse and insult by their neighbors.[20] Furthermore, in view of the economic plight of

---

15 Rosen, *The Forest, My Friend*, pp. 98–100.
16 Interview by author with Rachel Mizoc-Gewing. After the war, Rachel Gewing discovered that the man who had saved her and her sister by placing them in two separate houses that he owned had been executed by the local Ukrainian underground after it was discovered that he had concealed Jewish girls.
17 Brunowski, *They Were Few*, p. 161; see also letter Bronka Cohen, Tel Aviv, to Rabbi Herzog, December 30, 1945, Religious Zionism Archives (hereinafter: RZA), Rescue Files. The writer received a letter from the woman who had rescued her niece, informing her that she was interested in handing over the girl to Jews because her neighbors were harassing her. Testimony Yeshayahu Drucker, YVA, O.3/3249; testimony Leibl Koryski, OHD 15(68); Fogelman, *Conscience and Courage*, p. 277.
18 Testimony of Leibl Koryski, OHD 15(68).
19 Fogelman, *Conscience and Courage*, p. 278; Litvak, "JDC's Contribution," p. 343.
20 Gutman, *Jews in Poland*, p. 32.

post-war Poland, some Poles did not wish it to be known that they had rescued a child because this might make their neighbors covet the riches they
had presumably received for returning the youngster.[21] Their concern was
real. On more than one occasion, when an act of rescue became known, the
rescuers were harassed and threatened if they failed to hand over the gold and
silver they had ostensibly received from the Jews.[22] Several rescuers were even
murdered on these grounds. The fate of a peasant in Kraśnik County is a case
in point. The peasant had concealed two Jewish girls in a hideout he had built
for them under his kitchen floor. He took care of them faithfully without sharing the secret with his wife and daughter. When the Soviet forces arrived, he
kept the children in hiding and visited the occupying forces to determine their
attitude toward the Jews. After he found a Jewish doctor and officer among the
soldiers, his concerns were eased and he released the girls from the hideout.
When his wife complained about his having concealed the Jewish girls in their
home, the peasant appeased her by promising that they would now receive
benefits from the Jews. The fighting that then took place in the area forced
them to leave their home and move to another village. When their provisions
ran out, the peasant returned to the village with his daughter and Malka, one
of the Jewish girls, in order to gather potatoes from the field. The man encountered people on the way and boasted to them that, after the situation
calmed down, he would surrender the girls to the Jews and be well paid in return. Some time later, the peasant went to Kraśnik, told Jewish survivors there
about the girls in his home, and asked for a reward for having concealed them.
When the survivors asked him to produce the girls, he returned again, this
time with Malka, but rejected their request to leave her in their custody until
he received the money. When the peasant took a third trip and did not return,
it was assumed that he had been robbed and murdered. Indeed, several days
later, masked men visited the peasant's home, beat his wife, threatened the
girls, and demanded the money that he had "received" for them. Only then
was it universally realized that they had murdered the peasant.[23]

The end of the war and the Jewish concern for child survivors placed the
rescuers in a quandary as to whether they should relinquish the youngsters to
the Jews. Rescuers who had agreed to shelter children for economic reasons
and had been promised money and property after the war had an interest in

21 Testimony of Mira Bramm; Tec, *When Light,* pp. 87–88.
22 Fogelman, *Conscience and Courage,* p. 276.
23 Testimony of Malka Templer, YVA, O.3/4278.

returning the children.[24] They had played their part; now it was time to claim their due.[25] The existence of economic motives for rescue did not imply that the child had been mistreated or that the rescuer and the child had not formed an emotional bond. It did mean, however, that throughout the war, the possibility of eventual separation had hovered in the background: the rescuers had expected it and often, looked forward to it.[26] In some cases, however, the main motive for concealment had been financial but, due to the emotional bond that had formed, the rescuers were now unwilling to do anything that would mean parting with the children, including forgoing the promise of payment.[27]

Some rescuers — irrespective of the reason for their willingness to conceal the children — suggested to their charges that they should return to a Jewish environment in the belief that this would be in their best interests and even persuaded them to do so. Rescuers personally delivered younger children to Jewish institutions,[28] either feeling that the children did not rightfully belong to them, or concerned that a decision not to surrender them would be

---

24 Tec, *When Light*, pp. 88, 90. According to Tec, rescuers who had concealed Jews for monetary purposes did not note this in their testimonies; only the survivors' testimonies make this clear. After the war, these survivors did not feel that they owed their rescuers gratitude since the rescuers had considered their actions simply part of a "deal." By construing matters in this way, the survivors failed to take account of the danger that the rescuers had faced.

25 Letter Nachman Har-Zahav to Rabbi Herzog, November 5, 1946, RZA, Rescue Files, 191.

26 Dekel, *Remnants of the Sword*, pp. 567–568.

27 Child card of S. Liberman, Card 72, GFHA, Koordynacja card catalogue of children, File 800. During the war, the rescuer had received support from a Jewish organization for taking care of the child. She was sent to a camp in Germany later on, but before her deportation she managed to place the child in a Polish orphanage. After the war, she returned from the camp and reclaimed the girl.

28 Wasserstein-Blanker, "After the Holocaust I Did Not Want to Return to Judaism," p. 334. The girl remained with her rescuers until 1947; autobiography of Shoshana Wajman in Tenenboim, *One of a City and Two of a Family*, p. 218; interview by author with Rachel Kagan-Plodwinska, December 1989; interview by author with Lucia Milch-Rosenzweig. In her search for refuge, Lucia encountered a Polish teenager whom she had previously seen bringing food to her Jewish teacher, who was in the ghetto. The boy helped her find a house where she could work as a Polish girl. When the war ended, the teenager returned to her and told her that he had come to deliver her to the Jews. So it happened; Grynberg, *Księga Sprawiedliwych*, "Kuriata," p. 284; ibid., Gutowska, p. 172; testimony of Esther Mark, YVA, O–3/4168; Silver, *Secret Saints*, pp. 137–139; Neshamit, "The Koordynacja for the Redemption of Children in Liberated Poland," pp. 136–137: Lewinsky, "My Wanderings and My Rescuers," p. 19: the boy refused to leave his rescuer and stayed on with him for two additional years, during which the rescuer contacted Jews at his initiative and tried to persuade the boy to go with them.

a source of regret for themselves and the children all their lives.[29] Many of the rescuers found the need to make a decision excruciatingly hard.

Rescuers who had promised parents to return children to them, to relatives, or to Jews after the war, now had to keep their word. In their dilemma, their promise to the parents clashed with the bond that they had formed with the children.[30] An example is a girl who did not want to write to her uncle in Palestine, even though this had been her mother's last wish. She testified, "[...] In fact, [the rescuer and her sister] forced me; they said that they'd promised it to my mother." The rescuer also presented the facts in the same way but added that, although she knew it was her duty and acted accordingly, the decision was difficult and she had made it despite her feelings for the girl.[31]

Another factor that facilitated the decision to relinquish a child was sincere concern for the youngster and the hope that the release would generally be better for him or her, would give greater opportunities for study, and would provide the child with what the rescuers themselves could not.[32] For example, when after the war, a fourteen year-old boy refused to leave the peasant who had taken him in, the peasant told him, "You're an intelligent boy; it's a shame

29 Koryski, "These Are Our Children," *Farn Yiddishn Kind*, GFHA, File 798. Danuta was found by a poor Polish woman next to a railroad track in the Lublin area, where trains to Majdanek passed daily. She housed and raised the girl; thank-you letter from Child Care Department to Juliana Wojciechowski, September 18, 1946, in the matter of R.K., ŻIH Education Department, File 638; letter Education Department to Central Committee presidium, October 8, 1947, in the matter of Z.G., ibid.; autobiography of Ruth Alpher, in Tenenboim, *One of a City and Two of a Family* (Hebrew), p. 138.

30 Cheshin, *Adoptive Children* (Hebrew), p. 130; Dekel, *Remnants of the Sword*, p. 218. The rescuer even escorted the girl as far as Austria, where her aunt was living in a DP camp; Shulamit Magen, "First and Last Memory," written in 1992 and given the author by her husband; letter Immigrant Care Department, Mizrahi Organization in Palestine, on behalf of Nachman Posek, to Rabbi Herzog, January 15, 1946, RZA, Rescue Files; *Księga Sprawiedliwych*, "Kusuth," p. 257, story of Michael, in Küchler, *We Accuse*, pp. 157–164.

31 Tec, *When Light*, pp. 143–144. The witness noted that at that time she had been very angry with her rescuer, Ada Celka and her sister, for having forced her to get in touch with her uncle, and that this anger has stayed with her ever since.

32 Ibid., p. 144; Autobiography of Shoshana Wajman, in Tenenboim, *One of a City and Two of a Family*, p. 218; letter organization of Jews from Opoczno to Rabbi Herzog, March 31, 1946, RZA, Rescue Files; story of Reuven, in Küchler, *We Accuse*, p. 155. The boy recounted how his rescuer had taken him along when she had left her home and scraped together a living for both of them by knitting sweaters. After the war, she obtained a permit to take him to Warsaw, where she placed him in a children's home. Testimony of Aharon, ibid., pp. 219–220; Küchler-Silberman, *My Hundred Children*, pp. 206–209; Mahler, "Reclamation of Jewish Children from Their Non-Jewish Rescuers," pp. 36–37.

for you to stay here. Surely you'll be a doctor. Go to the Jewish children's home and they'll send you to study."[33] In a few cases, the rescuers made a condition for the release of the child on a promise, backed up with guarantees, that he or she would have a better future with family members than with them.[34]

Some rescuers wished to resolve the dilemma of allowing the child to grow up in a Jewish environment, thus keeping their promise to return them to the Jewish people after the war, and coping with the difficulty in parting from the children, by linking the two and joining them. Such an intention amounted to a readiness to put an end to their personal life up to then and establish a new life based on a wish to stay with the youngster and continue to protect him or her.[35] There were also rescuers who wanted to leave with the children but could not do so due to various commitments, and were left emotionally torn.[36] There were also cases where rescuers had asked for permission to accompany the child but the Jewish organizations refused. Sarid (Leibl Goldberg) described such a request, which the Koordynacja executive board rejected due to the anticipated hardship of the trip and the problem of obtaining permission to immigrate to Palestine. Ultimately, the boy remained with the Polish woman.[37]

Some rescuers surrendered children to Jewish organizations even though this had not been their original intent. The children had continued to live with them after the war and it seemed as though they would continue to do so, but the passage of time and changes in personal and family circumstances forced the rescuers to surrender them. For example, a judge

33 Interview by author with Ita Kowalska, 1995.
34 Letter Central Committee to Committee of Jewish Labor Party, New York, July 2, 1946, in the matter of M.G., ŻIH, Education Department, File 638.
35 Grynberg, *Księga Sprawiedliwych,* "Apolonia Ołdak," p. 387. Apolonia and the girl whom she had rescued moved to Israel in 1950, after her husband passed away; Yishai, *In the Shadow of the Holocaust,* p. 80; Dekel, *Remnants of the Sword,* pp. 230–231: The "mother" had lost her husband and daughter in the Polish uprising in Warsaw; Shner-Neshamit, *I Did Not Come to Rest,* p. 193; Paldiel, "Rescuers in the Footsteps of the Rescued," Gertrude Babilinska, p. 26; ibid., Apolonia Ołdak, p. 28; ibid., Helena Schmedt (Sarah Rubinstein), p. 29.
36 Hellman, *Avenue of the Righteous,* pp. 237, 249; Dekel, *Remnants of the Sword,* pp. 218–223. Several years later, the rescuer followed the girl to Israel; ibid., p. 203. The rescuer moved to Israel with the girl, who had been entrusted to him as a baby, when she was fifteen years-old; ibid., pp. 232–233. The manifest of the vessel *Exodus* included three women who sailed to Israel with the children whom they had rescued, as they had promised their parents.
37 *Mission to the Diaspora,* p. 89.

who had rescued a Jewish girl and raised her lovingly was forced to part with her in 1948 because the woman whom he had married did not want to keep her.[38]

The reasons for deciding not to return children were as numerous as those in favor of returning them. Even if the rescuers knew that they had been asked to protect the children only until the storm subsided, and they had originally intended to do so, time took its effect and they had established parental bonds of love with the youngsters and refused to give them up. From their standpoint, these were their children, whom they had continued to care for after the war as if nothing had changed.[39] They were not prepared to see the children placed in a children's home, where they would be just one among many, or sent to an unfamiliar relative who would be a stranger to them.[40] They believed that their years of service in raising the children had made them so significant in the life of the children that they were entitled to keep

---

38 Testimony Yehuda Bronstein, OHD, 25(68). The judge had spent the war in Lwów with the girl and moved to Wrocław, Poland, after liberation. See also letter Pawel Cypryanski, Słupsk, Poland, September 1995. During the Germans' retreat at the end of the war, Pawel's mother was shot and the children were left alone in the family's home. Pawel's father returned from Germany, where he had been imprisoned, and raised his three children and the girl, Henia, whom his wife had rescued and whom he had not known previously. In 1948, the father married a widow who also had three children. The new family, now with seven children, barely made a living. To his children's displeasure, the father decided to hand Henia over to a Jewish organization. The children's opposition to this soured their relations with their father; Jacoby-Frydman, "Testimony," pp. 57–58. The couple that had taken care of Tamar during the war was later joined by a brother and his five children and an elderly mother. Their apartment was very crowded; the family lacked basic necessities. Furthermore, the grandmother was an antisemite and harrassed the girl.

39 Kahana, *After the Deluge*, pp. 15–16; Dekel, *Remnants of the Sword*, pp. 138, 194; Ferderber-Salz, *And the Sun Appeared*, pp. 136, 170–171; letter Warsaw Committee to Central Committee, March 26, 1946, ŻIH, Education Department, File 638; letter Central Committee to Weiblatt, Britain, May 28, 1947, in the matter of S.H., ibid.; Grynberg, *Księga Sprawiedliwych*, "Julia Paja," p. 391. The girl remained with the family after the war. In 1955, her uncle arrived from the USSR and claimed custody. The rescuer refused, arguing that since so many years had passed, the girl was now part of the family. Eventually the uncle abducted her; interview by author with Yehuda Bronstein, September 1995. The rescuer gave Bronstein a photograph of the girl and provided details about her family but refused to hand her over, so she remained with him in Poland; letter Rabbi Findling, Haifa, to Rabbi Herzog, December 1946, RZA, Rescue Files.

40 Fogelman, *Conscience and Courage*, p. 280; organization of Jews from Opoczno to Rabbi Herzog, March 31, 1946, RZA, Rescue Files; letter Central Committee to Jewish Labor Party committee, July 2, 1946, in the matter of M.G.; letter Central Committee to HIAS, Warsaw, in response to letter March 8, 1946, in the matter of P. ŻIH, Education Department, File 638.

them.[41] Childless rescuers who had taken a Jewish child into their home believed that the fact that the war had ended was no reason to give him or her up.[42] Some rescuers had found "their" children wandering along the roads or had gathered them from orphanages; they therefore felt they had made no commitment to the youngsters' parents.[43] Other rescuers who were barely able to support their families after the war did not consider their economic plight a reason to relinquish the children.[44] There were those who thought that by officially adopting the children it would be impossible to remove them from their custody. At least, they assumed, the legal proceedings for their removal would be long drawn-out and in the meantime, the children would remain with them.[45]

There were rescuers who, when asked to hand over their children, would not take a stance that might jeopardize the trust they had established, believing that the youngsters should be allowed to make their own decision.[46] Others thought that the children should not be removed from families in which they felt secure and should have to make the decision only when they were older.[47] Several rescuers were even willing to educate the children so that they

41 Interview by author with Elżbieta Ficowska-Kopel; Benjamin Anolik, *In the Service of Memory* (Ghetto Fighters' House: Kibbutz Lohamei Hagetaot, 1990, Hebrew), p. 114.

42 Dekel, *Remnants of the Sword,* pp. 206–213; Neshamit, "The Koordynacja for the Redemption of Children in Liberated Poland," p. 134; Koryski, "The Zionist Koordynacja for the Redemption of Jewish Children in Poland," p. 26; letter Anatoly Dolski, Poznań, Poland, to Hofstand, Tel Aviv, August 15, 1945, RZA, Rescue Files. The letter, along with the request to have the matter dealt with, was sent to Rabbi Herzog's office; testimony Yehuda Bronstein, OHD, 25(68); Reicher, "The Priest Burst into Tears."

43 Depositions Szloma Besserman, Max-Murdoch Rozenfeld, and Chuma Hakman to attorney Heifetz, Canada, April 2, 1949, ŻIH, Legal Department; Neshamit, "The Koordynacja for the Redemption of Children in Liberated Poland," p. 134; record of deposition by Jopowicz at Central Jewish Committee, May 8, 1947, in the matter of L.H., ŻIH, Education Department, File 638.

44 Letter Warsaw Committee to Central Committee, April 25, 1947, in the matter of K.F.; letter Kaplinski, Youth Aliyah, Poland, to Youth Aliyah, Paris, March 14, 1947, in the matter of E. and J.F., CZA, L58/748.

45 Mahler, "Reclamation of Jewish Children from Their Non-Jewish Rescuers," pp. 36–37; Grynberg, *Księga Sprawiedliwych,* "Bańkowska," p. 45; Anolik, *In the Service of Memory,* p. 71.

46 For example, see description of the case of Irka from Lublin in testimony of Devorah Zilber, OHD, 27(68).

47 Interview by author with Halina Kowalska, Warsaw, September 1994; Dekel, *Remnants of the Sword,* p. 199.

would be aware of their Jewish heritage, thereby retaining them while eventually allowing them to make their own decision.[48]

Rescuers who had concealed children due to religious motives continued to raise them as "good Christians" after the war. One mother who came to reclaim her daughter had to retrace her footsteps after the village erupted in pandemonium, in the middle of which the local priest said that if she continued to insist, the villagers would prefer to see the boy die rather than surrender him. Another case concerned a woman who, in 1957, visited the offices of the Jewish community in Łódź together with a girl whom she asked to give into their keeping. The woman claimed that she had baptized the girl, but when the girl grew up and decided that she did not want to be religious, she realized that Heaven had rejected her gift![49]

There were children who had come to Polish homes during the war and offered themselves as workers. Some of them had not even identified themselves as Jewish. Those who had been taken in by peasants became integral parts of the families' economic life, helping with household and field chores, taking care of younger children, leading the cows to pasture, and sometimes doing work that was actually too strenuous for youngsters of their strength and age. After the war, some of them stayed on with their rescuers and continued to be part of the household, even though they were now old enough to understand that they were Jews. Although the rescuers profited from their presence, they also provided a sense of belonging. From the standpoint of the children, these were now their families.[50] Less understandable are cases in which the children continued to stay with families that had mistreated them even after the war had ended.[51]

---

48 Sarid, "Remarks about the Koordynacja," p. 19; testimony of Hannah Batista, YVA, O.3/5732, *Mission to the Diaspora*, p. 84.

49 Dekel, *Remnants of the Sword*, pp. 137–138, 201–202; See also Neshamit, "The Koordynacja for the Redemption of Children in Liberated Poland," p. 122.

50 Testimony Sabina Halperin, MA, A.201; testimony Zipora Minc, MA, A.262; Neshamit, "The Koordynacja for the Redemption of Children in Liberated Poland," pp. 143–144; recorded interview with Haviva Barak-Oveitz; interview by author with Lucia Milch-Rosenzweig.

51 Statement by Pawel Milczuk, June 14, 1947, GFHA, Correspondence File, 788–790; most testimonies that describe such exploitation of children were given by child-removal operatives. See Fleiszer, "The Rescue of 24 Children," pp. 300–304; testimony of Devorah Zilber, OHD, 27(68); testimony of Leibl Koryski, OHD 15(68); Dekel, *Remnants of the Sword*, pp. 54–56. For obvious reasons I did not find such testimonies from Poles. In the children's testimonies that I examined, the children described their continuing to live with their rescuers after the war as a direct continuation of their wartime lives.

According to the testimony of operatives in the field, negotiations with rescuers sometimes focused not on the surrender of children but on the terms for their surrender. Some of the Polish rescuers exploited the children as tools for extortion from the organizations — from "the Jews" — and in their tactics, played their strongest card: information about the children. By withholding information, they strengthened their negotiating position.[52] Some of them, convinced that the children's relatives and the Jewish organizations would seek to reclaim the children at any price, used the opportunity to profiteer. By contrast, others were totally committed to retaining the children and hoped to deflect the operatives by demanding an exorbitant sum. One rescuer, for example, claimed that she had demanded a huge sum of money from the father of the girl who lived with her, assuming that he could either not afford it or would refuse to pay. Thus, "the affair would drag on, even for a whole year," and meanwhile the girl continued to live with her. Eventually, however, the father was able to raise the money and gave the rescuer 75,000 zlotys. "I took the money," the woman testified; "The bills burned in my hands like the thirty pieces of silver for which Judas Iscariot betrayed Jesus. I didn't buy a thing for myself, but even so I was glad when the money was gone."[53]

When action was taken to remove children from the homes of rescuers, relatives and operatives recounted cases in which Poles in general, and rescuers in particular, incited children against their parents, the Jews, and Judaism. For example, one father who had returned to reclaim his daughter was subjected to a barrage of curses and accusations. His daughter claimed, among other things, that the Jews had crucified Jesus and that her father wished to

---

52 Küchler-Silberman, *My Hundred Children*, p. 191; Dekel, *Remnants of the Sword*, pp. 89–92.

53 Hellman, *Avenue of The Righteous*, p. 238; see also Dekel, *Remnants of the Sword*; Küchler-Silberman, *My Hundred Children*, pp. 190–193; *Mission to the Diaspora*, p. 88; Shner-Neshamit, *I Did Not Come to Rest*, p. 192; testimony Yehuda Bronstein, OHD, 25(68); testimony Devorah Zilber, OHD, 27(68); testimony Yeshayahu Drucker, YVA, O.3/3249; letter Israel Rosenberg to Youth Aliyah, Jerusalem, undated, in the matter of P.L., CZA L58/748; letter Drucker to Rabbi Herzog, April 27, 1947, in the matter of Z.S., RZA, Rescue File; letter Adolf Szeinfeld to Rabbi Herzog, November 21, 1946; ibid.; letter Katowice Committee to Education Department, March 21, 1947, in the matter of G.G., ŻIH, Education Department, File 638; letter Education Department to HIAS, July 24, 1947, in the matter of A.K., ibid. The documents and testimonies, which provide a detailed account of the case, show that there was no connection between the huge sum demanded and the nature of the deliberations, which created the grave impression of extortion, and the care and treatment of the child. Even rescuers who had showered "their" children with love and gave them appropriate care might attempt to extort money.

take her in order to make her blood into matzot.[54] Another girl related that after the liberation, two Jews came to the village and searched for Jewish children. The neighbors' children, who knew she was Jewish came and warned her that the Jews would take her away and use her blood for making matzot for Passover.[55]

Rescuers who continued to raise children after the war, and believing that nothing would be able to stop them doing so, responded desperately when operatives visited their homes and asked them to relinquish the youngsters. Affluent rescuers offered the activists large sums of money to leave them alone and allow the situation to continue;[56] others took action to thwart any change of custody and surrounded the child and the rescuer family with a wall of silence that was difficult to penetrate.[57] Some warned the activists that if they tried to remove the children by force, they would face public protests against the ingratitude of the Jews.[58] Others, in their despair, threatened to commit murder[59] or suicide.[60] These warnings were not idle threats; activists who came to remove children were often assaulted by people, armed with various implements, who came to help rescuers thwart the action.[61] Some

---

54 Dekel, *Remnants of the Sword*, p. 539. See also Küchler-Silberman, *My Hundred Children*, p. 211; letter Warsaw Committee to Central Committee, March 23, 1946, in the matter of K.F. and M.L.; and testimony Devorah Zilber, OHD, 27(68). Marysia recounted a case in which rescuers told a Jewish girl who had been in their care that the Jews would sell her for a price; see story of Ella in Küchler, *We Accuse*, pp. 190–191. When Ella's uncle came to remove her, the rescuer told her not to go with him because the Jews would take her to Palestine and kill her; Yerushalmi, *Children of the Holocaust*, pp. 88–89.

55 Interview by author with Rachel Wolf-Wajnsztok.

56 Testimony Leibl Koryski, OHD 15(68).

57 Letter Director of Legal Department, Adv. Gutmacher, to court registrar in Wrocław, May 19, 1947, in the matter of P.A., ŻIH, Legal Department; Szneiderman, "A Jewish Mother Struggles for her Daughter," pp. 71–72.

58 Koryski, "The Zionist Koordynacja for the Redemption of Jewish Children in Poland," p. 26.

59 Letter Joint Distribution Committee relative-search officer in Germany to Polish military legation in Berlin, June 25, 1946, in the matter of A.A.I.I., ŻIH, Legal Department; testimony Yehuda Bronstein, OHD, 25(68): description of an attempt to remove children from Garwolyn.

60 Koryski, "The Zionist Koordynacja for the Redemption of Jewish Children in Poland," p. 27.

61 Dekel, *Remnants of the Sword*, pp. 130–131, 161–162, 198; interview by author with Yosef Haezrahi-Bürger, with description of the removal of Marysia; Neshamit, "The Koordynacja for the Redemption of Children in Liberated Poland," pp. 122–125. Neshamit claims that the dissemination of rumors about activists who abducted Polish children sometimes escalated into blood libels; testimony Yeshayahu Drucker, YVA, O.3/3249. A case in which a child was removed from a village near Skarżysko-Kamienna; *Mission to the Diaspora*, p. 87.

rescuers complained to the authorities about operatives who had used force and they threatened to take up weapons,[62] hoping that the authorities would act to prevent the removal of children from their homes.

All rescuers — whether they handed the children to the Jewish organizations willingly or initially refused for various reasons but complied afterwards, including those who attempted to profiteer from the surrender of the child — found the separation difficult. It affected all of them to some degree, left them with a sense of loss, and imprinted them in some way.[63] Many rescuers described the period when they had saved Jews during the war as the pinnacle of their lives — a time of deep satisfaction despite the danger. Now it was over and finished.[64] In families where the rescuers had children of their own, it was these children that found the decision of the parents hard to bear. The children of the rescuers had rarely been involved in the decision to take in a Jewish child or the decision to return him or her. Meanwhile, the years had taken their effect and, in their eyes, they were losing their siblings. Sometimes the parents' decision to surrender the Jewish child drove a wedge between them and their own children.[65]

Not every separation was the product of preparation, indecision or decision. Sometimes children left, or were removed from the homes of the rescuers without saying goodbye. When children vanished under unknown circumstances and with the rescuer not knowing what had become of them, anxiety resulted. One boy, Moshe, for example, recounted that his rescuers found it hard to understand what had happened to him and why he had suddenly vanished. They asked shepherds in the area to look out for him, fearing

---

62 Interview by author with Yosef Haezrahi-Bürger. This incident led to his imprisonment.

63 Decision of municipal court in Łódź, Case 37/46, in the matter of E.R., ŻIH, Legal Department; letter Jadwiga Mazur, April 1994, in the author's possession. The writer described the suffering that the Woleński family endured due to having parted with the child, even though they had two children of their own; Fogelman, *Conscience and Courage*, pp. 282, 282; Tec, *When Light*, p. 144; response Skrzypak to letter Erma Szulginer, January 6, 1947, GFHA, Correspondence File, 788–790.

64 Fogelman, *Conscience and Courage*, p. 274. According to Fogelman, it was not only the stress of parting that caused the rescuers' difficulty; they also suffered due to the loss of the personal satisfaction that they had gained through doing a good deed for another person. Ibid., p. 279.

65 Testimony Yehuda Bronstein, OHD 25(68), description of the removal of a girl from Gdynia in 1948. The "mother," too fearful to tell the Jewish girl and her own children that she was relinquishing the girl for good, told them that she was merely sending her away for studies. Bronstein, who had been monitoring the mother and her children and observed the warm and loving treatment that the girl had received, described the parting as a tragedy; see also letter Maria Madej, Poland, April 21, 1995; letter Pawel Cypryanski, September 1995.

that something terrible had befallen him. Failing to find him, the parents were so distraught and anxious about the boy that they could not resume their routine lives.[66] In another case, a Polish rescuer answered a letter from the girl whom he had sheltered:

> When we read your letter, we were very sad about having lost you. You did not have to hide your identity from us because you know my political views. I loved you dearly and we will miss you. My wife was very concerned about your not writing and I thought you might have caught a cold and did not want us to know. I very much want to see you and I know that Zosia wants to as well. Try [to come] so that we can talk. A letter is not the same thing as a personal talk. I am happy that you found relatives but I would rather think of you as our daughter. I write no more; we want to see you again. Even though you never wanted to kiss me, I send you kisses and am waiting eagerly. Father.[67]

A woman rescuer expressed the sense of emptiness that filled her home after the departure of the girl whom she and her husband had raised:

> Lusia has already been gone for two weeks. It's very hard for me. Neither I nor my husband can eat or sleep. [Her] place at the table is empty, it's desolate at home and there's a buzzing in the ears. No one indulges himself, no one sings, I have no one to teach. The days go by monotonously. I tell the schoolchildren that Lusia has gone to Warsaw... I'll never see the girl again, never, ever.[68]

Some rescuers' lives were perceptibly changed by having concealed Jewish children; for them, the clock could not be turned back. Several had to change personal plans; a few became ill due to the stress. They drew a direct connection between cause and effect. For them, time could not ease the agony of the separation. The entire fabric of their lives was changed; it marked their

---

66 Frank, *To Survive and Testify*, p. 81. The boy had gone to Zamość to sell some merchandise. His uncle, who had met with him previously and asked him to come with him, did not accept his refusal and abducted him with the help of a Jewish officer; see also Rosen, *The Forest, My Friend*, pp. 149–155.

67 Letter Erma Szulginer, under the pseudonym Zosia Kowalczyk, to the Skrzypak family (with whom she had stayed during the war under a Polish identity) and their response to her, January 6, 1947, GFHA, Correspondence File, 788–790.

68 Grynberg, *Księga Sprawiedliwych,* "Vogelgesang," pp. 590–591; ibid., Jan and Bogumiła Chawiński, p. 73.

disconnection from the "reason" for the change that had been forced on them.[69]

Caregivers and single women who had provided for Jewish children during the war made desperate efforts to maintain their cover stories when the war was over. Having told neighbors, friends, and family about nonexistent marriages or relationships that they had formed, they now lived in fear of having their lies exposed. They were afraid that the child's parents or relatives would return and demand custody of the youngster whom they had worked so hard to present as their own. Now they had to face the difficulty of explaining his or her sudden disappearance, which made enduring their loss even harder. Although they had not given birth to the child, they had raised him or her as their own.[70] There were cases in which, after the war, one of the parents returned and joined the family with which the child was staying, leaving the denouement for a later time. Secretly, each side schemed to break off relations from the other. For example, a Jewish mother recounted, "I didn't tell [the caregiver who had concealed her daughter] that I intended to leave, she thought that my daughter would live with her forever. But I knew there was a rivalry for my daughter and I wanted to get her away."[71] Another mother remembered the parting from the woman who had taken care of her daughter:

> We were at the station and Marysia was helping me. I had some bundles and she came with me as far as the train. When I think about it now, I know that Marysia was wondering the whole time, 'Is she going to take

69 Letter of testament by Paula to her daughter, Helena Gurala; interview by author with Janina Chryc. After Gestapo officials removed from their home a mother and daughter who had been hiding with them for some two years, Janina's own mother suffered a fall and died at the end of the war. A week later, her father returned from Germany, where he had been a prisoner; see also *Mission to the Diaspora*, p. 89. A mother of three concealed a Jewish girl. When the matter was discovered her husband was executed but the girl survived; Gruss, *Child Martyrdom*, pp. 91–94. A woman who took in two children during the war refused to marry a man who had proposed to her due to concern that he would not love the children, she remained unmarried; Grynberg, *Księga Sprawiedliwych*, "Kuriata," pp. 284–285. A couple concealed two Jewish children and German forces came to search their home after they were denounced. The husband and wife were in the forest with the children at the time. The searchers, deprived of their quarry, set the house ablaze and the couple's elderly parents, who were at home, perished in the flames. See also interview by author with Yehudit Szwarcbach: her daughter's caregiver gave birth to a child whose father had pressured her into having sexual relations with him by threatening that if she refused he would reveal that the girl who was living in her home was Jewish; Tec, *When Light*, p. 144.
70 Fogelman, *Conscience and Courage*, p. 278.
71 Interview by author with Yehudit Szwarcbach.

me with her or not?' I did a really foolish thing; I should have taken Marysia with us to Israel. She had really raised Jacob and had bonded with him. She remained all alone; she never married and never had children of her own.[72]

Another rescuer related, "Had Bolik [her husband] not returned from the war, I would have taken the girl and moved far, far away. No one would have found me." Nevertheless, she knew deep inside that just as the girl's father had found her now, so he would have found her at some future time. In the summer of 1946, after they had been living together for about a year, the girl's father disclosed his decision to leave Poland. The rescuer's agitated reaction follows:

I was stunned by the blow. I couldn't imagine my life without her. Whom should I live for? And if she wouldn't be with me, who would take care of her? Finally I started thinking that if her mother were alive, I am sure we could have found a solution. We'd live together or I'd give her the girl — her daughter — unreservedly and with peace of mind. It would be enough for me to visit them and have them visit me. Together we'd see to her education. But to give her to a man whom she hardly knew, even if he was her father? Who would understand her? Who would show her the same patience and love? Who would wipe away her tears when she was sad or hurt? Men aren't made for that, they think

---

72 Interview by author with Ceisza Landau, January 1989. The rescuer had been the caregiver of Jacob and his older brother even before the war. When the family was sent to the Częstochowa ghetto, she went with them and continued to take care of the children. When the ghetto was eliminated, the woman moved out and took Jacob with her. When Jacob's father and older brother were executed, his mother, Seishe, left the ghetto and joined the caregiver and her son. The three of them moved to the Aryan side of Warsaw, where the caregiver supported them. After they left Poland, the mother and son continued to correspond with her. In 1986, Seishe and Jacob returned to Poland for a reunion with the caregiver, who was by then living in an old-age home. It was a painful encounter; the caregiver was not fully lucid and did not recognize them. Jacob was given a notebook that had been found among her possessions, in which she had documented various events related to him during his stay with her. See also letter Frania Langans, GFHA, Correspondence File, 788–790. In her letter, Frania, the biological mother, describes the caregiver's devotion to her son: she left her own home and moved to a distant locality so that he would not be recognized. She also stayed in contact with the boy's mother and visited her in her place of hiding. "To this day she takes care of him and considers him the only thing of value in her life. When I came to her and said that we were going, she fell ill. She begged me to take her with me. Otherwise [she said], her heart would not be able to withstand her longings."

more about their own comfort. Even the best father hasn't got maternal feelings.[73]

There were cases in which rescuers knew where the children had gone after their removal and visited them regularly. Every such encounter was difficult for both the rescuers and the children. Pinhas Krybus, an activist with the Koordynacja, testified that the meetings were occasions of heartrending crying. When rescuers in search of the children discovered that the youngsters had left Poland, they were distraught.[74]

It was very important for both rescuers and the rescued to stay in touch after the separation. Encounters or correspondence could ease the sense of loss and allow both parties to provide each other with support. In most cases, however, the Jewish organizations viewed such encounters with disapproval and prevented them from taking place, seeing them as impediments to the children's acceptance of the situation.[75] There was a palpable fear that the rescuers and the children would be unable to stand the separation and would wish to be reunited. A man living in Palestine asked Rabbi Herzog to expedite the removal of a child survivor from Poland, adding:

> According to reliable reports that I received recently, the girl is in continual danger of being returned to the home of the Christian woman in Tarnów. The girl misses the woman badly and considers her a mother,

73 Hellman, *Avenue of the Righteous,* pp. 235–236. Leokadia found the baby girl at the edge of a forest and took her in. Throughout the war, she cared for the youngster lovingly and endured many dangers and hardships. Knowing nothing about the girl, she never imagined that her father would knock on her door one day and demand that she be handed over.

74 Testimony of Pinhas Krybus, OHD 45(68); Dekel, *Remnants of the Sword,* p. 132.

75 Letter Maria Madej, April 21, 1995; story of Michael, in Küchler, *We Accuse,* pp. 157–164; records of Kolbuszowa municipal court, Mark P3345, September 12, 1946, about an agreement concluded in Niepolomice municipal court in the matter of Maria Anna Skrzydlewski, Section 3 of the agreement, GFHA, Correspondence File, 788–790; Dekel, *Remnants of the Sword,* pp. 132–133; letter Jakob Abramowicz to Rabbi Herzog, February 20, 1947, in the matter of S.H., RZA, Rescue Files. The rescuer lived in Tarnów, far from the children's home in Łódź; nevertheless, she visited the girl several times. Interview by author with Chana Martynowski-Gutmorgen. Henka was abducted by Drucker and her sister without being able to say goodbye to her rescuer. She wanted very much to see her again but they did not allow her to do so. Hanka wrote to her and was astonished when she received no reply. Only afterwards did she find out that the letters had been destroyed in order to deny the rescuer knowledge of her whereabouts; Neshamit, "The Koordynacja for the Redemption of Children in Liberated Poland," pp. 140–141. According to Neshamit, the Koordynacja made strenuous efforts not to allow "parents" to visit in order to help the children to overcome their longings and forget their previous "families."

because she never had the chance to know her own mother. The Polish woman with whom the girl grew up has visited her several times in Łódź and is willing to take her back at any moment. Unless a way is found to redeem the girl at once, there is reason to fear that she will be lost to her family and her origins for good, Heaven forbid... The only thing that matters is to expedite the rescue of this orphan from the claws of spiritual death [*shmad*] that beset her from every direction.[76]

It was no simple matter to evade the organizations or relatives who were searching for the children. The efforts of some rescuers to conceal children and prevent their return were successful, and they were able to continue to raise the youngsters to adulthood. These rescuers had to employ the stratagems they had acquired during the war. They changed addresses, invented stories about family relations, and were alert to anything that made them suspect that someone had found them out. In fact, at least in the first few years following the war, when activity in search of children was most intensive, the rescuers could neither return to their previous lives nor find the peace of mind they deeply desired.[77]

The operatives were in various minds with regard to the rescuers, depending on the difficulties they encountered in their search for children. It was easier to appreciate the noble-minded humanitarian feats of rescuers when they did as hoped for and relinquished the children to the activists or family members. It was harder to praise rescuers who confronted the activists belligerently when asked to return the children. In such cases, the rescuers were regarded in less gentle terms. Some activists accused them of extortion and trafficking in children; others saw them as having abducted children in the name of Christianity, or having failed to understand where "the best interests of the child" really lay. Still others tended to doubt if the rescuer's love for the children was genuine.[78] The activists were equally aware, however, that

---

76 Letter Jakob Abramowicz to Rabbi Herzog, February 20, 1947.
77 Interview by author with Elżbieta Ficowska-Kopel; letter Bozena Szaniewska, February 18, 1995, in the matter of Basia Glowacka; interview with Jerzy Dolmawski, Poland, in Berman, "Wanda's Lists"; Anolik, *In the Service of Memory*, p. 71; Reicher, "The Priest Burst into Tears"; Kempner, "Only the Baby," Fogelman, *Conscience and Courage*, p. 278.
78 Letter Koordynacja presidium to William Bein, director of JDC-Poland, November 15, 1946, JDC, microfilm from Poland; Küchler-Silberman, *My Hundred Children*, p. 190; Neshamit, "The Koordynacja for the Redemption of Children in Liberated Poland," p. 123; Koryski, "The Zionist Koordynacja for the Redemption of Jewish Children in Poland," p. 27.

there was considerable justice in the rescuers' unwillingness to part from the children,[79] even if it clashed with their own outlook and beliefs.

The children were caught in the middle, sometimes not understanding why they had become the objects of struggle. In Wolhynia, for example, a Polish woman had found an infant lying in an alley with a note attached — "Have mercy on this baby! Save him!" — and took him home with her. After the war, the child's uncle returned, discovered that the boy was alive, and claimed him. The woman refused; having rescued the baby, she now saw her as her own son. Furthermore, he was no longer Jewish. Even when the uncle brought reinforcements, the woman, undeterred, shouted, "I won't give him back alive!" As all this was taking place, the boy stood there as each party tugged on one of his arms, screaming, "Don't tear me in half!"[80]

Involvement of the Polish Judiciary with Regard to Jewish Children

> *The king said, "Cut the living child in two and give half to one and half to the other." But the woman whose son was the living one pleaded with the king, for she was overcome with compassion for her son. "Please, Oh Lord," she cried, 'Give her the living child; only do not kill him!" The other woman said, "It shall be neither yours nor mine; cut him in half!" Then the king spoke: "Give the living child to her," he said, 'and surely do not put him to death; for she is his mother." When the entire nation of Israel heard the king's judgment, they beheld the king with awe, for they saw that he possessed divine wisdom to render justice.*   I Kings 3:25–28

---

79 Testimony Leibl Koryski, OHD 15(68). In reference to the problem that had been presented to them concerning their rights regarding the children, Koryski claimed that the activists also believed that a mother who had raised a child was his or her de facto mother — the person who had decided to take in the child, care for him, and love him; Chasia Bielicki-Bornstein, "Back to the Bosom of Their People" (Hebrew), MA, D2.1. According to Chasia (the first caregiver of the group of older children at the Koordynacja), the activists knew full well that it would be no easy task to separate the children from their caregivers and that they would not surrender the children without a struggle; Neshamit, "The Koordynacja for the Redemption of Children in Liberated Poland," p. 130. Neshamit finds it wholly unsurprising that rescuers changed addresses to conceal the children in their custody when they discovered that the youngsters were being sought after: rescuers who had cared for children devotedly were not prepared to part with them.

80 Dekel, *Remnants of the Sword*, p. 437.

The courts had to intervene when two sides laid claim to the child and could not agree about who would be the youngster's parent for the rest of his or her life. These situations created an impasse between the rescuers with whom the children had lived and the parents, relatives, or Jewish organization that claimed custody of the youngsters. The most frequent claimant on behalf of the Jews was the Central Jewish Committee by dint of its status as the Jews' official representative body. The Committee was able to call on lawyers who had been hired by the various Jewish committees throughout Poland.[81] The Central Committee made its legal apparatus available both to individual Jews and to the Jewish and Zionist organizations that were operating in the country at the time[82]

The guidelines drawn up by the Committee's legal department with regard to orphaned children, or children who were considered orphans until proved otherwise, were based on three statutes: the Family Law, the Fostership Law, and the Marriage Law. The document was based on Polish laws relating to the children and on court rulings handed down in late 1945 and the first half of 1946, which already addressed themselves to the special circumstances of the war.[83] The document was required because the Committee members considered the issue of the children "one of the most difficult problems facing the community," as stated in the preface — a sentiment that was enough to explain its necessity. The document, which presented in concentrated form the information needed to understand the minutiae of the laws, was sent to all departments, institutions, and local committees that dealt with matters relating to the children. The topics presented in the document give an indication of the complexity of the legal issues involved.

The document is divided into three sections: (a) determining fostership (*Opieka*) of children; (b) parents' rights to children in the care of strangers; (c) the rights of distant relatives to children who had been left parentless.

81 Letter Education Department to Attorney Hoffer, via the community of Rzeszów, July 28, 1947, ŻIH, Education Department, File 638; letter Herszenhorn, Director of Central Committee Education Department, to Lublin Committee, July 3, 1949, in the matter of A.A.I.I., ŻIH, Legal Department; appeal by Goldfinger of decision by Tarnów municipal court, presented to district court in Tarnów, File OP16/46 (Icz361/46, November 22, 1946, in regard to Z.Z. and Z.C, known as Hubel, GFHA, Correspondence File, 788–790.
82 Testimony Leibl Koryski, OHD 15(68); decision of Lublin district court, February 7, 1947, in the matter of J.K. (S.R.), GFHA, Correspondence File, 788–790; decision of Łódź municipal court, File 37/46, in the matter of E.R., ŻIH, legal Department.
83 Legal document in the matter of Jewish children in the care of non-Jews. The court rulings were dated September 25, 1945, January 22, 1946, May 14, 1946, and May 21, 1946, ŻIH Legal Department.

Section A notes that in regard to "children whose parents have been lost, i.e., whose whereabouts are unknown or who were sent to camps, and whose death has not been legally confirmed, any interested party and also the Central Committee or branches thereof may apply for a granting of fostership." The applicant had to present documents or bring witnesses attesting to the child's identity. Further on, the document states, "The district court, in its role as the competent institution under the law, shall assign fostership of the child to a person who is related to him by kin or by a more distant relationship, or to a person who is related to the child or to his family and is fit for the assumption of guardianship." If the child was enrolled in one of the educational institutions of the Central Committee at the time of the application, "It is recommended that a representative of the Central Committee appear with a statement from the institution in regard to the party responsible for fostership."[84] This clause shows that the sides had plenty of maneuvering room. Any interested party could apply for legal certification of guardianship over a child; the court was entitled to decide upon the most appropriate person. Persons with a kinship connection had this right, but so did any person found suitable for other reasons. This would include people who had taken care of the children for years, saving their lives, protecting them and developing a relationship of dependency and love. To make sure the applications were free of any other intent, the document stated that if property registered in the name of the child's family was found, another individual should be placed in charge of the property.[85]

In Section B, dealing with the rights of parents to their children, the following appears:

> The parents of the child (mother or father) are legally entitled to demand the surrender of the child from persons who were not authorized to be the child's guardian. When children who were lost are being sought, parents may avail themselves of the legal authorities, police, local councils, etc., under Section 26 of the Family Law. Furthermore, all responsibility for care of children that was legally recognized in view of the prevailing situation at the time is null and void in the event that the parents (mother or father) had been imprisoned or in camps; in this case

84 Legal document in the matter of Jewish children in the care of non-Jews, Section A: "Determination of Fostership of Children," ibid.

85 See, for example, letter Education Department to Central Committee presidium, August 3, 1947, in the matter of P.S., ibid.; letter children's home in Otwock to Central Committee Legal Department, July 31, 1947, in the matter of C.F., ibid.

the children shall revert to the guardianship of the parents (mother or father). The legal authorities, the police, the courts, etc., will be available to parents who report to them in the event that they encounter refusal to turn over the child to their custody. In cases where the court legally ratifies the care of children by parties other than parents, and in cases where the parents demand custody of the child, they must apply to the district court, as the competent legal instance, in order to declare legal custody of the child.

This section of the document makes it clear that the primary right to the child if one of the parents remains alive, belongs to that parent and not to the person who has cared for the child, even if that person adopted the child legally or secured the legal right as a foster parent. This is valid only if the parents apply to the court in order to rescind any previous decision. It is noteworthy that the document charges all governmental institutions with the duty of helping parents in their search for their children.[86]

Section C, dealing with the rights of distant relatives to parentless children, broadens the limits of the rights to the child much as does Section A, but this time under the guiding principle of the "best interests of the child." This section establishes that if both parents perished but a relative survived (even though this, too, was uncommon under the circumstances of the war), it is not self-evident that that person is legally entitled to care for the child. The question is phrased as follows: "In cases where the parents are not alive, relatives of the children may apply to the district court for legal approval of fostership. The court shall rule in these cases, in the 'best interests of the child.'" However, "the court shall take into consideration kinship, close relations with the child or his family, or other circumstances, and shall decide to grant custody over the child to the most appropriate person. It should be emphasized that kin have a prior right over other persons."

The expression "close relations with the child" created a complicated problem because families had been scattered during the war. Some had fled to the Soviet Union or other locations when the war began; others were deported to labor or concentration camps. Under such circumstances, it was impossible to base judgment on "close relations with the child." After all, not all such children had known their relatives, and even if they had done, the time that had elapsed was of great importance in regard to their ability

---

86 Legal document in the matter of Jewish children in the care of non-Jews, Section B, "Rights of Parents to Children in the Care of Strangers," ibid.

to remember them. In many cases, rescuers had much closer relations with children than did their biological kin.

If custody of the child had been legally assigned to others, the relatives had the option of applying for release "from the current caregiver and for legal transfer of the child to the applicant or some other relative." However:

> It should be emphasized that the district court, as the guardianship authority, shall release the present guardian only if one of the following has been appointed as guardian: a person who (1) is unfit for the role; (2) lacks civil rights, parentage rights, or guardianship rights; (3) is in poor psychological condition; (4) did not obtain the right of guardianship from the parents (father or mother) while they were alive; (5) is found unsuited to be a guardian due to his characteristics or relations with the child or with his family.

In clarification of the fifth item, "characteristics or relations with the child," the following appears: "intimate relations, drunkenness, riotous behavior, immoral behavior, mistreatment of the child, and insufficient evidence that the child will be raised and schooled properly."

Thus, a person who applied to remove a child from a rescuers' home had to prove that the rescuer was flawed in one of these respects. This claim was liable to degenerate into a campaign of mutual recriminations, in which the means would justify the end — an ironic possibility where feats of rescue during the Nazi era were at issue.[87]

From the point of view of people wishing to remove children from the home of the rescuer there was something cynical about the fourth item. On the verge of annihilation, many parents desperately tried to find any person, anywhere, to rescue their children. They were willing to promise a potential rescuer anything, including an undertaking not to reclaim the child if they survived. Now, their relatives were liable to honor these promises.

The guidelines state that under Sections 41 and 43 of the Fostership Law, the district court, in its role as a fostership committee, shall recommend the suspension of the parents' custody of their children if it is found that the parents were unable for a lengthy period of time to care for their child, and will implement the decision under the law. The same applies in cases of parents who had perished, whose whereabouts were unknown, or had been deported to the camps, even if their death had not been legally proven. Section B of the document, in contrast, discussing the rights of parents to children in the

---

87 Ibid., Section C, "Rights of Distant Relatives to Parentless Children."

care of strangers, states that parents have the legal right to demand the surrender of children from persons who are unauthorized to have possession of them. Section B also states that if the responsibility of any person for the child had been recognized in the past, this responsibility is nullified if the parents' guardianship over the child was disrupted due to their having been in prison or in the camps. In all cases where the claimants are the child's parents, the court must be at their service in order to assign legal possession of the children to them. Thus, the law distinguishes between the right to fostership over the child and the right to possession.

The guidelines express a dual approach toward parents' rights to their children. On the one hand, they discuss a situation of child abandonment by parents; on the other, they acknowledge the special circumstances of the war. The difference between the two outlooks gave the judges broad latitude for rulings in accordance with their worldview and the way they understood the case before them. The following story shows how severely they were torn as they considered the need to rule in favor of one side or the other. A mother placed her infant daughter (born in April 1942) on the steps of a building in Lubartów. The mother survived the war and subsequently spent time in a DP camp in Germany, where she wrote the following:

> I had to hide in a forest without food or clothing. Three days passed and I realized that I could not continue that way for much longer. I became weak from hunger and cold and I nursed my daughter with blood and not with milk. Knowing that we could be shot like dogs at any moment, I decided to save my daughter. In my despair, I worked up the courage to crawl into town in the evening. I left my baby on the steps of a house and attached a note with her name.

A couple named Wisocki found the baby and took her home. In a home visit conducted in response to the mother's letter, it was found that the Wysockis, then aged about sixty, were living under modest conditions, loved the little girl dearly, and were providing her with excellent care. The rescuers demanded that the girl's mother come to Poland and prove that she was indeed the mother. This created yet another problem typical of the time: the need to produce witnesses who could attest to a biological relationship between the parent and child. From the point of view of the rescuers it was a logical demand, but if one bears in mind the conditions of the war and the ways in which parents had to relinquish custody of their children, together with the fact that most of Polish Jewry had been annihilated, obviously it was often impossible to find witnesses. In this case, the mother eventually came to Poland and her case was adjudicated by the court, which decided in her favor and ruled that the Wysocki family be given compensation.[88]

If the question of parents' right to their children was not contested, it did nonetheless occur with regard to relatives. The document states that their claims were to be litigated in court and each case should be examined on its own merits, bearing in mind "the best interests of the child." Although the law gave relatives prior rights over strangers, the court had to take into account the degree of kinship and relations with the child in choosing the people best suited to care for him or her. In such claims, the court was supposed to discharge the de facto foster parent only if she or he were found to be unfit for the task.[89] It was also determined that if the child had been staying with people whom the court had not yet authorized to serve as foster parents, the child's relatives were entitled to demand him or her from the de facto guardians — but only with the agreement of the court. If the child had relatives, their right, or the right of a person deputized by them for this purpose, to be foster parents for the child prevailed over the right of the rescuer, even if the child continued to live in the rescuer's home.[90]

One of the questions before the courts was the question of how to relate

88 Letter World Jewish Congress to Central Committee, June 31, 1946, ŻIH, Education Department, File 643; letter Central Committee to World Jewish Congress, undated, ibid.; letter Central Committee to HIAS, undated, ibid.; letter Education Department to Wysocki, Lubertów, undated, ibid.; letters Central Committee to Central Committee presidium, September 21 and November 19, 1946, ibid.; letter Education Department to Joint Distribution Committee, Warsaw, January 31, 1947, in the matter of E.F., ibid.; see also five letters from March to May 1949 in the matter of R.H., ŻIH, Legal Department. The boy was handed over to the Ursula convent in Łódź in 1943. Until 1944, the child's father was still alive and paid for his upkeep. Neither parent survived the war but a sister of the boy's grandmother, who had spent the war in the Soviet Union, asked to take possession of him. The court demanded that she bring witnesses that the boy's mother, Gittl née Blumenstein, was indeed his mother, since during the war she had lived under the false name of Juliana Chmielewska. The court wished to ensure that the mother was indeed Jewish and that the boy was her son. There was something absurd about this directive, since a Jew who had to live under a false name would not divulge his real name and his Jewish identity, let alone consort with his child and thereby place him in danger! See also minutes of Kolbuszowa municipal court in the matter of Maria Anna Skrzydlewska, R.K., GFHA, Correspondence File, 788–790. The girl's aunt brought two witnesses with her. While the identity of one of the witnesses was being checked, her papers were presented — one document from 1942, showing her Polish identity and her false name, and the other, her marriage certificate from 1946, in her Jewish name — to prove that she was indeed a Jewish woman who had been living under a borrowed identity during the war.
89 See five conditions for discharge of guardian, p. 242, ŻIH Legal Department.
90 See, for example, letter Central Committee Legal Department to court in Staszów, May 17, 1949, in the matter of S.H. ibid.

to the very act of surrendering a child during the war. Should it be seen as a temporary act of entrustment — "for safekeeping"– or should it be regarded as permanent? Another issue to be considered was the intentions of the parent when they relinquished the child under circumstances that now made it impossible to explore the issue with them. This question arose in full fury in a petition presented to the court in Kłodzko in 1946. When the court of first instance in Nowa Ruda heard the case, nine witnesses were called, Jews and Poles; each gave their own version of the way the parents, the Fuchsberg family who were no longer alive, regarded the relinquishing of their daughter. The lawyer who represented the claimant, the girl's aunt, argued:

> [If] one bears in mind that the will to live and the hope that it will be possible to survive annihilation is present in every person's soul, even in perilous situations, [the Court] should conclude that Fuchsberg, when he handed the girl to the Grzegorczyk family, believed that one day he would be able to reclaim her.

The lawyer reinforced this assertion by stating that no one would hand over their child "as a gift." Accordingly, in his opinion, it could not be assumed that parents would hand over their children without the possibility of reclaiming them. Nevertheless, in this case the court ruled in favor of the rescuers and only the district court, as court of second instance, reassigned the girl to her aunt.[91]

Parents and relatives of children realized that the litigation process would be protracted. Furthermore, by choosing this path they knew they would be entrusting the decision to a third party with legislative powers, that is, they would be violating the law if they did not accept its decision. Therefore, they usually tried to arrive at an agreement before trial. However, this too could be very time-consuming and might not end with the desired result.[92] For example, the father of a girl and her rescuer, each separately, asked an arbitrator to solve

---

91 Appeal of ruling by Nowa Ruda court, presented by Helena Fuchsberg to the court in Kłodzko, case mOP1/46, May 5, 1948, in the matter of L.F., who also appears as Grzegorczyk, GFHA, Correspondence File, 788–790.

92 Letter Central Committee to Staszów Committee, November 26, 1946, in the matter of S.H., ŻIH, Education Department, File 638; letter Central Committee to Reingerc, Argentina, January 8, 1947, ibid.; letters Central Committee to Weiblatt, UK, May 28, 1947 and August 29, 1947, ibid.; the letters show that the following persons dealt with the removal of the girl at the relatives' behest: the Central Committee, Rabbi Kahana's representative (presumably Drucker), and Rabbi Schonfeld of the UK. In its decision, handed down in 1948, the court ruled that the girl should remain with her rescuers but appointed a foster mother for the girl representing the Central Committee. See also letter Central Committee Legal Department to court in Staszów, May 17, 1949, in the matter of S.H., ŻIH, Legal Department.

the problem, knowing that all of them — the rescuer, her husband, the biological father, and the child — could not continue living together for long without a decision. The father turned to the prosecutor-general in Wrocław, who declared that although the girl was indeed his flesh-and-blood kin, he had abandoned her at the edge of a forest and in doing so had relinquished her, albeit unwillingly, to a stranger, who had cared for her with the utmost devotion during the war. This, in the absence of the girl's biological mother, made the rescuer her mother de facto. The prosecutor added that the rescuer had earned the status of a mother due to the expenses she had incurred on the girl's behalf during the war. The father was also told that the court would refrain from ruling in favor of the rescuer only if he could prove that she had taken the child against his wishes. Since the father was not prepared to make such an allegation — apart from it being false, he appreciated the rescue of his daughter by the woman — he chose not to pursue his claim in court. The rescuer, in turn, contacted a lawyer, who explained that she had nothing to gain by going to court since the law plainly favored the biological father. Thus, she, too, renounced her claim and the matter was not taken to court.[93] In other cases, family members acted on the feeling that they had no choice but to refer the matter to the court in the hope that it would recognize their rights to the children.[94]

The reasons for turning to the courts were many and not limited to issues of custody. It might happen, for example, when a family could not locate the address of a rescuer who evaded them at length in order not to relinquish the child in his or her care,[95] or when a rescuer denied having possession of a Jew-

---

93 Hellman, *Avenue of the Righteous*, pp. 236–238. Junisz and his wife placed their daughter Shifra, about eighteen months old, at the edge of a forest, hoping that somebody would take her in. Since Leokadia found her and took her home, Junisz did not think it fair to bring kidnapping charges against her. When he offered Leokadia a sum of money for surrendering the girl to him, it was as a sign of gratitude, Junisz claimed, but also as a counterweight to the prosecutor's argument about Leokadia's rights to the girl due to the sums of money that she had spent on her. Ultimately, Junisz took the girl and placed her in a children's home until he was able to leave Poland with her.

94 Autobiography of Withold Wajman, in Tenenboim, *One of a City and Two of a Family*, pp. 131–132. Withold knew that his younger brother was staying in a convent orphanage even though the sisters claimed that the boy had died in 1945. A police investigation showed that the boy was indeed alive and at the convent; accordingly, the older brother turned to the court. Testimony of Devorah Zilber, OHD, 27(68), describing cases in Tarnobrzeg and Mińsk-Mazowiecki; letter Bein, Joint Distribution Committee, Poland, to JDC-New York, October 24, 1946, in the matter of M.Z., JDCA, HZ/46/1133.

95 Letter Director of Legal Department, Adv. Gutmacher, to court recorder in Wrocław, May 19, 1947, in the matter of P.A. The claim, under Section 26/2 of the Family Law, was brought against the rescuer's father, who knew his son's address but refused to divulge it to the girl's mother. ŻIH, Legal Department.

ish child and no basis to allow negotiations to begin had been established.[96] Sometimes families turned to the courts in the hope that they would force recalcitrant children to rejoin them.[97] A demand for an especially large sum of money also served as a reason to go to court, the claimants hoping that the court would regard it as extortion and order the rescuer to surrender the child.[98] Often, however, the rescuers had also considered the possibility of an allegation of extortion and tried to keep their demands off the official record. One rescuer, for example, gave the Central Committee a deposition about his claims against the relatives of the girl but refused to sign it.[99] Another rescuer mentioned the sum that he wanted to receive only when speaking to the girl's family, but refused to do so officially to the Central Committee and other representatives who contacted him and tried to exert pressure on him to sign a deposition.[100]

If the status of parents regarding their children had been legally established, that of brothers and sisters had not. Neither rescuers nor the law regarded them as automatically entitled to reunite with their siblings.

96 Letter Education Department to World Jewish Congress, November 1947, in the matter of J.S., ŻIH, Education Department, File 641. The home of S. Jankowski was placed under lengthy surveillance. Although two witnesses testified in court that a girl had been with him during the war, no girl was observed in his company.

97 Letter Drucker to Rabbi Herzog, June 12, 1947, in the matter of A.N., RZA, Rescue Files.

98 Letter Central Committee to HIAS, July 1947, in the matter of A.K., ŻIH, Education Department, File 638. The boy was claimed by his grandfather. The rescuer demanded $2,500 for his return and the Committee handed the matter over to the Legal Department.

99 Record of deposition by Jopowicz. The Jopowiczes demanded assistance in the sum of $50,000, or $10,000 in moving to America, plus a house in the town of Wierzbnik that belonged to the Hirszman family. A letter from the Education Department to Kornwasser in Detroit, May 16, 1947 (on the same topic), stated in respect to the first demand that Jopowicz was interested in going to Detroit, where he had an uncle, and in regard to the third demand it was stated that he was interested, in addition to the Hirszmans' house, in a house that Kornwasser owned in Wierzbnik, ibid.

100 Letter Częstochowa Committee to Central Committee, July 3, 1946, ŻIH, Legal Department; letter advocates Rogoziński and Wertheim, Łódź, to Child Care Department, January 13, 1947, in the matter of Z.S., ibid.; letter Yaakov Etzioni, Tel Aviv, to Rabbi Wohlgelernter, during the latter's visit to Jerusalem, January 22, 1947, RZA, Rescue Files. The edge of the letter, where the date was written, is torn, but a subsequent letter that refers to this one indicates that it was dated January 22, 1947; letters Drucker to Rabbi Herzog, April 27, 1947, and June 12, 1947, in the matter of Z.S., ibid. The rescuer demanded $12,000 and the family's large real-estate holdings in Częstochowa. The attorney from Łódź wrote that only after the girl's uncle provided him with the correspondence with the rescuer, which apprised him of the huge sums that the rescuer was demanding for the girl, could he begin to take legal action.

Usually siblings had to go to court in order to obtain recognition of their rights.[101]

The legal proceedings usually differentiated between appointing the child's foster parent and determining where the child would be raised.[102] Therefore, relatives did not always file suit for the purpose of removing children from rescuers' homes. If the rescuer was taking good care of the child and the Central Committee did not expect to win the suit, the relatives first applied for the status of foster parents, thereby getting official access to the home where the child was being raised, in the assumption that they could eventually sue for custody. Even those who continued to raise children by court order, however, knew that they had no presumption of custody until a foster parent was legally appointed; therefore, they acted to obtain such an appointment for themselves.[103] From the legal standpoint, even if the rescuers had baptized the children and recorded them with the church under their own name, they were not considered the legal foster parent until the adoption was formalized.[104] It is hard to know how many rescuers were aware of this legal problem, but a review of the case files shows that even Poles in small rural localities were involved in such litigation, evidently considering it a necessary evil in order to achieve the desired purpose. However, many others were presumably oblivious to this legal issue.

Sometimes the Central Committee or other organizations concluded agreements with rescuers. The courts, however, did not always recognize these agreements if they had been concluded without court mediation. This gave each litigant the possibility of suing the other on the grounds of unfairness or use of pressure and manipulation. For the rescuers, this made it pos-

---

101 Draft of letter from Central Committee, addressee's name indecipherable, undated, in the matter of C.G., ŻIH, Legal Department. The girl had an adult brother and an aunt but the rescuer refused to surrender her to them on the grounds that she did not trust them. The court ruled in favor of the rescuer.

102 Minutes of Kolbuszowa municipal court in the matter of Maria Anna Skrzydlewska. At first the girl was left with her rescuers but the court assigned her a Jewish legal guardian, Mojzesz Grunbaum. GFHA, Correspondence File, 788–790.

103 Letter Central Committee Legal Department to court in Staszów, May 17, 1949, in the matter of S.H., ŻIH, Legal Department. In a trial held in 1948, it was decided that the girl would remain with her rescuers but that a representative of the Central Committee would be granted fostership. The rescuer, Czerny, neither attended the hearing nor expressed any objection to the fostership decision. In May 1949, Czerny, after having disregarded the court's ruling, asked the same court to declare him the girl's foster father.

104 See ruling of Kłodzko district court, File Icz24/48, October 13, 1948, in the matter of L.F., also known as Grzegorczyk, Section 3 of the judge's ruling, GFHA, Correspondence File 788–790.

sible to rescind their previous decision if they now regretted surrendering the child.[105] However, sometimes the courts, as the legal authority, became involved as guarantors for the carrying out of agreements that had been arrived at by rescuers and relatives before trial.[106]

As soon as the possibility of going to court arose, each side made the necessary preparations so as to improve its chances of success. The staff of the Central Committee Child Care Department, aware of the legal provisions concerning the possibility of revoking fostership if the foster parent was declared unfit, attempted to discover the child's living conditions in the rescuer's home, since this as well as the family's economic situation could be grounds for a suit. The Department also tried to determine whether the rescuers were interested in the child because they hoped to acquire money or property that the deceased parents had left behind.[107] However, there was a problem with this: when it was clear that the rescuers were treating the child well, obviously the likelihood of removing him or her from the home of the rescuers decreased.[108] In such cases, the Central Committee was in no hurry to file a claim for the custody of a child, knowing that if the rescuer won the suit, the decision could not be reversed until the child turned

---

105 Ruling of Łódź municipal court, File 37/46, in the matter of E.R.. ŻIH, Legal Department. The claimant (the rescuer) argued that she herself had objected to handing the child over to the Koordynacja; the initiative behind the act had been taken by her daughter who lived with her. She also asserted that since she was illiterate, her daughter had signed the relinquishment papers on her behalf.

106 Minutes of Kolbuszowa municipal court in the matter of Maria Anna Skrzydlewska, R.K., GFHA, Correspondence File 788–790. The judge realized that both sides could challenge the agreement: the rescuer for having been under-compensated and the girl's aunt for having overpaid. Therefore, he inserted the question of payment into the agreement drawn up between the sides. Section 2 of the agreement stated: "Leah Weinfeld [the girl's aunt] and Celina Dodzyńska [her rescuer] confirm jointly that Celina Dodzyńska has received in full the sum owed to her for having supported and raised the minor for five years and has no further claims. Leah Weinfeld, in turn, states that the consideration that Celina Dodzyńska received is reasonable, not excessive, and compatible with the actual expenses incurred, and that she, the aunt, waives any claim of overpayment or profiteering."

107 Draft of cable. On the basis of the response received, the cable seems to have been sent from the Central Committee to the Częstochowa Committee on July 3, 1946; cable from Częstochowa Jewish Committee to Central Committee, July 3, 1946, in the matter of Z.S., ŻIH, Legal Department; letter Central Committee to Katowice Committee, June 13, 1947, in the matter of O.K., ŻIH, Education Department, File 638; and letter, Central Committee to HIAS, July 1947, in the matter of A.K., ibid.

108 Letters Central Committee to Katowice Committee and HIAS, ibid.; letter Częstochowa Jewish Committee to Central Committee, ibid.

eighteen.[109] However, in fact, even if the child was receiving proper care, the rescuers' economic situation and the question of their ability to bear the expenses of raising the child to adulthood were of great importance in the eyes of the courts.[110]

Various measures were sometimes taken before resorting to litigation. In one example, the Koordynacia applied to the Registrar of Population before bringing suit and asked him to register a boy survivor, who had been registered under a Polish name, under his Jewish name, so that he could be recognized as Jewish.[111] In another case, a Polish woman who was sued for custody of the girl in her care by the girl's brother, hurriedly turned to the Registrar of Population in order to lower the girl's age by two years. Thus she could claim that the girl was too young, still needed her, and therefore should not be surrendered.[112]

In many post-1946 claims for children, Jewish organizations represented relatives who sought custody even though they were living outside Poland. From their experience in such cases, the activists believed that the chances of winning in court would be greater if the claim were presented by relatives, however distant, who lived in Poland, and they made strenuous efforts to locate such relatives.[113] If the Jewish organizations had made their claims "on behalf of the Jewish people," the chances of their winning the children decreased. The Central Committee, for example, lost a claim that it had presented to a municipal court on behalf of the Koordynacia and a subsequent claim

---

109 Letter Education Department to Bina Rybak, Łódź, May 13, 1947, in the matter of L.H., ŻIH, Education Department, File 638; letter Education Department to Kornwasser, Detroit, May 16, 1947, in the same matter, ibid.

110 Ruling of Łódź municipal court, File 37/46, in the matter of E.R., ŻIH, Legal Department.

111 Ruling of Lublin district court in the matter of J.K. [S.R.] GFHA, Correspondence File 788–790. The rescuer recorded the boy under a Christian name, the Koordynacja wished to have him registered under a Jewish name.

112 Interview by author with Chana Martynowski-Gutmorgen. Indeed, Hanka was left in the rescuer's custody.

113 Letters Drucker to Rabbi Herzog, January 27, 1947, and June 12, 1947, RZA, Rescue Files; letter World Jewish Congress to Central Committee, March 31, 1946, ŻIH, Education Department, File 643; letter Central Committee to Wysocki, Lubartów, undated, ibid.; letter Central Committee Child Care Department to HIAS, Warsaw, undated, ibid.; draft of letter evidently sent by Central Committee to World Jewish Congress, undated, ibid.; letters Child Care Department to Central Committee presidium, September 21, 1946 and November 19, 1946, ibid.; letter Child Care Department to JDC, Warsaw, January 31, 1947, ibid.

that it filed with Lublin district court. Ultimately, the rescuer was named the boy's foster mother.[114]

Although the court rulings were guided by the provisions of the law, they were distinct in the different emphases given to the facts and testimonies and the different ways in which the law could be interpreted. Some judges, for example, regarded the surrender of children by the parents as an act of forfeiture in favor of the rescuers. Other judges ruled that if the child had been handed over "at a moment of mortal danger and extermination by the German authorities, it [was done only] for safeguarding and education" and to save the child's life.[115]

At the time, the Jewish activists believed that the Polish courts, unlike those in the USSR, would usually recognize the prior rights of parents and relatives and ruled in their favor.[116] However, the rulings that I studied were very varied. One ruling handed down by a district court and upheld by the Polish Supreme Court, stated that a family that had taken in a Jewish boy after the war and had even adopted him lawfully should return him to his mother.[117] In another case, however, in which the claimant was a girl's older brother, the court ruled in favor of the rescuer.[118] Even when parents or relatives won custody, it was only after lengthy litigation.

114 Ruling of Lublin district court in the matter of J.K. [S.R.]. The Central Committee presented the first claim and the appeal in conjunction with the Koordynacja. See also working report of Teofilia Goldman; appeal to Tarnów district court in the matter of C.Z. and S.Z., GFHA, Correspondence File 788–790.

115 Ruling of Nowa Ruda municipal court, File mOP1/46, May 5, 1948, as deduced from appeal by Helena Fuchsberg to Kłodzko district court and the ruling of said court in the matter of L.F., ibid.

116 Letters Drucker to Rabbi Herzog, January 27, 1947, and June 12, 1947, RZA, Rescue Files; Kahana, *After the Deluge*, p. 53; Dekel, *Remnants of the Sword*, p. 101. A court in Ukraine recognized the paternity of a survivor who wished to reclaim his daughter but ruled that the girl should be left with her rescuers on the grounds that whereas her situation with the rescuers was good, her father was single and if he married there was no way to know how his new wife would treat the girl. Furthermore, her father intended to travel to Poland and thereafter to emigrate to Palestine. Ultimately, the father left for Poland without his daughter: see also ruling of Lithuanian Supreme Court, Civil Case 45–370-2, in the matter of A.F., GFHA, Correspondence File, 788–790. In this ruling, the Lithuanian Supreme Court thought differently and upheld the decision of Vilnius district court, Area 2–20, February 26, 1945, to return the boy to his mother.

117 Dekel, *Remnants of the Sword*, pp. 102–104.

118 Interview by author with Chana Martynowski-Gutmorgen. When the brother received an immigration visa for Palestine, he left Poland. In late 1948, the girl was kidnapped by Drucker and her sister, and when the two sisters moved to Israel after the establishment of the state, they were not able to reunite with their brother, who had been killed in 1947 in a battle in the north of the country.

Due to the differentiation that the law recognized between the person who would actually raise a child and the one to be declared his or her foster parent, court rulings sometimes established an indestructible bond between relatives and rescuers. For example, a young man who had sued for custody of his sister's daughter, lost in court. The ruling stated that the girl should remain with her rescuers, who were designated as her foster parents until the age of eighteen, and the uncle was declared a second foster parent.[119] The Łódź Municipal court, in contrast, appointed the town's Jewish committee, "the purpose of which is to protect the Jewish population that survived the war," as the foster caregiver of a girl whose rescuer could not afford to support and educate her, and appointed the rescuer as a joint foster parent, thereby giving her "the authority to control the case and report to the [fostership] authorities any event that requires their intervention."[120] There were cases in which the court, while stating that the Jewish relative should be the child's foster parent, required that the relative had to report to the court about the child's whereabouts whenever necessary. By so deciding, it ruled for all practical purposes that the child must remain in Poland.[121]

The court rulings against handing children over to their relatives were based on several types of reasoning. Some rulings stated that the parents who were raising the child had done so in the past and therefore were entitled to continue doing so in the future.[122] In other cases, courts noted that the claimant was alone and without family, whereas the rescuers maintained a united family cell, thereby providing a healthy home setting for the child.[123] Yet other rulings stated that good and affectionate care of the child, even without a specific religious orientation, were, practically speaking, what the child's parents would have wanted.[124]

In an appeal to the Tarnów district court, the appellant, a representative of the Central Committee, claimed that the municipal court had stated in its ruling that two sisters, one seven or eight years old and the other aged ten to

---

119 Testimony Devorah Zilber, OHD, 27(68).
120 Ruling of Łódź municipal court, Case 37/46, in the matter of E.R., ŻIH, Legal Department; Koryski, "The Zionist Koordynacja for the Redemption of Jewish Children in Poland," p. 28.
121 Neshamit, "The Koordynacja for the Redemption of Children in Liberated Poland," p. 125.
122 Kurek-Lesik, "*Udzial Żeńkich*," p. 350. In this case, the claimant was the girl's mother.
123 Testimony Devorah Zilber, OHD, 27(68).
124 Ruling of Lublin district court in the matter of J.K. [S.R.], GFHA, Correspondence File, 788–790.

twelve, should remain in a convent orphanage as the girls wished. Challenging this finding, the appellant argued:

> If we take into account, on the one hand, their background at the [convent] orphanage and, on the other, the psychological state of the girls, who had been persecuted during the occupation due to their Jewish origins and believe that in this manner they will be able to erase the traces of their origins and avert possible future difficulties in their lives... , then they cannot be expected to comprehend a new reality, in which a Jewish orphanage would assure them of a happy future.[125]

Despite this argument, the district court upheld the lower court's ruling and claimed that it was necessary to establish "whether the girls had made their decision freely and are sufficiently mature to make [such] a decision." Thus, the court summarized the reasoning behind its decision:

> In this session [of the court], the minors were questioned painstakingly and thoroughly about the course of their lives today and the circumstances of their rescue from death during the occupation. In view of this personal contact with them and on the basis of their statements, the Court has reached the conclusion that their intellectual level is sufficient and that they have a high level of practical wisdom. These circumstances suffice to entitle these minors to decide where they wish to remain and under what conditions they are to be raised"[126]

The ability to feed, house, and assure the future of children was very important in the reasoning behind the legal decisions. In the above litigation before the court in Tarnów, the judge expressed his opinion to the Jewish plaintiff:

---

125 Appeal to Tarnów district court in the matter of C.Z. and S.Z., GFHA, Correspondence File, 788–790.

126 Ruling of Tarnów district court, File OP/1646 (Icz361/46), in the matter of C.Z. and S.Z., known as Hubel, February 24, 1947, GFHA, Correspondence File, 788–790. During the litigation in the municipal court and in the appeal documents, the girls were also referred to under their Jewish surname, whereas the district court ruling mentioned them only under their borrowed identities. The reasoning of the district court makes no reference to the other claims about the flawed nature of the trial in the municipal court but addresses only the question of the acceptability of the girls' wishes. Notably, the girls were delivered to the convent only in March 1946, after having wandered around various villages during and immediately after the war; see also ruling of Lublin district court in the matter of J.K. [S.R.]. In this trial, too, the court stated that its decision to leave the boy with his rescuer was based on the wishes of the boy, who told both the municipal court and the district court that he wanted "to stay with Mommy," i.e., Maria K., ibid.

For the children's wellbeing and according to Christian and moral principles, children of Jewish origin should be under Jewish custodianship,
in Jewish orphanages that have adequate budgets from the United States,
from families of Jews who were murdered. [Then], without a doubt, the
children will enjoy a higher standard of living and also the possibility of
attending school and learning skills in accordance with their aptitudes,
so that they will enjoy good material conditions to assure their future
life.[127]

Nevertheless, despite this, for the reasons cited before, the judge upheld the
original ruling to leave the girls in the orphanage of the town convent.

In a trial in Łódź, the court explained its decision to give the local Jewish committee fostership over a girl and to transfer her to its children's home:
"[The committee] has financial sources that can assure the girl an appropriate
standard [of living], now and in the future." The court stated this after being
convinced that the rescuer lacked the wherewithal to raise her.[128]

In another case, Lublin district court ruled that the original ruling could
be overturned only if the appellant's witnesses had not been questioned or if
the minor's state of health had not been examined.[129] Studies of other appeals,
however, indicate that they were submitted to the courts both by Jews and by

---

127 Appeal to Tarnów district court in the matter of C.Z. and S.Z.
128 Decision of Łódź municipal court, File 37/46, in the matter of A.R.; testimony Leibl
    Koryski, OHD 15(68). In his testimony, Koryski described the judge as a "liberal." In the
    trial, a rescuer who had handed a girl over to the Koordynacja for payment demanded
    that the girl be returned to her. The court investigated the rescuer's ability to raise the girl
    and found that one of her daughters, who during the war had officially recorded the girl
    in the baptism papers as her daughter, was very ill and that her husband had disappeared
    in the Soviet Union after the war. The husbands of two other daughters were not working
    regularly and one of the daughters — who lived with her mother and had signed the docu-
    ments of surrender of the girl — was pregnant. The rescuer had no financial resources
    of her own and was supported by her children, who had shown no interest in the trial.
    Therefore, the judge ruled, the plaintiff lacked the wherewithal to raise the girl. However,
    "Mindful of the importance of the moral and emotional relationship between them [...]
    and after bearing in mind that Walerja Janiszewska protected the girl for six years, [the
    court decides] to grant her joint fostership."
129 Decision of Lublin district court in the matter of J.K. (S.R.). The judge decided to uphold
    the decision of the municipal court because the court of first instance had heard thirteen
    witnesses who testified that the rescuer was treating the boy well and had heard about
    the minor's state of health and living conditions from two expert witnesses, who gave a
    favorable opinion.

non-Jews,[130] for additional reasons based on various sections of laws dealing with the status of the children, and were litigated anyway. For example, one mother sued to reclaim her daughter and the municipal court ruled that the girl should remain in the custody of the person who had been raising her. The mother appealed to the district court, which, after taking the circumstances of the war into account, ruled that the girl should be returned to her mother.[131]

In an appeal before the court in Kłodzko, several arguments were raised against the decision of the court of first instance to award continued fostership and custody of a girl to her rescuer. The plaintiff, the girl's aunt, claimed that the Fostership Law gave relatives preference over rescuers and that the ability of the rescuers in the future to care for the girl was not clear. This contention was based on a remark by one of the witnesses, who said that the girl's father had told him that he was surrendering her to these rescuers for lack of choice, although he considered them "shady types." The plaintiff also claimed that the girl had a sister in Palestine who wished to be reunited with her and that the plaintiff wanted to be the foster parent of both girls; that the Fostership Law counsels against separating siblings; and that the court had heard nine witnesses but preferred the testimonies of the defendant's witnesses over those of the plaintiff. These claims aside, appellant's counsel redefined the specific case as one of general principle:

> The matter of nationality, which the municipal court disregarded without explanation, must not be overlooked. Obviously, a child whose nationality is other [than that of those who raise him], as in the minor and the Grzegorczyk family, has character traits that are other [than those of] random foster families. The character differences under the laws of heritage, the difference in worldview — which will become more and more evident over the years — and the differences in blood should also be taken into account in appointing a foster parent.[132]

---

130 Ibid.; appeal at decision of Nowa Ruda court, submitted by Helena Fuchsberg to the court in Kłodzko in the matter of L.P.; Dekel, *Remnants of the Sword*, pp. 102–104. The appeal was submitted by Poles who had adopted a boy after the war in response to the Polish government's urging to adopt children from orphanages. Afterwards, the boy's Jewish mother traced her son to the orphanage, sued to reclaim custody of him, and won the case.

131 Kurek-Lesik, "*Udzial Żeńkich*," p. 350.

132 Appeal at decision of court in Nowa Ruda, submitted by Helena Fuchsberg to the court in Kłodzko in the matter of L.P. The girl had spent around seven years with her rescuers. The remarks of the Jewish plaintiff's counsel might have been considered antisemitic had they been uttered by the Polish side.

At the end of the litigation, the district court overturned the ruling of the municipal court and, in consideration of the circumstances and the best interests of the child, appointed the appellant (her aunt) as her foster mother.[133]

In an appeal before Tarnów district court, the appellant claimed that the verdict of first instance had been "an error in judgment from the statutory, factual, ethical, moral, and Christian standpoints." The plaintiff, a representative of the Koordynacja, described a series of events in the judge's chambers during the three days preceding the trial and on the day the verdict was handed down, and suggested that the judge's decision had been tendentious. The judge, she alleged, had told her on the day the suit was filed that, in his opinion, Jewish children should be placed in Jewish children's homes and, furthermore, that these girls had relatives living abroad who wished to claim them. He gave her an invitation to the court for the next day and she personally delivered it to the nuns at the orphanage where the girls were living. When she arrived in court the next day, the judge told her that the matter had been deferred to a later hour. Later that day, however, she found out that the judge had discussed the case in her absence an hour before the time established and had decided to grant fostership to a Polish peasant whom the nuns had recommended, without allowing her, the girls, or any of the witnesses whom she had brought to present their case. When she asked the judge for an explanation the next day, he told her that his ruling in the matter of fostership was meaningless because concurrently he had ordered the girls to be handed over to a Jewish orphanage. Accordingly, the petitioner stated that she would reimburse the convent for its expenses on account of the girls. A day later, the girls themselves were brought to court and the judge upheld his decision to leave them in the convent — again without hearing the petitioner and without examining the documents and the girls' identity and age. When the appellant asked the judge to explain all this, he told her again that his conduct had caused no harm and that she should appeal the decision to the district court at once.[134]

---

133 Decision of Kłodzko district court in the matter of L.P.
134 Appeal in Tarnów district court in the matter of C.Z. and S.Z. See also working report Teofilia Goldman. The court records list the appellant as Teofilia Godlewska, whereas her family name was Goldman. In a report to the Koordynacja, the plaintiff wrote that before she had turned to the court she had contacted the mother superior of the convent and told her that relatives of the girls had contacted the Koordynacja and asked it to help them claim the girls, and the mother superior had expressed her consent and invited her to come and take them. When she came the next day, the mother superior told her that she could not relinquish them. The girls, frightened by the nuns' stories about the Jews, had tried to go into hiding and even to run away.

Thus, as opposed to family members who based their lawsuits and appeals on two grounds — the special circumstances pertaining to the war, the parents' wishes, and their right to the children, on the one hand, and the relatives' ability and suitability to be foster parents, on the other — the judges handed down their decisions in view of the "best interest" of the child as they interpreted it, sometimes regardless of the circumstances. The rationales in verdicts that favored the rescuers were based on the judges' interpretation of the "best interest of the child."[135] This concept itself, however, was dubious because it concerned not only who would raise the child but also in what religious atmosphere, Jewish or Christian. The rescuers, who were Christian, were on one side; parents or relatives who had survived the inferno and were, of course, Jewish, were on the other. Those who sued in court for custody of a child who was their kin, did so not only because they wished to reunite their families, but also because they believed that growing up among members of the child's own people was in the child's "best interest."

Every court ruling obviously left one of the parties dissatisfied, and when a verdict of co-fostering was handed down, presumably both sides were unhappy. The litigants did retain the option of continuing the battle in the courts and many did so, but sometimes the parties tried to change the decision out of court. Thus, there were cases where non-Jews who had been forced to surrender children to relatives emerged from the courtroom, instigated riots, and incited against the Jews so as to enlist public support and backing from the street.[136] In other cases, they fled with the child in order to avoid having to hand him or her over.[137] The Jewish side responded in various ways: the Central Committee favored continued litigation but some Zionist organizations called on the Bricha organization to remove children surreptitiously from the country and out of reach of the Polish authorities.[138]

---

135 This problem was not unique to Poland. See also Joseph Michman, "The Problem of Jewish War Orphans in the Netherlands," p. 409.

136 Dekel. *Remnants of the Sword*, pp. 206–213. In this case, the judge was asked to go into the street and explain his decision in order to calm the crowd that had gathered. Five years later, the girl's relatives in Israel discovered that the rescuer had been arrested as a collaborator with the Gestapo. At the trial, it was found that the man had done much to help Jews during the war but, unfortunately for him, a Gestapo operative discovered that a Jewish girl was staying in his home and applied extortion, promising safety for the girl in return for his collaboration; see also Neshamit, "The 'Koordynacja for the Redemption of Children' in Liberated Poland," p. 125.

137 Neshamit, ibid.; Kurek-Lesik, "*Udzial Żeńkich*," p. 350.

138 Koryski, "The Zionist Koordynacja for the Redemption of Jewish Children in Poland," p. 27; Dekel, *Remnants of the Sword*, pp. 104, 210; testimony Yeshayahu Drucker, YVA,

The children themselves did not always accept the verdict and could not be forced to do so. The situation depended, of course, on the children's age, their ability to take action against the decision, and assistance that they received from their surroundings. One girl, for example, objected to being handed over to her uncle, in accordance with the court ruling, and ran back to her rescuers. When her uncle failed to talk her into returning, he left Poland. In 1948, the girl was tracked down by her grandfather but refused to join him even after legal proceedings and a ruling in his favor. Police delivered her to her grandfather's home but she ran away again and again.[139]

A legal directive from the Central Committee, mentioned above, stated that if a child was found to own property of any kind, the court should appoint a custodian for the property — someone other than the foster parent — thereby ruling out the possibility that concern for the child was actually based on the chance to acquire the property.[140] Some non-Jews, however, regarded property registered in a child's name as their own, and the parents of the children whom they had rescued may have promised that this would be the case.[141] Usually, the Legal Department of the Central Committee dealt with matters related to custodianship of property in order to protect children from all kinds of "benefactors," Jewish and Polish alike.[142] In practice, it was not always possible to keep children and their property separate by litigation. Such a case involved a girl who had survived in Częstochowa. The girl's parents had owned a great deal of property and she was their sole heir. Immediately after the war, her rescuer contacted her uncle in Palestine and expressed an interest in the property, which by then had been recorded in the girl's name, "in

O.3/3249; see also testimony Drucker about the removal of S.S. in Kurek-Lesik, "*Udzial Żeńkich,*" p. 350; see also testimony Leibl Koryski, OHD 15(68), story of the girl A.R.; see also decision of Łódź municipal court, File 37/46, in the matter of A.R., ŻIH, Legal Department.

139 Dekel, *Remnants of the Sword,* p. 194.
140 Legal document on Jewish children in non-Jews' custody, Part A: "Determining Fostership of Children."
141 Working report Teofilia Goldman in the matter of R.P. Goldman received a letter from a woman named Nowaczyńska, from Krosno, in which the rescuer requested a sum of money for expenses related to a trial in which she had sued to have property of the girl who was still living with her to be transferred to her name.
142 Letter Education Department to Central Committee presidium, December 3, 1947, in the matter of P.S.; letters children's home in Otwock to Central Committee Legal Department, July 1947, in the matter of C.F., and 1948 in the matter of M.H., ŻIH, Legal Department; Shner-Neshamit, *I Did Not Come to Rest,* p. 207. Shner-Neshamit suspected a family member of a girl whom she had personally removed, of being interested in the girl only due to her wish acquire the vast property that had been recorded in the girl's name.

order to assure her future." The local Jewish committee hired a lawyer to deal with the property issue and three members of the rescuer's family and three Jewish townswomen were named custodians of the property. During the four years of litigation over custody of the girl, the rescuer earned income from the property. The discussions over the terms of the girl's surrender became more and more complicated until the suspicion arose that the lawyer dealing with the property was himself the main obstacle to the rescuer's consent to surrendering the girl in return for the property. Under his influence it was maintained, the rescuer was also demanding astronomical sums.[143]

Anyone could resort to the legal system but the system could not always solve problems within a reasonable period of time and, thereby, prevent a delay that could affect the child survivor's psyche. There were also cases that seemed to admit the possibility of a ruling in favor of one side or another but became increasingly complex. One such case involved Ita-Leah Igenfeld, a girl born on August 12, 1941, in Branew, Kraśnik District. When the Nazi aktions began, her mother fled with her into a forest where she encountered two acquaintances. When autumn arrived and the weather became colder, the girl came down with sores and cried frequently. Her mother realized that her condition was deteriorating and that she could no longer take care of her. She took her acquaintances' advice and placed the girl, now fifteen months old, on the stoop of a house in Rataj-Ordynacki village, along with a note: "This baby girl has been baptized in the name of Leonka." Before doing so, she left markings on the girl's back so that she could identify her. The mother and her acquaintances stayed near the village to keep it under observation, and another acquaintance kept track of her daughter on her behalf. From then until the end of the war, the youngster stayed with the Pyczes, a childless farmer couple. In July 1944, when the Soviets occupied the area, the mother visited the farmer in the company of her three acquaintances but the man refused to return her daughter and threatened to kill her if she were to return. The mother sued in Lublin but the trial was postponed again and again — due to the farmer's influence, the mother charged. The girl was examined and the markings that the mother had described could not be identified.

143 Letter Gwircman, Tel Aviv, to Rabbi Herzog, Jerusalem, December 11, 1945, RZA, Rescue Files; draft of cable based on response to the letter — evidently from Central Committee to Jewish committee in Częstochowa, July 3, 1946, ŻIH, Legal Department; letter Yakov Etzioni to Rabbi Wohlgelernter, January 22, 1947; letter Etzioni to Rabbi Herzog, March 19, 1947, RZA, Rescue Files; letter Gwircman, Tel Aviv, to Central Committee Legal Department, Warsaw, December 5, 1947, in the matter of Z.S., ŻIH, Legal Department.

The farmer continued to issue death threats against the woman, the legal proceedings got nowhere, and she decided to leave for Germany and continue the struggle from there. The mother spent all this time with a group of acquaintances from the forest and married one of them. To facilitate the legal proceedings, he adopted the girl legally. In 1948, the mother and her new husband moved to Canada, where they continued to struggle for possession of the girl. Because of the distance involved, the mother officially authorized Rabbi Kahana of the Council of Religious Communities in Poland to continue dealing with the matter and to represent her vis-à-vis the legal and judicial authorities. The Canadian Federation for Polish Jews also asked Rabbi Kahana to help her. In April 1949, the witnesses who had been with the mother during the war sent depositions from Canada. The Central Committee hired a lawyer, who found the matter hard to pursue due to "lack of evidence." After the cause gathered momentum and many Jewish organizations began to take an interest in it, the attorney who claimed that he had not been paid for his services, resigned. The mother, in her distress, sent off letters in many directions, expressing amazement that no one could return her daughter. In her despair, she wrote twice to the Pope but received no answer. A Jewish journalist in Canada mobilized for the cause, wrote a summary of her story, and published it in Jewish newspapers in North America; he also urged Jewish women and women's organizations to write to Eleanor Roosevelt[144] and ask her to intervene with Francis Joseph Cardinal Spellman of New York. They believed that if Cardinal Spellman was asked often enough, he would ask the Pope to help the mother reclaim her daughter. But time went by; Rabbi Kahana was about to leave Poland and the Central Committee's status changed. Letters from the World Jewish Congress to the Central Committee and Rabbi Kahana also went unanswered. The affair ended only in the mid-1950s, when the girl, now sixteen years old, was handed over to her mother in Canada by order of the Polish Supreme Court.[145]

144 The writer and journalist Eleanor Roosevelt was the wife of Franklin Roosevelt, U.S. president throughout World War II until his death shortly before the end of the war.
145 Letter JDC family tracing officer to Polish military legation in Berlin, June 25, 1946; handwritten note from an employee of the Central Committee named Szablowska, undated but evidently from 1946 in view of its contents; letter Central Committee to Justman, undated but presumably from 1946 in view of its contents; power of attorney from Rachel Igenfeld-Besserman, Canada, to Rabbi Kahana, Warsaw; letter Federation of Polish Jews in Canada to Rabbi Kahana, September 22, 1948; depositions of Szloma Besserman, Max Rosenfeld, and Chuma Hakman, signed in the presence of Adv. Heifetz, Canada, April 2, 1949; letter Adv. Jan Stalinski, Lublin, to Central Committee, June 10, 1949. The letter indicates that the matter was of interest to the Jewish committee in Lublin, JDC, the Koordynacja, and

Thus, perseverance and resolve could eventually be rewarded, but the passage of time and the sequence of events sometimes led to a painful outcome and raised doubts about whether the price of the lengthy struggle had been worth paying. Something similar happened to a mother who returned from Germany after the war to recover her daughter. The non-Jew with whom she had left her daughter told her that he had placed the girl in the courtyard of a building during the Warsaw Ghetto uprising and had no idea what had become of her. The girl's mother moved to Germany after the Kielce pogrom and emigrated to the United States in 1949. Over the years, she suspected that the Pole knew more than he was willing to divulge, and she continued to stay in touch with him, and even sent him money with which he should continue to look for her daughter. In the mid-1950s, the mother returned to Poland without telling the man that she was coming and, at the recommendation of the United States Embassy, hired a lawyer who informed the Pole that she had died and bequeathed some money to whoever managed to find her daughter. Then the Pole "suddenly remembered" where he had left the girl. The resulting inquiry discovered that the girl had been raised in a Catholic orphanage and had later been adopted by two unmarried sisters. The fiancé of the daughter, by now an adult, met with the mother and told

---

"a special emissary from Łódź"; letter Rachel Besserman, Canada, to Central Committee, June 27, 1949; letter Hirszenhorn to Lublin committee, July 3, 1949, in the matter of I.I.; letter Kurt Grossman, World Jewish Congress, New York, to Rabbi Kahana, September 8, 1949. The letter indicates that the mother had turned to eleven different organizations. Copies of this letter were also sent to the Central Committee, the Legal Department, and the Education Department. See ŻIH, Legal Department; Leiberman, "The Heartbreak of a Jewish Mother"; see also case of Z.S.: letters Gwircman to Rabbi Herzog, December 11, 1945, and April 2, 1946, RZA, Rescue Files; draft of cable, evidently from Central Committee, to Częstochowa committee, July 3, 1946, ŻIH, Legal Department; letter Częstochowa committee to Central Committee, July 3, 1946; letter attorneys Rogoziński and Wertheim Łódź, to Child Care Department, January 13, 1947; letter Yakov Etzioni to Rabbi Wohlgelernter, January 22, 1947; letter Etzioni to Rabbi Herzog, March 19, 1947, RZA, Rescue Files; cable Rabbi Herzog to the Bishop of Częstochowa, Dr. Kubina, March 20, 1947, RZA, Rescue Files; cable Drucker to Rabbi Herzog, April 27, 1947, ibid.; letter Adv. Etzioni to Friedman, Rabbi Herzog's bureau, Jerusalem, May 22, 1947, ibid.; letter to Adv. Yakov Etzioni, although it does not bear the sender's name, its contents indicate that it was sent from Rabbi Herzog's bureau, July 8, 1947, with attached letter Drucker to Rabbi Herzog, June 12, 1947, ibid.; letters Gwircman, Tel Aviv, to Central Committee Legal Department, Warsaw, December 5, 1947, and January 21, 1948, ŻIH, Legal Department; letter Central Committee Education Department to Central Committee presidium, March 12, 1948, ibid.; testimony Yeshayahu Drucker, YVA, O.3/3249. After the Supreme Court ordered the girl to be returned and the rescuer refused, she was forcibly removed and taken to Israel.

her that her daughter had been so traumatized by the event that she asked to be left alone. The mother did not give up and filed a lawsuit. The court ruled that before anything else the mother and her daughter had to meet. It was a very difficult encounter; the daughter cursed her mother, accused her of various misdeeds, and refused to live with her. The litigation continued at length, and as of late 1957 — when the story was reported — no solution had been found.[146]

Obviously, the courts were asked to settle only those cases where the parties involved had not been able to resolve the issues amenably. The time that had elapsed until the court was turned to, coupled with the length of litigation, only amplified the emotional burdens that accompanied the cases. In studying the arguments raised by the parties, the transcripts of the proceedings, and the judges' reasoning in their verdicts, we can appreciate the unbearable hardships caused by the Nazi occupation and the impossible human situations that were dealt with in these "Trials of Solomon."

The Catholic Church and its Attitude to the Return of Jewish Children to Judaism

Baptism of Jewish children during the occupation was mainly a ruse employed to conceal their identity so that they could assimilate into Christian society and avoid death. In principle, baptism did not make a Jew into a Gentile according to Nazi criteria, but in practice it allowed the child to integrate into the Christian surroundings. Baptisms were performed at various times during the war — at the beginning with the parents' explicit permission after the child was living with the rescuing family; or after the war, when the child was on his or her own. The act of baptizing a child during the war did not necessarily reflect a genuine intention to convert to Christianity. However, by living in a Christian community, enjoying the sense of security that it provided, and imbibing its religious atmosphere — as opposed to the decree of death that hovered over the Jews — children were often influenced actively to embrace Christianity.

To understand the nature of the controversy between Judaism and Christianity which, after the war, focused on returning baptized children to

---

146 Sznajderman, "A Jewish Mother Struggles for her Daughter," pp. 71–72.

the Jewish people, one must first assess Christian perceptions of the Jews and the issues of baptism and conversion.[147]

Two outlooks that derive from Christianity's general approach to the Jews underlie the attitude of Christians towards the Jews with regard to helping them during the war: (1) the need to put into practice the virtues of kindness, mercy, and altruism that Christianity demands of its believers, and (2) the perception of the Jews' fate as punishment for the ancient sin of the Crucifixion. Thus, when a Jew turns to a Christian for help, he or she may find a motive to provide assistance and an excuse to withhold it — both motives within the outlook of the Church.[148]

The Catholic Church has never changed its basic demand for universal adherence to Christianity. Even during the war, the Christian tradition of praying for the conversion of the Jews, as practiced since 1909 by order of Pope Pius X, continued. This prayer, which urges God to end the Jews' suffering, was included in a broader context of prayers for the global unification of the Church (that is, also the ingathering of non-Catholic Christians under the wings of Catholicism).[149]

The doctrine and canon law of the Catholic Church propounds two seemingly opposed principles: belief in the salvation of the world through Jesus Christ (affirmed by the Council of Trent in the sixteenth century) and the inalienable right of parents to determine how their children are to be raised, that is to say, personal free choice. "Salvation of the world through Christ" explains why baptism is a sine qua non for salvation according to Catholic doctrine; it also explains the baptism of children who are in mortal peril even if their parents object. The "free choice" principle explains the distinction in

---

147 In March 1995, I wrote to the head of the Church in Poland, Józef Cardinal Glemp, and Pope John Paul II, and asked them to help me understand several issues in the Church's attitude toward conversion of Jewish children to Christianity during the war, in view of the German death decree, and the Church's attitude toward the return of these children to the Jewish people. The Vatican did not reply but Cardinal Glemp's secretary in Poland, Dr. Andrzej Dziuba, sent me a formal response that failed to address any of my questions. Thus, here I base myself on Luc Dequeker's article about the attitude of the Church in Belgium and in general. See Luc Dequeker, "Baptism and Conversion of Jews in Belgium 1939–1945," in Dan Michman, ed., *Belgium and the Holocaust: Jews, Belgians, Germans* (Jerusalem: Yad Vashem, 1998), pp. 235–271.

148 Tec, *When Light*, pp. 137–139; Kahana, *After the Deluge*, p. 120. This is not to say that the religious motive was the only one that underlay the reaction of Christian rescuers.

149 Dequeker, "Baptism and Conversion," pp. 241, 243.

canon law between children younger and older than the age of seven, which the Church defines as the age of reasonable independent decision.[150]

The baptism of a child below that age is legal if two conditions are met: (a) the parents give their permission (thus the Church defends the right of parents to choose the nature of their children's religious education), and (b) the child receives a Catholic education after baptism. In exceptional situations — if the child is in mortal danger or if the parents cannot be located — the requirement of parental permission is waived. However, the Church's definition of "parents" includes aunts, and uncles. If any of them are alive and they have not waived rights to the child, the child is regarded as having been baptized illegally (unless he or she is in mortal danger at the time of baptism). In the absence of these conditions, baptism of a child younger than seven is considered illegal at the outset but valid thereafter, since it is one of the sacraments. Thus, if Jewish parents agree to a child's baptism for the purpose of protecting him or her but do not intend it to be an act of conversion to Christianity — even if they approve of a Church education for the child — the conversion is illegal but not invalid. According to the Catholic doctrine shaped by Pope Benedict XIV in the eighteenth century, which has never been rescinded, the Church asserts responsibility for the Christian education of children even if they are baptized without their parents' permission. The situation is different with regard to children who are baptized after the age of seven. The Church sees them as adults, that is, they cannot be baptized against their will. Furthermore, the baptism of an adult presumes the acceptance of religious study and education. Such a baptism can be performed only by the explicit decision of an archbishop.[151] Furthermore, according to traditional Church dogma, if the child is presented as having been baptized, the Church's right to him or her cannot be abrogated.[152]

With respect to the conditions during the war, the question now is whether both the rescuers and the Church viewed the baptism issue as did the Jews, that is, as a purely ad hoc measure. Might it have been the rescuers'

---

150 Ibid., p. 244.

151 Ibid., pp. 240–241, 245–246; see also encyclopedia entries about the Mortara Affair. On January 24, 1858, papal police kidnapped the six year-old (almost seven) Jewish boy Edgardo Mortara in Bologna, Italy, because a Christian maidservant in his home had secretly baptized him while he had been dangerously ill five years earlier. All the family's attempts to reclaim him failed. The Church claimed that the boy's baptism was valid even though it had been against his parents' wishes, because his life had been in danger when it was performed.

152 Dequeker, "Baptism and Conversion," p. 242.

surreptitious intention to "steal" souls — Jewish souls — for Christianity? Some claim that baptism and Christianity may not have been forced upon the children, even though this leaves unanswered the question of what motivated the clergy[153] — was baptism the purpose of the rescue or its means? Another claim that has been put forward is that some priests responded to requests from Jews to convert, even though the Germans had warned the Polish diocese not to baptize Jews, and that they obviously knew that the applicants had not approached them out of a genuine desire to become Christian. After all, the mission is a principal imperative in the Catholic faith. However, there were also priests who would not baptize persons who requested it, instead giving them false certificates of baptism and admitting them to the Christian community de facto but not de jure. With a Christian birth certificate, a Jew could obtain a *Kennkarte* (identification card) and circulate freely. Another assessment that has been expressed — apparently based on impressions and experience — is that some children were indeed concealed for reasons of mercy, but that most were hidden for the purpose of converting them to Christianity thereafter and prizing them away from their Jewish faith. Rabbi Kahana reasoned, "I believe the Catholic priesthood fully understood that the impetus to accept Christianity and the large number of applicants was not a consequence of an awakening to the Christian faith."[154]

The fact was that even if children had been baptized only to save them, they were living as Christians, were being raised as Christians, and had become part of the community in which they lived. From the standpoint of some of the clergy, such children were now Christian irrespective of the motive for the conversion. The question is whether one can truly discuss the baptism or conversion issue without relating to the conditions created by the Nazi occupation, and the prospects of survival by assimilating into the Christian community. That is, can one discuss only the final outcome — the fact that the child had been baptized, raised as a Christian, and lived with a Christian family — as though this were the point where the matter began? After all, if it was just a sincere attempt to help Jews as human beings, or to help the Jewish people to try to save individuals for the purpose of its continued

---

153 Such is the view of Nehama Tec. See Tec, *When Light*, p. 142.
154 See, for example, Kahana, *After the Deluge*, pp. 117, 121, 124. In 1942 (no exact date noted), an order forbidding the baptism of Jews was issued to the clergy. In any baptism ceremony, parents had to affirm in writing that the children who were to be baptized and all participants in the ceremony were of Aryan origin. Attached to the circular were regulations explaining who would be recognized as Aryan.

existence as a people, the problem of returning baptized children to Judaism would never have arisen.

Thus, the true test, in my opinion, is the outcome. We may attempt to gauge the general motivation of the Catholic clergy by observing the problems that arose as children were being removed — even though one cannot always infer the initial motive for the baptism from the way the clergy acted at the end of the process, by which time the children's Christianity was a fait accompli. The fact is that in some cases local clergymen or convents refused to return children to the Jews.[155]

Halakha (Jewish law) determines that *shmad* (loss of Jewish identity by defection to another religion), even in a time of emergency, is one of the situations in which a Jew should rather forfeit his life than transgress because the sanctity of God's name is at issue. However, it should be recalled that most of the Jews of Poland were religious to some extent or another, and that due to the agonies of the time, some observant Jews swerved from the dictates of halakha — as others had done in previous periods of Jewish history. Many Jews realized that baptism could mark their path to survival. However, some did express concern from the outset that identification with the new Christian identity which was so essential for survival, was a one-way path with no return to Judaism. The overwhelming thought, however, was to address the immediate problem first and to leave the question of returning to Judaism to the future — perhaps even to the child's own discretion upon reaching adulthood.[156] Some rabbis did tackle the painful dilemma and authorize baptism, in the hope that some family member would survive, reclaim the child, and return him or her to the Jewish people.[157] As for the issue of returning the child to Judaism, there was no question, because from the standpoint of halakha, Jewish identity from birth is never invalidated.

In April 1945, a month before the end of the war, Moshe Shertok (Sharett), head of the Jewish Agency Political Department, met with Pope Pius XII while visiting Jewish Brigade soldiers serving in Europe. When he returned to Palestine, Shertok reported on his meeting to the executive of the Jewish Agency and described his impression of the Pope's stance on the issues that he had raised in their conversation. One of these concerned Jewish chil-

---

155 See, for example, letters in the matter of R.H. from March 1949 onward, ŻIH, Legal Department. In this case, the suit was brought by a sister of the boy's grandmother, who had raised his mother after her own mother died when she was a child.

156 Tec, *When Light*, pp. 141, 144, 147.

157 Interview with Rabbi Kahana, in *Kurek-Lesik, "Udzial Żeńkich,"* p. 346.

dren in non-Jewish hands. Thus Shertok described what he said to the Pope and the latter's response:

> Now we need to demand the [reclamation of the Jewish] children who survived. I understand the view of the convents very well, but for us it is not just a question of saving Jews as human beings but also of saving them as Jews. They must return to the bosom of Judaism and the Jewish people. We hope to bring them all to Palestine and to allow them to live fully Jewish lives. [The Pope] said, "Yes, I understand." I saw that he was not meeting me for the purpose of holding a real conversation. He was meeting me as an expression of goodwill and his answer was only that and no more. The only outcome of the conversation was that I was able to say that I had met the Pope and had told him that we wanted the convent children back. He expressed no opposition.[158]

This meeting between a Jew and the Pope to discuss the return of Jewish children may have been the first of its kind but it was not the last. On his first trip to Europe after the war, Rabbi Herzog, the Ashkenazi Chief Rabbi of Palestine, stopped first in Italy in order to meet the Pope. The rabbi believed that the Vatican could help to alleviate the problems of European Jewry, foremost the rescue of children, noting that a large majority of surviving children were in non-Jewish hands, that is, in Catholic institutions or with Catholic families.

On February 10, 1946, the Pope agreed to receive the rabbi in audience. Rabbi Herzog used the occasion to describe the magnitude of the disaster that had befallen the Jewish people and, above all, the problem of orphans who were still in non-Jewish homes. He argued that even though the Jews were grateful to the children's rescuers, they could not acquiesce in the children's continued presence in non-Jewish surroundings, where they were cut off from their heritage. "Today," he added, "every child means a thousand children to us after our people's great disaster, while for the Christian Church with its millions of believers, an increase of that size is of miniscule value." Afterwards, the conversation turned to the rising tide of antisemitism in Poland, and the Pope expressed his puzzlement about why antisemitism still existed anywhere on earth. As for the demands which Rabbi Herzog had presented, the Pope asked for a detailed memorandum and promised to consider it with gravity. On February 17, before leaving Rome, Rabbi Herzog visited the Vatican secretariat, submitted the memorandum that the Pope had

---

158 Barlas, *Rescue during the Holocaust*, p. 169.

requested, and was told that his request to have the Pope issue a public manifesto urging all priests to furnish information about the whereabouts of Jewish children would be discussed. Pending a decision, the rabbi was assured that if he heard anywhere in his travels about the presence of Jewish children in Catholic institutions, and if he encountered obstacles in removing them, he was to contact the Vatican directly and ask it to intervene, and that the Vatican would help. However, the Vatican's assurance came with a proviso attached: the rabbi must visit the locations himself and investigate the situation personally — an absurd condition since the chief rabbi was based in Palestine. Rabbi Herzog was also given permission to use the Pope's remarks as a basis for his requests when he met with members of the clergy.[159] There is no evidence that the Vatican ever discussed the rabbi's request that the Pope issue a public manifesto to leading Catholic clergy.

Rabbi Herzog arrived in Poland again in early August 1946, but several days later hurriedly boarded a train to Prague. On August 21, he returned to Warsaw to meet the director of UNRRA, but two days later entrained to Prague again, this time from Katowice, escorting children who had been living in Jewish institutions.[160] Both of his visits to Poland were conducted in haste and he did not meet with Polish Church leaders on either occasion. Thus, he was unable to deal personally with cases in which clergy refused to return Jewish children.[161]

After the war, an apostolic nuncio (ambassador of the Vatican) visited the British occupation zone and met with the Central Committee of Liberated Jews to offer assistance in feeding and clothing the refugees. At the meeting, a representative of the refugees, Dr. Hadassah Rosensaft, told him,

> We are neither asking for food nor for clothing. I came from Poland, a Catholic country, and several survivors of Bergen-Belsen who re-

---

159 *The Rescue Voyage*, pp. 14, 16; Kahana, *After the Deluge*, p. 77; Fogelman, *Conscience and Courage*, p. 248, n. 2. According to Fogelman, Rabbi Herzog received assurances that the Vatican would use its influence in Poland and would spare no effort to release Jewish children from convents. In my opinion, the original text does not support this inference. Rabbi Herzog had been told at the Vatican secretariat that he could cite the Pope's name and would receive assistance, but not that the Vatican would apply its influence to support the initiative.

160 *The Rescue Voyage*, pp. 60, 72–73, 78–80.

161 It should be born in mind that the search operations for Jewish children took place during a period of nearly four years after the end of the war, and that Polish clergy refused to return children to Judaism throughout that time and not at any particular date. Rabbi Herzog visited Europe in 1946 and as stated, spent only a limited period of time there.

turned to Poland to [re]claim their children, who had been hidden with Catholic families, found out that the families were not prepared to give them back. We would like the Vatican to issue a public call to Catholics to return Jewish children to their parents or relatives or to Jewish organizations.[162]

However, all the various requests and communications from Jewish organizations to the Pope concerning the issue of a public call or a pastoral letter went unanswered. The Vatican addressed no such message to the clergy in the formerly Nazi-occupied countries.[163]

In the meantime, Jews who had been involved in the cause of returning children to Judaism were encountering new difficulties. After the liberation, rescuers' families began to ask priests to baptize concealed Jewish children who had not been baptized previously. For example, two sisters who had been taken to a convent in Tarnów were baptized after the war, and when a representative of the Koordynacja visited the mother superior of the convent and told her that the family of the girls, who lived abroad, had asked the Koordynacja to remove them, she expressed her consent. But when the Koordynacja operative came the next day to remove them, the mother superior said that the clerical authorities forbade her to relinquish baptized children.[164] In another case, operatives were told that if a boy had been baptized, he could not be returned unless the person who took him would undertake to continue raising him as a Christian.[165]

In one case, parents surrendered their baby boy to a non-Jew together with money and jewelry intended for his upkeep. The Pole appropriated the money himself and left the baby in a church without his parents' knowledge. The boy was baptized and raised in a convent. After the war, the priests discovered that the child's aunt was searching for him and had him moved to a succession of convents in order to keep him out of her hands.[166] In another case, a mother entrusted her son to her neighbor. She was subsequently deported to Auschwitz but survived and after the war claimed her son back. Had the

---

162 Fogelman, *Conscience and Courage*, p. 348, n. 2.

163 Ibid.; Kahana, *After the Deluge*, p. 77; *The Rescue Voyage*, p. 16.

164 Working report Teofilia Goldman.

165 Kahana, *After the Deluge*, p. 343.

166 Dekel, *Remnants of the Sword*, p. 695. The boy's aunt never found him. Years later, the non-Jew, troubled by his conscience, told the boy, Mietek, that he was Jewish. In 1961, Mietek emigrated to Israel. Similar events happened in western Europe, e.g., the stories of Anneke Beekman in the Netherlands, the Finally brothers in France, and Henri Elias in Belgium.

boy been with her, he would certainly have been murdered, for such was the fate of most children taken to Auschwitz. Even though the condition of "mortal peril" was unquestionably present in the surrender of the boy, the neighbor refused to return him. Since he had been baptized, the priest sided with the adoptive mother and even said that if the court were to decide otherwise, the boy should be put to death rather than be returned to the Jews![167] In cases where nuns or priests believed that Jewish children should not be returned, they stopped at nothing to ensure this outcome — hiding and smuggling the youngsters, lying about their fate, etc.[168] — and the removal operatives had to contend with such situations. When one of the women operatives, who was knowledgeable about Catholicism, heard rationales about the impropriety of handing baptized children back to the Jews, she fought back, arguing that since these children had been baptized without their parents' consent and for the obvious purpose of saving their lives, the reasoning was invalid from Christian theological perspective.[169] These verbal skirmishes, however, did not necessarily bring about the desired results.

The tension surrounding religious issues sometimes angered the Jewish activists without reason. For example, one operative in the Żegota Polish underground recalled that when the Central Jewish Committee was established after the war, she visited its offices with another activist in order to give the new organization lists of children whom Żegota had helped to conceal during the war. However the reaction of the Committee members was harsh, as if the underground activists had committed a crime in their "theft" of the Jewish children and having them baptized, and in so doing, had torn them away from their Jewish roots. They even told them, she says, that they were worse than the Germans: the Germans deprived Jews of their bodies but they were stealing their souls.[170]

For many families who had provided children with a home during the war, their Catholic faith and Christian upbringing were inseparable from

167 Bielicki-Bornstein, "Back to the Bosom of Their People."
168 Autobiography of Withold Wajman, in Tenenboim, *One of a City and Two of a Family*, pp. 131–132. During the war, Withold left his brother in a doorway and the boy was taken to a church orphanage. After the war, Withold applied to the convent and asked for custody of his brother, but the nuns claimed that the boy had died. Withold sued in court. At the time the testimony was given (1946), the matter had not been resolved.
169 Mahler, "Redemption of Jewish Children from Their Non-Jewish Rescuers," p. 39; Fleiszer, "The Rescue of 24 Children," pp. 300–304.
170 Interview with Jadwiga Piotrkowska, Kurek-Lesik, *"Udzial Żeńkich,"* p. 340.

membership in the family. Wherever this happened, children were raised and educated as Catholics — whether baptized or not.[171]

Since the Pope, as we have seen, did not issue a public manifesto concerning the surrender of Jewish children, his official stance on the issue is unknown (unless one construes his silence as tacit support of the clergy). The following are two cases in which the Pope himself was asked to help — even though we cannot generalize on their basis. When the father of a girl survivor asked the girl's Polish rescuer to surrender her, the rescuer turned to the Pope in the hope of securing support from the person whom she considered the supreme authority. The pontiff answered her request less than a month later, ordering her to return the girl to her father. If she continued to keep the girl deceitfully, the Pope explained, she would eventually regret it because ultimately the girl would discover the truth. He added that it was her duty as a Catholic not only to return the girl to her father but to do so graciously and humbly.[172] In contrast, a Jewish mother who twice turned to the Pope to help her reclaim her daughter from non-Jewish adoptive parents received no answer at all.[173] One may, of course, wonder whether the requests ever reached him — a question that is impossible to resolve.

The story of Z. Szczekacz demonstrates how hard it was for the Church to grasp the uniqueness of the fate of the Jews under Nazi rule, and the Jews' inability to fathom the spirit of Christianity. A girl was born in April 1942 in Częstochowa, the heartland of Polish Catholicism, and was given over to the Strzelczak family. After the war, Mr. Strzelczak contacted the girl's uncle in Tel Aviv, told him what had become of his family in the war, and noted that he was raising the girl as though she were his own daughter. The uncle, Avraham Gwircman, turned to Rabbi Herzog and asked him to help recover

171 One may gauge the importance of Christian education in devout Catholic families from Grzywacz's testimony: see Grzywacz, "To the Bosom of My People," pp. 62–64. The adoptive family that claimed the boy from the orphanage did not know he was Jewish; the first question they asked him was whether he was a pious Christian, since they were too. The warm care that they gave him affected him and reminded him of his own family so strongly that, unable to restrain himself any longer, he told them that he was Jewish. The adoptive family continued to shower him with affection anyway. However, when he reached communion age the family turned to a priest, who baptized him and gave him communion. When representatives of Jewish organizations persuaded him to emigrate to Palestine, he eventually decided to leave the family — but not the Church, as he thought it impossible to breach his covenant with Jesus and by doing so, to live as a heretic.
172 Hellman, *Avenue of the Righteous*, p. 237.
173 Letter Kurt Grossman to Rabbi Kahana, September 8, 1949, in the matter of I.L.I.B, p. 2 (list of organizations that the mother contacted for assistance).

the girl. Before the rabbi's second trip to Europe, Gwircman told him that he had legally adopted the girl and that her name was now Sabina Gwircman. In May 1946, Drucker contacted Strzelczak at Rabbi Herzog's request but nothing came of it. While in Poland, Rabbi Herzog wanted to go to Częstochowa and deal with the matter personally, but the Polish government refused to guarantee his safety (due to the pogroms that were occurring at the time). Since Strzelczak coveted the extensive real estate that belonged to the girl's grandfather in Częstochowa, the matter was handed over to the legal department of the Central Jewish Committee.

Investigating the matter in Częstochowa, the Committee found that that the rescuer had already presented Gwircman with his financial demands for the surrender of the girl. In 1947, with the sides unable to agree on the amount of compensation that the rescuer should receive, an appointed attorney from Łódź sought the backing of the Central Committee Child Care Department in suing Strzelczak. When he showed no intention of compromising, a person acting on Gwircman's behalf asked Rabbi Wohlgelernter of the United States to send a request for assistance to Dr. Teodoro Kubina, the Bishop of Częstochowa, because "Everyone is sure [… that only he] has influence over the Christian […] and if he summons the Christian and demands that he give back the orphan in return for all the property — the Christian will not refuse." Rabbi Wohlgelernter was also asked to request that the Chief Rabbi send Bishop Kubina an "appropriate letter" by air mail. It should be mentioned that many Jews regarded the bishop as a friend; after all, he had fearlessly condemned the July 1946 pogrom in Kielce. In March 1947, Rabbi Herzog received a copy of the letter that had been sent to Rabbi Wohlgelernter together with a request to act quickly because the girl's immigration visa to Palestine was due to expire at the end of the month. The next day, Rabbi Herzog cabled Bishop Kubina, asking him to help transfer custody of the girl to her uncle. In the meantime, Drucker (representing the Council of Religious Communities) met with the bishop, who rebuffed him, advising him to take up the matter with the rescuer. In response, Drucker informed Rabbi Herzog in April 1947, "One can no longer hope for any help from the bishop." A copy of the letter was sent to the girl's family, but they would not accept Kubina's refusal to help. In a letter to Rabbi Herzog's bureau in Jerusalem, they said, "As for continued action, I allow myself to suggest that you send a response by cable to Captain Drucker and ask him to meet with the bishop again and pressure him to summon the Christian for an inquiry in his presence." Drucker persisted in his contacts with Strzelczak but eventually realized that in view of the latter's financial demands ($12,000 plus real estate), there was no choice but to apply to the courts. Moreover, after visiting the bishop again he understood that he was not prepared to help.

Noting that more than two years had passed without any sign of a solution and chafing at the difficulties that were being thrown in his path, Gwircman asked the legal department of the Central Committee to have the trial moved to Warsaw:

> Since the management of the affair in Częstochowa, an especially devout city, has met with difficulties, especially by certain people who have the ability to slow things down, it would be inconvenient [to hold the trial in Częstochowa] due to the atmosphere. It could be problematic for the Jews who survived [the war] and are living in Częstochowa today.

The Child Care Department received Gwircman's request with understanding and undertook (in March 1948) to ask the Polish Ministry of Justice to have the legal proceedings moved to Warsaw "in view of the current situation in Częstochowa." Ultimately, Gwircman went to Poland in order to pursue the matter himself. In the last round of litigation (late 1949), the Supreme Court ruled in Gwircman's favor. When Strzelczak still refused to hand the girl over, Drucker removed her from Strzelczak's home with police assistance and she left Poland with her uncle after she was registered in his passport. According to Drucker, Bishop Kubina received him pleasantly in both of his visits but told him explicitly that he could not help him. In the official view of the Church, he explained, no force in the world can remove from the Church one who has received any of the sacraments because they cannot be undone. Thus, even though Kubina expressed his understanding and sympathy, he denied having the ability to intervene. The bishop then expanded on this line of reasoning, explaining to Drucker that a rabbi can wield the instrument of *herem* (excommunication) over any member of his community, and since herem was universally feared, the community accepted his decrees. The situation was different among Christians, said Kubina: a pastor has no such instrument. In fact, said Kubina, he could not contact the girl's rescuer, who had had her baptized and raised in the Catholic faith and ask him to release her, for this would be in contravention of canon law.[174]

---

174 Letters in the matter of S.Z. Gwircman (see n. 145); letters Gwircman to Rabbi Herzog, December 11, 1945, and April 2, 1946, RZA, Rescue Files; cable, evidently (given its contents) from Central Committee to Częstochowa committee, undated but, according to the reply, sent on July 3, 1946, ŻIH, Legal Department; letter Częstochowa committee to Central Committee, July 3, 1946, ibid.; letter attorneys Rogoziński and Wertheim, Łódź, to Child Care Department, January 13, 1947; letter Yakov Etzioni to Rabbi Wohlgelernter,

Conclusion

In our attempt to probe the attitude of the Polish state regarding the return of Jewish children, we found that "the Polish state" was an amorphous concept made up of various elements: private, governmental, and clerical. Each was motivated by, and acted on the basis of its own beliefs, outlooks, and emotions — and no less, by its interests. The new Polish regime was usually preoccupied with a profusion of internal problems that threatened its very existence. Even though it was fully aware of the problem of the country's Jewish survivors, it did not address itself explicitly to the problem of Jewish children who had been taken in to non-Jewish homes, a matter evidently of trifling concern to the government but so crucial for the Jews.

The courts acted in accordance with pre-war statutes and also consulted initial post-war verdicts that dealt with the specific problems that had been caused by the war. The judges in the courts system had vast powers of discretion, spanning the range between the laws, which had been written under ordinary living conditions, and the realities imposed by the war.

Most Polish people and Church officials found it hard to accept requests from parents and relatives for the reclamation of children because the youngsters had already been integrated into their "new" families and communities. They found the idea of demands from Jewish organizations for children on behalf of the "Jewish people" even harder to accept.[175]

From the theological perspective, Judaism and Christianity were situated on the opposite sides of a seemingly unbridgeable abyss. Canon law did not allow Catholic clergy to order Jewish children to be returned to Judaism

January 22, 1947; letter Etzioni to Rabbi Herzog, March 19, 1947; cable Rabbi Herzog to Bishop Kubina, Częstochowa, March 20, 1947, RZA, Rescue Files; cable Drucker to Rabbi Herzog, April 27, 1947; letter Yakov Etzioni to Friedman, Rabbi Herzog's secretary, May 22, 1948, ibid.; letter to Adv. Yakov Etzioni: although the sender's name does not appear, given its contents it was sent from Rabbi Herzog's bureau, July 8, 1947; letters Gwircman to Central Committee Legal Department, December 5, 1947, and January 21, 1948, ŻIH, Legal Department; letter Herszenhorn, director of Child Care Department, to Central Committee presidium, March 12, 1948, ibid.; testimony Yeshayahu Drucker, YVA, O.3/3249; interview by author with Yeshayahu Drucker.

175 This problem was not unique to Poland. In his article on the Church in Belgium, Dequeker quotes a report from a Benedictine priest, Bruno Reynders, concerning Zionism and Jewish nationality. Reynders did not accept the premise that any Jewish organization or community, such as CDJ, which is neither a religion nor a national group, had legal rights to the children. See Dequeker, "Baptism and Conversion," p. 249, and Brachfeld, *A Gift of Life,* p. 125.

after they had been baptized and raised in the faith. The problem, then, devolved on local clergymen, each of whom acted in accordance with his own *Weltanschauung* and the way he construed the initial reason for the child having received refuge in the bosom of the Church. Jewish law, in contrast, saw no impediment to the reacceptance of those born Jewish but who had been converted to Christianity. Both emotionally and nationally, the Jews found it difficult to accept the Christians' arguments in favor of keeping the children, at a time when every Jewish survivor was so vital for a resurgence of the decimated Jewish people.

CHAPTER 6

The Attitude of the Rescued Children

Anyone who was an adult during the war absorbed and remem-
bered places and people and at the end of the war sat down and
counted them and recounted them. He will surely do this to his
dying day. For children, it was not the names that were absorbed
into memory but something totally different. For them, memory
is a pool that never empties. It is replenished over the years and
becomes clearer and clearer. It is not a chronological memory but
a flowing and changing one, if one may say such a thing.

Aharon Appelfeld[1]

A
fter the war, as we have described in previous chapters, many and diverse Jewish bodies organized to search for and remove refugee children who had survived under various circumstances and in different localities. The children had separated, or had been separated, from their parents during the war. Some had found refuge in the homes of non-Jews or in convents; others had wandered on their own under false identities among the villages and towns of Poland.[2] The period that the children spent on the Aryan side until the end of the war was very significant in their life stories.

When operatives visited the homes of rescuers with the purpose of claiming these children, the negotiations were generally conducted between the adults and the outcome did not usually depend on the children or their wishes. That is not to say that the children's wishes were totally ignored; after all, they could be more easily removed if it were done with their consent. In most cases, however, their refusal was not considered sufficient reason to

---

1   Aharon Appelfeld, *Life Story* (Jerusalem: Keter, 1999, Hebrew), p. 85, published in English as *The Story of a Life* (New York: Schocken, 2004).
2   Chapter 1 describes their feelings and memories of this parting.

leave them with the rescuers. The operatives had the feeling that in view of the children's appalling wartime experiences and their craving for stability, they were not mature enough to make decisions that would determine their future.[3] Furthermore, the situation and atmosphere in Poland at the time, especially the attitude toward the Jews, reinforced the belief that the children would be best off outside the country.

The Jewish organizations operating in Poland established children's homes and staffed them with caregivers and educators. The staff members, most of whom had themselves experienced the war, did their best to make the facilities as pleasant as possible for the children. However, most of the children found it difficult to make the transition from a home and family setting to collective life in an educational institution.[4] There were some children who found the adjustment so daunting that they had to be transferred to a Jewish family for an interim period.[5] In retrospect, some operatives believed that more children would have made a better adjustment had they too been relocated to a family setting.

The war left many of the children with physical and mental scars. Some youngsters had been concealed in narrow, cramped, and dark hideouts in homes or courtyards; and as poor as their physical condition was, their psychological condition was even worse.[6] Others, although hidden under conditions that were not especially harsh, were in deep psychological distress due to the continual fear of being discovered. Their feelings did not ease even

3 Interview by author with Sarah Shner-Neshamit.
4 Dekel, *Remnants of the Sword*, pp. 645–651; Renia, for example, found the transition extremely difficult; she hated the children's home so badly that she tried to escape by leaping from a balcony, ibid.,p. 236; Sarah Shner-Neshamit, "Characteristics of the Spiritual Image of Redeemed Children," in Bornstein, ed., *Redemption of Jewish Children*, pp. 73–74. Sarah Neshamit recounted the story of a girl who spent all her time standing at the door of the children's home, as if expecting a family member to come and claim her. Once, when Sarah visited the children's home, the girl turned to her and said, "Ma'am, would you like to be my mother?"; see also the story of Yoram, ibid., pp. 76–77; *Mission to the Diaspora*, p. 90; Mahler, "Redemption of Jewish Children from their Non-Jewish Rescuers," p. 36; Shlomi, "Organizational Actions by Jewish Survivors in Poland after World War II, 1944–1950," p. 531.
5 Wasserstein-Blanker, "After the Holocaust I Didn't Want to Return to Judaism," pp. 334–355. Esther did not thrive in the children's home and planned to escape and return to her rescuers; in response, friends of her family took her into their home in Warsaw; Hochberg-Marianska, "I Cared for Child Survivors," p. 13; recorded interview with Haviva Barak (Luba Owjec).
6 "This is How we Began," *Farn Yiddishn Kind*, p. 1; GFHA, File 798; Küchler-Silberman, *My Hundred Children*, p. 262; Cheshin, *Adoptive Children*, p. 131; testimony Irene Haber, Łuków, "Upside-Down Roots."

after the war ended; their emotional antennae remained razor-sharp and they reacted with acute distrust to anything that might augur change. For this reason, the children found it very difficult to trust the "strangers" who had come to take them away.[7] Displacement from their rescuers' homes inflicted psychological shock and compounded their distress. For example, one girl who was brought to a children's home maintained, "The Polish woman who took me in also misled me in the end; she had promised to take me to a Polish orphanage but instead handed me over to the Jewish Committee."[8]

The Children: Between Hammer and Anvil

During the war, the children had formed relationships of varying degrees with their rescuers. Accordingly, they responded to the postwar circumstances in different ways, depending on their personal situation: their age, nature, and their place in the homes of the families of their rescuers. They cannot, therefore, be regarded as one homogeneous group.

Children who had been separated from their parents in infancy knew no "parents" other than those who had raised them, and had no idea about their Jewish identity. Those born on the eve of the war may have retained faint memories of some other family, but the memories steadily faded over time. These children could not conceive as to why they needed to leave the families with whom they had bonded and to whom they were attached. Drucker, who had much experience of such situations, likened the removal of children of this age as being "torn away" from the home and culture in which they were raised.[9] Slightly older children were in a state of emotional conflict. On the

---

7   *Mission to the Diaspora*, p. 83. According to Sarid, the children who reached the children's home were confused and frightened; afterwards he regretted the absence of professionals who could have provided care in such situations. According to Granatstein (*Days of Genesis*, pp. 122–123), most of the children believed that they were being removed for the purpose of making them work and that they would receive food and clothing only in return for labor; Yerushalmi, *Children of the Holocaust*, pp. 92–94; Cheshin, *Adoptive Children*, p. 131; testimony Baruch Mann, MA, A.399; autobiography Erich Holder, in Tenenboim, *One of a City, Two of a Family*, pp. 95–96; Neshamit, "The Koordynacja for the Redemption of Children in Liberated Poland," p. 87.

8   Bielicki-Bornstein, "Back to the Bosom of Their People," p. 322; see also Mahler, "Redemption of Jewish Children from their Non-Jewish Rescuers," p. 36.

9   Interview by author with Yeshayahu Drucker; see also Shner-Neshamit, "Characteristics of the Spiritual Image of Redeemed Children," p. 80; testimony Yehuda Bronstein, OHD 25(68), about the girl whom he removed from Gdynia; Koryski, "The Zionist Koordynacja

one hand, they did not wish to leave their safe havens; on the other, with the abrupt change in their lives they slowly began to recall details of their previous life and their real parents' homes — details that had been repressed or banished from memory during the war. The result was emotional turmoil.[10]

Some older children expressed the wish to leave their rescuers as soon as they knew the war was over. A few of them even took the initiative to leave, as if eager to be released from the pressure of a life of secrecy and false identity. These children, young in years but adult in life experience, carried memories of their homes and parents and knew that they were Jewish.[11] Some had gone through the war without disclosing the secret of their Jewish identity to their rescuers, who never faced the issue overtly even if they had suspicions.[12] Some children could not muster up the courage to reveal their Jewishness to their rescuers even as they left, possibly due to fear that the rescuers would react negatively. One girl, for example, wrote to her rescuers after she left:

> My dear loved ones, I imagine that the content of this letter will be a big surprise [for you]. The situation forced me to spend four years acting out a comedy. I am Jewish. My parents and my entire family disappeared in 1942. I was left totally alone. At first, I was in such despair that I was ready to take my own life but the will to live was stronger. I lived a lie and this allowed me to reach you. It was hard for me to live in fear that the truth would come out. There were moments when I was ready to tell everything but I held my silence because I was afraid that I'd lose the connection with you, so I remained silent. Not long ago I got word from relatives of mine in Palestine; they want me to come to them. I'm really sorry to be leaving you. I'm really sad that you'll bear a grudge

for the Redemption of Jewish Children in Poland," p. 29; Frederbahr-Salz, *And the Sun Rose*, p. 167; when the mother came to reclaim her daughters, she found that her oldest daughter remembered her and was delighted to see her but that her younger daughter shared in neither the memories nor the delight.

10 Koryski, "The Zionist Koordynacja for the Redemption of Jewish Children in Poland," p. 29.

11 Testimony Jacob Lutner, MA, A.402; letter Gabryel Maszanski to Koordynacja, Łódź, October 22, 1947, GFHA, Correspondence File, 788–790; Koryski, "The Zionist Koordynacja for the Redemption of Jewish Children in Poland," p. 29; Hochberg-Marianska, "I Cared for Child Survivors," p. 12.

12 Koryski, "The Zionist Koordynacja for the Redemption of Jewish Children in Poland," p. 29; interview by author with Sarah Shner-Neshamit; interview by author with Chasia Bielecki-Bornstein; testimony Mira Bramm; Hochberg-Marianska, "I Cared for Child Survivors," p. 12.

against me. But believe me, all I want is to repay you for the favor that you did me. I hope that my family's situation will let me repay this favor. I ask you again: don't be angry with me. Forget every bad moment that we had. And as for the New Year, I bless you and kiss you and hug you. Kisses to Aunt Basha and to everyone.[13]

This girl left her rescuers of her own volition after the war. Others, however, refused to leave. In March 1945, about two months after the liberation of Warsaw, one of the newspapers in Palestine published an article under the title, "Jewish Children from Warsaw Hidden by Christians Refuse to Return to their Parents." The article reported the following:

> According to emissaries whom the Central Committee recently sent to the liberated Polish subdistricts in order to distribute relief to the surviving Jews and record their names, Jewish children from the Warsaw Ghetto who were found [in Christian homes] are refusing to return to their Jewish parents. These children, who have not seen their parents for years, do not believe in their Jewish origins and disavow their legal parents.[14]

Refusal to part from rescuers was not only typical of the immediate months after liberation, but persisted throughout the period in which the Jewish organizations were active. Numerous testimonies of children, rescuers, and operatives suggest several reasons for this. The main ones follow:

a. **Fear of change**: During the war, the children had been living under norms of behavior that they had to acquire over time and that helped them to survive. Since these norms had become part of their personality, the children found it difficult to shed them in one stroke at the end of the war. Lena Küchler, director of the Central Jewish Committee children's homes in Rabka and Zakopane, claimed that the children did not clearly understand the transition from war to peace. As long as the war still raged, she explained, the children knew that disclosing their real identities could be fatal whereas lying and evasion could keep them alive. Therefore, the

---

13 Letter Irma Shulginer, under the alias Zosia Kowalczyk, to the Skrzypek family with whom she had spent the war under a Polish identity, GFHA, Correspondence File, 788–790. Since P. Skrzypek's reply to Irma was written on January 6, 1947, the letter presumably was written ahead of Christmas and the New Year, in December 1946.

14 *HaMashkif,* March 5, 1945, CZA, J25/100.

children were loath to relinquish this weapon, on which their self-confidence was founded.[15]

Some children lacked the mental fortitude to cope with the change that the transition from one setting to another would create. Older children remembered their separation from parents and the loneliness and yearnings that followed. They had also acquired experience of life on the run — the terror of flight and seeking refuge in hideouts — and were frightened that they would have to go through it again. The rescuer families had given them a framework to which they could cling; the threat of parting from it rekindled their worst memories. Paradoxically, many children regarded their wartime environment as a safe and stable place and that any subsequent change might undermine and endanger the stability they had gained.[16]

One man who was aged twenty at the end of the war, described it thus: "I treated Christianity as a game. I knew I was Jewish and I never ignored my Jewishness. Just the same, [after the war] I went back to the village and began to teach children in return for various commodities. I even thought about staying there. The villagers wanted to marry me off, and I almost believed that it should be that way. It took strength to get up and go."[17]

This was the state of mind of an "adult child"– one who already knew his own mind and who, in theory, could decide for himself. Furthermore, he says, he knew he was Jewish and realized that his Christianity was a "game." If this is how an adult felt, younger children found it all the more difficult to endure the uncertainty that the change would entail. Some children saw no reason to replace someone whom they knew, whatever their nature, with someone unknown. A girl described this feeling: "The war was over and I was still staying with the Szyteks. I was afraid to return to Radzymin where there were now no Jews. I was more and more con-

---

15 Küchler-Silberman, *My Hundred Children*, pp. 177–178 (in Hebrew edition). On the eve of the war, Lena Küchler was a Ph.D. student in education at the University of Kraków. To treat the children who were under her care after the war, Küchler attempted to understand their behavior in view of the reality that they had endured.

16 Remarks of Chasia Bielicki-Bornstein, caregiver and counselor for the first group of children at the Koordynacja children's home in Łódź, published in a pamphlet, "Gathering of the Koordynacja Children," Kibbutz Lehavot Habashan, October 1985 (Hebrew), given to me by Chasia Bielicki-Bornstein.

17 Interview by author with Moshe Tuchendler; see also interview by author with Lucia Milch-Rosenzweig.

vinced that I'd do best to stay with this family in the village because, after all, it was the only family I had."[18]

A boy described what he felt: "A little bit out of habit and a little for lack of choice, I stayed in the village. I tried to carry on with routine life (of course, with less tension and without the dangers). I found it psychologically hard to reveal my real identity and, truth to tell, I saw no point in doing so." Just the same, when he occasionally visited Zamość to sell merchandise, he would meet with Jews.[19]

Some teenagers turned down the request for removal because they refused to let an adult decide what was best for them. The war had matured them and had subjected them to ordeals that even older people found difficult to endure; nevertheless, they had survived and the crucible of time had made them more independent than ordinary youngsters. Thus, they felt that the decision on whether to transfer their lives to a new setting should be made by themselves and not by a stranger. Above all, they were unwilling to forgo their own freedom of choice.[20]

b. **Rapport with rescuers**: Most children retained the sense of intimacy with their rescuers that they had acquired at the beginning due to the protection, defense, and shelter and food that the rescuers had provided. As time passed, these feelings intensified in at least some of the children, as the perception of their rescuers as their protectors deepened into a sense of belonging and love. Therefore, when the war ended, children who had enjoyed human warmth did not wish to disengage from the people who had filled the void that had come about in their emotional world. For the most part, the rescuers responded in kind.[21]

18 Wasserstein-Blanker, "After the Holocaust I Didn't Want to Return to Judaism," p. 334.
19 Frank, *To Survive and Testify.* p. 78.
20 Interview by author with Sarah Shner-Neshamit.
21 Tec, *When Light,* Danuta Bril, pp. 143–144. Danuta related that she knew several members of her family were in Palestine. Her mother had given her the addresses of her brothers and asked her to write to them after the war. She did not do so, however, because she did not wish to leave the two women who had rescued her; interview by author with Chana Martynowski-Gutmorgen. Chana knew that her rescuer was not her mother and even remembered her own family. Even so, when her brother came to take her, Chana refused to go and stayed with her rescuers; testimony Shoshana Beiman, "Gathering of the Koordynacja Children"; letter Rabbi Findling, Haifa, to Rabbi Herzog, December 1946, in the matter of L.A., RZA, Rescue Files; Neshamit, "The 'Koordynacja for the Redemption of Children' in Liberated Poland," p. 130; Grynberg, *Księga Sprawiedliwych*, p. 172.

In contrast, younger children, who did not remember their parents at all, or had only dim memories of them, had grown up with their new families and knew no other kinship.[22] Their world-view centered on the people with whom they had spent their formative years — a landscape that encapsulated the families, their surroundings, and their childhood.

Notably, some children did not wish to leave their rescuers for reasons that were greater than just the sense of bonding: they also considered their rescuers exemplary human beings who had taken them in unconditionally, demanded nothing of them, took responsibility for them, and had endangered themselves on the child's behalf. A case in point is a girl who had found refuge during the war with the sister of a priest. The family had treated her well and respectfully, even telling her, "Jesus, too, does not want the Germans to harm the Jews." In view of the entire family's humane attitude, the girl bonded with them strongly and when her uncle came after the war to take her away, she refused to go. "I didn't have the will-power to part with all the people whom I loved and admired," she said.[23]

Children sometimes glorified their rescuers by comparing them with their parents, "who wanted to get rid of us."[24] One girl expressed this in a conversation with a friend: "I really like this aunt [the rescuer] even more than my mother. My mother abandoned me; my aunt took me into her home."[25] Even though the explanation had little to do with reality, it was also a way of explaining something to herself that the girl found impossible to understand.

c. **Sense of indebtedness to rescuers**: Some children refused to leave their rescuers because they felt indebted to them. Although this feeling originated in the emotional bond that had been formed, it is not self-evident in itself and should be considered an additional layer of the relationship. Many rescuers were impoverished when they took the youngsters into

---

22 Fogelman, *Conscience and Courage*, pp. 278–279. Fogelman claims that from the standpoint of the young children who did not remember their parents, the encounter with them was in fact a meeting with strangers. The only bond they knew was the one they had established with their rescuer "parents"; see also Shner-Neshamit, "Characteristics of the Spiritual Image of Redeemed Children," p. 81. Sarah described a case which she witnessed, of a girl who cried and refused to return to her father; Koryski, "These Are Our Children," *Farn Yiddishn Kind*, p. 3; Granatstein, *Double Life*, p. 13; testimony Matti Greenberg and remarks of his rescuers' son, in Berman, "Wanda's Lists."
23 Dekel, *Remnants of the Sword*, pp. 190–194.
24 Shner-Neshamit, "Characteristics of the Spiritual Image of Redeemed Children," p. 86.
25 *Mission to the Diaspora*, p. 88.

their care. Some were alone and their plight had been worsened by damage caused by the war. Nevertheless, they risked their lives to rescue the
children, shared their food with them, and supported them for better or
for worse. The children's refusal to abandon their rescuers at the end of
the war had nothing to do with an awareness of their Jewish identity, but
was a result of their choice to link their fate to that of their rescuers so
as not to betray them and abandon them in their troubles. A boy named
Aharon, for example, remained with the peasant woman who had concealed him. After the war, the woman fell ill and her children, who had
not known of Aharon's existence during the war, abandoned her. Even
though Jews whom he encountered frequently asked him to join them,
Aharon refused, preferring to continue to take care of the peasant woman.
Only after the woman herself talked him into leaving did Aharon set
out for Kraków.[26] Practically speaking, a child like Aharon underwent a
transformation from "supported" to "supporter."

d. **Fear for the fate of the Jews**: There were children who refused to leave
their rescuers and safe homes precisely because they knew they were Jewish. They retained memories of Jewish realities and culture from their
parents' homes but also recalled the circumstances that had brought them
to their new surroundings. Their senses, having absorbed the horrors of
the war, had taught them that Jews were people who got evicted from
their homes and were beaten, abused, and killed. Therefore, the prospect
of reconnecting with the perceived Jewish fate terrified them. These children usually denied their Jewish identity and objected to the very idea of
living among Jews. The Jewish survivors reminded them of the woes that
had befallen them and rekindled old fears. One of the survivors, today a
Catholic priest, described the phenomenon: "After the war, I was afraid
to reveal that I was Jewish. The fear stayed with me but I always thought
about Jews. On Lubartówska Street in Lublin there were Jews after the
war. I would go there to hear Yiddish, to see Jews. But I didn't tell [any-
one] that I was Jewish."[27] This fear persisted even after the youngsters

26 Testimony of Aharon in Küchler, *We Accuse*, pp. 219–220; see also interview by author
   with Yosef Haezrahi-Bürger about brothers who had been concealed in Treblinka village;
   Koryski, "The Zionist Koordynacja for the Redemption of Jewish Children in Poland,"
   p. 29.
27 Testimony Zvi (Hersz) Gryner, today Father Grzegorz Pawlowski, in Łuków, "Upside-Down
   Roots"; see also interview by author with Rachel Frank-Friedberg, March 1993. Rachel, a
   caregiver at the first children's home of the Jewish committee in Lublin, testified that when
   the children discovered that they were Jewish, most were badly upset; Granatstein (*Double*

were taken to children's homes. A caregiver at the Koordynacja's children's home reported sometimes hearing children crying at night. When she attempted to comfort the children, they claimed that they could not fall asleep because they were afraid to be among Jews.[28] Their new home and the devoted care that they received did not suffice to calm them.

e. **Acceptance of the Christian faith**: Familiarity with Christian ritual was an important part of the children's false wartime identity. The more knowledgeable a child was, the less the danger of his or her identity being revealed. This made Christian observance an inseparable part of the children's new identity, and their familiarity with the new faith became greater as time passed. For many children, identity evolved into identification; the outward practice of Catholicism for reasons of safety became the acceptance of Christianity as a faith. The contrast of memories of suffering, attacks, and fear, and the security that Christianity provided, augmented by their identification with their rescuers and the acceptance of their way of life, created a sense of refuge under the wings of Christianity. For example, one girl survivor described what she felt after the war:

> Right after the war, I had a problem with my identity. I didn't want to go back to Judaism. I was a Christian girl. I prayed. I believed. I couldn't believe in [a Jewish] God. For me, it was a fact that God hadn't helped me and Jesus had... I thought of my grandmother as the embodiment of justice on earth. And they'd killed her... They murdered the Jews, but the Christians — no... Then what kind of God was he?

Life, pp. 13, 14–15) retells the case of a child who, for several days after having been taken to the Agudath Israel children's home, behaved wildly and insisted loudly to anyone within hearing distance that he was not Jewish, did not wish to be Jewish, and would not calm down until he was returned to his "parents" in the village; Mahler, "Redemption of Jewish Children from Their Non-Jewish Rescuers," pp. 35, 36–37. When a girl named Marysia realized that the operative had come to take her to the Jews, she trembled from head to toe, as if suffering from a high fever. She remembered being separated from her parents and recalled things that the Germans had done, and was afraid. She refused to respond and turned her face to the wall; Küchler-Silberman, *My Hundred Children*, p. 88–89. When a five-year-old girl heard her rescuer disclosing her Jewishness at the headquarters of the Jewish committee in Kraków, she was gripped with fear, cried loudly, and pleaded with her not to hand her over; Koryski, "The Zionist Koordynacja for the Redemption of Jewish Children in Poland," p. 29. In another case, after lengthy negotiations, a boy who was about to be surrendered blurted out to his rescuer, "For that [to surrender me to the Jews] you shouldn't have saved my life."

28 Testimony Chasia Bielicki-Bornstein, in Łuków, "Upside-Down Roots."

Jesus was OK, he helped, he saved people. The God of the Jews didn't care about his Jews...[29]

Another girl survivor testified:

The [Christian] faith was so strongly planted in my soul that no force in the world could dislodge it. Magia and Pacewicz [her rescuers] talked about faith and truly believed in it, so who could argue with them? Certainly not my mother, who wants to bring me back to the Judaism from which I'm fleeing with all my heart, I'm already a goy and that's what I want to remain.[30]

Some children suffered psychological distress due to the need to choose between Judaism and Christianity — a decision that entailed a spiritual matu-

---

29 Testimony Pola Weinstein (b. 1933) in Dror (interviewer and editor), *Pages of Testimony*, C, p. 1002; see also Mahler, "Redemption of Jewish Children from their Non-Jewish Rescuers." A nine-year-old girl said, "The Jewish God killed my parents and burned down my home, and only Lord Jesus saved me;" Kurek-Lesik, "*Udzial Żeńkich;*" interview with Drucker. Drucker told the researcher that he often escorted youngsters from the children's home to church. These children did not want to hear anything about their Jewishness and hated Jews. Their reasoning was: "If they were Jews, why did Jesus save them and not the Jewish God?" Drucker testified that he found this rationale difficult to counter.

30 Shulamit Magen, "First and Last Memory," written in 1992 and given to me by her husband; see also Tec, *When Light*, pp. 142, 144. Tec stresses in her study that baptism and the Christian faith were not necessarily forced upon the children; the testimony of a boy named Shlomo gives one an idea of the sense of safety that Christianity provided. See Grzywacz, "To the Bosom of My People," pp. 62–64; see also testimony Cipora Minc, MA, A.262. The decision to be a Christian was made at the girl's initiative. Her rescuer applied no pressure and expressly left the decision up to her. When the removal operatives came to converse with her, the girl denied she was Jewish; see also the story of Zvi (Hersz) Griner, today Father Grzegorz Pawlowski, in Łuków, "Upside-Down Roots." Zvi related that during the war he was under Christian influence and it was his practice, together with other orphans who were with him at the various children's homes, to recite the prayers. By the time he reached high school, he had become a "strong believer;" see also Perlberger-Shmuel, *This Girl is Jewish*, pp. 59–65; Shner-Neshamit, "The Spiritual Character of the Redeemed Children," p. 84. As Shner-Neshamit escorted a group of children from Poland to Prague, one of the girls turned to her at the Prague railroad station, removed a picture of the Virgin Mother from around her neck, hung it on her escort's neck, and told her, "I'm leaving Poland and I'm no longer in danger. You're going back to Poland, where they're still murdering Jews... The Holy Mother protected me throughout those years of war. Now I want her to protect you." Shner-Neshamit was moved by the girl's decision to give her the object that she treasured above all others. As they parted, the girl placed a letter in her hand and asked her to send it to her rescuer. When she reached Łódź, Shner-Neshamit opened the letter and read it: "Dear Aunt, the Żydzy are hauling me off to their Palestine. But I promise you that I won't forget what you taught me and I'll always remain true to our holy Catholic faith."

rity that was beyond their age. The boy who subsequently became a priest described the feeling: "After I had already become a neophyte, I went to the priest to make confession.... I told [him] that until I was fourteen I'd committed no sins, because I'd been a Jew. He told me to forget what had been before. [Nevertheless], I cried at night when I thought about what had happened."[31]

The younger children did not "convert" in the accepted sense of the term; they had simply grown up in the Christian faith.[32] According to Tec, children who had lived even among rescuers who did not treat them well found refuge in Christianity and therefore found it difficult to relinquish it. In other words, they distinguished between Christianity and Christians.[33] Their place in familiar surroundings had a favorable effect on them.[34] For this reason, many children remained Christian after the war even after they had been removed from Christian surroundings. Some continued to recite Christian prayers, refused to relinquish the crucifix they wore round their necks, and maintained Christian ritual even in the children's homes. They continued to conceal their origins and repudiated their Jewish names. Some even wished to continue going to church.[35] One of the survivors testified: "Since I'd become a Chris-

---

31 See Łuków, "Upside-Down Roots; see also Grzywacz, "To the Bosom of My People," p. 63. As the war came to a close, Shlomo disclosed his Jewish identity to the family that had adopted him from the orphanage. Since he had become a choir boy by that time, the rescuers reported this to the priest, who baptized him. Some two years after the war, when he told them that he had been offered an opportunity to leave Poland for Palestine with Jewish children, the family and the priest were immensely agitated. However, when Shlomo eventually decided to leave, the priest gave him his blessings; Shner-Neshamit, "Characteristics of the Spiritual Image of Redeemed Children," p. 73. Shner-Neshamit told the story of a girl who sent a picture of herself in nun's attire to her father in Australia and expressed sorrow about the anguish that she had caused him.

32 Tec, *When Light*, p. 142; interview by author with Yeshayahu Drucker.

33 Tec, *When Light*, p. 143.

34 Koryski, "These Are Our Children," *Farn Yiddishn Kind*, p. 3. In the article, subheaded "Testament of an Unhappy Mother Must be Honored," Leibl Koryski told the story of a mother dying in a hospital who asked to have her daughter restored to Judaism. The girl refused, saying, "My mother is very dear to me but I cannot do as she asks. I know I was Jewish but now I've found a lovelier and better faith and that's how I survived"; see also Mahler, "Redemption of Jewish Children from their Non-Jewish Rescuers," p. 35.

35 Frank, *To Survive and to Testify*, p. 81. Moshe testified: "Even though I was with my uncle, I said the Christian prayers every day, morning and evening; I continued to believe in Jesus;" Dekel, *Remnants of the Sword*, pp. 645–651. Dekel states that Renia continued to wear a crucifix and recite Christian prayers and that other youngsters at the Jewish children's home rebuked her for doing so; Granatstein, *Double Life*, p. 15. When young Bolek was removed from his rescuers' home, he continued to protest loudly that he was not Jewish. He did this even in the children's home. He avoided the company of the older youngsters in the home, shirked his duties, genuflected and recited prayers, crossed him-

tian according to the rules of the faith, I couldn't breach the covenant that I'd concluded with Jesus and become an apostate." Even when he eventually decided to leave his rescuers and move to Palestine, he vacillated about how to continue being a "loyal, observant Christian" "because I'd been filled with the Christian spirit and believed in it with all my heart."[36] In the Christian doctrine, one who accepts Jesus and subsequently repudiates him is a sinner who forfeits any possibility of atonement. Children who had been living in a Christian environment were deeply afraid of the punishment for apostasy.

Nevertheless, the children who were taken to the Jewish children's homes slowly began to return to their Jewish identity. Each of them, at his or her own pace, went through the process of replacing Christian religious values with Jewish and Zionist values, whether religious or secular.[37] On the other hand, most of those who remained with their rescuers, irrespective of the reason, remained assimilated in Christian society and did not return to Judaism.[38] The roots they had found in Christianity had become the source of their strength.

The children who, at war's end, were old enough to have retained memories of their parents, carried with them the pain of having been parted from them. Even if at the time, they had understood the necessity of separation,

self, and kissed the crucifix. Granatstein testified that the boy was confused, disillusioned, and embittered; letter Yehuda Grünbaum to Rabbi Herzog, April 1946, RZA, Rescue Files. The correspondent says that when the girl's father came to claim her after the war, she refused to speak with him and shouted, "What does this Jew want from me, tell him to go to hell"; Shner-Neshamit, "Characteristics of the Spiritual Image of Redeemed Children," p. 78: At the Koordynacja children's home, "Christian" children were treated very cautiously, they were not prevented from reciting Christian prayers and were allowed to hang the crucifix over their beds. The other children were warned not to provoke them. The counselors knew that only an understanding attitude and pleasant words might induce them to return to Judaism. The religious bodies also understood the children's psychological quandary and their need to continue attending church. At the Council of Religious Communities children's homes in Zabrze and at that of Agudath Israel in Łódź, children who wished to go to church were taken to Sunday Mass. Over time, the Jewish faith replaced the Christian one. See Granatstein, *Days of Genesis*, p. 123; interview by author with Yeshayahu Drucker; Kolodny, "Captive Children."

36 Grzywacz, "To the Bosom of my People," p. 64. See also testimony Sarah Lederman, OHD 50(68). Lederman describes the fears of a girl whom she had removed. The girl repeatedly asked her in tears, "What will become of me? You're saying that I'm Jewish and that I can't pray on my knees any more... and how will my life be without prayer?"

37 Hochberg-Marianska, "I Cared for Child Survivors," pp. 12–13.

38 Story of Zvi (Hersz) Griner, today Father Grzegorz Pawlowski, in Łuków, "Upside-Down Roots"; Reicher, "The Priest Burst into Tears"; Śliwowska, *Dzieci Holocaustu Mówią*, "Marjanna Adameczek," pp. 11–12.

their subsequent hardships, together with the safety they had found with their rescuers, caused some to be angry at their parents for having abandoned them and consigning them to an unknown future. For example, a woman I met in 1994 (when she was about fifty years-old) told me, "My mother should have taken me with her. You don't leave a girl behind in that way." Observing my reaction, she added, "She didn't think about me, she thought only about herself, she couldn't endure my death. It was a very egoistic thing. She should have taken me with her."[39] Evidently, time did not ease the agony of separation and its aftermath and the perceived lack of mother's love.

Many Jewish children had spent the war in surroundings that were antisemitic to one degree or another, and had slowly imbibed the atmosphere as they adjusted to their new environment.[40] One of the survivors testified:

> They were antisemitic but they were against murdering people. They were willing to save anyone and to endanger themselves for him. At home, a large copper relief hung on the wall, with a table and a child lying on it, and Jews with long beards were sitting around the child, each with a straw in his mouth, stuck into the body of the child, and they were sucking his blood. It was clear to everyone that this was accurate.[41]

Children who had absorbed the antisemitic atmosphere could not identify with the new Jewish surroundings in one stroke. Some were disgusted by the

39 Conversation of author with Theresa Rychlik, December 1994. The talk took place in Kraków in the presence of her fifteen year-old son; see also Brachfeld, *A Gift of Life*, p. 113. In 1991, while attending a conference in New York of children who had been hidden during the Holocaust, Brachfeld witnessed an incident in which a woman born in the Netherlands burst into tears on the stage as she testified about having parted from her mother. "I would have preferred to be deported with her than to be left behind," the woman said. "She lied to me. She didn't come back to claim me"; see also Tec, *When Light*, p. 144; "A Jewish Mother Fights for Her Daughter," pp. 71–72. The daughter challenged her mother: "Why did you leave me if I'm so important to you?!"

40 Yishai, *In the Shadow of the Holocaust*, p. 80; Yerushalmi, *Children of the Holocaust*, pp. 88–89; Neshamit, "The Koordynacja for the Redemption of Children in Liberated Poland," pp. 136–137; Shner-Neshamit, "Characteristics of the Spiritual Image of Redeemed Children," p. 83.

41 Magen, "First and Last Memory"; see also Paldiel, *Whoever Saves One Soul*, p. 23. Paldiel, director of the Righteous among the Nations Department at Yad Vashem, claimed, "The Righteous among the Nations were not always motivated by philosemitism; some did what they did despite their objections to the Jews and their own antisemitic leanings, but considered the idea of the sanctity of life a supreme principle."

very concept of a "Jew."[42] For a few children, this internalization of antisemitism led to eruptions of rage and frustration against those who had them removed from their new families and, indirectly, undermined the sense of stability and safety that they had managed to attain. These encounters were accompanied by antisemitic remarks.[43] For example, one seven year-old girl who had been brought to the "kibbutz" in Warsaw threw a violent tantrum: "I don't want to be a Jew, I hate Jews. Jews want to kill me." When one of the women told her, "But you're Jewish," the girl replied, "So, I hate myself."[44] There were children who hated the Jews for having "crucified Jesus," and blamed all the woes that had befallen the Jews on their opposition to Christianity.[45] Some continued for some time to believe that Jews use the blood of Christians to make matza. For example, one girl blurted to her father, "Dirty Jew, you [in the plural] crucified Jesus the Messiah. [Now] you want to make matza out of me."[46] Koryski, the Koordynacja operative, testified that at the Seder dinner on the first Passover in the children's home (spring 1946), some children burst into tears when they saw the matza on the table and refused to touch it.[47]

42 Story of Hella, in Küchler, *We Accuse*, pp. 190–191. Hella's rescuer told her not to go away with her uncle because the Jews would take her to Palestine and kill her there. The girl believed this and refused to go; Bielicki, "Back to the Bosom of Their People," MA, D2.1. Chasia Bielicki-Bornstein recalls that in the midst of preparations for the Passover Seder, Marysia brought an eleven year-old girl to the children's home and called her a "tough case." The girl said that she would rather throw herself under a streetcar than be with Jews; Neshamit, "The Koordynacja for the Redemption of Children in Liberated Poland," p. 131. Neshamit told the story of a boy named Stanisław Munczynski, who burst into tears when he discovered that he was about to be handed over to a Koordynacja operative and said, "To the Jews? If that's the way it is you shouldn't have saved me at all"; story of Sabina, proceedings of conference of hidden children in the Holocaust. While in the children's home, Sabina avoided all activities because she was ashamed to be seen in the company of the other children. When they sang songs in Hebrew, she pounded the walls and created disturbances.

43 Dekel, "Along the Paths of the Bricha," p. 432. The girl protested that her father wanted to take her in order to make matza out of her; *Mission to the Diaspora*, p. 87. When the father came to claim his daughter, the girl shouted that she did not want to be Jewish and to be the daughter of an anti-Christ, and even threatened to commit suicide.

44 Sarid, "Remarks about the Koordynacja," p. 19.

45 Yishai, *In the Shadow of the Holocaust*, p. 80; Shner-Neshamit, "Characteristics of the Spiritual Image of Redeemed Children," p. 83.

46 Dekel, *Remnants of the Sword*, p. 539.

47 Koryski, "The Zionist Koordynacja for the Redemption of Jewish Children in Poland," p. 29; see also Magen, "First and Last Memory." Magen attested that on the first Passover that she celebrated with her mother after the war (when she was eight years-old), she refused to touch the matza on the table and informed her mother that she would not eat it because it was made with Gentile blood.

There were children who remained undecided long after the war about whether to stay with their adoptive families or rejoin the Jews. After the war ended and they had received word about Jewish survivors, theoretically they did not have to stay with their rescuers. They could choose either option but the choice and the action that it called for, demanded mental strength that they found hard to generate on their own. For example, one of the boys testified, "This sentence [that he had to return to his people] by Bronek [his rescuer] tapped an inner conflict that I had been repressing for a long time. On the one hand, I was a boy who had finally found a home and family and knew how much danger lay in wait for him away from this home; on the other hand, I could not forget my family and my Jewishness."[48] Even if amid their vacillations the children remained with their rescuers and felt wanted in their homes, neither they nor their rescuers always considered this their "last stop." In some cases, the family atmosphere soured some time later, or some event served as an impetus for the children's departure. The availability of a different option and a new setting helped children and rescuers to change their decisions in response to changing circumstances. Thus the boy continued his story: One day in late 1946, his rescuer's wife, in a momentary fit of anger, called him a "Jew son of a bitch." Bronek struck her in rage but the boy decided to leave. "Something really extreme had to happen to push me out," he testified.[49]

---

48 Lewinsky, "My Wanderings and My Rescuers," p. 19: nevertheless, Tuvia spent another two years or so with his rescuer; see also testimony Sukha Shmueli, MA, A.217. The boy stayed with his rescuers for almost two years after the war (in the Western Ukraine), parting with them only when he moved with them to Poland under the repatriation arrangement; Grzywacz, "To the Bosom of My People," pp. 63–64. The boy knew that he was Jewish and even became interested when he had heard that Jews were returning from Russia. However, he had bonded with his rescuers very strongly and did not want to part from them. Indeed, he stayed with them until 1947; Wasserstein-Blanker, "After the Holocaust I Didn't Want to Return to Judaism," p. 334: after the war, the girl spent another two years or so with her rescuers. Even after she moved in with a Jewish family, she missed her rescuers and continued to visit them in the village.

49 Lewinsky, "My Wanderings and My Rescuers"; see also Tamar Jacobi's answers to my questionnaire: Tamar's rescuers treated her well and continued to raise her, knowing that her mother had not survived. Afterwards, the rescuer's grandmother, brother, and five nephews moved in with them. The grandmother was an antisemite who harassed the girl. In view of the worsening economic situation and the grandmother's treatment, Tamar agreed to move to the Koordynacja children's home; interview by author with Yehuda Bronstein, 1997; testimony Yehuda Bronstein, OHD 25(68). A judge who had rescued a girl remarried after the war. His new wife did not want her; she treated her roughly and urged her husband to get rid of her. After much indecision, the girl agreed to move to the Koordynacja children's home.

Sometimes the removal of children from rescuers' homes was initiated by older siblings, themselves teenagers. They had decided to return to the Jewish fold but wanted their younger siblings, still living with their rescuers, to join them. Usually these were siblings who had been together when their wanderings had begun during the war, but had been forced to separate some time later. When the war ended and before they learned about their parents' fate, the youngsters took action to remove their siblings. One such "removal operative" was a boy born in 1931 who after the war was staying at the children's home in Zakopane, near the Slovakian border. The boy knew no peace of mind until he set out to search for his sister; eventually he discovered her in Sopot, in northern Poland on the Baltic coast, and took her to Zakopane. Returning to the home, the boy related, "She didn't want to be Jewish but she came with me."[50] These older children actually imposed their own decisions on their siblings.

Some children marked the moment of liberation with profound disappointment. In their hard times during the war, they had fantasized about the liberation and their lives that would follow. In a certain sense, they expected liberation to bring great relief and a feeling of happiness "in return" for the hardships that they had endured and their daily struggle for survival. Reality, however, had something else in store for them. When they realized the magnitude of the disaster and their personal loss, they were stricken by a sense of emptiness that made them feel overwhelmed and helpless. It was as if they accepted the verdict of fate and froze in their tracks. These adolescents were able to be on their own, look for work, change residence, and establish lives of

---

50 Story of Wiktor in Küchler, *We Accuse*, pp. 71–72; see also autobiography of Sabina Shtickgold in *Tenenboim, One of a City, Two of a Family*, pp. 24–25. Sabina remembered the place where her sister had been in Warsaw. When she came to search for her, she found the city in ruins. After a great deal of searching, she did find her sister but the latter refused to join her. Sabina persisted, and after much persuasion the two set out to the children's home in Toruń; see also interview by author with Chana Martynowski-Gutmorgen. After the war, Hanka's older brother found her and her older sister and tried to talk them into coming with him. When she and her rescuer refused to separate, her brother took the matter to court. He lost and had to leave Poland, but before he left he instructed the older of the two sisters to have Hanka removed; see also interview by author with Haim Edelstein. After the war, Haim encountered his uncle and joined him. He knew the whereabouts of his younger brother and pleaded with his uncle to claim him too. The uncle procrastinated, offering various reasons. When they set out from Ukraine to Poland, he promised to go back for Haim's brother after they settled in — but he did not keep his word. To this day, Haim is troubled by the feeling that had he been more persistent, his uncle would have taken his brother as well. The brother remained in Ukraine; see also interview by author with Rachel Mizoc-Gewing.

freedom. However, they did not initiate the change; instead, they continued to live as they had lived during the war and in the same surroundings. It took the operatives two or three years, if not longer, to find some of them, and it was they who established contact with the children and took the initiative to remove them. Other children, who did not avail themselves of the operatives' initiatives and could not muster the fortitude to bring about change, continued to stay where they had been during the war.[51]

As we have seen, every separation of children from their rescuers was difficult. Some of the youngsters missed their rescuers even many months after removal and rejoiced whenever the rescuers contacted them.[52] To some extent, however, children who had totally lost contact with rescuers' families were better off than those who for various reasons were not able to part. The act of separation, however agonizing, sent a message of finality. Theoretically, it gave the children more emotional freedom and psychological readiness for the process of starting over. In contrast, those who did not realize that they would never re-encounter their rescuers and would have no chance to part with them carried long-lasting sorrow and guilt feelings. A girl whose mother reclaimed her from her rescuers related that, years later in Israel, her mother told her that after she had gathered her, she would continue to visit her rescuers during school vacations. The girl did not remember these visits; it was as though they had been erased from her memories of the time. The survivor summed up what she felt: "It was very hard. I never really parted from them and I've always missed them."[53]

51 Neshamit, "The Koordynacja for the Redemption of Children in Liberated Poland," pp. 123, 133; Maria (b. 1930) came to Poland under the repatriation arrangement together with the peasant who had sheltered her during the war. The peasant sent her away to learn a trade and she spent about two years doing odd jobs. Afterwards, she moved to Bytom, where she found work as a domestic. She lived among Poles and saw no chance of changing her situation; Śliwowska, *Dzieci Holocaustu Mówie*, "Marjanna Adameczek," pp. 11–12. When Marjanna (b. 1930) heard that the war had ended, she was elated. She and a friend went to the nearest large town and encountered Jews. She described her feeling: "I had no one to approach and no one took an interest in me. Then I thought to myself, freedom, what's in it for me?" Marjanna and her friend returned to their familiar environs and hired themselves out for labor. Marjanna married a Polish man at an early age, established a family, and is still living in Poland; autobiography of Halina Wengrowska, in Tenenboim, *One of a City, Two of a Family*, pp. 217–218.

52 Neshamit, "The Koordynacja for the Redemption of Children in Liberated Poland," p. 130.

53 Magen, "First and Last Memory"; see also Frank, *To Survive and to Testify*, p. 81. The boy's uncle ambushed him when he came to town on market day and, with the help of a Jewish officer, took him away without allowing him to return to the village and see the peasant again. According to his testimony, the matter troubled his conscience long afterwards;

There were children who learned in their efforts to survive during the war how to fit in comfortably and, thereby, to be desired in their surroundings. Thus their character was shaped by and tailored to the new and frequently-changing situations that came about. These youngsters also responded to their removal from the families with acceptance, and even if they were amazed by or initially opposed to the idea of being handed over to strangers, they did not persist in their refusal — as if realizing that the matter was not up to them. Such a girl summed up the change in her life in a nutshell: "I accepted the verdict without questioning and without complaining; the main thing was to survive!"[54]

Some children attended the negotiations that concerned their fate but did not understand the give-and-take and the absolute nature of its outcome; it was simply too much for them to comprehend. They also did not understand why they had to leave their homes and the people who had raised them and why they had to go away with someone else. Even though the newcomers treated them kindly and explained the issue, it did not make sense to them and they seemed to want it both ways. One boy, for example, burst into tears after he was removed from his rescuers' home, shouting that he wished to return to them. When the removal operative attempted to comfort him — by saying that he was his uncle and even promising to buy him lots of treats — the boy answered, "If you're my uncle, take me back to them and come to visit me."[55] A girl who had been promised that she would be taken to Palestine, after hearing the operatives praise the country lavishly, asked to have her "mother" taken to the new homeland with her.[56] Another girl suggested to an operative who told her that her "mother" was too poor to support her, that she give her

---

Rosen, *My Friend the Forest*, pp. 143–155. As the war ended, thugs began to visit Olina, Donya's rescuer, at her home, but by then she had managed to send Donya elsewhere. When the Russians approached, Donya emerged from her hideout and made her way to them. She encountered Jews and set out with them without parting from Olina; interview by author with Chana Martynowski-Gutmorgen. Hanka spent three days crying incessantly and pleading to return to her rescuer; for years afterward she bore the anguish of having left her without saying goodbye.

54 Responses by Tamar Jacobi to my questionnaire; see testimony Fredza Rothbard in Łuków, "Upside-Down Roots"; autobiography Erich Holder, in Tenenboim, *One of a City, Two of a Family*, pp. 95–96; story of Michael in Küchler, *We Accuse*, p. 164; story of Reuven, ibid., p. 155; story of Wiktor, ibid., p. 72.

55 Testimony Yeshayahu Drucker about the removal of Avigdor Baranowicz from his rescuers' home, in Berman, "Wanda's Lists."

56 Interview by author with Halina Kowalska.

money so that she would not be poor. That way, the girl reasoned, she could continue living with her.[57]

Most children who had been privileged to have a home during the war were grateful to their rescuers — even if in return for this they had been asked to contribute to the household or perform strenuous house and field chores. Whether or not they understood at the time what the act of rescue had entailed, they understood that they had been protected. When the war ended and the economic situation in Poland took a turn for the worse, the children saw their adoptive families' economic hardships and felt obliged to them. When the operatives came to remove them, some drew a connection between the difficulties and the "economic opportunity" that was being presented to them. Thus, they asked the operatives to provide their rescuers with aid for having saved them, or even conditioned their departure on the rescuer's receiving financial compensation. For example, a rescuer persuaded a boy whom he had saved that he would be best off returning to Jewish life, and even invited a Jewish acquaintance to remove him from the village. When the acquaintance came, however, the boy agreed to accompany him only with the proviso that his rescuer be paid for all the years that he had cared for him. When the Jewish acquaintance told the child that it was none of his business, the boy became so angry that he picked up a pitchfork and prepared to strike the Jew with it. Only the rescuer's intervention thwarted a disaster. The boy stayed with his rescuer for another year and a half after the incident, and when he finally decided to leave, again he made a condition that his rescuer be paid. Notably, according to his testimony, this was his initiative.[58] A girl, having heard that the Central Jewish Committee was offering assistance to people who had rescued a Jewish child, told her rescuer, "For once, at last I've got a chance to exploit the Jews because I'm Jewish. I'll take whatever I can." In her testimony, this girl also noted with emphasis that her rescuer had not ordered her to claim the relief, although she agreed to accept it.[59]

---

57 Testimony Devorah Zilber, OHD, 27(68); Mahler, "Redemption of Jewish Children from Their Non-Jewish Rescuers," pp. 36–37; see also Hellman, *Avenue of the Righteous*, pp. 238–239. Shifra's rescuer vacillated about how to tell her that they had to part. Finally, she made up a story that she had to go to hospital and therefore could not continue to keep her. The girl promised to return after her convalescence.

58 Lewinsky, "My Wanderings and My Rescuers."

59 Testimony Sabina Halperin, MA, A.201; see also letter Regina Kuper to Central Committee, May 18, 1945, ŻIH, Education Department, File 645: In her letter, the girl retold the story of her rescue and recounted that after having been denounced during the war for staying with her rescuer, the latter had to find her a hiding place with an acquaintance and paid a monthly sum of money for the new hideout. Toward the end of the war, the

The youngsters did not find it easy to acclimatize to the children's homes. Each child had a special life-story and his or her presence in a group of children created emotional difficulties. Since many of them had been placed in children's homes against their will, some expressed the wish to escape and threatened to do so at the first opportunity.[60] A caregiver at the Koordynacja children's home claimed that even though the caregiving and educational staff spared no effort to offer the children a warm home, this was not enough to convince at least some of them to stay; instead, they continued to wish to return to "their" families.[61] In some cases, operatives who took children to children's homes warned about the possibility that the new arrivals would attempt to run away and asked staff members to watch their movements carefully.[62] The staffs of the children's homes were vigilant, keeping doors locked and the children under surveillance so that they could not carry out their threats. Whenever children disappeared anyway, the staff hurriedly searched for them in the city streets and railroad stations in order to track them down before they could get far.[63] Some children tried to escape again and again, using new ruses each time. For example, a girl at the Koordynacja children's home in Łódź rushed into the street about two weeks before Passover and cunningly began to shout that the Jews had grabbed her and wanted her blood for making matza. She knew her remarks would fall on attentive ears and indeed, a large crowd gathered at once and began to hurl stones at the windows of the home. The girl had evidently planned to exploit

rescuer's situation deteriorated and she terminated her payments and promised to pay up when she could. The girl asked that her rescuer receive assistance in repaying her debts; Shner-Neshamit, "Characteristics of the Spiritual Image of Redeemed Children," p. 88. Shner-Neshamit wrote that the children continued to wish to reward their rescuers even after they had been placed in children's homes; Yishai, *In the Shadow of the Holocaust*, p. 80; Koryski, "The Zionist Koordynacja for the Redemption of Jewish Children in Poland," p. 29.

60 Testimony Devorah Zilber, OHD, 27(68). Marysia testified that after she brought Irka to the children's home, the girl refused to eat and spent all her time standing at the door, ready to run away the moment it opened. Her tenacity influenced the other children, creating a climate of escape attempts; Mahler, "Redemption of Jewish Children from Their Non-Jewish Rescuers," p. 38.
61 Bielicki-Bornstein, "Back to the Bosom of Their People."
62 Testimony Devorah Zilber, OHD, 27(68); testimony Zipora Minc, MA, A.262.
63 Testimony Chasia Bielicki-Bornstein, a caregiver and counselor at the Koordynacja children's home in Łódź, "Gathering of the Koordynacja Children"; Mordechai Bahat, "Redeemed Children On their Way to Palestine," in Bornstein, ed., *Redemption of Jewish Children*, pp. 95–100. Bahat writes that the children's home doors were kept locked for two reasons: fear of street antisemitism and the wish of many children to run away.

the commotion to run away but the caregivers called the police; the police-man who reported to the scene dispersed the crowd and the girl was forc-ibly returned to the home.[64] A caregiver at a Koordynacja children's home described a different kind of scheme. After a boy in her care failed to escape by talking her into letting him go, he changed his strategy: he began to take part in social activities, speak pleasantly about his new place of residence. The caregiver, noticing the change in the boy's attitude toward the home, let her guard down; the boy took advantage of this and ran away.[65] Events involving escapes caused much stress and frustration among counselors and caregivers. The same caregiver related that in the summer of 1946, shortly before she left Poland with a group of children, a boy disappeared while the staff of the home was busy packing for the trip. They could not tell the police because the inves-tigation might reveal the illegal nature of their departure from Poland. Thus, the caregiver formed a group of boys and together they set out to search for the child. The searchers spotted him some time later but when they called his name, Staszek, he began to run away. One of the older members of the search party chased him down. Sobbing, Staszek explained that he did not wish to go to Palestine with them and wanted to return to his "aunt." Then he began to shout, endangering everyone. The caregiver concluded her testimony: "It was

---

64 Shner-Neshamit, "Characteristics of the Spiritual Image of Redeemed Children," p. 85; see also testimony Leibl Koryski, OHD 15(68). Koryski testified about children who had fled and complained to the police that the Jews had abducted them against their wishes; testimony Moshe Jeruchamzon, OHD 44(68), who described the case of Yitzhak Gandel-man. After being removed from his rescuers, the boy asked to use the toilet and then fled, returning only after Jeruchamzon threatened him with a pistol; testimony Zipora Minc, MA, A.262.

65 Bielicki-Bornstein, "Back to the Bosom of Their People"; see also removal operative's clari-fication report in the matter of Grandmother Cyngiser, February 23, 1947, GFHA, Cor-respondence File, 788–790.. The report was written by an operative who had delivered two brothers to a children's home after after they had run away from him during the removal operation. After three days at the home, the children managed to escape. The writer sus-pected that the boys had fled to the village where they had been living and he proposed to wait a month or two and then search for them again in the same location; letter from Bein, Poland, to Koordynacja, Ichud, and Hehalutz, August 12, 1947, JDC, microfilm from Poland. Bein requested an inquiry about what was being done about a girl who had fled back to her rescuers; see also undated list of twenty-five children in care, JDC, microfilm from Poland. One of these children was a boy who had fled from the Agudath Israel child-ren's home and returned to his rescuers, who now refused to send him back to the home; Dekel (*Remnants of the Sword*, p. 198) reported about a boy who had fled from the Koor-dynacja children's home after three weeks and returned to his rescuer's home. Additional attempts to remove him failed; Koryski, "The Zionist Koordynacja for the Redemption of Jewish Children in Poland," p. 29; story of Leah, in Dekel, *Remnants of the Sword*, p. 194.

the first time... that I used uneducational means. I lied to him: I said the train would stop in Lublin on the way to Palestine and we'd take him to his 'aunt.' He believed it and came back [to the home] with us."[66]

To thwart continued relations between children and rescuers and shorten the process of disengaging from the past, the staff of the children's homes tried to prevent mail correspondence between the sides without the children's knowledge. The youngsters continued to write but the counselors opened the letters, read them, and decided whether to forward them or not depending on their contents.[67] The children expected a response and were disappointed when they failed to receive it; they were amazed about how the very people who had established a relationship of belonging with them were now ignoring them. One girl wrote the following to her rescuer: "[. . .] I am very curious [to know] whether you've been receiving my letters. If you don't want to answer now, I don't want an answer because today I'm here and tomorrow I'll be somewhere else..."[68] The same girl apparently tried to assuage her disappointment by attempting to blame the non-arrival of the letters on communication difficulties. Another girl, however, wallowed in guilt feelings and blamed her rescuers' cold shoulder on herself and her behavior. Thus she wrote them: "I have already written lots of letters to my aunt [the rescuer], did my aunt receive them? I asked my aunt to forgive me for having been so ungrateful and a bad [girl], but now I regret it very much."[69]

For some children, time and distance neither eradicated nor healed the yearnings for rescuers and the way of life the rescuers had provided them during the war. The activists thought these residues could be overcome by removing the children from Poland and distancing them from their rescuers, from the Polish and Christian reality, and from antisemitism. This proved to

---

66 Bielicki-Bornstein, "Back to the Bosom of Their People," p. 330.
67 Bahat, "Redeemed Children en Route to Palestine," p. 95. Mordechai Bahat, a counselor at the Koordynacja children's home in Łódź, reported on a group of girls at the home who organized and wrote to their Polish rescuers that the Jews were holding them against their wishes. The letters were confiscated and not sent to their addressees; see also interview by author with Chana Martynowski-Gutmorgen. Chanka wrote many letters to her rescuer but her sister and a lifelong friend, living on a "kibbutz" (collective) in Silesia while waiting to emigrate to Palestine, confiscated them. They did not want the rescuer to trace them down because Chanka had been taken from her by deception, without realizing that the two would never see each other again.
68 Letter from a girl at the children's home in Lyons, France, to her rescuer, MA, D1 459-1. Instead of signing her name, the girl wrote "Fa Fa Fa Ca 122" at the bottom of the letter, a code that her rescuer's family evidently knew.
69 Letter Roma to her rescuer, written at the children's home in Lyons, MA, D1 459-2.

be correct for some children but not for all. One girl was removed from Poland and placed in a Youth Aliyah children's home in France — from where she ran away. A letter to Warsaw described her escape as follows: "She had many difficulties in acclimating there. Since she had become very antisemitic while staying with the non-Jewish family, she caused Youth Aliyah lots of problems. She was very ill at ease and ran away a short time later." The information was sent on to Warsaw because the counselors suspected that the girl would make her way to a Polish family that lived near Paris and knew her "parents" and assumed that these people would help her make contact with her rescuers.[70]

Two girls from the children's home in Lyons also wrote to their rescuers in Poland, expressing three emotions: nostalgia for the family, antisemitism, and Christian piety — as if they were inseparably related. Thus one of the girls wrote (in the third person in the manner of a polite Polish child):

> My dear aunt, why did my aunt hand me over to these murderers, these bandits, these *parchów*?[71] My aunt would have done better if she'd turned me over to the Germans. These Jewish *parchów* have sprouted horns already. The Germans killed too few of them and they're sure that they're taking us to that horrific place, Palestine. As soon as they led us across the Czechoslovakian border, I began to cry. Then the Jewish *parchów* [said]: "Oy vey, go back to the goyim." That's because they never say Poles but always — goyim. So I answered, *parchów* Jews, if only the Germans had killed you off. My aunt has no idea how miserable I am now. One of those she-monkeys wanted to beat me up and I can't even tear off their sidelocks.... . I also forgot to write that in Łódź I bought some rosary beads, a medallion, a booklet [of prayers], and a novena[72] to the

70 Letter JDC-Paris, to JDC-Warsaw, May 17, 1948, in the matter of T.S., JDC, microfilm from Poland, XI; see also Dekel, *Remnants of the Sword*, p. 200. Fourteen-year-old Mira vacillated at length about whether to leave her rescuers, who had left the decision up to her. After lengthy conversations that her aunt also attended, Mira decided to move to a children's home and was removed from Poland shortly afterward. Although she appeared to be well accepted by her new friends, she must have entertained regrets because she disappeared from a hostel near Paris, turned to the Polish consul, and asked to be returned to her Polish "parents." Attempts to return her to the children's home failed.

71 The expression *parchów* is a Polish (and Yiddish) slur that suggests someone who suffers from boils.

72 This word originates from the Latin *nov*, denoting the number nine. A novena is a cluster of prayers devoted to a certain purpose and is performed over a period of nine days, weeks, or months. The purpose of the prayers may be a request for divine mercy related to some event, e.g., a person's death or a child's safe trip. Often the purpose is printed on a card that carries the likeness of a saint. The idea is that anyone who recites this prayer should focus on the subject.

Holy Mother. I can't go to church now but I'll always remain Catholic and Polish, and I'll return to Poland.[73]

The second girl appealed to her rescuers in the first person, calling them "Mother" and "Father."

> Beloved Mother... Mother, it would have been better if you had handed me over to the Germans than to these Jews so that they would torture me so badly, or if you had drowned me. Anything not to hear *oy vey mir, git, vusi* [words in Yiddish] any more. Even so, I'll get back at them yet. I go around as filthy as a chimney sweep because they don't let me do laundry. You have to go around with lice. In the meantime, I don't have lice. But I think they know that I'm carrying a medallion. Three girls, one of them is named Roma, the others are Irena and Marysia, and I'm the fourth. They have prayerbooks, rosary beads, and medallions. I'm sorry I don't have beads.[74]

Neither letter reached its destination; the counselors at the children's home in France confiscated both without the girls' knowledge. Several features stand out in the letters: the wish to curry favor with the rescuers, much anger and confusion, refusal to acquiesce in the change imposed on them, and immense antipathy toward Jews.

With these letters in the background, one may understand why one of the rationales cited by operatives (of all Jewish organizations — Zionist and non-Zionist) in justification of what they did to remove children from non-Jews' homes was the concern that these of all children, the last remnants of Jewish families that had been murdered due to their Jewishness, would become antisemites.[75]

73 Letter Roma, MA, D.1. 459-2. Notably, Roma stayed in a children's home of the Hashomer Hatza'ir movement, where the counselors did not wear sidelocks; that, however, is how she pictured Jews. As for her remark about the word *goyim* [Gentiles], Chasia, a caregiver at the Koordynacja children's home, said that most children who had lived with loving families found the parting difficult. "To us they were goyim but to the children they were parents." See interview by author with Chasia Bielicki-Bornstein.
74 Letter by a girl from the children's home in Lyons to her rescuer, MA, D.1. 459-1. I have tried to preserve the spirit of the girl's writing but added punctuation. The letter was composed in childish penmanship and in one paragraph that was unpunctuated except for a few periods at ends of sentences. Capitalization was also lacking.
75 Shner-Neshamit, *I Did Not Come to Rest*, p. 204; idem, "Characteristics of the Spiritual Image of Redeemed Children," pp. 81–82; interview by author with Yeshayahu Drucker.

Conclusion

The transition from one period to the next in the children's lives depended, as stated, on each child's position at the starting line and the pace of change. Some children lived in both worlds for a while — sometimes briefly, sometimes longer. On the one hand, residues of the customs and beliefs of their wartime ways of life endured; on the other, the youngsters found themselves in a new setting.[76] Other children, especially those who had returned to Judaism voluntarily, left behind the evidence of their former surroundings, as if shedding an unwanted garment, and draped themselves with the reality and culture that the Jewish children's home imparted.[77] For children who did not wish to leave their rescuers and the realities of the new life, and who persisted in their refusal even if they were already staying in children's homes, the adjustment was difficult and very painful.[78]

Some children had led harsh lives in their wartime places of residence; they had worked hard, were exploited, and grew up without affection and a caressing hand. Nevertheless, for them, too, these places of refuge had been a home, a place to hide, and a shelter. Others had been privileged with love, affection, warmth, and a sense of intimacy. There were children who even during the war understood the magnitude of their rescuers' action on their behalf; others learned to appreciate it at a distance of years. Donya Rosen's book came out in 1954. Rosen had been found hiding in an isolated cabin owned by Olina, a strange hermit of a woman whose own family, not to mention the peasants in her surroundings, considered her "a little mad." Olina fought with all her soul against anyone who tried to menace the girl. Whenever danger loomed, Olina moved Donya into a hideout deep in the forest.

76 Magen, "First and Last Memory." Shulamit Magen wrote her memoirs in 1992, while severely ill. "To this day," she wrote, "whenever I am frightened or in severe pain, instinctively I cross myself on the head. I ask God to help, but equally I ask Jesus;" see also interview by author with Sarah Szczekacz-Gwircman-Tsur, May 2000.

77 Interview by author with Mira Bramm-Ehrlich, May 2000; interview by author with Zvi Ksiazenicki-Harel, May 2000; interview by author with Erella Hilferding-Goldschmidt, May 200.

78 Dekel, *Remnants of the Sword*, p. 236; Magen, "First and Last Memory." Shulamit Magen describes the adjustment as having been so lengthy as to have continued, at times, after she had reached a kibbutz in Israel: "I don't care if the whole world is against me. The children, the teachers, and all the kibbutz members, for whom I'm an antisemite." She continues: "Time has its effect. I'm softening up and learning the language. I read lots of books and approach the children, but I'm always vigilant, ready to attack and to defend myself"; see also interview by author with Sarah Szczekacz-Gwircman-Tsur.

She stayed in touch with the girl, brought her food, and boosted her morale in difficult moments. Upon liberation, Donya was away from Olina's home and the two never saw each other again. Donya dedicated her book to Olina and wrote the following in the introduction:

> Dedicated to Olina and all the nameless Olinas who risked their lives to save Jewish children. To Olina: Dear, unforgettable Olina, if I were a sculptor I would make a monument to you, I would commemorate your exalted image — the image of a mother who is willing to suffer cruel afflictions for her children, willing even to sacrifice her life at any time and moment. For you were a mother to me — a mother whom I lost at the dawn of my childhood.
>
> Unfortunately, I am neither a sculptor nor a poet. My grasp suffices only to hand you this modest gift — this memoir, written out of a profound psychological need, one arising from the heart. Accept it, dear Olina, as an expression of my immense love for you, an expression of my gratitude and appreciation. Dear, beloved Olina — I will never forget you.[79]

Unlike Donya, Leah was an infant when her parents surrendered her to an acquaintance who placed her in an orphanage a short time later. The Jopowiczes claimed her from the orphanage and raised her until after the war, when her aunt tracked her down and had her removed from her rescuers' home by court order. In 1998, Leah published a book of poetry titled *Lemi she'asafani* ("To those who gathered me in.")[80] She concluded one of her poems as follows:

> My father and mother left me [cf. *Psalms* 27:10]
> to whomever it was who gathered me.[81]

Even though several people and institutions "gathered" Leah in during her lifetime, the first to do so were the couple who chose her from the other children in the orphanage. In her poem "Wet Nurse," Leah refers to the woman who took her into her home and addressed the following to her:

---

79 Rosen, *The Forest, My Friend,* dedication page at the front of the book.
80 Leah Nebenzahl, *To Those who Took me in, Cycle of Poems* (Tel Aviv: Eked, 1999, Hebrew).
81 Ibid., p. 20.

[. . .]

And today I return to you
With
The historians' scalpel
And a matriculation certificate.

I invite you
To come in
Through the front door

To understand what you are for me
While
I dwell
Among my people.[82]

Donya's words to her rescuer attest to the enduring nature of the pain of separation; Leah's poem, in contrast, is written from a position of self-confidence, evidently grown over the years, that allowed her to cope with the past.

These girls, and other children like them, carry the baggage of their childhood and continue to work through the events that they endured. This is a natural, inevitable, and perhaps also an important process.[83]

Most of the children were quickly removed from Poland to other countries. The need to integrate in a new location and grow up in a new society ostensibly distanced the children from the events of the past — but only ostensibly. The disengagement from parents and separation from rescuers was, and remains, part of their mental reality. In fact, when we examine the children's personal stories (not only after the end of the war but also from the time the war began to affect their lives and childhood), we realize that their burden was too heavy for a child to bear. On the one hand, one may argue that, at least from the children's perspective, the actions to remove them were problematic in human terms. On the other, one must ask whether it would have been better to leave them behind, uprooted from their cultural origins?

In any event, the operatives were mindful of the price that the children were paying even as the removal actions were taking place. Although they were guided by the national perspective and the need to revive Jewry (in whatever form), they also regarded their actions as "in the children's best interests." However, their work involved much indecision, especially when they

---

82 "Wet Nurse," ibid., p. 4.
83 Aharon Appelfeld makes the same point. See Appelfeld, *Life Story*, p. 85.

witnessed moving human moments between adoptive parents and children. Addressing himself to the dilemma of removing children from their rescuers' homes to Jewish children's homes, Drucker said the following: "It's as though I stole [the child] from his parents and made him into the child of the collective."[84] This consciousness, however, did not weaken the urge to be involved in the operations. At the time, the children were deemed immensely important for the rehabilitation of the Jewish people, to whom their parents had belonged — even if the operatives realized that the children's own rehabilitation was no less important. Thus, the operatives lived with the duality but allowed the collective consideration to prevail. Notably, every organization made every effort to ease the children's crisis of transition back to their Jewish identity.

It is hard to know whether taking the children away from their rescuers and Poland was indeed in their "best interests." The many talks that I held with child survivors living in Israel in the course of this study gave me the impression — although it is only an impression and not a statistical finding — that despite the difficulties that they endured, the erstwhile children consider themselves part of the environment and culture that they inhabit today and do not believe it should have been otherwise. Recently, a woman who returned from Poland after an encounter with her childhood "siblings" told me, "I cannot imagine not having been found and having stayed there!" – even though she was deeply impressed by their attitude toward her.[85] In contrast, a woman who had been born in the Warsaw Ghetto and spent her entire life in Poland stressed, in her conversation with me, that she is happy that her adoptive mother did not hand her over to the Jewish organizations. She said she had enjoyed a happy childhood and had enjoyed the privilege of a mother's boundless love.[86] One is free to construe both claims as rationalizations meant to justify the situation. Just the same, the majority seem to endorse their return to a Jewish environment as correct. As evidence, we note the many requests in recent years from children who had survived and remained in Poland for assistance in searching for relatives and learning about their Jewishness. For most people, the need for roots is a central imperative in the shaping of a lasting personal reality.

84 Testimony Yeshayahu Drucker, in Berman, "Wanda's Lists."
85 Interview by author with Sabina Kagan-Heller, September 2000.
86 Interview by author with Elżbieta Ficowska-Kopel.

Conclusion

In this study I have examined the topic of Jewish children who survived the Holocaust in the homes of non-Jews and the actions taken by various post-war Jewish bodies to locate and remove them, and place them in Jewish institutions. I examined the organizations involved and their ideological identity, the methods used by each body, what was common and what was unique in the methods, and where the organizations obtained the funding to do what they did. I also found it necessary to study the background of these operations — the political situation in Poland, the prevailing states of mind among the Polish population, and the attitude of the Polish government regarding the removal of the children. Finally, I tried to shed light on the human-emotional aspect of the actions taken, from the standpoints of the Polish rescuers and the children themselves. Below are the main issues that were examined in this study.

Estimates of the Number of Jewish Children Entrusted to Non-Jews in Poland during the War and the Likelihood of their Survival

In general, the concealment of Jewish children took place at the stage of the Nazi occupation when the Jews confined in the ghettos realized that their compatriots were being murdered and communities were being annihilated in what became known as the "Final Solution" (in German: *Endlösung*). Up until then, as long as they did not feel themselves to be in mortal danger, parents were very reluctant to part with their children and attempted to keep their families intact. In most of the relatively few instances of concealment that preceded this time, non-Jewish caregivers or acquaintances took in one or several children to ease the plight of the parents and children, or parents sent children out of the ghetto to make a living on their own because they were unable to support the whole family. However, as the deportation rumors began to gain credence, many Jewish families tried to establish some form of contact with non-Jews in order at least to save their children. The German occupation authorities in Poland, foreseeing such a development, terrorized both Jews and Poles by threatening with the death penalty anyone who helped Jews, and backed the threat by carrying out public executions of both bene-ficiaries and benefactors of such assistance, as a deterrent. They also began to search for people in hiding. The dangers on the Aryan side of the ghettos came not only from the Germans but also from Polish informers and extor-tionists. Nevertheless, in view of the looming menace of extermination, many parents attempted to make some kind of connection with people outside the ghetto. Whenever a refuge for a child was found, the youngster had to cope with the difficulties of acculturation with a new family and strange surround-ings. The children's very survival hinged on a plausible cover story and the ability to assimilate into Polish society, as well as to familiarize themselves with the realities of life in a Catholic environment. A "Jewish appearance," lack of fluency in Polish, unfamiliarity with Polish cultural and religious in-dicators, and a Jewish accent — could be their undoing.

I will not make the mistake of attempting to estimate the number of Jewish children in Poland who found shelter in non-Jews' homes. Any such estimate cannot be born out with enough evidence to support even an ap-proximate number. Since the initiatives to save children (except by those of Żegota) were taken by individual parents and with a maximum of discre-tion; one cannot quantify it. However, if we take account the total number of Jews in Poland on the eve of the Holocaust (over three million) and the large number of testimonies about parents' attempts to save their children, we may assume that many youngsters, of all ages, found their way out of the ghettos.[1] Just the same, the difficulties of concealment were such that the number of children who left the ghettos cannot possibly bear any relation to the number who survived the war.

Nevertheless, the activists in the organizations that engaged in the re-moval of the children after the war had the impression that a "large number" of youngsters had survived. To gauge the meaning of a "large number," one

---

1 By comparison, in pre-war Belgium there were some 66,000 Jews, of whom about 4,000 children were placed in hiding. Admittedly, the degree of persecution was very different to that in Poland and the odds of survival were greater. Just the same, the number of con-cealed children attests to the willingness of parents to part with their children at the time of the deportations.

can examine the estimates cited in correspondence among the organizations about actions in which they were involved. Since by then, some children had already been removed, the estimates concern the possibility of finding additional children. One report stated: "There are around 1,200 children with non-Jewish families who need to be redeemed for us."[2] "...We have to [remove] another 5,000 children fast... . In the meantime, dozens of goyish women who have Jewish children are pounding on the doors and people approach us every day saying that there are children here and there."[3] "[. . .] Quite a few children still remain in the homes of Christians and in convents. One may say without exaggeration that there is hardly a village in Poland without one or more children in Christian homes. Additional names of places where Jewish children are to be found are reported frequently."[4] "Today it has become possible to liberate many more children from Christian families. We have [lists of] people with whom we are negotiating. Two hundred children are listed and hundreds more await liberation."[5] "...Hundreds if not thousands are about to be redeemed from non-Jews."[6]

These reports were always written in the context of descriptions of the correspondents' work and the shortage of money to finance the operations; therefore, the writers may be suspected of overstating their case in order to secure greater support. However, one cannot ignore the feeling of the activists that Jewish children were still in hiding in many localities across Poland and that there were more such children than the operatives were able to remove.[7]

---

2   Report Moshe Yishai, Jewish Agency emissary, March 12, 1946, *Jewish Agency News* (June 1946), CZA, S25/5262. Yishai distinguishes in his estimate between children who were staying with non-Jewish families and those in convents.

3   Letter Leibl (in view of the contents — Leibl Goldberg) to Hans Beit, Youth Aliyah-Warsaw, July 18, 1946, CZA, L58/595.

4   Letter Federbusch, Mizrachi secretariat, to Freimann, New York, with copy to Warhaftig, May 21, 1947, YVA, P.20/8. Federbusch quoted reports that he had received from Poland; letter Birzinski, World Mizrachi secretariat, Jerusalem, to Gruenbaum, Jewish Agency Rescue Committee, May 21, 1947. The letter quotes an excerpt from a letter that Drucker sent from Poland to the Mizrachi secretariat, CZA, S26/1317. The contents are identical to those of the quotation in Federbusch's letter, except for a minor change in phrasing.

5   Letter Koordynacja presidium, Abraham Berensohn, Shaike Zszukowski, and Menahem Kunda, to Jewish Agency Rescue Committee, Paris, August 10, 1947, CZA, S26/1424.

6   Letter Jewish Agency Rescue Committee to South African Jewish war appeal, part of a report on the use of funds raised in South Africa, November 24, 1947, ibid., S26/1291.

7   Our remarks do not deal with the question of whether Polish society could have mobilized more vigorously to rescue Jews who were being exterminated on their doorstep or whether more children could have been saved. After all, even if thousands had been saved, it would still be a negligible share of the number of Jewish children who had been in Poland shortly before the war. See Krakowski, "Jewish-Polish Relations," pp. 251–256; see also Teresa Prekerowa, "The 'Just' and the 'Passive,'" *Yad Vashem Studies* 19 (1989), pp. 369–377.

Influence of the Political Situation in Poland on the Child-Removal Operations

The child-removal operations were not undertaken in a void; in many ways, they depended on the social and political situation in Poland. The authorities were busy rebuilding the state from its ruins and faced a proliferation of internal problems — economic, social, and political. The issue of the Jewish survivors was important to the government for two reasons: a genuine awareness of their needs and the feeling that the western countries regarded the issue as a litmus test of how the Polish regime and population would treat the Jewish survivors. Thus, it was possible to search for, trace, and remove Jewish children with very little interference. However, due to internal problems, the government did not offer concrete assistance nor did it initiate legislation that would mandate the registration of Jewish children who were living in Polish homes. Obviously it would have been easier to trace the children had there been such legislation, but under the circumstances benign neglect was also helpful.[8]

Where there were difficulties in carrying out operations, they came from political entities on the far Right and citizens who, due to incitement, regarded Jews as collaborators with the new regime. Furthermore, many Poles were afraid that the return of Jews to their towns would be followed by demands for restitution of property. For these and other reasons, Jews were attacked and injured and even murdered in various locations and on the roads. All the operatives noted in distress that it was virtually impossible to visit some localities in Poland without risk to life and limb. Thus, the search and tracing of children took place under especially difficult conditions, with virtually no cooperation from the population and even less from those who had rescued children.

The changes that took place in Poland from 1947 onward and the process of becoming a "people's democracy" magnified the difficulties and led to a sense of urgency in the task of removing children who remained in the country. For their part, rescuers who had not handed over Jewish children in their custody by then made even more strenuous efforts to hide them from the searchers. The operatives' concern was justified, since by now the authorities were hindering the activities of all the Jewish organizations, irrespective of affiliation and, in 1948, began to order the organizations to desist from

8   In Belgium, too, an attempt to pass legislation requiring disclosure of custody of a Jewish child failed. See Brachfeld, *A Gift of Life*, p. 124.

their operations. Nevertheless, the operations continued on a limited scale for another year or so, after which the closure of the organizations' offices and the lack of funding finally brought them to an end.

Extent of the Removal Operations

Various Jewish organizations as well as private individuals were involved in tracking down, and removing Jewish children from the homes of non-Jews. Relatives sometimes took the initiative on their own (the number of such cases cannot be estimated) and sometimes also sought the assistance of the organizations. The amount of such assistance varied from case to case.

Some organizations that dealt with removing children did so as part of their general activity among the survivor population. Examples are the Child Care Department of the Central Committee of the Jews of Poland, the Zionist youth movements, and Poalei Agudath Israel. Others were organized solely for this purpose, for example, the Koordynacja; Yeshayahu Drucker's activities on behalf of the Council of Religious Communities; and Sarah Lederman's actions on behalf of Rachel Sternbuch, representing the Rescue Committee of American Orthodox Rabbis.

Actions to find and reclaim children began with local initiatives by the survivors themselves. In the immediate post-liberation period, they realized that Jewish children remained in non-Jewish homes throughout Poland and tried to gather them up. Some time later, the organizations were set up and the operations took on a more institutional character. Apart from the Koordynacja, established at the initiative of an emissary from Palestine who had come to Poland, and apart from the actions undertaken by Sternbuch, who was based in Switzerland, all the organizations came into being at the initiative of the survivors. Each of them developed its own method of gathering up children. Although the methods had a common denominator, each was also unique in some way, influenced by the ideology and worldview of its executive body. Many Jewish organizations outside Poland were also involved indirectly, by providing the operatives with moral and material support.

It is worth bearing in mind that very few people were actually engaged in removing children. For example, all the actions sponsored by the Council of Religious Communities were carried out by one man. Action on behalf of the American rabbis' rescue committee was also the work of one person. Two people operated on behalf of Poalei Agudath Israel and about ten people acted at different times on behalf of the Koordynacja. Other activists, of course, did office work, received requests, and gathered information.[9] All the activity took place under conditions of pressure. At times, the operatives had to make repeated trips to an outlying location in order to effect the removal of one child, even though it was clear that a Jewish child could be found in almost every village and that many children were still waiting for removal.

It is difficult to take an unequivocal stance as to whether the fragmentation of operations among the organizations was beneficial or detrimental. On the one hand, rivalry inspired the organizations to seek different ways of locating and removing children and it also spurred their resolve. Some organizations acted strictly in accordance with the law; others, exploiting their unofficial status, allowed themselves to act in ways that did not receive the governing institutions' approval. On the other hand, the rivalry led to an immense waste of energy and led to tactics that sometimes included the "theft" of children from each other. However, it is only fair to note that in some instances, the operatives overcame their disagreements and cooperated. After the fact, when the operatives themselves were asked how valuable it might have been to unify operations, they raised arguments both for and against. One may conjecture that mutual recriminations over work methods and claims of lack of cooperation were due mainly to frustration over the inability to remove some children despite all the efforts, and not necessarily due to the sincere belief that a common denominator could be found and joint action taken.

In my research on the activities of the various organizations, I could not determine any absolute disadvantage in the fact that the bodies ran separate operations. Furthermore, disagreements and differences in outlook among the organizations could not be overcome. Had the financial resources that the different organizations allocated to the operations been pooled, or, at least, subjected to the review of an oversight committee, the cause might have been favorably affected. However, such a committee would have been subjected to massive pressure from the Jewish public, as well as to supervision by the security agencies of the Polish government.

As for whether more could have been done, in theory the answer is yes. However, more money, a more efficient organizational apparatus, and a larger pool of workers would have been needed. Even then, one should not overstate

---

9   It is difficult to know how many people in the Central Committee were involved. Most of the actions were undertaken through the head office in Warsaw but the Committee also made use of Jewish committees at the local and district levels. The number of people who served this cause on behalf of the various Zionist youth movements, both at the secretariats and in the "kibbutzim," also cannot be determined.

the case by saying that the results might have been dramatically different. The Jewish organizations did not operate in a void and success did not depend on their efforts alone.

Estimates of the Number of Children Removed by the Organizations

As we have said, the number of children who found shelter with non-Jews after the war cannot be estimated accurately. Nevertheless, various authorities judged it to be about 5,000.[10] Leibel Sarid confirms this: "When I reached Poland [in late 1945] and began to investigate, I was told that the number of children was around 5,000. I do not remember the source of this estimate. In any event, it was the accepted figure at the time."[11] It was this estimate that served as a goal, and objective for the organizations in the field.

The number of children removed from non-Jewish homes was smaller. Many reports about the subject were written at various stages of the operations[12] but they are not in sequence and cannot serve as a basis for a clear numerical progression. Furthermore, some of the organizations did not submit reports at all. The operatives' estimates of the total number of children removed also lack a common denominator. Drucker, for example, believed that all the

---

10 Letter Leibl to Hans Beith, July 18, 1946: "The Koordynacja has already removed about 1,000 children from Poland and another 5,000 have to be [removed]"; see also Warhaftig, *Refugee and Survivor*, p. 427: "The number of children who survived by being placed with Christian families and in convents is estimated at 5,000."

11 *Mission to the Diaspora*, p. 91. However, there were also lower estimates, such as those of the Jewish Brigade members who reached Poland in 1945. See Habas, "Report from Visitors to Poland," p. 2; Yishai report.

12 *Mission to the Diaspora*, pp. 91–92. According to Sarid, 200 children were removed from families and convents in 1946 (238 additional children were claimed from Polish orphanages, bringing the total to 438); see also letter Koordynacja presidium to Bein, director of JDC-Poland, November 15, 1946, JDC, microfilm from Poland. The document, originating in the ŻIH archive in Warsaw, was given to me by the director of the JDC archive in Jerusalem. The Koordynacja reported that 1,000 children, including 250 reclaimed from the custody of non-Jews, had been gathered up; letter Koordynacja presidium to Jewish Agency Rescue Committee, August 10, 1947. The letter states that more than 1,000 children were removed during the entire period of activity. Two hundred and thirty were reclaimed from April 1946 to January 1947 and sixty-three followed in January–August 1947, bringing the total to 293; letter Jewish Agency Rescue Committee to Jewish war appeal, November 24, 1947. The letter states that the Koordynacja reclaimed more than 300 children during its eighteen-month tenure.

organizations together removed 2,000–3,000 children from non-Jewish homes (not counting "repatriation children"),[13] whereas Sarid estimated the total number of children removed from families and convents by all organizations and relatives at no more than 1,000.[14]

The estimates about the number of children removed by each organization also vary. Warhaftig accepted Kahana's total estimate of 2,500 and broke it down into 1,000 removed by the orthodox, 1,000 by the Central Committee, and 500 by the Zionist Koordynacja.[15] Drucker, who carried out the actual removal of children for the Council of Religious Communities, testified that 600–700 children passed through the Council's children's homes[16] (including children of other organizations), but there is no clear information about how many children the other religious groups may have gathered. According to the list of children who stayed at the Central Committee children's homes, the total number of children removed from families throughout Poland was 427[17] while, according to the Koordynacja records, 191 of the 968 children who stayed in its children's homes had been removed up to April 1948.[18] We do not know how many children were removed by the Zionist youth movements. Thus, the overall total seems to have been smaller than 2,500.

The greatest unknown is the number of children who were removed by private individuals: relatives, acquaintances, or strangers who encountered children and helped them to leave the homes of their rescuers. The number seems to have been large. However, even though there are some documented cases in which organizations helped private individuals to claim children, centralized lists of such cases do not exist. If such children were placed in children's homes for an interim period, they appeared on the home's lists. Others, who were taken by family members or sent to relatives outside Poland, cannot be tracked down, except for a few cases that merely indicate that the phenomenon existed. Thus, records that would allow us to draw numerical conclusions simply do not exist.

---

13 Testimony Yeshayahu Drucker, YVA, O.3/3249; Kahana (*After the Deluge*, p. 55) put the figure at about 2,500.
14 *Mission to the Diaspora*, p. 91.
15 Warhaftig, *Refugee and Survivor*, p. 428.
16 Testimony Yeshayahu Drucker, YVA, O.3/3249.
17 Totals compiled by Ita Kowalska, Warsaw, on the basis of the "Blue Catalogue" (records of the Central Committee Education Department), provided to me by Kowalska and in my possession.
18 Koryski, "The Zionist Koordynacja for the Redemption of Jewish Children in Poland," p. 32.

How Many Children Remained in Poland after the Organizations Ceased their Activities?

There is no doubt that Jewish children remained with their non-Jewish rescuers despite all the steps taken by the various Jewish organizations. Not only did some children remain undiscovered, the operatives themselves claimed that as they concluded their activities, they still had lists of children who had not yet been, or could not be, removed.[19] Nevertheless, vague estimates have been suggested, such as "very few"[20] or "many."[21]

It has been argued that, in addition to survivors who remained in Poland under false identities, "one should count several thousand children who were adopted by Polish families or found shelter in convents or residential institutions, whose traces were lost despite the efforts to discover and redeem Jewish children."[22] This estimate is evidently based on remarks by operatives who expressed conjectures about tens of thousands. Kahana, head of the Council of Religious Communities, claimed, for example, that he could state from experience that thousands if not tens of thousands had survived in Christian homes in Poland.[23] In another estimate, he stated that thousands of children had survived in Poland and tens of thousands remained in the eastern areas that had been occupied by the Soviet Union.[24] Sarah Shner-Neshamit, in contrast, responded to Sarid's estimate as follows:

---

19 Interview by author with Yeshayahu Drucker. Drucker says that in his last year of work (1949–1950), after the children's home in Zabrze had been closed, he continued to stay in touch with children whom he had not managed to remove; see also *Mission to the Diaspora*, p. 91. According to Sarid, quite a few children (although he offered no number) remained in Poland; for examples of reasons for leaving children behind, see ibid., pp. 87, 89; see also interview by author with Yehuda Bronstein, 1997; testimony of Leibl Koryski, OHD 15(68).

20 Dekel, *Remnants of the Sword*, p. 697. On p. 13, however, Dekel claims, "There is no doubt that many Jewish children were lost to us; they were unable to discover anything about their origins and we were never able to redeem them."

21 Barlas, *Rescue during the Holocaust*, p. 106. Barlas included children throughout Europe: in Poland, France, Switzerland, Netherlands, and Belgium.

22 Gutman, *Jews in Poland*, p. 13.

23 Kahana, *After the Deluge*, p. 16; letter Jewish Agency Rescue Committee to Jewish war appeal, November 24 1947. The letter, reporting on the activities of the Koordynacja, states, "Hundreds if not thousands [of children] are about to be redeemed from the Gentiles." This information about the potential outcome of the child-removal actions had apparently been forwarded to the Jewish Agency Rescue Committee in the Koordynacja's reports.

24 Kahana, *After the Deluge*, p. 55. Note that Kahana is referring to children who survived in the former Polish territories and not in the Soviet Union proper.

I believe... the number of 2,500–3,000 Jewish children who were saved by Poles and remained in Poland is exaggerated. If it were true — one could call the Polish people the saintliest of the saintly! But we know the bitter truth... The Poles themselves have a strong interest in proving that they saved Jewish children and they publicize every case about which they can obtain information (or misinformation!). Never has such a large number of Jewish child survivors in Poland been reported.[25]

As we have stated, information about the possible whereabouts of Jewish children was received in various ways. Unlike the Koordynacja and Agudath Israel, which initiated searches for children, the Council of Communities and the Central Committee based what they did mainly on information that found its way to them. Even so, they had their hands full. If we bear in mind the efforts that parents made to remove children from ghettos (and considering the many dangers that this involved), the number of survivors who had information about the matter and bothered to hand it over after the war, and the reasons for difficulties in conducting searches in the absence of information, we may only conclude that more survivor children remained in Poland than were removed by the organizations.

In recent years, a widespread phenomenon has developed in Poland of adults who search for information about themselves and their families after their adoptive parents, or someone else, told them that they were Jews who had survived the Holocaust as children.[26] Who can be sure, however, that all

25 Shner-Neshamit, remarks about Sarid's testimony. Shner-Neshamit reports that in the 1960s she received a list, drawn up by the Jewish Agency Rescue Committee in 1947, of 347 children who had not yet been removed. This number and Sarid's estimate vary too widely, she says. Importantly, however, the Rescue Committee's list was of children who were known not to have been removed, not of children about whom nothing was known. I assume that Sarid, in this testimony, estimated the number of children removed at 2,500–3,000 because Shner-Neshamit referred to this number in her testimony. I was unable to locate Sarid's testimony and Shner-Neshamit does not remember how it came into her possession.

26 See testimony Teresa Wiczurk, Elżbieta Ficowska, Jerzy Dolmawski, Konrad Skyczynski, Anna Zlonka, and Jan Czartoryski, in Berman, "Wanda's Lists"; the story of a Polish sculptor, in Anolik, *In the Service of Memory*, p. 71. At her request, Anolik did not cite the sculptor by name because the account of her Jewish identity is known only to her and her husband and has not been divulged to her daughter; story of Lubka Limanowski-Czeslak, ibid., p. 114; final report of the Association for the Restoration of the Lost Remnants of the Holocaust," Warhaftig, *Refugee and Survivor*, p. 454; Szneiderman, "A Jewish Mother Fights for Her Daughter," pp. 71–72; Reicher, "The Priest Burst into Tears"; Klinger, "Jewish Baby;" will from Pola to her daughter, Helena Guzala; Anika's story in Dekel, *Remnants of the Sword*, p. 693; Irena's story in Łuków, "Upside-Down Roots." A list of names of others in Poland who did not discover their Jewishness until adulthood is in my possession.

adult "children" in this situation received this information? I know of people who became aware of their Jewishness after family members in Israel or elsewhere began to search for them again, or who took this initiative themselves after having suspected it or received a hint that their adoptive parents did not deny.[27] Even if there are no more than a few dozen people of this kind, it is evidence not of the extent of the phenomenon of left-behind children, but only of its very existence.[28]

Whose Children Are These?

When asked the loaded question of whether the removal of the children from their rescuers was the right thing to do, bearing in mind the youngsters' "best interests," most operatives and other people involved answered unequivocally: Jewish children should be returned to the Jewish people. The child-removal operations were motivated by a national view of the Jewish people as a corpus in need of protection and assurance of survival,[29] coupled with the terrible feelings that were a result of the annihilation of most of Polish Jewry. Furthermore, the children were perceived as the future of the Jewish people precisely because they were young.[30] These motives and thoughts kindled in the operatives the sense that they were performing a holy mission on behalf

27 Kempner, "Only the Baby Survived"; Miron, "Because of That War," story of Slawayes and Maria in Dekel, *Remnants of the Sword,* pp. 694–695.
28 In August 2000, Henryk (who uses the surname of the Polish family that adopted him from a Polish orphanage after the war) asked me to try to track down relatives in Israel. Henryk (probably b. late 1937) was able to give me only a few details about his family. In a previous search that he had conducted in the Jewish archives in Warsaw, he had found nothing. In early September, I located a cousin of his father who was living in Israel and the two established contact. Shortly afterwards, I located another relative. This case shows that even if surviving children knew they were Jewish, they lacked the tools with which to conduct a search (or did not believe that they could find anything) and, therefore, continued to live their adult lives in Poland (with some disquiet in a corner of their heart). Presumably Henryk is not the only example.
29 For a discussion, see Michman, *Holocaust Historiography: A Jewish Perspective,* pp. 396–397.
30 Testimony Leibl Koryski, OHD 15(68); Dekel, *Remnants of the Sword,* p. 13. Dekel quoted remarks at a Bricha conference in March 1946; Litvak, "JDC's Contribution," p. 367; Rubinstein, "Reckoning of an Era," p. 185; Shner-Neshamit, *I Did Not Come to Rest,* p. 204; letter Koordynacja presidium to Jewish Agency Rescue Committee, August 10, 1947; "All the Children Must Be Repatriated," *Farn Yiddishn Kind,* GFHA, file 798; Session 21, XXII Zionist Congress, p. 414.

of both the Jewish people and the parents who had perished — the honoring of a last will and testament as it were.[31]

The operatives' work was also strongly influenced by the fact that most of them were themselves Holocaust survivors and had suffered desperately from the way the Poles had treated them during the war. Even though they greatly appreciated the humaneness of rescuers who had incurred personal risk to save Jewish children, they regarded them as exceptional individuals in a society whose culture was underlined by such strong antisemitic feelings that it could not possibly assure the children of a satisfactory future. Accordingly, they viewed the removal of the children not only as a national imperative but also as a personal and human matter rooted in their own harsh life experience. Moreover, they found unendurable the possibility that Jewish children who would remain in non-Jewish homes might themselves become antisemites.[32] For these reasons, the operatives saw no contradiction between the concept of "the best interest of the child" and the Jewish people's right to reclaim Jewish children. They believed that by returning the youngsters to the bosom of their people they were ultimately serving their best interests. Zionists and non-Zionists alike shared this view and categorically rejected the notion, asserted by Jews who professed a universalist outlook, that it was in the children's best interest to leave them with their rescuers.[33]

31 It was in Poland of all places that a body such as the Central Jewish Committee was allowed to place Jewish children in Jewish institutions. This was due to the sensitivity of the authorities to prying eyes in Western countries about the treatment of the Jewish survivors, coupled with the authorities' preoccupation with their own problems. This was not the case in Belgium (see Brachfeld, *A Gift of Life,* p. 123) and the Netherlands (see Michman, "The Problem of Jewish War Orphans in the Netherlands," pp. 408–412).

32 Shner-Neshamit, *I Did Not Come to Rest,* p. 204. Relating to the concern that the children would grow up to be antisemitic, Shner-Neshamit added, "After all, we endured no little suffering in our lengthy history from apostate Jews of various kinds"; interview by author with Yehuda Bronstein, 1997. Bronstein claimed that he had gone into the matter with no doubts whatsoever: "I had lost my whole family and it was important for me to reclaim every child possible"; testimony Devora Zilber, OHD, 27(68); testimony Sarah Lederman, OHD 50(68); Kahana, *After the Deluge,* p. 49. Kahana claimed that the imperative of redeeming the children was one of the most important actions taken at the time, especially since there were so painfully few Jews in Poland, and any Jewish child who was uprooted from the Jewish people was likely to assimilate into Polish society and abandon his or her Jewish faith; Rubinstein, "Reckoning of an Era," p. 185. Rubinstein complained about rescuers "who managed to instill in the children's hearts hatred of the Jewish people and of everything that should be holy and close to a Jewish child's heart."

33 See discussion of the matter in Chapter 3, the section titled "Disagreements and Rivalries among the Organizations."

Despite the resolve that this outlook generated, it is noteworthy that doubts and heretical reflections occasionally surfaced in the course of the operations, especially when the activists saw the warm and healthy relations between rescuers and children and observed the distress of all the sides in parting. However, these doubts never evolved into crises that challenged their basic outlook.[34]

---

34 Berman, "Wanda's Lists." Drucker reported having found it difficult to observe the agony of adoptive parents who loved "their" children as he transformed the youngsters into "collective property;" see also testimony Yeshayahu Drucker, OHD 28(68). After the fact, Drucker asked, "If they hadn't removed the children, how many souls would have been lost to the Jewish people, 2,500? It might have been better; a large proportion of [the children] went through a major crisis." As the operations were taking place, however, Drucker served the Council of Religious Communities indefatigably, as a "one-man factory"; see also testimony Leibl Koryski, OHD 15(68); testimony Devora Zilber, OHD, 27(68). Marysia says that the first time she removed a girl (from a locality near Lublin) she banished all doubts from her mind: "If I'm going to be so sentimental, I won't be removing anyone. It'll be this way with all of them. Every child will want to stay where he is. He doesn't know me and he won't want to go with someone he doesn't know. It's impossible." Later in her testimony, Zilber discloses the fatigue that she suffered afterwards due to the stress that her work had caused. She reports having thoughts about stopping but resumed her travels after a few days of rest: "I couldn't accept the thought of leaving the children without assistance"; Sarid, for example (*Mission to the Diaspora*, p. 88), admits having entertained regrets in cases where the children had been treated well. However, beset by the feeling that removing the child was his or her parents' wish, and concern that the child would be brought up among murderers of Jews, he flagellated himself for those "moments of weakness." Sarid added, "A person's biological relationship with the Jewish people needs no apology"; see also Shner-Neshamit, *I Did Not Come to Rest*, p. 204; idem, "Characteristics of the Spiritual Image of Redeemed Jews," pp. 80–82. Shner-Neshamit recalls having wrestled prodigiously with the question of the operatives' right to remove children from loving homes and place them in institutions, "where they will yearn for a home of their own and a mother's love. I believed we were causing the children a great injustice because it creates a painful human problem that dwarfs the national or religious rationales. After all, we're only punishing the child, not redeeming him. And he's young and defenseless." However, she went on to claim, "As time passed, I freed myself of the pangs of conscience over the removal of children from their adoptive [families'] homes." Two events led to her change of heart: the Kielce pogrom, which made her doubt the possibility of assuring that the children would not be raised as antisemites and themselves take part in future pogroms against Jews; and the case of a girl from Kraków, years later, in which a Polish mother scolded the girl whom she had adopted and raised, telling her that her misbehavior originated in her being Jewish (in response, the girl leaped out of the apartment window and was injured); see also Warhaftig, *Refugee and Survivor*, pp. 425–426. Warhaftig responded to operatives' testimonies about their dilemmas by criticizing them, accusing the hesitant of a lack of understanding of the historical perspective. They did not realize, he said, that acquiescence in leaving children with their rescuers amounted to surrendering to Hitler's plan to annihilate the Jewish people. He added, "Sometimes they were misled into believing that what a child wanted was best for him; but a child's desires are susceptible to influence, to rapid changes."

If there was near-unanimity about the Jewish people's right to the children, there were serious ideological disagreements about the branch of Judaism to which the children should be returned. The rivalry among the entities involved, which kept them from uniting around the common goal, focused among other things on the kind of education that the children would receive[35] and where they would live in the future. Furthermore, the issue of the children was part of the broader web of post-Holocaust rehabilitation, and at the time views were divided about the ways and means of rehabilitating and assuring the convalescence of the Jewish people. By implication, the struggle over the children became part of the philosophical struggle for primacy.

Due to this rivalry, the remarks of some of those involved may be construed as slights against, if not dismissal of, the importance of the actions of the other bodies and later claims about the degree of success of one entity relative to that of another.[36] This was not always done systematically and there are differences among testimonies that the same people gave at different times. Even if this behavior sometimes seems offensive, it does not diminish the investment of effort that all protagonists made at the time.[37]

---

35 The question of education persisted after the end of the war. Zvi Zameret, *The Melting-Pot Days: The Frumkin Commission on the Education of Immigrant Children (1950)* (Ben-Gurion Heritage Center, Sde Boker, 1993, Hebrew), pp. 8–18.

36 Warhaftig, *Refugee and Survivor*, p. 430. Warhaftig quoted Drucker as having claimed, "The orthodox were more successful in redeeming children because they demonstrated greater devotion to the job," thus countering Moshe Yishai, the Jewish Agency emissary, who said that the orthodox had managed to remove more children because they had paid more (ibid., p. 429).

37 Sarid ("Initial Deployment," p. 315) inveighed against the Central Committee for "leaving thousands of Jewish children in the hands of Poles and Ukrainians and abandoning them, practically speaking, to spiritual annihilation... Only an emissary from the Yishuv who lives a fully Jewish life, an outgrowth of organic unity, can fathom this divisive phenomenon"; Sarid (*Ruin and Deliverance*, pp. 402–420) describes the Koordynacja's actions as unique and regards them as a direct outgrowth of the actions that partisans and demobilized soldiers undertook on behalf of children. Elaborating on these remarks, Sarid added, "It is important to emphasize this fact in order to refute the commonly expressed mistake that the redemption actions began only with the establishment of the Koordynacja. The redemption of children was started by activists in the movements before the emissaries arrived." Sarid does not mention in this context any other body that dealt with the issue, as if only the movements and the Koordynacja were involved; Fridenson and Kranzler do the same (*Heroine of Rescue*, p. 163) in describing the motives of Sternbuch, delegate of the Rescue Committee of the Orthodox Rabbis in the USA, in going to Poland and working for the removal of children. They stated that no one else was taking action in the matter — as if nothing had been done before she arrived in 1946 and while her actions were under way; Rubinstein ("Reckoning of an Era," p. 185) describes the doggedness of the Mizrachi and Torah va'Avoda operatives without mentioning other organizations, creating the impres-

In contrast to some views expressed today,[38] I found in my research that not only the Zionist organizations carried the stigma of the "war for the children" and the interpretation of how and where they should be raised. All the organizations that were active in Poland, without exception, represented ideologies that dictated their actions in all areas of life to an exaggerated degree; their interpretation of the most appropriate approach to the children

sion that only the Mizrachi movement was doing anything; Warhaftig (*Refugee and Survivor*, pp. 429–430) claims that most of the actions were undertaken by the Koordynacja, the Council of Religious Communities, the Mizrachi movement, and Hapoel Hamizrachi. He does mention Lederman (Agudath Israel) and notes that she removed several dozen children, but he totally overlooked the youth movements. As for the Central Committee, Warhaftig alleges that it was totally uninvolved in removing children. As for the fact that more children stayed in the Committee's children's homes than anywhere else, he explains that the local Jewish committees received children who had been delivered at the initiative of non-Jewish families; Lederman's testimony mentions no other body except for "the Communists" (i.e., the Central Committee) in the context of abducting children from their children's homes; in 1993, I interviewed Yosef Haezrahi-Bürger, one of the Koordynacja removal operatives. The talk centered on the Koordynacja's activities. When I asked him what the Central Committee had been doing, Bürger claimed vehemently that the Central Committee had not removed any children at all. I dared to tell him that I had documents proving the opposite — even before the Koordynacja had come into being. Enraged, he called my research dangerous because it distorted reality, argued that even if such documents existed all the archival material must have been "planted" (i.e. false) — and asked me to leave his house. Before I left, Bürger, in my presence, phoned Menahem Kunda (today a lawyer), who had represented the Ichud on the Koordynacja secretariat and was one of the three members of the Koordynacja presidium, and complained about me. Afterwards, I had a talk with Kunda and told him about the documentation in the archive in Warsaw. He said it was definitely possible that the activists of the Koordynacja were unaware of the nature of the Central Committee's activities. Clearly, these one-sided testimonies fool anyone who does not investigate the matter in depth. For example, Litvak ("JDC's Contribution," p. 352), relating to the question of the Jewish children, contrasts the activism of the youth movements and the Koordynacja with the passivity of the non-Zionist organizations and the Central Committee, leaving unanswered the question of whether his definition of "non-Zionists" includes Agudath Israel. What about the Mizrachi activists, who did not participate in the Koordynacja? Exactly how passive was the Central Committee? Did Litvak make sure that the information he had received from Zionist activists was true and accurate?

38 For example, Grodzinski, *In the Shadow of the Holocaust*, pp. 1–113. For an analysis of the issue, see Dan Michman, "'Desroyers of Zionism,'" the Principles of the 'Post-Zionist' Outlook in Contemporary Israeli Society," in Dan Michman (ed. and foreword), *'Post-Zionism' and the Holocaust: the Israeli Public Polemic on "Post-Zionism" in 1993–1996 and Where the Holocaust Fits into it — a Reader* (Ramat Gan: Bar-Ilan University, 1997, Hebrew), p. 15; I do not belittle the feelings of people who believe they have been harmed by this or that ideological decision; historical justice demands that they be given a forum. For a balanced historical perspective, however, the broader context and the prevailing *Zeitgeist* of the time should be kept in view: not everything was done in an arbitrary and obtuse manner.

was no exception. Obviously the choice of remaining in Europe would have created many problems that were not the case in Palestine, and subsequently in the State of Israel, as the unfolding of events in the first decades after 1945 shows. Those who favored aliya were not "Zionists" in today's sense; they included some members of Agudath Israel, who were ideologically anti-Zionist.[39]

Child-Removal as Part of the Effort to Revive the Jewish People

The elation that erupted with the end of the war, especially among the survivors but also among Jews the world over, was accompanied by the deep shock of the horrendous loss. The agony was both personal and public, but since there were Jews who had survived the war, the need to support and care for them, both morally and materially, surfaced from the very beginning. Poland was the main focus of this multifaceted rehabilitation effort. On the eve of the war, Polish Jewry, with its more than three million persons, was a major center of Jewish culture for the entire Jewish world. After the war, only about one percent of this population remained. Despite the immense blow, Poland still had a substantial number of Jewish citizens. However, the socio-political situation in Poland at that time severely hindered the ability of the survivors to rehabilitate themselves and handicapped the relief actions that were taken.

Within the range of problems current at the time, the cause of the Jewish child-survivors received great attention. Most of the children were completely unable to help themselves, and this motivated everyone who was dealing with the issue. For them it was a proactive choice, and its importance to the survivors themselves can be understood by the remarks of Eliezer Ludowski, a leader of the Jewish partisans in the forests of Wolhynia. In March 1944, at the first meeting of Jewish partisans in Równe after the town was liberated, Ludowski told his comrades, "I want us to decide today that we are going to operate among the Jews... Let's begin acting as Jews among survivors who are in hiding with Gentiles. As for the children, as Jews first of all, they'll have an address to turn to for assistance."[40]

---

39 Interview by author with Jechiel Granatstein, 1996. Granatstein, secretary of Agudath Israel in Poland after the war, saw no point in exchanging one exile for another and believed that the children should be brought to Israel.

40 Sarid, *In the Test of Song and Deliverance*, p. 15.

The activists who searched for Jewish children considered it vital to try to reclaim as many youngsters as possible. The establishment of a high number of reclaimed children as an indication of success was understandable at the time. In retrospect, however, the importance of these actions for Jewish revival seems to have centered not only on the quantitative aspect but on two other facets: moral values and morale. From the standpoint of moral values, the actions taken were compatible with the target of assuring collective Jewish continuity. Although opinions concerning the children's future were diverse, most operatives felt that the regeneration of the Jewish people called for an effort to track down each and every child. The object of paramount importance was not the numerical total, but rather each individual, who added one more brick to the Jewish edifice and one more link in the collective endeavor. The documentation of the operatives and the organizations that supported them abounds with expressions of this feeling.

The actions were no less important for Jewish morale. The very survival of Jewish children against all odds was considered a "victory over Hitler." A child survivor was like a ray of light that pierced the darkness, bolstering self-confidence and showing that the Nazi decrees could be defeated.

One may get an idea of the relationship between these two senses from remarks made at the first postwar Zionist Congress (late 1946) with reference to a photo album about child survivors in Poland that was presented to the president of the Congress: "... This is indeed a guarantee that the attempt to make Europe *Judenrein* was in vain. [It shows that] there is a generation to be saved and this generation, the successor generation, will be among the creators of our people's future."[41]

The very fact that the issue inspired such rhetoric, however, makes us ask yet again why the actions undertaken by the Jewish organizations were not more united. If we examine this question only from the narrow perspective of the issue of the Jewish children, which was close to the heart of Jews everywhere and elicited warm emotions, then the inability to work together evokes bewilderment and the feeling that those involved must have been hard-hearted. But if we look at the issue through a wider prism, we realize that it was just one component in the debate over the overall concept of the Jewish people, the question of its destiny, and the details that made up the concept. These questions have always been a source of friction among Jews of different convictions, and so they were to an even greater extent at this

---

41 Session 21, Remarks by the Chair, Yehudit Epstein, Twenty-Second Zionist Congress, p. 414.

critical moment in Jewish existence. The cause of the Jewish children did not lead to a modification of convictions, just as other issues at the time failed to overcome disagreements.

One may also gauge the perceived importance of removing Jewish children from the homes of rescuers and returning them to their Jewish identity by considering the terminology that was used at the time. Some of those involved termed the removal of children as "rescue." It was not enough for children to have survived the inferno, although this alone was seen as a victory over the Nazi decrees. In most cases, it was also considered essential to remove them from their "goyish" habitat and integrate them into the Jewish community, in whatever version it might be. Some of the bodies that operated in Poland referred to the removal operations as *pidyon*; others termed them *geula*. (Both are translated into English as "redemption" although each has a slightly different connotation in Hebrew.) It was not by chance that they invoked these concepts, since the terminology expressed a clear ideology.

The immediate postwar era was marked by rapidly escalating needs: of the destitute survivors who were returning to their previous home, of those still in the DP camps in Europe, of groups of refugees who had reached different countries and needed aid from local communities, and of the Yishuv in Palestine, which was fighting for Israeli independence.[42] Those who found themselves in any of these situations understood their own needs. The total resources available, however, were limited and every decision by a funding body to support one of the many causes was tantamount to depriving others of that support. Even though the child-redemption activists were scathingly critical of the institutions, the documentation shows that, in fact, their cause commanded a great deal of attention and held a special position in the eyes of the Jewish institutions both in Palestine and around the globe. The issue was widely discussed, its importance emphasized in numerous meetings, and it was funded from a large number of sources, even if ultimately the demands made at the field level were difficult to meet.

---

42 In regard to the World Jewish Congress' support of Palestine as the most appropriate setting for the Jewish resurgence, see Frimerman, "Activities of the World Jewish Congress in 1938–1946," p. 154.

The Human Aspect: the Rescuers and the Rescued

As we have seen, rescuers and children responded to the removal operations in different ways. It is therefore, important to recount some of the personal stories so that the human element can be revealed; dispassionate analysis at the institutional or ideological level is not enough. The children had experienced a war that had torn them from their families and they had endured great difficulties in adjusting to the non-Jewish society that had given them shelter. Those who had to conceal their identities and live under pseudonyms, and those who worked hard to remain with their new families, were given refuge, protection, and food. For those who had found warm homes and loving families, the privilege was all the greater. Children in both categories acquired a sense of belonging and eventually found their place in their new surroundings. Non-Jews who had endangered themselves by taking in Jewish children now regarded these youngsters as part of their family, even if they were not always aware of it. In most cases, it was not easy to sever the knot, and in those cases where the two sides had developed loving relationships, it seemed altogether impossible. The surrendering of children to the Jewish organizations was a traumatic experience for children and rescuers alike, and often no less for the removal operatives.

Obviously one should not generalize by saying that everyone who had concealed a Jewish child found it difficult to return him or her to the Jews at the end of the war. There were plenty of rescuers who rejoiced at the opportunity to receive material aid from the Jewish organizations in return for giving up the youngsters. The children themselves, however, found the parting difficult unless the initiative for leaving was theirs to begin with. It was their second parting within a relatively short period of time, and naturally it frightened them. When the relationship between rescuers and rescued had been deep and significant, both sides struggled to live with the experience of separation. The existential and ideological significance of returning children to the Jewish people was not relevant at the individual level and was of no help in calming stormy emotions.

More than sixty years have passed since these events took place. The children grew up and themselves became parents; most of the rescuers have passed away. During the intervening decades, all involved carried with them the emotional burden of that period and the act of concealment; each dealt with it in their own way and in accordance with the circumstances of his or her life. Some of the children remembered faces, events, feelings, and experiences, whereas for others that era was tantamount to near-oblivion, as though wishing to leave room only for whatever occurred from then on. In recent years, however,[43] the whole episode has experienced an awakening; we witness the phenomenon of rescuers searching for the children whom they saved[44] and the "children" seeking out their rescuers,[45] as well as any shred of information about their biological families so as to discover roots and identity, to attain some sort of closure and to illuminate fragments of memory.[46] Furthermore, the survivors seem to be more appreciative of the actions of the rescuers now that they can see them through adult eyes and from a distance of decades. Although the passage of time made the search more difficult, those who had the good fortune of finding what they had sought feel that the effort was worth it.

43 Why now, of all times? First, relations between Israel and Poland allow survivors in Israel to visit Poland and communicate more easily. Second, not only the "children" have grown up but so have *their* children. Thus, they are more at leisure to deal with their past, more confident in coping with it, and more interested in filling in missing links in their personal stories.

44 Letter Maria Madej, Poland, October 7, 1995; letter A. Walaczynska, Poland, March 1995; letter Roma Jarska, Poland, April 20, 1995; letter Pawel Cypryansky, Poland, August 5, 1995; file of documents in the matter of S.K., transferred to the ŻIH Archives in Warsaw in 1999 by Stanisława Rostropowicz, daughter of Józef and Natalia. An extract of the contents of the file was forwarded to me so that I could track down the "girl." The woman was located in the United States and established contact with the rescuer's children.

45 Interview by author with Zvi Ksiazenicki-Harel, August 1998; interview by author with Hanita Leshem, May 1996; interview by author with Erella Hilferding-Goldschmidt, August 1993; letter Yaron Eduardo Gruder, February 24, 1995; interview by author with Mira Bramm-Ehrlich, August 1994; Argaman-Barnea, "Girl of War"; interview by author with Henia-Tamar Wiszniewska-Mukhtar, May 1995; conversation by author with Sabina Kagan-Heller, July 2000.

46 Letter Bugomila Maria Kordzikowska, April 24, 1995; letter Bozena Szniewska, Poland, April 1995; letter Maria Magdalena Kruczalowa, Poland, April 20, 1995; Reicher, "The Priest Burst into Tears"; Meron, "Because of That War;" Klinger, "Jewish Baby"; documents received by the author from Erella Hilferding-Goldschmidt, Shadmot Devora, originating with the ŻIH. Erella located the two families that had concealed her and was given a passport that her mother had left with one of them. Although the name was false, the photograph was of her. After the photograph was shown on Polish television, childhood friends of her mother's who had copies of the same picture came forward and gave her details about it. Erella's friend, Eva, located Erella's paternal aunt in South America; interview by author with Pnina Modlen, August 1996. When asked what had prompted her to conduct her searches, Pnina explained that she could not live with her ignorance but added that as she grew up, troubling questions about her family's genetics had floated to the surface. Erella and Pnina founded families; both died recently.

The Child-Removal Issue in its Broader Context

This study concerns itself only with the removal of Jewish children from the homes of non-Jews in Poland, for reasons discussed in the Introduction. Notably, however, the problems we have discussed here are not unique to Poland; similar problems occurred in Belgium, the Netherlands, and France.[47] Of course, Poland was unique in several ways, such as the proportion of Jews in the general population on the eve of the war; the attitude of the local population towards the Jews; the brutal laws and penalties that the Nazis invoked to deter anyone from helping Jews; and, finally, the postwar political and social situation. But with regard to the removal of children from non-Jewish rescuers we see that despite the differences, the activists in the liberal countries of western Europe faced essentially the same difficulties.

The rehabilitation of these children — the few survivors of a human collective entity that had been doomed to extinction — was, to the best of our knowledge, unique in human history. The fact that from the moment of liberation, while the battles still raged, there were organized initiatives to locate and remove Jewish children wherever they could be found, and not only to track down those who had relatives, attests to a special collective consciousness that hallmarks the Jewish people. Discord about the methods of action cannot diminish the value of the initiatives themselves and of the consciousness of belonging to that collective.

The appreciable aid that Jewish organizations outside of Poland provided proves that the international relief and assistance systems developed by the

---

47 Brachfeld, *A Gift of Life,* pp. 66–122; idem, *Children of the Living,* pp. 141–146; Michman, "The Problem of Jewish War Orphans in the Netherlands," pp. 399–418; Poznanski, *To Be a Jew in France,* pp. 600–602; precisely because various entities and organizations harshly criticized the Central Jewish Committee in Poland, as though the staff of this body preferred to leave Jewish children in the homes of non-Jews, we present here an example of a similar problem in France: the newspaper *Libération* (December 1944) published an article by the Jewish-French journalist Alex Danan that contained the following exhortation to Jewish parents who had survived the war: "You who still live, if you still exist somewhere, in a concentration camp in Poland or Czechoslovakia, if you love your children, let them enjoy life where they are; otherwise they will resent you for having come back... The children no longer want to know about their history. If you haven't died yet, your children died for you." The article is quoted in Warhaftig, *Refugee and Survivor,* p. 425. I know of no article as vehement that was published in a general-circulation newspaper in Poland. Even if these or similar views were expressed, they were not widely publicized and the main debate took place among Jews. These views, prevalent mostly among some Jewish socialists and communists, were also expressed in Belgium (see Brachfeld, *A Gift of Life,* p. 123) and the Netherlands (see Michman, "Jewish War Orphans," pp. 409–410).

Jews in the modern era[48] served as a safety net that, however problematic, was able to provide almost immediate help. That these organizations were prepared to mobilize on behalf of child-removal initiatives in several European countries, and sometimes even to change their methods as time progressed in order to adjust to new situations, demonstrates — as the rabbinical saying has it — that "no generation of Jews, even this one, is orphaned."

In the attempt to reconstruct the issues and problems confronting me in this study, I found that the range of events relating to the Jewish children from the beginning of the war to the end of the formal search operations for them in the late 1940s — a period of about ten years — was strewn with human anguish. It suffices to mention just some of these situations: the parents' desperate clinging to their children; the fear that evil would befall them and the indecision about whether to surrender them to Gentiles; the desperate search for Polish people who would be prepared to receive the youngsters and the hope that the choice would not prove to be mistaken; sending the children into the unknown; the fear that the likelihood of meeting again was tantamount to zero and the self-restraint that parents had to employ in order to stifle their fear at the moment of parting; the effort that the children had to make in order to integrate into their new homes; and the hardships that other children had to endure to survive while wandering and searching for refuge, with no respite in their yearnings for a parent's caress; the rescuers' everyday struggle to conceal the children's origin both from their own people and from the Germans, in the knowledge of how easily the rescuers could be denounced.

The liberation itself brought on new dilemmas: the rescuers' uncertainty about whether to surrender a child who had been a secret for so long; the conviction that guided the activists as they came to gather the children on behalf of the Jewish people; the heartache that beset the operatives as they witnessed the rescuers' and the children's parting agonies; the need to decide what was in the "best interests of the child;" and the children's struggle to shed the identity, religion, and culture of one society and to re-acclimatize themselves to another — that of their parents.

All this left behind divided hearts.

---

48 See Michman, *Holocaust Historiography*, pp. 58–88.

None of the dilemmas was simple; the choice of one path over the other was almost insurmountable. Nevertheless, the decisions that were taken seemed right at the time they were taken. The decades that have elapsed since then have not blunted the intensity of the emotions that are aroused by personal and public events. More than half a century after the end of the war and the Holocaust, the aftermath of these dilemmas still occupy us.

*   *   *

> *In the 1980s, my mother, Aliza Kuperman-Nachmani, visited Poland several times to try to locate twins who, she was told, had been born to her sister during the war and had been handed over to non-Jews. The male twin, she discovered, had almost certainly died during the war, but his sister had survived and was evidently living in a village not far from the town where they had been born. Aliza ran into a wall of silence and could learn no more. When asked why she still considered it important to find the girl at the expense of her routine life and that of her family, Aliza answered, "It's important for me that she should know what her mother sacrificed in order to save her."[49] The story remains gripping; time does not heal.*

49 Interview by author with Aliza Kuperman-Nachmani, June 1986. The family's home town is Sobienie-Jeziory, Garwolin District. After the twins were handed over, their mother (Kuperman-Nachmani's sister) and her oldest son, then aged thirteen, went into hiding in an attic with the assistance of an acquaintance. After the Aktzion in Sobienie-Jeziory, in September 1942, the hideout was denounced to local Gestapo operatives and its occupants were removed and shot in the town center. Many others were motivated by the need to continue searching for children who had been handed over by family members. In the aftermath of a television program (Vered Berman, director and producer, "Lost Identity: The True Story," Israel Television, Channel 1, April 17, 2000), in which I assisted with preparatory research and the filmed journey that followed the findings, many people contacted me and asked for assistance in searching for children who had been surrendered or left behind in various locations in Poland during the war. Interestingly enough, some of the inquirers were the offspring of parents who had remarried after the war and had told their children, the products of their second marriages, about having handed over children from their first marriages. The motivation to search originated with the children in Israel and represented the honoring of a final testament so to speak. See also Kempner, "Only the Baby Survived."

APPENDICES

The Value of the Zloty

The Polish economy was in dire straits after the war. Vital commodities were scarce and the new regime struggled to establish national-level systems of production, supply and marketing. When banking services resumed in late 1945, the official dollar exchange rate was set at twelve zlotys to the dollar. The black-market rate was much higher and in 1946, under its pressure, the official rate was increased to 100 zlotys to the dollar.[1]

The assistance of the Joint Distribution Committee to the survivors was initially tendered almost exclusively in goods. When banking services resumed, JDC faced a dilemma in regard to transferring dollars to Poland. If JDC were to transfer dollars at the official rate, it would have had to convert them via the Polish state treasury resulting in limited gains for the needy Jews for whom they were donated.[2] After Dr. Josef Schwartz, director of JDC-Europe, met with officials at the Polish Ministry of Finance, the government granted JDC a special exchange rate (unlike anything received by other institutions): every dollar brought into Poland by JDC would be exchanged for 100 zlotys.[3] In June 1946, the "JDC rate" was increased to 140 zlotys, and later on, increased again to 170.[4] Only in January 1948 did the Polish Finance Ministry establish a standard rate of 400 zlotys for dollars that were brought in for welfare purposes or as gifts.[5]

Although throughout the early post-war years, the black-market dollar commanded much more than the official rate, the actual rate is difficult to estimate with precision and, to the best of my knowledge, has not been researched thus far. The American currency fluctuated on the free market with the rise and fall of supply and demand, making the exchange rate fluid.

---

1 Bauer, *Out of the Ashes*, pp. 77, 118.
2 Litvak, "JDC's Contribution," p. 340.
3 Ibid., p. 342; Bauer, *Out of the Ashes*, p. 118.
4 Bauer, *Out of the Ashes*, p. 118.
5 Litvak, "JDC's Contribution," p. 342.

Goldberg (the Koordynacja activist, who engaged in fundraising) described the situation tellingly: "It depended on the dollar exchange rate [at the time] and where the exchange takes place."[6] Since my sources of information are limited and cannot provide accurate information, I will use them only to give an indication of the gap between the official and the free-market rates. Thus, from summer 1945 to spring 1946, the unofficial rate climbed from 250 zlotys to the dollar[7] to 300,[8] 400,[9] and even 500.[10] The rate stood at 870 zlotys in August 1947 [11] but receded to 800 in October.[12] In view of the large differences between the official and the black-market rates, obviously the black market flourished.

A summarizing report on the Koordynacja's income and expenditures (evidently from late 1947) seems to indicate that the Koordynacja officials took money from foreign sources to the free market in order to convert it to their best advantage. The revenue side of the report shows a value of 620 zlotys to the dollar (this apparently being the average exchange rate in these conversions). In contrast, a report on the sum remaining in the Koordynacja exchequer after expenses shows a rate of 280 zlotys to the dollar.[13] (This is because the Koordynacja people could not know what the dollar exchange rate would be at the time of conversion.)

The ultimate measure of citizens' income is its purchasing power. Thus, for example, the monthly salary of a cooperative employee in 1947 ranged from 4,300 to 11,900 zlotys. A free-market price list from May 1947 shows that a one kilogram loaf of bread cost 100 zlotys, a kilogram of flour 120, a kilogram of soap 600, and a kilogram of beef 320.[14] In view of retail prices and delivery problems, it was hardly possible to survive without shopping in the black market.

6   Margoshes, "How to Redeem Jewish Children in Poland."
7   Testimony Devorah Zilber, OHD, 27(68).
8   Bauer, *Out of the Ashes,* p. 118.
9   Litvak, "JDC's Contribution," p. 340; Yishai, *In the Shadow of the Holocaust,* p. 66.
10 Margoshes, "How to Redeem Jewish Children in Poland."
11 Koordynacja income report, August 1947, CZA, S26/1424.
12 Drucker report on operations of the Council of Religious Communities, September 22, 1947, ibid.
13 Koordynacja report for October, evidently 1947, ibid.
14 Litvak, "JDC's Contribution," p. 357.

APPENDIX 2

The Personal and Human Aspects

The research material available to me was copious and diverse. It was also unique in that every document encapsulated a human life at a time when life was so valuable as to be almost unattainable. There follows a selection of documents that will give the reader some idea of my research sources as seen from various aspects. They serve to give a voice, as it were, to the people with whom the research work deals.

Sala Działoszyńska Surrenders Custody of her Daughter[1]

In January 1943, Sala Działoszyńska surrendered custody of her only daughter, Janina-Teresa, to a Polish couple, the Wittkens. The terms of the relinquishment were finalized orally four days later, and the following document was drawn up and signed in April. Even though it is phrased like an official contract, one can sense between its lines the horrors of the time, the despair, the concern for the girl, and the mother's acceptance of the likely outcome: that she would never be able to recover her daughter or bring her back to Judaism — all of this for the sole purpose of enabling her to survive. Presumably the document was written because the rescuers found the mother's oral consent insufficient and demanded an agreement signed in the presence of witnesses (!), even though sharing the secret with them might endanger the girl and themselves. The mother, for her part, must have had a great deal of composure and resolve to write what she called "my last request."

---

1   YVA, M.49/2938 (original in ŻIH).

My last request

I the undersigned, Sala Działoszyńska, was born in Kalisz on May 15, 1916. [I am] the daughter of Ick-Majer and Fajga née Zyngier, who married Działoszyński. In full command of my faculties, of sound mind, and in the presence of the witnesses Jan Ruciński and Wiktor Lukas, I hereby express my last request.

1. Destitute and homeless due to the occupation, I entered the ghetto of my own volition with no hope of surviving and for the purpose of rescuing my only daughter, Janina-Teresa, who was born of my marriage to Eljasz Librach, son of Majer and Esther Bykowski. The wedding took place in Kalisz on November 20, 1938, and was certified by a certificate from the Municipality of Kalisz. On January 20, 1943, I surrendered my daughter to the couple Bronisław and Lucyna Wittken of Lukasów, who live in Częstochowa, at 228 Narutowicza Street, and to them only, to their custody and not to be reclaimed, and I confirm that they will give her their family name and convert her to Christianity. Concluded on January 24, [1943] and today I confirm the surrender [of my daughter] in writing.

2. As the heir to a property in Kalisz at 7 Majakowski Street, recorded as No. 684 in the Land Registry, and to the plot and a house that remained there after the tragic death of my parents, Ick-Majer and Fajga née Zyngier, who married Działoszyński, I state today before the Wittkens that if I should die I waive, from this day to some unforeseen date, all my rights to the property noted herewith in favor of Messrs. Wittken and to their sole benefit. I am convinced that no harm will befall my daughter.

3. The couple Bronisław and Lucyna [Wittken] accept this document that I have written today and undertake to use this property for the education and schooling of the girl to whom I gave birth and whom they are adopting, Janina-Teresa.

4. This document, which fully corresponds to my wishes, was signed today in the presence of witnesses and by the members of the Wittken family.

Sala Działoszyńska-Librach
Częstochowa, April 12, 1943
Bronisław Wittken, Lucyna Wittken, and witnesses: Wiktor Lukas,
Jan Rucyński

Letter from a Jewish Mother to her Daughter[2]

The following letter was written by a Jewish mother to her daughter, who was staying with her rescuers, on the eve of the family's deportation to an "unknown destination." The letter was deposited with the rescuers so that they could give it to the girl when she grew up. The mother was torn between her wish to see her daughter again and the knowledge that such an encounter might endanger her by leading to her discovery. In her remarks, the mother addresses her daughter in two voices: one from the heart and one from the mind. Her parting comments bind the two together.

July 7, 1944

My dear and very beloved daughter!

When I gave birth to you, my beloved one, I did not think that I would be writing you a letter six and a half years later with contents such as these. The last time I saw you, on December 13, 1943, it was your sixth birthday. I entertained the delusion that I would see you yet again before our trip, but now I know otherwise. Father, Paula, and I are going with fifty-one other families to an unknown destination. I don't know, my dear daughter, whether I will see you again. I am taking your image with me from home, I am taking your precious chirp, the innocent scent of your little body, the sound of your innocent breathing, your laughter, and your crying. I am taking with me your terrible fear, which your mother's heart was unable to soothe. I am taking with me the memory of my last sight of you on December 13, 1943, the grown-up look in your eyes, the taste of your childish kisses, and the embraces of your tiny hands, my tiny, tiny one. So, I am taking all these things with me for the trip. May it be that [Divine] Providence will let me survive this horror and reclaim you, my treasure. If it happens, I will explain to you many things that you don't yet understand and maybe will never be able to understand, since you are in different surroundings and are being raised in an atmosphere of [normal] human beings.

My dear daughter! I want you to read this, if the good God permits it, after you grow up and will be able to take an objective look at what we did

2 Letter from Sarah and Jechiel Gerlitz to their daughter Dita, YVA, O.33/2129. All three survived and moved to Israel. The letter appears in Hebrew translation in Yehudit Kleiman, ed., *Letters from "Nowhere": Last Letters of Jews from the Nazi Occupied Countries* (Jerusalem: Yad Vashem, 1988, Hebrew), pp. 26–27. See also Sarah Gerlitz testimony, YVA, O.3/4430.

for you. My hope is, my daughter, that you will not disapprove of us, that you will love the memory of us and of our entire reviled people, of which you are a part. I want you, my dear daughter, not to be ashamed of your origins and not to repudiate them. I want you to know that your father was a man of an uncommon type in this world and you can be proud of him. He lived his entire life for the sake of doing good for people. May God bless him, watch over his steps, and let him reclaim you. My dear treasure! You are your father's whole world, his only ambition, his compensation for all the suffering. So, if our fate does not end well, I want you to remember him fondly. I want you to remember your wonderful grandparents, your aunts and uncles, and the whole family. Remember us always and do not judge us. As for me, your mother... forgive me, forgive me my dear daughter for having given birth to you. I wanted to give birth to you for joy and honor and it is not our fault that things turned out differently. So I beg of you, my only and precious daughter, do not judge us. Try to be good, like your father and your father's fathers. Love your parents who are caring for you and [love] their family; they will certainly tell you about us. I would like you to appreciate the sacrifice that they are making on your behalf, so that they will never have reason to regret what they undertook of their own good will. There is one more thing I would like you to know: your mother was a proud person even though our enemies ostracized us, and if I die, it will be without weeping and wailing, but rather with a smile of contempt on my lips. I hug you warmly and kiss [you] and bless [you] with all of a mother's strength and love.

Your mother

What can I write to my daughter, my dearest treasure in the world? You have to open your heart and look inward, for no pen in the world can describe what is raging in there now. I wholeheartedly believe that all of us will come through this time and that our hearts will be reunited.

Your father

Young Buzio's Testimony[3]

Buzio's testimony, given immediately after the war was over when he was nine years old, describes only two scenes among the ordeals that he and his sister

3   YVA, M.49/2881 (original in ŻIH).

experienced during the war. Nevertheless, it awakens us to the tragedy of young children who were forced to wander alone among villages and lets us sense their yearnings for their parents' caressing and protective arms. With a mere wave of a hand, a six-year-old boy became responsible for his four-year-old sister; thus Buzio led her among villages and across fields in a trek of survival. From what seems to be an adult perspective the boy describes his sister's yearnings for her mother's love.

Look, you know that there were 6,000 Jews in our town, maybe more. They called out to us to leave our homes — so they could kill us... Then anyone who could escape to the forest began to do so.... When Father escaped and Mother ran... I escaped, too! Should I have stayed with the Germans?! I was already six years old by then and my sister Shulamit wasn't four yet — she also followed us. Meanwhile, the Germans began to shoot into the forest. We lost our parents — and they're still gone. The two of us began to wander around in the villages and in the area around us. The peasants gave us bread, they weren't mean, but no one let us come into their home and let us sleep there, no one let us. So we learned to sleep in the fields, in an apple orchard under a tree. But sometimes we managed to sneak into some stable. One night we found a stable that was unlocked. We sneaked in very quietly and lay down on the pile of straw. My sister Shulamit noticed a cow that was taking care of a calf that was lying next to her, so she turned to me and said, "Look, Buzio! Look what a wonderful mother this calf has. Look how she's licking her ears, her eyes . . . . Oh, if only I was a little calf, too . . .!" Then, her dreamy eyes began to examine her index finger, smiling at her index finger...

But I don't want to tell anybody about that...

A Father's Thoughts[4]

The document that follows was written in the autumn of 1942, shortly after the writer's daughter was transported from the Warsaw Ghetto in the great deportation. The daughter evidently perished in Treblinka.

The Jews debated with each other about whether, in view of the extermination program and the fact that the children were in the greatest danger, whether the children should be handed over to non-Jews, even though the adults knew that they might be lost to the Jewish people. The more extreme

4   ŻIH, 301/283.

rejected this possibility categorically. The more lenient considered it an opportunity that should not be lost; only time, they said, would tell whether the children could be reclaimed for their relatives or for Judaism. There were a various range of views between these two poles. Of course, in many cases the outcome was decided not by logic but by emotions — how could one accept the possibility of extermination while looking into the frightened eyes of a child?

The author of the document discusses the problem of absolute and uncompromising faith. He argues with the holders of various views and feels the pain of the reality and of his own personal loss — his daughter. Maybe writing this provided him with some consolation even though it could not bring his daughter back. He wrote in Hebrew.

There must not be found among you anyone who makes his son or daughter to pass through the fire... (*Deut. 18:20*).[5]

Dedicated to my beloved daughter, Miriam Sarah
Who was taken from us on September 5, [19]42

The Menace of Spiritual Annihilation

When Hitler's army entered and occupied Poland, the Jews faced an onslaught of total violence. As time passed, the tide of assault gathered force.

Decrees and persecution, riots and looting, torture and slaughter — all steadily worsened. Polish Jewry, powerless against its Polish oppressors before the war, now fell into despair and helplessness. A time came, the likes of which had never existed in the history of our people, our brothers and sisters, so persecuted by history and so drenched in blood.

People started to leave the struggle. One by one they began to commit suicide and leave their faith. The first phenomenon was not very common but conversion was. Even though the Nuremberg Laws barred apostate Jews from becoming German until the third generation for they were still considered Jews, those who converted thought never-

5   The quotation is from Deuteronomy. 18:10, not 18: 20. The verse in full reads: "There shall not be found among you anyone who makes his son or daughter to pass through the fire or who uses divination, a soothsayer, a sorcerer, an enchanter, a witch, a charmer, a medium, a wizard, or a necromancer."

theless that by accepting the yoke of the new faith they might obtain
some relief, maybe even a great deal, because it would shelter them and
provide a respite, more or less, under the wings of the new divine presence. Whether their hopes were dashed or not did not matter. What
counted was that the menace of *shmad* [spiritual annihilation] had gone
away exactly as it had come, leaving no impression among us [unclear
word].

We drew sighs of relief, confident that the threat of shmad had
passed over for good, knowing that the step of conversion, if taken, was
taken solely for reward and not for no reward, and if the convert did not
receive some kind of reward he would not be quick to exchange his faith
for another.

Unfortunately, we miscalculated. This menace, the menace of
shmad, reappeared and in a different and more severe form. It came in
connection with the deportations they call *Umsiedlung* ["resettlement"].

Since the decree of deportation applied to all Jews — men, wom-
en, and children — some of them, due to concern and pity for their
children, the fruit of their loins, began to hand them over to Poles to
be raised and educated. However, this was very, very expensive, so expensive that even the affluent Jews could not afford it. Furthermore, not
everyone had the necessary connections with the world outside the
ghetto. Therefore, they began to place children in convents and other
religious institutions for schooling, telling themselves, as it were, "Look,
we're doing this solely to save our children, Jewish children, and [as the
saying has it] a person who saves one Jewish soul has saved a whole
world. What is more, it is only until the storm blows over, is it not?
Because, it never really occurred to me to raise my son or daughter in
the Christian faith, which is alien to me and my spirit. What I am doing
now is only a means to the end of survival and, as we all know, the end
justifies the means. This trend of thought struck roots in many hearts
among our people and they began to endorse it. It captured the thinking
of many of us, and even the leaders and spokesmen of national parties
deferred to them and agreed to the rescue of Jewish children by surrendering them to convents, thinking that by so doing they would be able
to save a number of Jewish children.

So the question is, "Body or soul: which is preferable?"

One who surrenders his children to a convent for schooling may
be sure that he has saved their bodies from the claws of the yellow beast,
but he is endangering their Jewish souls. After all, who doesn't know that

the convent has one goal — to win souls for the Christian church? It is impossible to imagine that a boy or girl of tender years who is raised by clergy in the spirit of Christianity will remain loyal to the Jewish spirit. The soul is burnt while the body is sustained. Who dares to say that it is worth doing?

Our forebears knew that leaving the faith is a transgression that one should rather die for than commit. Willingly and happily they went to the pyre. They were killed and slaughtered in the sanctification of God's name. Yes, their bodies were obliterated but their pure souls survived. The parchments were burned but their letters floated into the air and were not desecrated. Here we are encouraging the opposite: to abandon the soul and save the body, to burn the letters and save the blank parchments, or worse still, to record different letters on them, letters totally foreign to us and our heritage.

Anyone who knows a little about the nature, traits, and ways of the priests will realize that they accept these children with open arms for a reason. Buying souls for Christianity has always been their way. And if they now wrap themselves in a mantle of mercy and humaneness and wish to raise our children in their institutions on behalf of these [virtues], then our eyes have not yet glazed over so badly as to overlook the main reason for their doing so: nothing but the making of souls or, in other words, fishing in turgid waters. They wish to exploit the parents' fear for their children, their beloved ones, and take them into their institutions. Their goal, however, is plain: to bring the children under the wings of the Christian presence.

It is clear that the priests' pity for our children is not motivated by the altruism preached by the man from Nazareth. If that were the case, they would pity not only the children but also old people who need help. Thus far, we have not yet heard that they'll help [adults] who escape from the ghetto walls and pound in vain on people's doors in search of shelter. Nor have we heard thus far about pleas from the priests in favor of the Jews, [promising] not to exploit them or denounce them to the authorities.

For generation after generation, our people has resisted the influence of this alien spirit. An entire literature has been devoted to this struggle, from the days of the Maccabees up to the Middle Ages; at the time when youngsters were kidnapped and drafted in to the Russian Army and afterwards, in the era of the menace of national assimilation. Shall we now undo all of this in one stroke?

Shall we betray the Eternal One of Israel and sell our offspring into barrenness?

I am confident that if we could ask this question at this time, the entire nation would answer in unison that we should not pass our sons and daughters through the alien flame.

A. H.-K.

Warsaw

Hanukka, 5703 [December 1942]

[Text added later, in identical handwriting but with a different pen] This document was written with regard to a proposal from a youth emissary to save children by handing them over to convents and Christian schools for education, at a fee of 10,000 zlotys per year for each child. Some leaders of the Zionist Movement almost accepted the offer. A few wavered while others opposed it flatly.

Irena's Testimony[6]

Irena (b. 1938) gave her testimony in Wrocław in June 1948 — the testimony of a girl who had been separated from her parents when she was four years-old and from her rescuers when she was about ten. As brief as the testimony is, it sheds light on the difficulty of parting from the people she loved. Since the two separations were six years apart, the descriptions of the experience of parting are different. The account of her separation from her biological parents is typified by individual scenes. The account of the hardships of parting from her rescuers, and of their feelings at the time, is fuller.

> I remember when I was in the ghetto with my parents, we shared our apartment with a lot of strangers. We often felt hungry. I was afraid of the Germans because I knew they were killing Jews, and my father, my real father, the Jewish one, told me that they were also killing Poles. This Polish woman came to us in the ghetto, and my father asked her to take me in. I remember him and the Polish woman talking. She lived in town and was too scared to let me stay with her, so she took me to her brother in a village near Lublin. Father told me not to call him Father any more but to call him Sir, because this man in the village would be my father.

6   YVA, M.49/3786 (original in ŻIH).

From that moment on, I thought these were my parents. Sometimes this used-to-be mother visited me, took me in her arms, and kissed me. I asked my father, the new one, why this woman, my used-to-be mother, wasn't living together with us, and he told me it was impossible. I loved this woman; she was my real mother, as I found out later on. It was good in the village. I wasn't hungry, I went to confession at church and took the Holy Communion, and I dressed well. They brought me up like their only daughter. I really was their only daughter. I wore nicer dresses than other girls in the village. I loved my father and mother very much.

Two years ago, in 1946, this man came to us and asked me if I was willing to go away with him, but I didn't want even to hear about separating from my parents. All his talks with Father were quiet and they told me to leave the room so I wouldn't hear. Once this man told Father, "We'll weigh the girl and give you her weight in gold, OK?" Father said that he didn't want gold and wouldn't give me over. I was really happy that Father didn't want to give me to this man because I didn't want to leave my parents. Once I came home from school and saw my parents really upset. Mother told me that my aunt in Warsaw had told the police about us. My parents cried and I didn't understand what it was all about.

At night I heard Father and Mother crying. In the morning, Mother took me into her bed and told me that the woman who used to visit me sometimes was my real mother and that my real parents gave me to them so that they'd bring me up. But the Germans killed my parents and now my relatives are coming and demanding that they give me back and it looked as though they would have to do it, because they were calling the police. The man who came here all the time is my uncle and he was going to force my parents to give me back by getting a court order. I cried and said that I wouldn't go. A few days later, as I was coming back from school, this uncle waited for me in the street and invited me to get into a bus. I refused because I wanted to walk home. I was afraid that he'd take me somewhere and I didn't want to go. My parents were in town, shopping for the holidays. After I came home, they forced me into the bus and Father agreed to this. It was terrible! I can't even think about it!

I went to Wrocław with my uncle. I couldn't get used to it no matter what, even though the uncles were good to me. I really missed my parents. I was very sad. They sent me to the school in Wrocław and I went there as a half-dormitory student. I still wear the dress and the shoes that my adoptive parents bought me. My uncle isn't rich; he makes only a little money. My uncles have a little boy and they pamper him because he's little. Another aunt lives with my uncle; she has no children and she loves me a lot. It was very hard for me to leave my adoptive parents but I'm young and I couldn't oppose it. I was helpless and cried all the time. My parents cried, too, but they had to give me back because the police and the court said they had to. Now I think the Jews are doing better than the peasants in the village and I'll be able to learn something from them. I've made peace with what happened to me.

The Travails of a Mother and Son[7]

The following testimony was written by a Jewish mother who gave it to the Koordynacja activists before she left Poland. It describes her survival in Warsaw and that of her son, the sense of being trapped, the attempt to break through the ring of death, and everyday achievements on the way to the long-awaited day of liberation.

Our lives began to turn into hell on August 20, 1940, when they took away my husband, the father of my son. In his last letter, sent from Pawiak [Prison], he made me swear never to part from the boy because he would never see us again. A few days later, I received a telegram telling me that he had died in Auschwitz. I was living on Chopin Street and I had to move from there to the ghetto. I found a place on Leszno Street. The first Aktzion began on August 1, 1942, at 5:00 p.m [*sic*]. The area between Leszno Street and Karmelicka Street was surrounded and the Germans, shouting, ordered everyone to go down to the courtyard. I was in despair. I knew what I had to do but didn't have the strength to take the boy to the *Umschlagplatz* [deportation area]. I looked out of the window and saw all my acquaintances and their children gathering in the courtyard. I found out that families of policemen were being released. Since my mother had a card saying that she belonged to a policeman's family, I didn't think much and handed over the boy to her. I said goodbye to them and asked them to send the boy to my sister-in-law. I was led to the Umschlag.

My despair about what would happen to my son was overwhelming. Just then I saw a friend, a nurse. She comforted me and promised that I'd be coming home in a nurse's uniform the next day. God must have been looking out for us, because if I had taken my son with me I would not have managed to get out of that hell. The next day, I went home. On the way, I bumped into my brother [the policeman], who told me that they hadn't honored mother's card and had led her away, but she had the presence of mind to turn to a Jewish policeman and beg him to take the boy and hand him over to her daughter-in-law, attorney Dyzenko [the policeman's wife]. It must have been the hand of fate that the policeman knew the Dyzenkos and lived with them in the same building. That very day, my sister-in-law sent me back my son. From then on, I managed to go into hiding whenever the Germans came, until the day when all the Jews had to leave their homes and move in to Miła Street. Masses of people set out and walked to Miła Street, and we were among them. It was terribly hot, my son began to cry and I didn't have the strength to carry him. Without thinking much, I grabbed him by the hand, ran with him into a building, and found a hiding place, and that's what saved us.

The last Aktzion began on April 20, 1943 [*sic*]. All the buildings on Leszno [Street] had already been burned down. Only our building, where supplies were being stored, was guarded by four soldiers and an officer. It drove me crazy to know that now I would have to die with my son. But God looked out for us.

On April 26, 1943, the last day of the deportation [*sic*], I set out with my son and didn't know how we would survive. My son was unusually good-looking and an officer who passed by noticed him. He approached me and asked if I realized that by tomorrow our house would be destroyed and the people in hiding would be killed. I had no choice but to ask for his assistance. He said that he felt bad about such a lovely boy and that his driver would be going to Prosta Street and I could go with him. I went home and told my relatives, but they all said it was a trap and tried to stop me doing it. But I felt I had to go, and without giving it another thought I said that here I'd be facing certain death and there I'd have some hope. An hour later, the German came by and said that the car was waiting for me. I said goodbye and went. Next to the ghetto, on Prosta Street, a guard detail stopped the car and when they saw a Jewish woman they ordered me to get out and stand by the wall. Suddenly I overheard a conversation between a Polish policeman and a Jewish policeman who suggested that he turn to his superior and beg them to let me and the boy go. A few minutes later, a German came over to me and asked if I had money. He removed my wedding ring and another ring from my finger and let me go.

So I went on to Prosta Street. From there I moved to the Aryan side and I reached a woman and stayed with her for one month. At 5:00 on Saturday morning, six extortionists pounded on the door, came in, took our money, and left us. The woman said I had to leave the apartment. I went to another acquaintance of mine but she refused [to let me in]. I intended to walk away, but then a friend of the landlady's came by, and when she saw how desperate I was and she saw my son, she came over to me and said we could visit her that evening. I went back to the first building to get my suitcase and just as I was about to leave, there was suddenly a loud ringing of the bell and a moment later four Germans came in. There were six of us there; they searched us and took 2,000 zlotys. Suddenly the officer asked who the boy belonged to. I answered: to me. He said that thanks to this boy he'd let us live and he slipped the 2,000 zloty into my coat pocket. After this happened, I left the apartment and walked to the woman, who was already waiting for us, and she took care of us from then on.

She sent me to a friend and took care of my son by herself. Since she couldn't live with him in Warsaw, she closed up her apartment and moved to a place outside Kraków. Every month she'd come to Warsaw to meet me. The devotedness of this woman knew no limits. After everything I had was finished, she worked to support herself and my son. She's been taking care of him to this very day and apart from him she doesn't think her life is worth anything. When I came to her and told her that we were going, she fell ill. She begged me to take her along with us because otherwise she'd miss him so badly that her heart would break.

Everything I've written here doesn't even begin to express the whole story that I could tell. If we go, please God, remember what I said: God is looking out for this boy. His father had a noble personality and extraordinary talents.

In brief, my son believes in the greatness and future glory of the Land of Israel.

Frenia Langans

<h1 style="text-align:center">Testimony of Karola, a Rescuer[8]</h1>

On the eve of the war, Karola worked as a caregiver for three Jewish children. She managed to save two of them by protecting them from the Germans and no less from her Polish neighbors. With immense resourcefulness, loyalty, and love, Karola was like a mother to them. Their rescue was a cause to which she devoted the war years.

The recorder of the testimony added a note to the record: [The rescuer] never married due to concern that her Polish husband would not be good to the Jewish children.

> Our family [the Jewish family for which she was caregiver] was made up of the parents and three children. The youngest was Samos; then there was a girl, Salusia, and the first-born, Izio Hochheiser. I raised the children. In the first year of the war, they killed the [children's] father. We were separated when they put all the Jews in the ghetto. I went to the ghetto every day; I visited the children as much as I could because I missed them badly. I related to them as if they were my own.
>
> Whenever it wasn't quiet in the ghetto, the children came to me and stayed until things calmed down. They felt at home with me. In 1943 they began to liquidate the ghetto. By chance, the little boy was staying with me in the village just then. That day I went to the gate of the ghetto, which was surrounded on all sides by SS men and Ukrainians. People were running around like madmen; mothers with children were being pushed helplessly towards the gate. Suddenly I saw the mother with Salusia and Izio. She saw me, too, and whispered into the girl's ear, "Go to Karolicja." Salusia didn't waste time thinking and like a mouse she eluded the heavy boots of the Ukrainians, who by a miracle did not see her. She ran over to me with her arms wide. I froze all over and walked with Samos and Salusia toward my village, Witanowiec, near Wadowice.
>
> The mother and Izio were deported and we never heard from them again. Life was hard and the children survived only by a miracle. At first I let them go out of the house, but when things got worse I had to hide them inside. But even that didn't help. The people around us knew that I was hiding Jewish children, and then I began to be harassed and

---

8   YVA, M.49/579 (original in ŻIH).

threatened from all directions so that I would hand the children over to the Gestapo. Otherwise, [people said] [the Germans] would burn down the whole village, murder people, and so on... The mayor was friendly to me and sometimes he calmed me down. I silenced the attackers with a gift or a bribe. But that didn't last for long.

The SS men sniffed around and riots broke out. One day they [evidently the villagers] announced that the children had to be driven out of this world. Their plan was to put them in a barn and smash their heads with an axe when they fell asleep. I ran around like a crazy woman. My old father was very worried. What should we do? What should we do?

Thee poor kids knew about the whole thing. Before they went to sleep, they asked me, "Karolicja, are they going to kill us today?" and I froze all over and decided not to give them up for anything. Suddenly I hatched an idea of how to save them. I loaded them onto a cart and told everyone that I was taking them out of the village in order to drown them. I drove all over the village. Everyone saw us and believed it. That night, I went to a neighbor and hid the children in her loft.

It was July; it was very hot. The children lay there, contorted on a layer of dust that was half a meter thick. These poor, wretched creatures. Terrible pus covered their bodies. Their toenails and fingernails fell out. They literally rotted. My heart ached. I felt that I couldn't hold on. But I fought. I had to work so that the children would at least have some food and so I could pay for the hideout up there. Those poor things, they went through three months of agony that way. Somehow I managed to cure them of the pus. They were pale as corpses, especially the girl. You could see the fear in her eyes. The boy was tougher.

I ran out of money and couldn't continue to pay [for the hideout]. I had to take the children out and I put them in a stable. I had no other way to do it. Once, SS men searched the area and one of them went into the stable. I was sure that it was all over, everything was lost. Then Samos had a sudden idea: he ran out to get some straw and arrange it for the cows to lie on. We were all stunned. Where did the kid get such resourcefulness? Salusia stood in the corner, pale.

From then on, things were quiet until the Red Army arrived. The children were happy and I was happier. I won't be parted from them. Even if they go to the end of the world, I'll go with them. They're like my children. I love them more than anything and there's nothing I won't do for them.

Testimony of the Rescuer Katrzyna Wolkotrup[9]

Katrzyna Wolkotrup (b. 1888) gave her testimony in 1946 to the chairman of the Jewish Historical Committee in Białystok, who recorded it (in the third person).

The laconic testimony unfolds the tragedy of the loss of her own family — the price they paid for helping Jews. She had not chosen from the outset to save a Jewish child, but at the critical moment she took him in. When she discovered that only the two of them were still alive, she decided to protect him.

> The witness remembers the Jewish couple who lived in her building: Michael and Chana. Michael was a poor craftsman.
>
> In 1941, during the German occupation, they had a son. The witness and her family were on very good terms with the neighbors. When the ghetto was established in Baranowicze, the daughter of the witness advised the Jewish couple to go into hiding in the cellar of the building, where they kept potatoes. They hid there for a week but then a neighbor denounced them to the Germans. The Germans came and surrounded the apartment. In the meantime [before the Germans came] the baby's mother asked the witness to hold him because he was crying.
>
> Even before the Germans entered the flat, the witness took the boy and went out with him to calm him down. She heard the Germans demanding that her daughter hand over the Jews who were there. The daughter insisted that there were no Jews in her home and that they had already left. The Germans, knowing full well where the Jews were — the neighbor who had informed on them had made this clear — pointed to the location of the hideout under the floor. When the witness overheard the threats, she took the boy to the countryside and spent the next two days there with him. When she returned to her home, she saw that everyone had been killed. Laying there were the corpses of the Jewish husband and wife, her daughter, her son-in-law, her two sons, her daughter-in-law, and their eight-year-old boy. The witness left the apartment and went to the village. She spent the rest of the war there, supporting herself on handouts and raising the boy as if he were her own son. When the Red Army arrived, she went to Baranowicze, and from there, as a Polish refugee, to Sierpiec.

9   Ibid., M.49/1959 (original in ŻIH).

She has spent the past year in Sierpiec; the Jews there are supporting her and helping her at their initiative. They are the ones who advised her to go to Białystok and contact the local Jewish committee. She reached Białystok on September 16, 1946. The boy is growing up and is handsome and healthy. The witness would like to continue taking care of him.

Signed: Katrzyna Wolkotrup

Magister M. Turek, Chairman of the Jewish Historical Committee in Białystok

The concluding sentence of the testimony, "The witness would like to continue taking care of him," indicates that the decision about whether to take the boy away from her had not yet been made. It also reflects the grave dilemma that the staff members of the Jewish committees faced: awareness of the duty of gathering up the children in order to revitalize the Jewish people, as opposed to their immense appreciation of rescuers and their actions during the war. This is an extreme case, since both the witness and the child had lost all their families and were left with nothing on earth but each other.

Letter from a Rescuer to the Mother of the Girl she Saved[10]

The baby's mother, Janina Danzig, and the daughter of the rescuer, worked in the same factory during the war. When the girl's mother sought a shelter for her daughter, her workmate suggested that she hand the baby over to her mother, Maria Asanowicz.

Both parents survived the war and came to the rescuer to reclaim their daughter. The following letter was written after their first visit and before the rescuer returned the girl, then aged two-and-a-half, to their custody.

Before the rescuer handed the girl to her parents, she dressed her in a blue undergarment into which she had sewn an amulet to protect her from evil. The amulet carried a little note: a pink piece of paper bearing several lines of writing in unfamiliar characters and in a language that the parents did not understand. Since the rescuer was of Tatar origin, the amulet was presumably written in Tatar.

---

10 I received this letter from Edith Danzig-Orimian, the child survivor.

Dear Madame Janina!

Forgive me for having treated you coldly while you were with us. You must understand that I didn't behave that way on purpose; at the time, I wanted to shout and bang my head against the wall. For a year and a half I loved Lala ["doll– the girl's nickname] as a mother loves her daughter and didn't think you would now take her from me. After the war, I was sure it would happen but now I thought everything would be different: I would come along with her so that we would be together for a while, and afterwards things would carry on normally. But now it took me by surprise, like a bolt of lightning out of a clear sky. But there's no choice; I'm happy that she'll be with her parents because that's good for her. It's too hard for me to uproot her from my heart, which she penetrated with her every fiber, shoes and all, it is too hard for me. But there's no other way; I have to accept it.

It may seem strange to you. You're thinking, "What of it? She took care of her for a while and now it's over." But for me it's as though I've lost my own child. There was a time when I didn't sleep at night. There were nights when I woke up twenty times for her but I didn't get angry at her. But then, when she began to talk, I loved every day and every hour with her more and more. Somehow she managed to make me happy, to give me energy, because I thought about how to keep her healthy. In the summer, many people suffered from dysentery and people died in every home. When this danger passed and a different disease broke out, again I worried about how to keep her safe. Now they're taking her from me in one go. I couldn't sleep for two nights. I envy you because you're happy. You found a healthy girl and you're able to take her — you sleep quietly, whereas I slept only three hours the first night and again tonight. I cry all day long, but what's the use of that? At least I have a clean conscience because I never did her any wrong and gave her everything I could. If anyone gave me anything — an apple, a cake, a biscuit — I always took it home for her. If I could keep her for the rest of my life, I'd do the same thing again. But praise be to God, she has parents.

I have one request — let me know now and then how she's doing, and send me a picture of her at the first opportunity. If she's in danger, you must find a way to send her or bring her to me, because it would be a shame if everything I did for her would be in vain. Truth to tell, it was so hard for me at first, she was so restless at night that if you'd taken her from me then, I wouldn't have been sorry. But now that she's begun to grow so nicely, to talk, to develop generally, and to sprout teeth — it's all worth something; now you can get some pleasure from it. To lose her for good now is very hard, but there's no choice. I entertained crazy thoughts about not returning her to you and taking responsibility before God and my conscience, but I can't. Somehow I'll overcome the loss.

But I ask you to write to me so I'll know that she's alive and well and still remembers me, her "mother," even though she's a stranger. I can tell you in so many words that there are lots of mothers who love their children less than I loved her. I will always remain the same "mother" for her as I've been so far.

If fate doesn't place me too far from you, please bring her to visit me — whether she'll recognize me or not. But if fate does take you far away, please, I request, send me her picture. If it could have been done here, in Korzec, I would have done it long ago. I ask of you, since unless I receive letters from you, I'll be sure that you've already forgotten me. In your first letter, please tell me everything, how the trip went, what she did, what she talked about, how she behaved, and in one word, everything. You can write about Lala in the third person. I won't stop thinking about her and she'll always be on my mind. I may not have much time left to live because that's how times are today, but please, write as long as you can.

The whole thing can really drive a person mad. I won't do such a thing again. Forming a relationship with a strange girl is something that only a foolish woman like me can do. I ask again: write to me about everything, at length and in clear language. If you don't like what I sewed for her, you can throw it away, but I did it with thought and tears so that she'd remember something of her "mama." You can cover her with the blanket. If you have to travel in the winter you can cover her because she likes to sleep under a blanket, covered up to the nose... but [unclear word] lovely that will stay with her, she has bonded with them. When she grows up, she'll forget them. I'd like you to keep "Nunio" as a gift that her "mama" gave with all her heart. I will always pray to God for her health: may He watch over her and may I be privileged to see her again.

Be well. If I offended you — maybe I didn't raise the little one properly — you can start over because, after all, she's still a little girl. I don't think I did anything bad to her.

The moment of parting from my beloved little daughter is approaching. Who knows, maybe it's for the best. She'll forget quickly because she's a little girl, but it'll be hard for me. May God protect her. In your letters, please call her "the little one." I'll wait with bated breath for the first letter about the trip and then I'll be more at ease. Please write lots about her, tell me how the trip went, in a word — everything, what she said and how she reacted to the changes.

May it be God's will that if she's ever lacking for a mother, may she be brought to me and she'll find the same mother again.

If she ever needs shelter, please do whatever you must so that she'll come to me, and she'll find me as I have always been.

Maria

The Danzigs moved to Poland under the repatriation settlement; subsequently, they also helped the rescuer, Maria Asanowicz and her family, to cross into Poland. The family remained in Poland until the mid-1950s and stayed in touch regularly with the rescuer.

Letter from the Rescuer Pola to Young Helena Guzala[11]

This letter was written by a Polish woman, Pola, who took a Jewish girl into her home and her heart during the war and continued to treat her like a mother after the war had ended. When she contracted an incurable illness and began her final decline, she wrote a letter to the girl and entrusted it to Bolek, her husband, so that he would give it to her when she became an adult. The letter teaches us a great deal about her devotion to and love for the girl, the difficulties that she faced, and her conviction that the stress that she had endured during the war had brought on her illness. However, it also explains her decision to continue raising the girl after the war and not to tell her about her Jewish origins.

March 1954

My dear daughter, I am writing this letter to you on your supposed birthday, but I confess that I don't really know when your birthday is.

My dear daughter, don't cry as you read this letter of mine, because you will be surprised by what you are about to read. Before I die, I'm writing to you to tell you that you are not my birth daughter. To the best of my knowledge thus far, you belong to a Jewish family. You are a Jew! Your real name is Halinka. A Jewish woman told me this, but she was

11 I received the letter from Helena Guzala, the child survivor.

not your mother because I never saw your mother with my own eyes. Your stepfather, meaning my husband Bolek, brought you [to me]. I am dying but Father lives. When you grow up, he will tell you everything because he swore to me in God's name that he would tell you everything about yourself. We, Father and I, experienced much human evil in your wake. We are concealing the fact that you are not our daughter because we had a girl like you when you were a baby. My beloved daughter! I loved you with all my heart, so passionately that it was like a blow to the chest. Unfortunately, I became ill with cancer but I did not hand you over to the Germans. I wrote a letter to my friend Francuska, asking her to treat you as though you were her own daughter. This letter will not be sent, but I wrote it because not all people are good and bad people might take you. My dear daughter, your sisters do not know that you are Jewish; only Francuska knows it. My dear one, my beloved daughter, I am close to heaven and I am dying. Swear to me that when you receive this letter from Owniska you will not look for your parents, because even our Poles persecute Jews. We were evicted from our home, treated with contempt, and beaten, but we did not hand you over. My dear daughter, I know you will cry when you read this letter. Please don't cry. I, Mama Pola, know that you are still young, you need a mother. I love you so much. If your real parents, the Jewish ones, had survived, they almost certainly were good people, because I once had a Jewish friend and she was a good woman.

You have your name, Halinka. We don't know your surname. Believe us, my daughter, there was a war. My daughter, I say goodbye to you and kiss you hard and thank you for having taken care of me in my illness. It is God's will. You have repaid your debt. Don't cry, my daughter Halinka, my dear treasure, my daughter.

I love you with all my heart, but I'm dying.

Your mother, Pola

Documents Concerning Ita-Leah Igenfeld-Besserman

In the course of my archival research in Israel and Poland, I came across numerous stories with great human interest. Sometimes the name of a certain child recurred in documents in different archives, and I adduced from this that various organizations were searching for and trying to reclaim the same child. On other occasions, only one document existed, telling part of a personal story of which the beginning and the end were unknown to me.

At the Jewish archives in Warsaw, I repeatedly encountered documents about a girl named Ita-Leah Igenfeld. The story they told captured my heart and I gathered the documents together. Several things about the story surprised me: the mother had survived but did not manage to reclaim her daughter even though she knew her whereabouts. I did not find contemporary documentation about her first efforts; only later documents filled in this gap. I discovered that the mother had left Poland (first to Germany, subsequently to Canada) but continued to struggle to reclaim her daughter even while she was living abroad. Most of the material belonged to the late 1940s, at the time when the Jewish organizations were winding up their activities in Poland. The material suggests that by that time the girl was living in a small Polish village.

The story continues: first, however, I present the reader with the documents that were made available to me. They are shown in chronological order; where they were undated, I arranged them on the basis of where they seem to fit into the story.[12]

Letter from JDC Branch in Berlin to Polish Military Legation in Berlin[13]

Date: June 28, 1946

Madame Stayeńska:
We wish to take an interest in a matter that deserves top priority due to its importance.

Mrs. Rachel Igenfeld-Besserman turned to the JDC office in Munich and asked them to establish contact with her five year-old daughter. Mrs. Igenfeld left her daughter, Ita-Leah Igenfeld, then sixteen months-old, on a path in Poland in the realization that this was the only way to save the girl's life. She herself went into hiding in a nearby village and found out that the baby had been taken in by a non-Jew, who afterwards placed her in the home of Józef Pycz, a wealthy Christian who lived in Rataj, a village near Kraśnik. The foundling was given the name Leonka. After the Germans left Poland, Mrs. Igenfeld visited Józef Pycz and demanded that he return her daughter

---

12 The names of the participants in this affair are spelled variously in different letters. The variants may be due to the different languages in which the letters were written. It is also possible that each participant pronounced the names differently.
13 ŻIH Legal Department (original in Polish).

to her, but the farmer refused and threatened to kill her in order to keep the girl in his custody.

Mrs. Igenfeld took the matter to court but the hearings were continually delayed because of the farmer's influence. Then, fearing for her life because of frequent threats from Józef Pycz, Mrs. Igenfeld fled to Germany. Before she surrendered her baby daughter, she had made several markings on her back so that she could recognize her afterwards.

In January 1946, Mrs. Igenfeld contacted our offices in Poland, but a letter that we wrote almost certainly got lost.

Dear Mrs. Stayeńska, we would be grateful if the Polish Military Mission in Berlin could help us with this matter.

Larry Lubeski
Relative Tracing Officer

Central Jewish Committee in Poland, Undated Internal Document[14]

Re: Igenfeld, Ita-Leah

Two years ago, the [girl's] mother came to claim her through legal proceedings. Markings [on the girl's back] that she reported did not match and the girl was not given to her.

[The adoptive parents] are not demanding money [to have the girl returned].

[Signed] Szablowska

Letter Central Jewish Committee to Citizen Justman, Cieszin[15] [undated]

We inform you that we made a field visit to learn about the case of the girl Ita-Leah Igenfeld. Józef Pycz, the peasant who has been caring for the girl, reported that two years ago her mother came to claim her with the assistance of a lawyer. Special markings that the mother reported were examined and were not found to match.

Thus far, the girl has been with Citizen Pycz, who is not prepared to relinquish her.

Attached is a deposition from Citizen Mina.

14 Ibid. (original in Polish handwriting).
15 Ibid. (original in Polish handwriting).

Letter from the secretary of the Canadian Federation for Polish Jews to Rabbi Kahana[16]

September 22, 1948

Dear Rabbi Kahana:

As you will see in the enclosed power of attorney (*Pelnomocnictwo*), in connection with the case of Mrs. Igenfeld-Besserman, which is no doubt familiar to you, I feel that it is unnecessary to appeal to you to take an interest in such a case of *pidyon shevuyim* ["redemption of captives"; the writer wrote the words in Hebrew]. You are doubtless aware of this since our generation has received more than its share of these tragedies. There is no need to use superfluous words to declare the prayer too constantly offered by us, at this time — *aseh lema'an tinokot* ["Act for the sake of our babies"; written in Hebrew]. However, we ask you to do the utmost within your power, on behalf of the Federation for Polish Jews and for this unfortunate mother.

For the past few months we have contacted various agencies with regard to the redemption of the child:

Ita-Laja Igenfeld (Leonka),

who can now be found with:Józef Pycz, wies Rataj

Gm. Kawenczyn

Pow. Kraśnik

Wojw. Lulelskie, Poland

[in Rataj village, Kwęczyn Council, Kraśnik County, Lublin District, Poland]

These agencies advised us that this matter should be handled by you, as the Chief Rabbi of Poland. We are, therefore, forwarding this to you, trusting that you will spare no effort to see that this mother is reunited with her child.

Your prompt reply will be anticipated with deep appreciation and sincere gratitude.

With greetings for the High Holydays,

N. Shemen, Secretary

16 Ibid.

Power of Attorney[17]

I the undersigned, Rachel Igenfeld-Besserman, née Fefferkuchen, born in 1918 in Janów Lubelski in Kraśnik County, and living in Toronto, Canada, hereby bestow power of attorney on Dr. David Kahana and empower him to take my daughter whose name is Ita-Laja, today Leonka, who was born in the village of Branew in Chrzanów Council, Kraśnik County, on August 12, 1941. The girl is living with Józef Pycz, who lives in Rataj village, in Kwęczyn Council near Kraśnik.

The possessor of this power of attorney shall be empowered on its basis to present claims on my behalf and on behalf of claimants on my behalf, and to represent me before the authorities and all other representative offices.

I affirm that I personally surrendered the girl on November 7, 1942. Next to the baby I placed a note bearing the following written message: "This baby girl has been baptized in the name of Leonka."

I affirm that the girl carries the following markings: several red stains the size of seeds on her back and a healed scar on her buttocks.

Toronto, April 20, 1948

Deposition of Canadian Notary before whom Witnesses to the Surrender of the Baby Appeared[18]

April 2, 1949

Deposition

I, Solomon Heifetz, a Notary Public in York County, hereby affirm that in 1949, the following people who were strangers to me appeared before me at my offices on 143 Queen West Street, Toronto, Canada: (1) Szlama Besserman, domiciled at 403 Spadina Ave. Toronto, Ont, (2) Max Rosenfeld, domiciled at 262 Laurier West, Montreal, and (3) Chume Hakman née Fefferkuchen, domiciled at 407 Spadina Ave., Toronto, Ont. The aforementioned testified before me that a woman named Rachel Besserman, presently domiciled in Toronto, summoned them as witnesses to a trial in which she is suing a [Polish] citizen named Józef Pycz, domiciled in Rataj village in Kwęczyn Council, Kraśnik County, Poland, to compel him to return to her her baby

---

17 The power of attorney was written five months before it was attached to the letter from the secretary of the Canadian Federation for Polish Jews. It may also have been sent directly.
18 ŻIH Legal Department (original in Polish).

daughter, who had been handed over during the war so that she might survive. These people wished to present me with a written deposition because they are unable to [appear] before the court in Poland.

[The identity of the people was verified by means of photographs and personal documents.]

1. **Deposition of Szlama Besserman**: I am a Polish citizen, I was born in Janów Lubelski in 1906, and I was in Poland until 1945. I came to Canada this year [1949]. From 1939 to 1944 I was in Branew, Chrzanów Council, Kraśnik County. A family named Fefferkuchen lived in this village. In 1941, their daughter, Rachel Igenfeld (currently my wife) came to them from the Warsaw ghetto. She was pregnant at the time and had a daughter several months later. The daughter was given the Jewish name Ita-Leah. We lived in the same village until 1942. When all the Jews in the area were deported, I had the good fortune, as a tailor, of going into hiding in peasants' homes. In November of that year, in the evening, Rachel came to me and told me that she could no longer keep her daughter in the forest hideout because the girl was suffering from malnutrition and cold, and under such conditions she would surely die soon. Rachel said that she had placed the baby in the neighboring village, Wólka, at the door of the home of a peasant named Jan Fac. Rachel hid and saw someone come out of the house and take the girl. She told me on this occasion that she had not put the girl down in Branew because she was afraid that they would recognize her, and [she] also [told me] that next to the girl she placed a note saying that the baby had been baptized into the church and that her name was Leonka. She did this so that it would be easy and possible to recognize the girl afterward. She also told me that [the baby] had another identifying birthmark on her back and a scar from a wound on her buttocks. Rachel asked me to try carefully to find out what had become of the baby. Rachel assumed that since I was circulating among the peasants, it would be easy for me to find out something about the girl. Indeed, I soon discovered that people from Wólka village had taken a baby girl to Kwęczyn Council, and this council, at the order of the Germans, handed her to a woman named Burczyn. She was to have received assistance from the council for this purpose. Gossip about the case left no doubt in my mind that this was Rachel's baby. About a year later, I found out that a man named Józef Pycz had taken the girl and adopted her. At the end of the war, I met with Rachel in Kraśnik and she asked me to go with her to claim her baby. I agreed willingly, and we were joined by Mordek

Rosenfeld (today Max Rosenfeld) and Chume Hakman. The four of us visited Kwęczyn Council. The local police commander and two policemen joined us. When we reached [the home of] Józef Pycz, he was not at home and his wife did not want to give up the girl. When Pycz returned, he also refused to hand over the girl and even cursed Rachel: What kind of mother are you who throws away her baby? [The witness' signature follows]

2. **Deposition of Max Rosenfeld:** I am a Polish citizen. I was born in Janów Lubelski in 1908. I stayed in Poland until 1945. I reached Canada in 1948. My name in Poland was Mordek. From 1939 to 1942, I lived in Branew together with my wife and my two children. In 1942, my wife and children were exiled to Torobina. I remained in hiding in the area because I wanted to get some food for my family. Soon afterward, the Germans murdered all the people in the area, including my family. I wandered in the forests in the vicinity and stayed in hiding until 1944. In July of that year I was liberated. I met Rachel Igenfeld in Branew in 1941. She had come from the Warsaw ghetto to her parents, the Fefferkuchens, who lived in Branew. Soon after that, she gave birth. I hid out together with her and the baby girl. I couldn't look the baby in the eye. She cried day and night, almost certainly because of hunger and the sores that she got because of dirt, because there wasn't any water to clean the sores. I suggested to Rachel that she leave the baby somewhere near people. At first she wouldn't hear of it — she didn't want to be separated from the baby. Eventually the hunger and the cold got so bad that she decided to give up the girl and placed her in November or December 1942 near the door of Jan Fac in Wólka, Kwęczyn Council. I went with her and waited nearby until someone came out of the house, saw the baby, and took her in. Then I found out that the Council gave the girl over to be raised. After the liberation in 1944, I went with Rachel Besserman and Chume Hakman to Józef Pycz to get her [back]. With my own eyes I saw that when Rachel lay the baby down she wrote a note about how the baby had been baptized into the church and her name was Leonka. She slipped the note into the baby's coat. Then she showed me a birthmark on the baby's back, and for that reason I went together with Rachel to take the baby [back] in order to be a witness. But Józef Pycz flatly refused to give her up. He said in my presence that he knew the girl was Rachel Igenfeld's daughter but he wouldn't hand her over because he loved her. [The witness' signature follows.]

3. **Deposition of Chome Hakman**: I am a Polish citizen, born in Janów Lubelski in 1927. I was in Poland from the day I was born until 1945. I reached Canada in 1949. During the war, I lived in Branew, Chrzanów area, Kraśnik County. From 1941 on, I was together with Rachel Igenfeld and I know exactly how the thing took place. In September 1942, they wiped out all the Jews in the vicinity — those who didn't manage to go into hiding. My parents were murdered, too. I spent a short time hiding on peasants' farms as a cattle herder. I knew that Rachel had run away to the forest with the baby and that she was hiding there. Afterwards, that autumn, I decided to hide in the forest, too. I found Rachel and the baby in ghastly condition: both of them were starving, exhausted, dressed in tatters. Seeing how she was suffering, I advised her to lay the baby down near some house because that was the only thing that might save her from dying of cold and starvation. Eventually Rachel agreed. A man named Mordek Rosenfeld also went with us; now he's a resident of Canada named Max Rosenfeld. We placed the baby a short distance from Jan Fac's barn in the village of Wólka, a place that we knew before the war. We decided to wait until somebody would take the girl. Fortunately, a little while later we heard the baby crying and someone came out and took her into a little house. We went back to the forest with the [girl's] mother. We decided to stay near the village in order to see what would become of the baby. The girl's name was Ita-Laja. She was sixteen months old and had blue eyes, a round face, fair skin, and light-colored hair. When we were liberated in July 1944, I joined Rachel when she visited Józef Pycz to take the child. Szlama Besserman and Mordek Rosenfeld went with us. Then I had an opportunity to hold the girl in my arms and I recognized her right away. The peasant didn't want to give her back. He said he loved her and wouldn't give her up. [The witness' signature follows]

I recorded the testimonies of the witnesses Szlama Besserman, Max Rosenfeld, and Chume Hakman. They read the depositions and confirmed that they were compatible with the testimonies that they had given in my presence and then they affixed their signatures. Toronto, Ontario, April 1949.

Solomon Heifetz, Notary Public, York County

Letter from Attorney Jan Steliński, Lublin, to Central Jewish Committee in Warsaw[19]

June 10, 1949

Today I received a second letter from the Central Committee of the Jews of Poland in regard to information about the case of Rachel Besserman née Igenfeld.

Thus far, I have given detailed information on this matter to (1) the District Committee in Lublin; (2) the JDC in Warsaw; (3) the Koordynacja for the Affairs of Jewish Children in Poland in Łódź; and (4) a special emissary from Łódź who contacted me in March this year.

I have asked [you] to give me the evidence that I need and have not received to this day, which is why I cannot take care of the matter.

I have asked [you] several times to take care of the advance that you promised me as part of my remuneration, or to pay me for what I have done thus far. Up to now, however, I have received nothing despite your promise.

Since several other organizations have been taking an interest in the matter and are demanding information from me, I already have a general idea about who holds the power of attorney to be in contact with me in this matter.

Given this state of affairs, I hereby state that I waive the power of attorney that I was given and will no longer handle this case.

Letter from Rachel Besserman, Toronto, to Central Jewish Committee in Poland[20]

June 27, 1949

Dear important friend:
Why haven't you written me about the trial involving my beloved daughter, even though I sent all the documents and testimonies three months ago?

For me, every day is an eternity. For you, it moves ahead so slowly. What is the reason? Is it the situation or is it my luck? If the problem has to do with money, write to me and tell me everything. I'm willing to do my utmost so that this young soul will be with me — the one whom I am suffering so much for, the one for whom I yearn endlessly. My young life is worthless in Canada;

19 Ibid. (original in Polish).
20 Ibid. (original in Yiddish).

all the Sabbaths and Jewish festivals are gone for me. I hope and understand that you're doing everything; you must have a lot of work to do in connection with the Jews in Poland. Still, I'm also one of those badly suffering souls. Five years have passed since my liberation and I'm fighting in all situations and in all kinds of countries. My pain knows no limit, my thoughts and worries for my dear girl are making me sick. Therefore, I beg you: have pity on me, help me. At this time, only you can help me by doing something that you'll be proud of. It is your great duty as Jews who deal with public affairs to restore a child to her mother — a Jewish child to the Jewish people.

Write to my lawyer so that he'll get the trial going. Maybe hire another lawyer. I'll send you money. Write to me about how to send the money. Please, once again, answer me quickly. A word about my daughter gives me the strength to live. Do something for a miserable mother.

Rachel

Letter from Director of Education Department, Central Jewish Committee in Poland, to Lublin District Committee[21]

July 3, 1949

In regard to the letter of resignation from Attorney Steliński of Lublin, who dealt with the matter of Rachel Igenfeld's daughter, due to lack of documents and mainly because he did not receive the advance that he had been promised, the Education Department wishes to appoint a chief representative who will try to persuade this attorney to continue handling this case by promising to arrange payment.

Signed: Herszenhorn, Director of Education Department
Bitter, Member of staff, Legal Department

---

21 Ibid. (original in Polish).

Letter from Kurt R. Grossman, World Jewish Congress, to Rabbi Kahana[22]

New York, September 8, 1949
Re: Child of Mrs. Besserman

Dear Rabbi Kahana:
You will recall our cooperation last year in Montreux when you were a member of the Committee on Relief and Rehabilitation and Reconstruction at the second plenary session of the World Jewish Congress.

At that time you expressed special interest in all cases where Jewish children were retained in non-Jewish homes.

I know that you are very well acquainted with the case of Mrs. Rachel Igenfeld-Besserman, c/o I. Platner, 4141/2 Spadenew Avenue, Toronto, Ontario, Canada. Her child's name is Ita Igenfeld now living with a peasant family, Mr. and Mrs. Joseph Pic in the village Rataj, district Kaweczyn. Mrs. Besserman has put all her hope in your ability and tenacity to regain the child for her and for the Jews as a whole.

I am now informed that you are going to leave Poland and go to Israel. I would be most grateful to learn what arrangements you have made for this case; that it should be taken care of by your successor. I would appreciate it if you would kindly inform me without further delay.

I have written to the Central Committee of Jews in Poland as per attached copy.

Very sincerely yours,

Kurt R. Grosman

Appendix to this letter:
Mrs. Besserman appealed to the following in regard to her child.
1. Central Committee in Lublin.
2. "Joint" in Warsaw.
3. Central Committee in Warsaw.
4. Rabbi Dr. Kahana in Warsaw.
5. Łódźer Committee.
6. Historical Comission in Łódź.
7. Berlin "Joint."
8. Polish Consulate in Berlin.

22 ŻIH, Education Department, File 677.

9. Polish Consul in Frankfurt am Main.
10. Central Committee in Munich.

All these organizations could not help her. In final desperation, she decided to write to His Holiness, the Holy Father, the Pope, in Rome. Maybe he would help her. He didn't. In fact, two letters were written to him and not one was answered. After all this, the author, C. Leiberman was notified of all the facts in the story by Rachel.

Mr. Leiberman urges that every Jewish woman in America and every Jewish woman's organization in America should write to Mrs. Eleanor Roosevelt about Rachel and her child, and urge her to bring this matter up personally with Cardinal Spellman of N.Y.

The idea is to have Cardinal Spellman write to the Pope in Rome so that he may have the child returned to Rachel. The child is now seven years old.

The Heartbreak of a Jewish Mother

Written by C. Leiberman
Translated by S. Smith

The author begins by urging every Jewish mother to listen to his story.

The story is about a Jewish mother named Rachel Besserman of 4/3 Spadina Avenue, Toronto, Ontario, Canada. This woman has been living in Canada for one year and is part of a group of DPs who came to Canada as tailors. As yet she has not settled herself because of great anguish brought on by the loss of her child.

It seems that in the year 1940, the Nazis were making life very touch [*sic*] for the Jews in Poland. Rachel Besserman and her husband were sent to the Warsaw ghetto. Late in 1940 Rachel's husband died, leaving her pregnant. Mrs. Besserman decided that, since she was blond and looked a little Aryanish, she would try to escape. This she accomplished with the help of forged papers. She fled to her ancestral home of Branevka, in the province of Kraśnik, where her mother was. It was there in July of 1941 that she had her child, a girl. It was named Lunka. Towards the end of 1941 the Nazis began conscripting Jews in the Branevka area. Mrs. Besserman feared for her life and the life of her child. She decided to run away and hide in the woods. This she did and in November 1942 when the child was sixteen months old, Rachel was faced with the greatest decision she ever had to make. The winter was the worst in 50 years and her supply of canned milk had run out. She was desperate. Her child was dying in her arms. After careful consideration she decided on abandoning the child, not entirely, just so that it would have a place to live. Since there wasn't any paper to be had for the purpose of writing a note, the inside of an empty cigarette wrapper had to suffice. On the note she wrote: "This child is already baptized. Her name is Lunka." Rachel placed the child in the barn of a man by the name of A. Fatz. Mr. Fatz found the child the next morning and brought it to the town authorities. The town authorities notified the Gestapo and the Gestapo sent two agents over to see it (the child).

The agents looked at the child and decided that since it was a girl and that so many children have already died, they would let this one live. Also, the child did not look Jewish. The authorities turned the child over to some sort of welfare agency and in turn the agency turned the child over to Mrs. Burtsen, a super-devout Catholic. The child was brought up in the Catholic tradition. She lived with Mrs. Burtsen for one year and after a year she was given to a rich farmer named Mr. Pick. Mr. Pick rebaptized the girl Stanislava and entered in the record that he was her foster father. All this time Rachel had kept track of her child through observation and through friends. In 1945 when the Russians liberated Poland she complained to the Russian authorities. The authorities decided against Mr. Pick and levied a fine against him. However, the child was not returned to Rachel. After a few weeks she decided to ask for the child again. Mr. Pick was very adamant about the whole thing and threatened Rachel with violence and death, if she didn't leave him alone.

Shortly thereafter the Kielce pogrom commenced and Rachel and her second husband Solomon Besserman were forced to flee, first to Germany and finally to Canada where they are now.

Letter from Kurt R. Grossman, World Jewish Congress, to Central Jewish Committee in Poland[23]

New York, September 8, 1949
Re: The child of Mrs. Besserman

Dear friends:
I have today written to Rabbi Kahana in above-mentioned case and hope that my letter will reach him before his departure for Israel.

---

23 Ibid. The letter was written in English but the wording at the bottom of the page was translated into Polish in handwriting. This phrasing appears in several copies and was evidently sent by the Central Committee to various departments.

In any case, I am sending you this letter with the suggestion that you be good enough to assist in Mrs. Besserman's understandable desire to regain her child.

May I expect your reply on action you have taken? Thank you for your kind cooperation.

Very sincerely yours,

Kurt R. Grossman

These are the documents that I found in the archives. From the way they flowed, it was clear to me that they did not take into account all the letters, documents, and papers that had been written on the topic; they were merely the ones that had made their way to the archives. In my research, I found that Rabbi Kahana had left Poland in September 1949; therefore the letters sent to him from the United States that month did not reach him. I also learned that political changes in Poland were sapping the strength of the Central Jewish Committee so badly that about a year later the Committee reformed itself into the National Association for Jewish Culture.

After Rabbi Kahana left Poland, his aide, Yeshayahu Drucker, stayed behind to continue dealing with the cause of Jewish children who were still living with non-Jews — his area of expertise with the Council of Communities since late 1945. I contacted Drucker and asked him what he knew of the case of the girl Ita-Leah Igenfeld-Besserman. To my surprise, he knew nothing about it (even though Rabbi Kahana had involved him in all matters related to the Jewish children, and in 1948 the girl's mother had given the rabbi power of attorney via the Federation of Polish Jews in Canada).

Driven by curiosity (a human trait), I wanted to know how this story ended. Was the girl (now an adult) living in Poland or had she joined her mother in Canada? For several years I considered taking advantage of one of my many trips around Poland and stopping at Rataj Ordynacki and a neighboring village, Wólka Ratajska, and enquiring… After much indecision, I did so in the late 1990s. I planned it meticulously, lest I offend the woman if the locals were unaware of her Jewish identity. I decided "just" to ask whether the daughter of Józef Pycz was living in the village. On the main road, a peasant whom I encountered (and who turned out to be from a neighboring village) told me that Pycz's daughter had gone to her mother in Canada in the mid-1950s following a court ruling. To my surprise, he knew the details of the story and claimed that everyone knew about it and had followed the case as it developed for years. A local woman who joined in the conversation led me to the home of an elderly woman who had been a friend of Leonka's adoptive parents. The latter told me that the Pyczes' home had been standing empty since the girl's parents died. (They had had no children of their own.) She told me that the girl, aged sixteen, had spent only a short time with her mother because her mother's wish for her to return to Judaism had destroyed their relationship. The girl returned to Poland some later time and married a villager, after which the two of them went back to Canada. My interlocutor described the broken hearts of the girl's adoptive parents, the lengthy years of the trial, and the void that the girl's departure had left behind.

Before Holocaust and Heroism Remembrance Day in April 2000, a journalist for an Israeli daily newspaper interviewed me. Among other things, I retold Ita-Leah's story as an example of a tragedy in which no one wins. Some time later, I received a phone call from a woman in central Israel who told me that her late father had been a cousin of Mrs. Igenfeld-Besserman. In the 1950s, she continued, his cousin, Rachel, had sent him letters telling her story and had enclosed some photographs. After the war, Ita's mother had given birth to two daughters with her second husband but allowed herself no rest until she could see the daughter whom she had left behind in Poland. One of the photos was a copy of one that had been sent to her from Poland, when Ita was ten years old. The girl's mother wrote the following on the back of the photo: "This is a picture of my beloved daughter, for whom I have shed a great many tears, and who remains in the coarse hands of an antisemite to this day. Her name is Ita-Leah Igenfeld and she is ten years old." Another photo was taken in early 1957, when Ita and her mother were reunited. The girl's mother wrote the following on its back:

"I send you this picture, I [...] together with my redeemed daughter, after fifteen years of war and suffering.

Your happy cousin, *Imma* [mother] Rachel

Ita's mother passed away in the 1980s. A relative in the United States helped me to track Ita down. I contacted her and she asked me to send her a copy of the documents presented above.

A year later, during one of the festivals marking the Jewish new year, Ita-Leah sat down with members of her Jewish family. Although she does not live as a Jewish woman, the encounter was notable for its family atmosphere.

Recently, I also met with one of her half-sisters, born to her mother after the war, and I also gave her copies of the documents.

Sources and Bibliography

Archives

American Jewish Joint Distribution Committee Archive, Giv'at Ram, Jerusalem

Box B12 file C61.013 transfer of children; file C61.019 Hehalutz–Poland 1947–1948; file C61.023, Łódź kibbutzim, Poland 1947–1949; file C61–055, Children's homes — Poland 2– 14 1948

Microfilms from Poland II, VIII, XI, documents photocopied from the files of JDC's archives in Warsaw and transferred to JDC's archives in Jerusalem

Files from JDC's archives in Warsaw brought from Poland by the head of JDC's archives in Jerusalem; given to me and in my possession

Bar-Ilan University, Ramat Gan, Institute for the Study of Religious Zionism (RZRI)

Record Group V.s The movement in the forefront of the rescue of children after the war. Files s. IV.21; s.V.21; s.IV.19; s.IV.20

Gonjondzki (Gonen) archive s.IV.22

Central Zionist Archives, Jerusalem

Record Group C25, Political Department of the Jewish Agency, files 5262, 10513, 5241

Record Group S25, Rescue Committee 1939–1948, files 1266, 1291, 1317, 1424, 1451

Record Group S86, Department of Emissaries 1946–1964, file 73

Record Group C6, Israeli office of the World Jewish Congress, files, 111, 113

Record Group L58, Continental office of Youth Aliyah, Polish branch, files 358, 382,428, 516, 575, 578, 595, 748, 810

Record Group J25, delegation of Polish Jewry in Israel, file 100

Ghetto Fighters' House Archive

Correspondence files 788–790 Activities of the Koordynacja in Poland
Card index Koordynacja children file 800
Koordynacja newspaper, *Farn Yiddishn Kind* ("For the Jewish Child"),
one-time issue, November 1946, Poland, file 798

Hebrew University, Jerusalem, Institute of Contemporary Jewry, Section for Oral Documentation

Record Group 68, redemption of children:
 Bronstein, Yehuda 25
 Drucker, Yeshayahu 28
 Jeruchamzon, Moshe (Mstisław Jankowski) 44
 Kaplinski, Baruch 21
 Koryski, Leibel 15
 Krybus, Pinhas 45
 Lederman, Sarah 50
 Zilber, Devorah (Marysia) 27

Lavon Institute, Tel Aviv, Labor and Pioneering Archive

Record Group Va'ad Hapoel secretariat — correspondence with Hechalutz centers, file of political parties and different organizations 364-4-209 IV
Record Group Va'ad Hapoel of the Histadrut — secretariat, file of Committee for Polish Refugees 3802-1-208 IV

Massuah Archive, Kibbutz Tel Yitzhak

Record Group Private Collections, Moshe Kolodny (Kol) Archive
Record Group Testimonies:
 Mara, Anton 25/27
 Packer, Naphtali 1/23

Moreshet Archive, Giv'at Haviva

Record Group D1, certificates and documents section
Record Group D2, manuscripts section
Record Group A, testimonies:
 Friedman, Avraham 403
 Halperin, Sabrina 201
 Lutner, Yaakov 402
 Mann, Baruch 399

Mintz, Tzipporah 262
Orlowicz-Reznik, Nesia 353
Shmueli, Sukha 217
Wildstajn Cyla, 485

Religious Zionist Archives, Mossad HaRav Kook, Jerusalem (RZA)
Rescue files 1–4

Yad Vashem Archives, Jerusalem
Private collections record group, Zerach Wahrhaftig collection, P.20/8
Red Cross card index, Arolsen
Testimonies Department, O.3:
Awrucki-Mandelberger, Hannah 5773
Batista, Hannah 5732
Blustein, Benyamin 8058
Brawer, Aviva 4509
Bronstein, Yehuda 5130
Drucker, Yeshayahu 3249
Hoter, Bella 5708
Kurc, Moshe 4290
Lindenbaum, Arie 5112
Lustigman, Rivka 4152
Marek, Esther 4168
Miller, Mordechai 3653
Nekryc, Miriam 3921
Templer, Malka 4278
Timyanski, Lyuba 5131

Żydówski Instityut Historyczny Archives, Warsaw, Poland;
Centralny Komitet Żydów w Polsce-Wydział Oświaty
(Department of Education)
Boxes 601–635, 636, 637, 638–641, 642–652, 668–677
Education Department booklet A-B: list of children not yet located
Instructions leaflet for staff of education department concerning interviewing children and completion of questionnaires
Leaflet on activities of the Central Committee of Jews of Poland from 1 January to 30 June 1946
Record Group, legal department of the Central Committee — 105
Record Group, reports of rescuers (reports written after the war when

children where handed over to the children's homes of the Central Committee)

Documents with the provisional notation RSLF; (during compilation of the sources for this book, these documents were in the process of being classified and computerized)

Various certificates, testimonies and documents given to the author by their owners

Barak-Owiec, Haviva, Kibutz Yiftach: recorded memoirs

Bielicka-Bornstein, Chasia, Kibbutz Lehavot Habashan: personal notebook written by her in the children's home in Łódź with details of children who arrived in the homes; notebook "Conference of Koordynacja children," Kibbutz Lehavot Habashan, October, 1985

Bramm-Ehrlich, Mira, Tiv'on: transcript of interview with her carried out in the children's home in Kraków, 1945, no. s-342

Bronstein, Yehuda, Ramat Gan: authority to work issued by children on behalf of the Koordynacja

Chryc, Janina, Poland: will in a letter to Helena Guzala written in 1954 by her adoptive mother

Farber, Nava, Kibbutz Yiftach: recorded interview with Antonina Falk, Poland

Gruder (Edward) Yaron, Herzlia: Children's home card

Gutmorgen-Luster, Ruszka, Kiryat Ata: invitation to her wedding with Captain Drucker (a fictitious invitation that was printed so as to gain the release of her younger sister from her rescuer)

Hilferding-Goldschmidt, Erella, Shadmot Devora: memoirs of Elżbieta Miszczyk, letters and documents relating to her

Książenicki-Harel, Zvi, Kibbutz Mizra: letter from Anna Sąchocka, granddaughter of his rescuer

Lavie, Tami, Haifa: testimony of Genia Düstenfeld

Lewinsky, Tuvia, Kfar Vradim: booklet "Memoirs: My Wanderings and My Rescuer"

Magen, Gideon, Kibbutz Ein Shemer: notebook of Shulamit Magen, "First and Last Memory"

Reisner, Yehiel, Poland: file of documents concerning Sabina Kagan-Rostropowicz

Shner-Neshamit, Sarah, Kibbutz Lohamei Hagetaot: comments on testimony of Arieh Sarid on his mission to Poland; list of Koordinacja children and comments on their life histories; interviews with Hanoch Levin and David Shirman — educators at the Koordynacja children's homes

Simchai, Iko, Kibbutz Hagoshrim: child's card issued in her name; photograph and caption from the Koordynacja album

Interviews

Interviews carried out by the author and in her possession

Barak-Owiec, Haviva-Luba, Kibbutz Yiftach
Bein-Avni, Tova-Ogenia
Bielicka-Bornstein, Chasia, Kibbutz Lehavot Habashan
Bram-Ehrlich, Mira, Tiv'on
Bronstein, Yehuda, Ramat Gan
Chryc, Janina, Jastrzębia, Poland
Drucker, Yeshayahu, Holon
Edelstein, Chaim, Upper Nazareth
Ficowska-Kopel, Elżbieta, Warsaw, Poland
Finkelstein, Rina, Bnei Brak
Frank-Friedberg, Rachel, Holon
Goldberg-Sarid, Leibel-Arieh, Afula
Granatstein, Jehiel, Bnei Brak
Haezrahi-Bürger, Yosef
Halperin, Sabina, Kibbutz Shoval
Hilferding-Goldschmidt, Erella, Shadmot Dvora
Jarska, Roma, Kraków, Poland
Kagan-Heller, Sabina, Los Angeles, USA
Kagan-Plodwinska, Rachel, Tiv'on
Kowalska, Halina, Warsaw, Poland
Kowalska, Ita, Warsaw, Poland
Książenicki-Harel, Zvi, Kibbutz Mizra
Kuder, Jan, Kraków, Poland
Kunda, Menachem, Herzliya
Kuperman-Nachmani, Aliza, Yokneam Moshava
Landau, Ceisza, Tel Aviv
Lichtman, Erich, Kibbutz Usha
Martinowsky-Gutmorgen, Hannah, Kiryat Ono
Milch-Rosenzweig, Lucia, New York, USA

Mizocz-Geving, Rachel, Kibbutz Mishmar Ha'emek
Modlen, Pnina, Kibbutz Shluchot
Neuberg, Sabina, Ramat Gan
Plonsky, Ala, Kibbutz Meggido
Plonsky, David (Yurek), Kibbutz Meggido
Ramon, Eli, Jerusalem
Schwartzbach, Yehudit, Haifa
Shner-Neshamit, Sarah, Kibbutz Lohamei Hagetaot
Szczekacz-Gwircman-Tzur, Zoshia-Sarah, Ramat Gan
Tuchhandler-Chandler, Moshe-Morris, Michigan, USA
Waldbaum-Leshem, Chanita, Jerusalem
Wisniewska-Muchtar, Henia-Tamar, Tel Aviv
Wolff-Weinstock, Rachel, Holon

Interview carried out by Shlomo Bargil

Goldberg-Sarid, Leibel-Arieh, Afula

Questionnaires

Rotbard, Fredzia, Kibbutz Gan Shmuel
Sternbach, Chaim, Kfar Yedidiya
Ya'akobi, Tamar, Kfar Hess

Correspondence with rescuers and others

Balcerzak, Maria, Tomaszów Mazowiecki, Poland, April and September, 1995
Chruściel, Władisława, Nowa Sól, Poland, April and August, 1995
Cypryański, Pawel, Słupsk, Poland, August and September, 1995
Jarska, Roma, Kraków, Poland, April, 1995
Kordzikowska, Bogumila Maria, Nowa Wieś, Poland, April, 1995
Kruczalowa, Maria Magdalena, Tarnów, Poland, April and September, 1995
Kuder, Jan, Kraków, Poland, April, 1995
Madej, Maria, Gdańsk, Poland, April and September, 1995
Mazur, Jadwiga, Warsaw, Poland, May and August, 1995
Szaniewska, Bozena, Milanówek, Poland, 1995
Walczyńska, A., Kraków, Poland, March, 1995

Newspaper articles
(in Hebrew unless otherwise indicated)

Argaman-Barnea, Amalia: "Girl of War," *Yediot Aharonot*, 7 Days Magazine, pp. 84–5, 96, June 11, 1993

Habas, Bracha: "Report from Visitors to Poland," *Davar*, p. 2, 28 August, 1945

Kempner, Mali: "Only the Baby Survived," *Yediot Aharonot*, 7 Days Magazine, pp. 31,33,56, 8 June, 1990

Klinger, Noah: "The Jewish Baby who was Thrown from the Warsaw Ghetto Walls is now in Israel," *Yediot Aharonot,* 10 April, 1989

Margoshes, Shmuel: "How to Redeem Jewish Children in Poland," *Der Tog*, p. 7, 2 August, 1945 (Yiddish)

Meron, Gideon: "Because of that War," *Yediot Aharonot*, 7 Days Magazine, pp. 50–4, 9 June, 1995

"Our Children in Belgium will be returned to Judaism," *Hatzofeh*, p. 1, 19 March, 1946

Reicher, Amit: "The Priest Burst into Tears in the Confessional Booth: 'I am Jewish," *Yediot Aharonot*, pp. 16–17, 17 July, 1992

Shpiesman, Leib: "New Marranos in Poland," *Der Tog* weekly English supplement, 7 April, 1946 (English)

Television

Berman, Vered (producer and director): "Wanda's Lists," Israel Television first channel. Part 1, 22 November, 1994, part 2, 22 June 1995

(producer and director): "Lost Identity — the True Story," Israel Television first channel. 15 April, 1997. Joint production of Israel Television and Polish State Television. In Poland the program was called *Kim jestem?* ("Who am I.") Part 2 was based on the continued research and reactions to Part 1 and was shown on Israel Television only on 5 May, 1997. I participated in the research of both parts of the program.

(producer and director): "Lost Identity — the True Story," Israel Television first channel, 17 April, 2000. I participated in the research

Lukow, Bracha (researcher and director): "Upside Down Roots," Israel Television first channel, 1989

Books and Articles in Hebrew

Anolik, Benjamin, *In the Service of Memory*, pp. 95–100, Kibbutz Lohamei Hagetaot: Ghetto Fighters' House, 1990

Armony, Lydia, "Testimony" in *Reclamation of Jewish Children from Christians in Poland after the Holocaust,* edited by Shmuel Bornstein, pp. 64–68, Kibbutz Lohamei Hagetaot: Ghetto Fighters' House, 1989

Bahat, Mordechai, "Redeemed Children on their Way to Palestine" in *Reclamation of Jewish Children from Christians in Poland after the Holocaust,* edited by Shmuel Bornstein, pp. 95–100, Kibbutz Lohamei Hagetaot: Ghetto Fighters' House, 1989

Bar-Gil, Shlomo, *Looking for a Home — Finding a Homeland: Youth Aliyah in the Educating and Rehabilitating of the Holocaust Victims, 1945–1955,* Jerusalem: Yad Yitzhak Ben-Zvi, 1999

Barlas, Haim, Rescue During the Holocaust, Kibbutz Lohamei Hagetaot: Ghetto Fighters' House, 1975

Beck-Chaim, Meir, "Testimony: How a Shtetl was Destroyed," in *The Book of Kraśnik* pp. 225–233, Tel Aviv: Association of Kraśnik Survivors in Israel and the Diaspora, 1973

Ben-Shem, Reuven, "From a Diary of the Warsaw Ghetto," in *Massua 10,* pp. 33–52, 1982

Berman, Adolf Avraham, *From the Days of the Resistance*, Tel Aviv: Hamenorah, 1971

Bielicki-Bornstein, Chasia, "Back to the Bosom of their People," in Dror Levy, ed., *Hashomer Hatza'ir Book*, pp. 316–344, Merhavia: Sifriat Poalim, 1961

Bornstein, Shmuel, ed., *Reclamation of Jewish Children from Christians in Poland after the Holocaust,* Kibbutz Lohamei Hagetaot: Ghetto Fighters' House, 1989

Brachfeld, Silvain, *A Gift of Life: The Rescue of 56 Percent of Belgian Jewry During the Nazi Occupation*, Tel Aviv: Yediot Aharonot and Hemed Books, 2000

Children of Life: Survival of Five Hundred Jewish Children from the Talons of the Gestapo in Occupied Belgium During the Holocaust, Tel Aviv: Ministry of Defence, 1991

Carlebach, Azriel, ed., *The Anglo-American Committee of Enquiry Regarding the Problem of European Jewry and Palestine*, Tel Aviv: Leitzmann, 1946

Cheshin, Shneor Zalman, *Adoptive Children*, Ramat Gan: Massada, 1955

Dekel, Ephraim, *Along the Paths of the Bricha B*, Tel Aviv: Ma'arachot, 1969

Remnants of the Sword: The Rescue of Children during and After the Holocaust, Tel Aviv: Ministry of Defence, 1983

Dror, Levy, ed., *Hashomer Hatza'ir Book,* Merhavia: Sifriat Poalim, 1961

Dror, Zvika (editor and interviewer), *Pages of Testimony: 96 Members of Kibbutz Lohamei Hagetaot Tell their Stories* A-D, Kibbutz Lohamei Hagetaot: Ghetto Fighters' House, Tel Aviv, 1984

Drucker, Yeshayahu, "One Man's Actions in the Redemption of Children," in *Reclamation of Jewish Children from Christians in Poland after the Holocaust,* edited by Shmuel Bornstein, pp. 35–37, Kibbutz Lohamei Hagetaot: Ghetto Fighters' House, 1983

Eliash, Shulamit, "Relations between the Chief Rabbinate of Palestine and the Mandate Government, 1936–1945," doctoral dissertation, Bar Ilan University, 1979

Encyclopedia of the Holocaust, Jerusalem and Tel Aviv: Yad Vashem and Sifriat Poalim, 1990

Engel, David, *Between Liberation and Escape: Holocaust Survivors in Poland and the Struggle for their Leadership, 1944–1946,* Tel Aviv: Tel Aviv University and Am Oved, 1996

Fleiszer, Devorah, "The Rescue of 24 Children from Christian Hands," in *Szebreszyn Community Memorial Book,* Haifa: Association of Szebreszyn in Israel and the Diaspora, pp. 300–304, 1984 (Yiddish)

Frank, Moshe, *To Survive and Testify, the Holocaust Trauma of a Jewish Boy From Zamość,* Tel Aviv: Ghetto Fighters' House and Hakibbutz Hameuchad, 1993

Frederber-Salz, Berta, *And the Sun Rose,* Tel Aviv: Naye Leben, 1968

Frimerman, Shmuel, "Activities of the World Jewish Congress in the Years 1938–1946," MA thesis, Bar Ilan University, 1995

Frister, Roman, *Without Compromise,* Tel Aviv: Zmora Bitan, 1987

Granatstein, Jehiel, *Double Life,* Bnai Brak: Pe'er, 1991
    Yemei Bereshit ("Days of Genesis,") Bnai Brak: Pe'er, 1997

Greenbaum, Yitzhak, *In Days of Destruction and Holocaust,* Jerusalem and Tel Aviv: Haverim,1946

Gruss, Noah, *Child Martyrdom,* Buenos Aires: Tsentral Farband fun Poylishe Yiden in Argentine, 1947 (Yiddish)

Grzywacz, Shlomo, "To the Bosom of My People," in Ghetto Fighters' House Bulletin No. 20, pp. 59–65, April 20, 1958

Gutman, Yisrael, "Jews of Poland in the Holocaust," in *The Broken Chain: Polish Jewry Through the Ages,* edited by Yisrael Bartal and Yisrael Gutman, Jerusalem: Zalman Shazar Institute, 1997, pp. 451–506

"Polish Jews from Liberation to Emigration 1944-1948," in *East European Jews — Between Holocaust and Redemption, 1944-1948*, edited by Benjamin Pinkus, Sde Boker: Ben Gurion University, 1987, pp. 113-123

Jews in Poland after World War II: Studies on Polish Jewry, Jerusalem: Zalman Shazar Center, 1985

Haran, Arye, ed., and Stern, Ruth, interviewer, *What we Remembered to Tell: 24 Members of Kibbutz Meggido Testify*, Tel Aviv: Moreshet and Sifriat Poalim, 1988

Hebrew Encyclopedia, Jerusalem and Tel Aviv, 1951

Janisz, Gershon, "The Epic of my Rescued Daughter Shifraleh 'Bagumila,'" in *Radzymin Memorial Book* in *Encyclopedia of the Jewish Diaspora* edited by Gershon Hel, Jerusalem and Tel Aviv: Encyclopedia of the Jewish Diaspora, 1975 (Yiddish), pp. 336-348

Kahana, David, *After the Deluge: Attempts to Revive the Religious Communities of Poland After World War II, 1944-1949*, Jerusalem: Mossad HaRav Kook, 1981

Kleiman, Yehudit, ed., *Letters from "Nowhere": Last Letters of Jews from the Nazi Occupied Countries*, Jerusalem: Yad Vashem, 1988, pp. 26-27

Koryski, Leibl, "The Zionist Koordynacja for the Redemption of Jewish Children in Poland," in *Reclamation of Jewish Children from Christians in Poland after the Holocaust*, edited by Shmuel Bornstein, Kibbutz Lohamei Hagetaot: Ghetto Fighters' House, 1989, pp. 23-33

Küchler, Lena, *We Accuse, Testimony of Children from the Holocaust*, Merhavia: Sifriat Poalim, 1963

Küchler-Silberman, Lena, *The Hundred [Children] to Their Borders*, Jerusalem and Tel Aviv: Schocken, 1969

Levinsky, Akiva, "Children Redeemed under the Auspices of Aliyat Hanoar," in *Reclamation of Jewish Children from Christians in Poland after the Holocaust*, edited by Shmuel Bornstein, Kibbutz Lohamei Hagetaot: Ghetto Fighters' House, 1989, pp. 101-106

Lewinsky, Tuvia, "Testimony" in *Reclamation of Jewish Children from Christians in Poland after the Holocaust*, edited by Shmuel Bornstein, Kibbutz Lohamei Hagetaot: Ghetto Fighters' House, 1989, pp. 101-106

Litvak, Yosef, "The JDC's Contribution to the Rehabilitation of the Jewish Survivors in Poland, 1944-1949" in *Eastern European Jewry — From Holocaust to Redemption, 1944-1948*, edited by Benjamin Pinkus), Sde Boker: Ben Gurion University, 1987, pp. 334-388

Mahler, Ella, "Redemption of Jewish Children from their Non-Jewish Rescuers," *Yad Vashem Bulletin* 29, July, 1962, pp. 34-40

Michman, Dan, "Destroyers of Zionism: the Principles of the 'Post-Zionist' Outlook In Contemporary Israeli Society," in *"Post-Zionism" and the Holocaust: the Israeli Public Polemic on "Post-Zionism" in 1993–1996 and Where the Holocaust Fits into it — a Reader*, Ramat Gan: Bar Ilan University, 1997, pp. 11–26

Michman (Melkman), Joseph, "The Problem of Jewish War Orphans in the Netherlands," in *Michmanei Joseph: Studies on the History and Literature of Dutch Jewry*, Jerusalem: Center for the Study of Dutch Jewry, and the Hebrew University, 1994, pp. 399–418

Mission of Rescue: The Journey of the Chief Rabbi of Eretz Israel, Rabbi Isaac Halevy Herzog to Europe, Jerusalem: Dfus Haivri, 1947

Mission to the Diaspora 1945–1948, Yad Tabenkin, Ghetto Fighters' House and Tel Aviv: Hakibbutz Hameuchad, 1989

Morgenstern, Arieh, "The United Rescue Committee of the Jewish Agency and its Activities, 1943–1945," *Yalkut Moreshet 13*, June 1971, pp. 60–103,

Nebenzahl, Leah, *To Those Who Took Me In — A Cycle of Poems*, Tel Aviv: Eked, 1994

Neshamit, Sarah, "The Koordynacja for the Redemption of Children in Liberated Poland," in *Research on the Holocaust and the Revolt*, second collection, Kibbutz Lohamei Hagetaot: Ghetto Fighters' House, February, 1952, pp. 116–148; See also, Shner-Neshamit

Orlowicz-Reznik, Nesia, *Mother, Can I Cry Now?* Merhavia: Moreshet and Sifriat Poalim, 1965

"The Children's Home of Hashomer [Hatzair]," in Dror Levy, ed., *Book of Hashomer Hatza'ir*, vol. 2, Merhavia: Sifriat Poalim, 1961, pp. 316–311

Paldiel, Mordechai, *Whoever Saves One Soul: The Righteous Among the Nations and their Uniqueness*, Jerusalem: Yad Vashem, 1993

"Rescuers in the Footsteps of the Rescued: Righteous Gentiles Living in Israel," in *Moreshet 41*, June, 1986, pp. 36–7

Peltel-Miedzyrzecki, Wladka-Feigel, *From Both Sides of the Wall, Memoirs of a Courier in the Resistance,* Tel Aviv: Hakibbutz Hameuchad, 1993

Perehodnik, Calek, *The Sad Task of Documentation: A Diary in Hiding*, Jerusalem: Keter, 1993

Perlberger-Shmuel, Miriam, *This Girl is Jewish (Memoirs of Marysia)* (Haifa: Association of Survivors of Wieliczka and the Vicinity in Israel, Carmelit, 1985)

Rubinstein, Eliezer, *Reckoning an Epoch: Mizrachi Movement and Torah vaAvodah in Liberated Poland*, Łódź, in *On the Paths of Rebirth*, 1989, pp. 179–188

Samet, Shimon, *When I Came the Day After: A Journey to Poland, 1946*, Tel Aviv: Z. Leinmann, 1946

Sarid, Levi Arieh, "The Beginnings of the Activity of Jewish Youth Movements among Polish Jewry and the Emissaries from Eretz Israel, 1944–1946," in *Eastern European Jewry — From Holocaust to Redemption, 1944–1948*, Sde Boker: Ben Gurion University, 1987, pp. 274–333

Ruin and Deliverance: the Pioneer Movements in Poland Throughout the Holocaust and During its Aftermath, 1939–1945, Tel Aviv: Moreshet, 1997

"The Koordynacja" in Shmuel Bornstein, ed., *Reclamation of Jewish Children from Christians in Poland after the Holocaust*, Kibbutz Lohamei Hagetaot: Ghetto Fighters' House, 1989, pp. 15–22

Schirman, David, "Management of Redeemed Childrens' Homes," in Shmuel Bornstein, ed., *Reclamation of Jewish Children from Christians in Poland after the Holocaust*, Kibbutz Lohamei Hagetaot: Ghetto Fighters' House, 1989, pp. 39–46

Shlomi, Hannah, "The Jewish Survivors in Poland Become Organized after the Second World War, 1944–1950," in Yisrael Bartal and Yisrael Gutman, eds., *The Broken Chain: Polish Jewry Through the Ages* (in Hebrew: *Continuity and Crisis: the History of Polish Jewry*, 1997), Jerusalem: Zalman Shazar Institute, 1997, pp. 523–547

"Organizational Activities by Jewish Survivors in Poland After World War II" in *Gal'ed: Collection on the History of Polish Jewry*, 2, 1975, pp. 287–331

"Actions of Polish Jews to Renew Jewish Life in Poland, January–June, 1945," in *Gal'ed: Collection on the History of Polish Jewry*, 10, 1988, pp. 207–225

Shner-Neshamit, Sarah, *I did not Come to Rest*, Kibbutz Lohamei Hagetaot: Ghetto Fighters' House, 1986, pp. 73–93

"The Spiritual Character of the Redeemed Children," in Shmuel Bornstein, ed., *Reclamation of Jewish Children from Christians in Poland after the Holocaust*, Kibbutz Lohamei Hagetaot: Ghetto Fighters' House, 1989, pp. 73–93; See also, Neshamit, Sarah

Sznajderman, S.L., "A Jewish Mother Fights for her Daughter," in Moshe Tamari, ed., *Węgrów Memorial Book*, Tel Aviv: Former Residents of Węgrów in Israel together with Survivors of Węgrów in Argentina, 1961, pp. 71–72

Sompolinsky, Meir, "The Anglo-Jewish Leadership: the British Government and the Holocaust," doctoral dissertation, Bar Ilan University, 1977

Tenenboim, Benyamin, *One of a City, Two of a Family: Selection from One*

Thousand Autobiographies of Jewish Children in Poland, Merhavia: Sifriat Poalim and Hakibbutz Ha'artzi-Hashomer Hatza'ir, 1947

Turkow, Jonas, "On the Rescue of Children from the Warsaw Ghetto," *Pages on the Study of the Holocaust and the Uprising*, second series, collection A, 1970, pp. 256–265

Once There Was a Jewish Warsaw, Tel Aviv: Education and Culture, 1969

Wasserstein-Blanker, Esther, "After the Holocaust I Didn't Want to Return to Judaism," in Gershon Hel, ed., *Radzymin Memorial Book* in *Encyclopedia of the Jewish Diaspora*, Jerusalem and Tel Aviv: Encyclopedia of the Jewish Diaspora 1975, pp. 331–335

Weg, Claudine, *I Didn't Manage to Say Goodbye: Children Saved in the Holocaust tell their Stories*, Tel Aviv and Jerusalem: Schocken, 1982

Yacobi-Friedman, Tamar, "Testimony" in Shmuel Bornstein, ed., *Reclamation of Jewish Children from Christians in Poland after the Holocaust*, Kibbutz Lohamei Hagetaot: Ghetto Fighters' House, 1989, pp. 55–60

Yahil, Leni, *The Holocaust: The Fate of European Jewry, 1932–1945*, Jerusalem: Schocken and Yad Vashem, 1987

Yishai, Moshe, *In the Shadow of the Holocaust: Memoirs of a Mission to Poland, 1945–1946,* Tel Aviv: Ghetto Fighters' House and Kibbutz Hameuchad, 1973

Yerushalmi, Eliezer, *Children of the Holocaust,* Haifa: MeMa'amakim, 1960

Zameret, Zvi, *The Melting Pot: The Frumkin Commission on the Education of Immigrant Children, (1950)*, Sde Boker: Ben-Gurion Heritage Center, 1993

Zionist Congress, Twenty-Second, Basel, 9–24 December, 1946, stenographic report, Jerusalem: World Zionist Executive, 1947

Zuckerman, Yitzchak, *The Polish Exodus on the "Bricha" and the Reconstruction of the Pioneer Movement*, Tel Aviv: Ghetto Fighters' House and Hakibutz Hameuchad, 1988

Zuroff, Efraim, "The Orthodox Public in the United States and the Destruction of European Jewry: Rescue Committee of the Orthodox Rabbis during the Holocaust, 1939–1945," doctoral dissertation, Hebrew University of Jerusalem, 1997

Books and Articles in English

Bartoszewski, Władysław and Lewin, Zofia, *The Samaritans: Heroes of the Holocaust*, New York: Twayne, 1970 (first published by Znak, Kraków, 1966)

Bauer, Yehuda, *Flight and Rescue: The Brichah*. New York: Random House, 1970

Out of the Ashes: The Impact of American Jews on Post-Holocaust European Jewry, Oxford: Pergamon Press, 1989

Bauminger, Arieh, *The Righteous Among the Nations*, Jerusalem: Yad Vashem, 1990

Blakeney, Michael, *Australia and the Jewish Refugees 1933–1948*, Sydney: Croom Helm, 1985

Blatman, Daniel, *For Our Freedom and Yours: The Jewish Labor Bund in Poland, 1939–1949*, London: Vallentine, Mitchell, 2003

Bronowski, Alexander. *They Were Few*, New York: Lang, 1991

Dequeker, Luc, "Baptism and Conversion of Jews in Belgium, 1939–1945," in Dan Michman, ed., *Belgium and the Holocaust, Jews, Belgians, Germans*, Jerusalem: Yad Vashem, 1998, pp. 235–271

Encyclopedia of the Holocaust, New York: Macmillan, 1990

Fogelman, Eva, *Conscience and Courage: Rescuers of Jews During the Holocaust*, New York: Doubleday, 1994

Fridenson, Joseph and Kranzler, David, eds., *Heroine of Rescue: The Incredible Story of Recha Sternbuch who Saved Thousands from the Holocaust*, New York: Mesorah, 1984

Grodzinski, Joseph, *In the Shadow of the Holocaust: The Struggle Between Jews and Zionists in the Aftermath of World War II*, Monroe Maine: Common Courage Press, 2004. (Called *Good Human Material* in Hebrew. The text of the English edition differs from that of the Hebrew original. The page numbers quoted refer to the Hebrew)

Hellman, Peter, *Avenue of the Righteous*, New York: Atheneum, 1980

Hochberg-Marianska, Miriam, "I Cared for Child Survivors," *Yad Vashem Bulletin* (Hebrew), no. 1, April 1957, pp. 15–16

Kermish, Joseph, "The Activities of the Council for Aid to Jews (Żegota) in Occupied Poland," in Yisrael Gutman and Efraim Zuroff, eds., *Rescue Attempts During the Holocaust*, Jerusalem: Yad Vashem, 1977, pp. 367–398

Krakowski, Shmuel, "Relation Between Jews and Poles During the Holocaust: New and Old Approaches in Polish Historiography," in *Yad Vashem Studies*, 19, 1988, pp. 317–340

Kranzler, David and Hirschler, Gertrude, eds., *Solomon Schonfeld: His Page in History: Recollections of Individuals Saved by an Extraordinary Orthodox Jewish Rescue Hero During the Holocaust Era*, New York: Judaica Press, 1982

Küchler-Silberman, Lena, *My Hundred Children*, London: Pan Books, 1963. (The text of the English edition differs from the Hebrew original. The page numbers quoted refer to the Hebrew)

Michman, Dan, *Holocaust Historiography: A Jewish Perspective: Conceptualization, Terminology, Approaches and Fundamental issues*, London: Vallentine Mitchell, 2003. (In Hebrew the book was called *The Holocaust and Holocaust Research: Conceptualization, Terminology, Approaches and Basic Issues*)

Poznansky, Renée, "Retrieving the Children," in *Jews in France during World War II*, Waltham: Brandeis University Press in association with the United States Holocaust Museum, 2001

Prekerowa, Tereza, "The 'Just' and the 'Passive,'" in *Yad Vashem Studies,* 19, 1988, pp. 369–377

Ringelblum, Emanuel, *Polish-Jewish Relations During the Second World War*, New York: Howard Fertig, 1976. (In Hebrew the book was called *Last Writings: Polish-Jewish Relations, January 1943–April, 1944*)

Rosen, Donia, *The Forest, My Friend*. New York: Bergen-Belsen Memorial Press of the World Federation of Bergen-Belsen Associations, 1971. (The text of the English edition differs from the Hebrew original. The page numbers quoted refer to the Hebrew)

Silver, Eric, *The Book of the Just: the Silent Heroes who Saved Jews from Hitler*. London: Weidenfeld and Nicolson, 1992

Tec, Nechama, *When Light Pierced the Darkness: Christian Rescue of Jews in Nazi-Occupied Poland*, New York and Oxford: Oxford University Press, 1986

Wahrhaftig, Zerach, *Refugee and Survivor: Rescue Efforts during the Holocaust*, Jerusalem: Yad Vashem, 1984. (The text of the English edition differs from the Hebrew original. The page numbers quoted refer to the Hebrew)

Yahil, Leni, *The Holocaust: the Fate of European Jewry*, New York: Oxford University Press, 1990

Zuckerman Yitzchak (Antek), *A Surplus of Memory: Chronicle of the Warsaw Ghetto Uprising*, Berkley, Los Angeles, Oxford: California Press, 1993. (In Hebrew the book was called *Those Seven Years*)

Books and Articles in Polish

Grynberg, Michał, *Księga Sprawliedliwych*, Warsaw: Wydawnictwo Naukowe PWN, 1993

Kurek-Lesik, Ewa, "Udzial Żeńskich Zgromadzeń zakonnych w akcji ratowania dzieci Żydówskich w Polsce w latach 1939–1945," doctoral dissertation, *Lublin: Katolicki Uniwersytet Lubelski*, 1989

Sliwowska, Wiktoria, ed., *Dzieci Holocaustu Mówią...*, vol. 1, Warsaw: Nakładem Stowarsyszenia Dzieci Holocaustu w polace, 1993

Index